The Baroque Violin & Viola

The Baroque Violin & Viola:
A Fifty-Lesson Course

Volume I

The Historical, Cultural, and Musicological Background
of Violin Music from the Seventeenth and Eighteenth Centuries
with Detailed Observations, Musical and Technical Analyses,
and

One Hundred Twenty-Five Specially Devised Exercises

Being the Author's Gift to Those Lovers of Baroque Music Wishing to Learn
to Play the Baroque Violin or Viola

by

Walter S Reiter

Professor of Baroque Violin, The Royal Conservatoire of The Hague,
The Netherlands

Professor of Baroque Violin, Trinity Laban Conservatoire of Music and
Dance, London

OXFORD
UNIVERSITY PRESS

OXFORD
UNIVERSITY PRESS

Oxford University Press is a department of the University of Oxford. It furthers
the University's objective of excellence in research, scholarship, and education
by publishing worldwide. Oxford is a registered trade mark of Oxford University
Press in the UK and certain other countries.

Published in the United States of America by Oxford University Press
198 Madison Avenue, New York, NY 10016, United States of America.

Library of Congress Cataloging-in-Publication Data
Names: Reiter, Walter, author.
Title: The baroque violin & viola: a fifty-lesson course / Walter Reiter.
Other titles: Baroque violin and viola
Description: New York: Oxford University Press, 2020. |
Includes bibliographical references and index. |
Identifiers: LCCN 2019056320 (print) | LCCN 2019056321 (ebook) |
ISBN 9780190922696 (v. 1; hardback) | ISBN 9780190922702 (v. 1; paperback) |
ISBN 9780190922726 (v. 1; epub) | ISBN 9780190922733
Subjects: LCSH: Violin—Instruction and study. |
Violin music—17th century—Interpretation (Phrasing, dynamics, etc.) |
Violin music—18th century—Interpretation (Phrasing, dynamics, etc.) |
Viola—Instruction and study.
Classification: LCC MT271 .R45 2020 (print) | LCC MT271 (ebook) |
DDC 787/.193071—dc23
LC record available at https://lccn.loc.gov/2019056320
LC ebook record available at https://lccn.loc.gov/2019056321

To my students, past, present, and future, to my parents and teachers, to my wife, to my children, and to my grandchildren.

"I have learned much from my masters, more from my colleagues . . . and more from my pupils than from all the others."

Talmud

CONTENTS

Foreword • xi

Inspirational Quotes • xvii

Questions and Answers • xix

About the Companion Website • xxiii

Acknowledgments • xxv

PART ONE THE BASICS

Lesson 1 Prelude • **3**
Choosing a Violin or Viola • 4
Choosing a Bow • 5
Strings • 6
Pitch • 9

Lesson 2 Holding the Violin • **11**
How to Hold the Baroque Violin: A Beginner's Guide • 19
Postlude • 21

Lesson 3 The Bow, Creator of Sound • **23**
Holding the Bow • 23

Lesson 4 First Sounds: Celebrating Our Vocal Heritage • **27**
Searching for Our Vocal Roots • 29
Exploring the Rhythm of Words • 30
Postscript • 34

Lesson 5 Copying the Human Voice: Sweelinck's Garrulous Little Swallow
(1612) • **36**
Vowels • 39
Diphthongs • 40
Single and Double Consonants • 41
Bowings • 42
Postscript • 44

Lesson 6 Five Exercises to Help Accustom You to 'Chinless' Playing • **45**
Recalling These Exercises in a Performance Situation • 49

Lesson 7 More Basic Concepts and Techniques: "A Division on a Ground" by
Mr Faronell, from *The Division Violin*, London, 1684 • 51
The Importance of the Bass Line • 52
Tempo and Rhythm • 53
The Hierarchies and the Bow Impulses • 54
Observations • 55
Variation 1: Dotted Notes • 58
Variation 2: Good Notes and Bad Notes • 60
Variation 3: Varying the Articulation • 61

Lesson 8 Learning to Feel: Developing a Heightened Awareness of the Emotional Power of Sound and the Intervals • **66**
Emotional Information: What Sound Tells Us • 67
How to Prepare: Manipulating Our Emotions • 71

Lesson 9 The Inner Life of Sound: "Messa di voce" • **74**
Postscript: Additional Study Material • 83

Lesson 10 Applying the Messa di voce. Arcangelo Corelli: Adagio from Sonata, op. 5, no. 3 • **85**
Dissonances and Consonances • 86
Observations • 88
On Trills • 89
In Praise of the Second Position • 91
Hemiolas: To Be Heard as Well as Seen? • 93
A Note on Chromatic Fingering • 93
Sound and Expression • 95
Summary • 97

Lesson 11 Temperament and "Historical" Intonation: An Outline • **99**
How Do We Learn "Pure" Intonation? • 101
Leopold Mozart on Overtones • 102
Peter Prelleur's Fingerboard • 105

Lesson 12 Chinless Shifting: Technique and Application • **108**
Section One: Toward a Methodology of Shifting • 108
Section Two: Applying Pure Intonation to Geminiani's Scale Studies from His *The Art of Playing the Violin* (1751). • 120

Lesson 13 Bringing Fast Notes to Life: The Inequality of the Equal. Albinoni: Sonata, op. 6, no. 2, Allegro • **127**
How to Play Equal Notes in a Flexible and Subtle Way • 127
The Three Flexibilities • 128
Observations • 132
Adding Slurs: A Misdemeanor? • 133
Sequences • 134
Summary • 138

Lesson 14 Learning to Feel Comfortable on Gut Strings: The Bow • **139**

Lesson 15 Learning to Feel Comfortable on Gut Strings: The Left Hand • **146**
The Fingers: Slaves of Our Inner Voice • 147

PART TWO RE-EXAMINING THE FAMILIAR: SONATAS BY VIVALDI AND CORELLI

Lesson 16 The Starting-Point of Interpretation: Learning to Observe. Arcangelo Corelli: Sonata, op. 5, no. 7 • **155**
Interpretation: A Question of Taste? • 155
Editions or Facsimiles? • 157
Instrumentation in Corelli's op. 5 Sonatas • 157

Means of Expression • 158
Choosing a Convincing Tempo • 158
Preludio • 159
Afterthought: What Happens Within • 167

Lesson 17 Corelli: Sonata, op. 5, no. 7 • **169**
Corrente • 169
Sarabanda • 177
Giga • 181

Lesson 18 Transforming Musical Decisions into Sound • **185**

Lesson 19 In the Footsteps of Corelli. Antonio Vivaldi: Sonata, op. 2, no. 1, Preludio • **193**
Observations • 193
Gesture • 195
Shifting: How, When, and Whither? • 197
Open Strings: Use or Misuse • 198
Notes Essential and Notes Ornamental • 200

Lesson 20 In the Footsteps of Corelli. Antonio Vivaldi: Sonata, op. 2, no. 1 (Conclusion) • **202**
Giga. Allegro • 202
Sarabanda Largo • 206
Corrente • 210

Lesson 21 Nurturing Spontaneity: Ornamentation, Module One • **216**
Ornamentation: Diversion or Essence? • 216
Overcoming Our Fear of Playing the Unwritten • 218
Ornamentation and National Styles • 219
Composed Ornamentation • 220
First Steps in Ornamenting: Corelli's Sarabanda • 222
Ornamenting the Second Half of the Sarabanda • 225
Corelli's Sarabanda Ornamented by Dubourg • 225

Lesson 22 Straight from the Heart: The Great Vibrato Debate • **227**
Conclusions • 237

Lesson 23 Rhetoric: The Power to Persuade • **239**
The Origins of Rhetoric • 239
Rhetoric and Music • 240
The Musician as Orator • 241
Rhetorical Playing versus Pure Instrumentalism • 243
Some Rhetorical Figures • 244

Bibliography • **255**
Index • **265**

FOREWORD

The study of the Baroque violin and its sister instrument the Baroque viola is an expansive undertaking. To facilitate the reader's progress through the various stages of study, I have considered it best to divide this course into two volumes.

Volume I contains Parts One and Two, a total of twenty-three Lessons. It comprehensively covers the basic musical, technical, and philosophical concepts of Baroque violin playing. Blending the informative with the practical, it provides in-depth analyses of repertoire from the early seventeenth century to sonatas by Corelli and Vivaldi and includes ninety-two exercises.

❦ ❦ ❦

After more than half a century spent teaching and playing the violin, the last thirty of which have been devoted almost exclusively to the Baroque violin, the author wishes to offer this course as a gift to all violinists and violists curious to share the modest musical insights he has gathered thus far along the way, pertaining to the performance of music from the Baroque period.

It is my belief that these two volumes may also be of interest to those who have chosen, as I did, to dedicate their student days to mastering the great Romantic concertos, but who are curious to understand why a specific repertoire of seemingly much easier music needs to be studied separately at all. Perhaps they will recognize that the change that has come over the world of classical music since the days of my youth, when Brandenburg Concertos were performed by vast symphony orchestras composed entirely of gentlemen, represents not merely welcome social evolution but an aesthetic revolution that even now is anything but on the wane.

The title of this course is perhaps misleading in that it claims to contain just fifty lessons, the equivalent of some two years of study in a conservatory. In fact, the contents of many of the lessons could never possibly be communicated in a single hour, at least not by me, even if the poor student were to sit patiently listening to a rapid outpouring of information without ever playing a note.

Whether you are an experienced professional violinist or violist or an interested amateur, a conservatory student seeking the kind of enlightenment your regular course of study does not provide, or a teacher hoping to learn how better to inform your pupils, these two volumes will teach you how to play key works from the repertoire of the seventeenth and eighteenth centuries in a historically informed manner, with technical and musical guidance at every step of the way. The course takes the form of a carefully designed, step-by-step series of lessons that both mirrors and magnifies my teaching program in the vast and wonderful HIP Department of the Royal Conservatoire of the Hague, in the Netherlands.

In my professional experience as a teacher of the Baroque violin and viola, I have found that the most fruitful results are achieved through detailed examination of carefully selected seminal works from the early 1600s through to J. S. Bach in which stylistic, musicological, and technical issues are explored in depth. Some years ago, however, it became clear to me that too much classroom time was being taken up in examining these works with each individual student in turn. A more efficient way to teach, I decided, would be to provide the student with as much written data beforehand as was deemed necessary for an informed and convincing performance, offering background information, quoting relevant historical sources and drawing attention to the myriad details within the text as well as an understanding of their implications. This written lesson would enable students to work in depth and in their own time, before coming to the classroom with a well-considered performance.

The results of this experiment were so encouraging that I decided to form the lessons into a book that, over a period of a decade, has gradually metamorphosed into this two-volume course. I have been most fortunate, throughout these years, to have ample opportunity to test the lessons on a constant flow of students; their feedback, patience, and helpful criticism has amounted to a continual process of correction, for which I am truly grateful.

Of course, the imparting of information and ideas is only one aspect of the teacher's role: the other part is that of drawing out the natural innate musicality of each individual student, encouraging initiative even when the outcome is questionable, respecting and nurturing that uniqueness which is every emerging artist's cherished birthright. Such a task is easier in the classroom than in the context of the written word; nevertheless, I have attempted to minimize this shortcoming by giving indications and devising exercises intended to help the reader develop his or her inner voice and to convey that voice into the world of sound.

The order of the lessons is not haphazard. In Part One we explore basic concepts and techniques: how to hold the instrument, how to play words, what is meant by 'interpretation,' the basics of rhetoric and temperament, what the affects are and how to sensitize ourselves to the emotional information inherent in the musical text.

In Part Two, we examine sonatas by Corelli and Vivaldi: this familiar and accessible music is excellent material for a deeper exploration of interpretive and technical aspects of Baroque violin playing.

Volume II begins with Part Three, in which we take a step back in time, studying the vocal roots of the first experiments in sonata writing before tackling three of the sonatas themselves. We return to Corelli in Part Four, enriched and inspired by our experiences of working with the composers who preceded him.

In Part Five, we study sonatas by Schmelzer and Biber before setting off to Versailles to encounter the sophisticated world of French Baroque music and in particular the music of one of its most exquisite exponents, François Couperin. Our journey ends in Leipzig with the music of J. S. Bach, the culmination and arguably the climax of our Baroque journey.

All repertoire to be studied in these two volumes has been especially transcribed, complete with the figured bass line, as published in their original edition; these parts, as well as transcriptions for viola players, may be downloaded and printed out from the course website.

There is very little original solo repertoire for the Baroque viola, but a good Baroque violist is one who is equally at home in all of the various styles he or she will be called upon to play, from Monteverdi via Schmelzer and Biber to Bach. For that reason, I teach Baroque viola students exactly the same repertoire as the violinists and I encourage all violinists to play the viola. Violists may well find it more convenient initially to work through the lessons on a violin before applying what they have learned to the viola transcriptions.

Most technical tips in these two books are offered on musical grounds, for it is my belief that the finer technical details are engendered by the demands of the music: a specific musical goal demands a specific technical solution, and every musical nuance causes a subtle technical change of which the player may or may not even need to be aware.

At every step of the way there are specially devised exercises. Many of these provide a methodological solution to the teaching of specific techniques gleaned from the historical sources, while others focus on the removal of physical barriers of the kind I commonly encounter in the classroom.

Central to the role of the Baroque musician is the ability to improvise: this is dealt with in five modules distributed throughout the course. Many well-trained musicians, perhaps precisely because they *are* so well trained, experience feelings of anxiety and inadequacy when asked to play anything that is not meticulously notated. For this reason, we start with ways of tackling inhibitions, using simple astylistic improvisation, before setting off to work through manuals of ornamentation from the mid-sixteenth century through to the Style Galant of the middle to late eighteenth century.

A true understanding of Baroque music cannot, I believe, be achieved merely by practicing within the confines of a sealed studio: I have therefore included four 'Interludes,' set in Florence, Rome, Versailles, and in Germany, that provide information on the historical, political, and cultural backdrop to the repertoire under discussion. A visit to Bernini's studio, where we learn to transfer visual images into sound, has proved an especially enjoyable exercise.

Much of the information in these two books is equally relevant to other instrumentalists making their initial journey into the Baroque repertoire: this includes recorder players, cornettists, flautists, and oboists as well as keyboard players, cellists, and double bassists. Moreover, just as many of the early treatises were written with both singers and instrumentalists in mind, there is a great deal of information here of relevance to vocalists.

∞ ∞ ∞

In the early seventeenth century, an instrument used mainly for accompanying voices and playing dances, not always in the most genteel of milieux, came storming onto the European stage as one possessing the power to express human emotions to a degree of which only the human voice had previously been considered capable. That instrument has been rediscovered in our time and is now known as the 'Baroque' violin.

Music played on this and other period instruments in a manner considered "authentic" today draws enthusiastic audiences in all corners of the globe. The historically informed performance (HIP) movement has resurrected a vast array of repertoire previously languishing silently on dusty library shelves and, using the instruments and techniques understood to have existed at the time, has brought this repertoire into the world's concert halls. No longer an eccentric ideology challenging the musical establishment, its reasoning and methodology are being gradually adopted and absorbed into the musical mainstream as 'conventional' musicians take on board its aesthetic and technical hallmarks.

Some symphony orchestras, particularly in Europe, now have Baroque orchestras embedded in their midst and there are chamber orchestras whose stylistic regeneration has allowed them to challenge the best of the well-established period instrument groups. Sadly though, in my view, musicians who find themselves called upon to play in a more 'historically acceptable' manner merely by imitating what they hear 'specialists' do are rarely convincing—for imitation and understanding, if they are at all related, are at best distant cousins.

Johann Joachim Quantz, whose *Versuch* (1752) is one of our principal sources of information on performance practice, was aware of this problem when he wrote (Introduction, § 9), *"The student must avoid a master who is not in a position to explain clearly and thoroughly everything that the student finds difficult to understand, and seeks to impart everything by ear, and through imitation, as we train birds."*

If you do not feel ready to commit to learning the Baroque violin or viola but wish to enrich your knowledge of HIP and of the repertoire, you may choose to work through some of this course on your modern instrument using a Baroque bow. However, your experience of the course will, I fear, merely shadow that of the more committed readers seeking to place themselves alongside their colleagues of yesteryear and to rediscover the sounds with which they transfixed their audiences.

Every one of us has a path to follow: many of today's Baroque violinists and violists started off as 'modern' performers and only became interested in the early repertoire after some years of professional activity. Some of my students take Baroque instrument lessons as a secondary subject, finding that it enriches both their modern playing and their total experience within the conservatory. Others decide on a "coup de coeur" that the Baroque instrument, with its wonderfully varied repertoire and intriguing sound world, is closer to their hearts than the modern one and find themselves with no other option than to elope to the Early Music Department.

❦ ❦ ❦

In most lessons of this course there is an opening section on general matters pertaining to the piece under examination, followed by a bar-by-bar analysis of the music and detailed suggestions on how to play it. Working through the 'Observations' section of each lesson will require patience and toil, but it will make for convincing performances and will set in motion ways of thinking that will stand the reader in good stead when working independently.

I have tried to justify as many of these 'Observations' as possible by quoting from the historical texts and treatises we refer to reverentially as "the sources." We cannot of course learn to play from these sources alone, for they are by no means books of rules, except perhaps when written by a composer in relation to his own compositions; but they do guide us along our way, beams of light shining into the darkness of bygone ages.

Some quotations I have included are specific to a composer, a type of dance, a place or a short period of time in an age of constantly changing musical fashion. The reader may object that others are anachronistic in the context that I have placed them; if I am guilty of this, it will be because such quotations seem to me to be both time-specific and worthy of more universal application.

While appreciating the undoubted value of treatises, we should nevertheless be aware of their subjectivity: they inevitably reflect the taste and preferences of the author and may occasionally criticize practices of which they personally did not approve but which, by implication, were commonplace at the time. Hence, phrases oft-heard today such as "*they* would never have done that in Rome in 1744" used to criticize a musical decision or "*they* did it like this in 1672 in Salzburg" used to defend one, must surely raise the question in our minds as to which *"they"* is being referred to.

There is no 'correct' way to play the violin, to interpret a sonata, to shape a phrase or to color a single note. The independent-minded student will derive much benefit from thoughtfully challenging what I have written: perhaps that freedom of dissent is one of the advantages of learning from a book. I am well aware that there is much in these volumes that is personal and subjective: it could not be otherwise. All teachers impart information and viewpoints that have become theirs through a process of study and ex-perience, gradually maturing ideas or sudden flashes of enlightenment. An exciting new book on the latest musicological research may enrich their knowledge or disprove what they have hitherto believed and taught; a problem arising in a single student may trigger a new avenue of enquiry; sometimes, a useful image comes from a poem.

ᛋᛋ ᛋᛋ ᛋᛋ

There were a great many self–help violin tutors around in the seventeenth and eight-eenth centuries, but not until the mid-eighteenth century, with the publication of the works of Geminiani (1751), Leopold Mozart (1756), and others, was any serious amount of technical information disclosed. Most previous 'Methods' were written for the am-ateur musician, with such enticing titles as *The Gentleman's Diversion* by John Lenton (1693) or my favorite *Nolens volens, or You Shall Learn to Play on the Violin Whether You Will or No* by an unknown author (1695). Even the more informative books can be vague or even silent on actual technical instruction. Take Michel Corrette's *L'École d'Orphée* (1738), for example, a Method described on the front cover as being *"useful to beginners."* Chapter I, entitled "How to hold the violin" and Chapter II, "Different ways to hold the bow" take up just a single page, the only useful tip on sound production being *"one must use large bow-strokes up and down, but in a gracious and pleasant manner."*

One reason for this scarcity of detailed written information is that, in an age rife with plagiarism, as we shall see, and free from copyright laws and permissions, teachers saw no reason to write books in which the cherished secrets of their art, would be re-vealed to the wider public.

Many composers did write material with a primarily didactic purpose but they contain no specific instructions. Vivaldi, for example, wrote sonatas and concertos for the young ladies of La Pietà and Tartini wrote variations on a theme of Corelli (*L'arte dell'arco*) which every aspiring violinist would be well advised to work through, as well as sonatas that might be said to have more technical than musical value. Similarly, Telemann wrote his *Methodical Sonatas* as study material while Leclair, in the introduction to his first book of violin sonatas (1723) writes that *"these works may be used as Études for those that need them."*

Had they foreseen that musicians in the distant twenty-first century, their ears ringing with the sounds of György Kurtag and Philip Glass, would once again seek to interpret their music and reproduce their sound-worlds, the great composers, performers, teachers, and treatise writers of the Baroque period might well have been a little more forthcoming with their information.

This course of study humbly attempts to rectify some of their omissions and to weave together the disparate strands of available information into a single, detailed pedagogic work. Once the curious and diligent reader has worked his or her way patiently and conscientiously through it, he or she will, I believe, be well placed to explore further and with greater confidence the wonderfully rich repertoire of the Baroque period.

London, 2010–2020

INSPIRATIONAL QUOTES

"The Intention of Musick is not only to please the Ear, but to express Sentiments, strike the Imagination, affect the Mind, and command the Passions."

Geminiani

"Rhythm and harmony penetrate deeply into the mind and have a most powerful effect on it."

Plato

"Many excellent musicians have distinguished themselves who have had no other master than their great natural ability and the opportunity to hear much that is good. These musicians have advanced further through their own effort, industry, diligence and constant inquiry than many who have been instructed by several masters."

Quantz

"Taste flows from feeling, it adopts what is good, rejects what is bad."

Rameau

"It is to be stated, however, in the first place, that precepts and treatises on art are of no avail without the assistance of nature, and these instructions, therefore, are not written for him to whom talent is venting any more than treatises on agriculture for barren ground."

Quintilian

"Nothing fundamental can be learned without time and patience."

C. P. E. Bach

"For it is impossible to devise rules which will meet all possible cases, so long as music remains an inexhaustible ocean of options, and one man differs from the next in his appreciation."

Marpurg

"Concerning such would-be luminaries who believe that music has to follow their rules, when in truth their rules have to follow the music, one can rightly say: *"Faciunt intelligendo ut nihil intelligant"* (they manage their thinking to understand nothing")."

Mattheson

"Anyone who does not wish to trust my taste, which I have diligently endeavoured to purify through long experience and reflection, is free to try the opposite of that which I teach, and then choose what seems best to him."

Quantz

"The reader is warned not to read it hastily but with thought and deliberation, if he is to derive from it full profit and satisfaction."

Tartini

"He who wishes to dedicate himself to music must feel in himself a perpetual and un-tiring love for it, a willingness and eagerness to spare neither industry nor pains, and to bear steadfastly all the difficulties that present themselves in this mode of life."

Quantz

"Hence we maintain . . . that the universal axiom of all music, on which we build all other conclusions regarding this science and art, would consist of the following four words: Everything Must Sing Properly"

Mattheson

"Nor let the scholar ever end a lesson without having profited something."

Piero Francesco Tosi

QUESTIONS AND ANSWERS

Q. Is there a correct way to play Baroque music?

A. No! There never was and there never will be, although there are some wrong ways.

Q. Can a book be a substitute for a teacher?

A. Up to a point, yes; but it surely can be a substitute for no teacher.

Q. From reading this book, one could assume that all your pupils play in exactly the same way. Is that true?

A. Absolutely not! Bringing out the special qualities of each pupil is always uppermost in my mind when teaching. Obviously, such discernment is not possible in a book.

Q. But if one hundred people put into practice every detail of one of your lessons, surely they must all end up playing in an identical way?

A. No. They may play in a similarly informed way, but they will all sound different. That is one of the mysteries of violin playing—and one of the joys of teaching.

Q. What would you say if someone read your suggestions and then did exactly the opposite?

A. That too is possible. The teacher's job is to inform and inspire, not to dictate.

"No lesson should be abandoned before the pupil knows it as well as possible. The pupil's progress is not measured by the number of his pieces, but by (his) ability to play them gracefully and fluently."

Marpurg, *The Art of Harpsichord Playing* (1750)

ABOUT THE COMPANION WEBSITE

www.oup.com/us/thebaroqueviolinandviola
Username: Music5
Password: Book1745

Oxford has created a password-protected website to accompany *The Baroque Violin &*
Viola: A Fifty Lesson Course. Scores of all the pieces discussed in this book, with the exception of the two unaccompanied Bach works, may be downloaded from the website in
versions for both violin and viola and can thus be printed out and placed on your music
stand. For your greater convenience while studying, each measure has been individually
numbered. Violists may find it easier to work through the 'Observations' sections on the
violin before turning to the viola transcriptions.

You will also find eight appendices on the website: a list of the specially devised
exercises contained in the course, an article on the controversy surrounding the introduction of wire strings in the early twentieth century, *Le tableau des energies des modes*,
Charpentier's table of tonalities and their affects (1690), biblical texts relevant to the
two sonatas by Biber examined in Lessons 32 and 33, some thoughts on the particular
challenges of the French Baroque repertoire, a short essay on the art of teaching and another on stress and ways of dealing with it. Finally, I have appended seven exercises for
the prevention and relief of physical tension.

The website also contains some helpful video and audio clips: these are indicated in
the text with the following symbol ⏵.

ACKNOWLEDGMENTS

Art Works

Lesson 2

Figure a   Adriaen Matham, (1620–1660), *Oude Vioolspeler*. By courtesy of the Rijksmuseum, Amsterdam.

Figure a   Gerrit van Honthorst, (1592–1656) *The Violin Player* (1626). Oil on Canvas. With kind permission of the Mauritshuis, The Hague.

Figure b   Johann Strauss, Statue in Vienna. Credit: iStock.com

Figure c   Corrette, *L'Ecole d'Orphee. Methode pour Apprendre facilement à joüer du Violon*, Paris, 1738. By kind permission of Anne Fuzeau Facsimiles.

Figure d   Frontispiece to Corrette's *L'Art de se perfectionner dans le Violon* (1782) By kind permission of Anne Fuzeau Facsimiles.

Figure e   Portrait of José Herrando. By kind permission of Anne Fuzeau Facsimiles.

Figure f   Portrait of Leopold Mozart, Engraving by Andreas Fridrich Jacobs (1684–1751) / De Agostini Picture Library / A. Dagli Orti / Bridgeman Images.

Figure g   Portrait of Leopold Mozart, Figure II from Leopold Mozart's *Gründliche Violinschule*, 1770. Engraving. British Library, London, UK / © British Library Board. All Rights Reserved / Bridgeman Images.

Figure h   Francesco Maria Veracini (1690–1768). Copper engraving, 1744, after Franz Ferdinand Richter. / Granger / Bridgeman Images.

Lesson 3

Figure a   Gerard Dou (1613–1675). Violinist, detail. Courtesy of Rijksmuseum, Amsterdam.

Figure b   *Der Fehler*, Figure V, from Leopold Mozart's *Gründliche Violinschule*, 1770. Engraving / British Library, London, UK / © British Library Board. All Rights Reserved / Bridgeman Images.

Figure c   Leopold Mozart, *Violin School*, violin virtuoso / De Agostini Picture Library / A. Dagli Orti / Bridgeman Images.

Lesson 7

Figure a   *The Division-Violin: containing a choice collection of divisions to a ground for the treble-violin. Being the first musick of this kind ever published*, 1684. Engraving, English School, seventeenth century / British Library, London, UK / © British Library Board. All Rights Reserved / Bridgeman Images.

Lesson 9

Figure a   Leopold Mozart: Bow Division, from his *Violin School*, French edition in the Bibliothèque nationale de France, Paris. By kind permission of Anne Fuzeau Facsimiles.

Figure b   Essempio XX, from Geminiani, *L'art du Violon* in the Bibliothèque nationale de France, Paris. By kind permission of Anne Fuzeau Facsimiles.

Figure e   Leopold Mozart: Bow Division, from his *Violin School*, French edition in the Bibliothèque nationale de France, Paris. By kind permission of Anne Fuzeau Facsimiles.

Lesson 11

Figure a   Annotated finger-board from "The Art of Playing the Violin," from *The Modern Musick-Master; or the Universal Musician* by Peter Prelleur, 1731. British Library, London, UK / © British Library Board. All Rights Reserved / Bridgeman Images.

Lesson 21

Figure a   Baroque altarpiece, Peterskirche, Vienna. Credit: iStock.com/Artist's.

Quotations

Permission to use Ernest C. Harriss's translation of Mattheson's *Der Vollkommene Capellmeister* was graciously granted by Elaine Harriss.

I have also quoted extensively from *On Playing the Flute*, by Joachim Quantz, translated by Edward R. Reilly, by kind permission of the University Press of New England.

Oxford University Press granted permission to quote from the following books:-

1. *A Treatise on the Fundamental Principles of Violin Playing* by Leopold Mozart
2. *The History of Violin Playing from Its Origins to 1761, and Its Relationship to the Violin and Violin Music* by David Boyden (1990)
3. *Arcangelo Corelli: "New Orpheus of Our Times,"* by Peter Allsop (1999)
4. *The End of Early Music: A Period Performer's History of Music for the Twenty-First Century* by Bruce Haynes (2007)
5. *Bach's Works for Solo Violin. Style, Structure, Performance,"* by Joel Lester (1999)
6. *An Eighteenth Century Musical Tour in Central Europe and the Netherlands*, by Charles Burney, edited by Percy Scholes (1959)
7. Christoph Wolff, *Bach, The Learned Musician.*

Oxford Journals gave permission to quote from the following articles in Early Music:

1. David Watkins, "Corelli's op. 5 sonatas: 'Violino e violone o cimbalo'"?
2. William Christie, "The Elusive World of the French Baroque."

Sources used by permission of W. W. Norton:

1. C. P. E. Bach, *Essay on the True Art of Playing Keyboard Instruments.*
2. Hans David and Arthur Mendel, *The New Bach Reader.*
3. Oliver Strunk, ed., *Source Readings in Music History.*

Tosi's *Observations on the Florid Song* is also frequently referred to; my gratitude to Andy Chart of Dodo Press.

Little and Jenne's *"Dance and the Music of J.S. Bach,"* by kind permission of Indiana University Press. David Ledbetter, *Unaccompanied Bach: Performing the Solo Works* (ISBN: 9780300141511). Publisher: Yale Representation Limited. Reproduced with permission of The Licensor through PLSclear.

Pierre Baillot's *L'art du violon*, translated by Louise Goldberg, is quoted by kind permission of Northwestern University Press.

My thanks to Boosey & Hawkes for allowing me to quote extracts from the *Exercises* of Ševčík. The Prefaces to the works of Rognoni are quoted by kind permission of the author, Bruce Dickey.

My thanks to Professor Victor Anand Coelho, director, Center for Early Music Studies, Boston University, School of Music, for allowing me to quote from "The Players of Florentine Monody in Context and in History, and a Newly Recognized Source for Le nuove musiche," *Journal of Seventeenth-Century Music* 9, no. 1 (2003).

The booklet notes to my recording of Biber's Mystery Sonatas are quoted by kind permission of the author, Peter Holman and of Steve Long, CEO of Signum Records.

My thanks to Taylor and Francis Books Ltd., UK, for permission to quote from *The Instrumental Music of Schmeltzer, Biber, Muffat and Their Contemporaries* by Charles E. Brewer.

Cambridge University Press gave permission to quote from the following three publications:

1. Hiller, Johann Adam, *Anweisung zum musikalisch-zierlichen Gesange* (1780). Translated and edited by Suzanne J. Beicken, University of Maryland. as *Treatise on Vocal Performance and Ornamentation*, Cambridge University Press, 2004.
2. Burney, Charles, *The Present State of Music in France and Italy: Or, the Journal of a Tour through Those Countries, Undertaken to Collect Materials for a General History of Music,* 1771. Cambridge University Press, 2014.
3. Bernard Brauchli, *The Clavichord.* Cambridge Musical Texts and Monographs, Cambridge University Press, 2008.

All quotes from Frederick H. Martens's *Violin Mastery, Talks with Master Violinists and Teachers* and Joseph Joachim's *Violinschule* are reprinted by permission of Forgotten Books.

Lesson 22: Galeazzi quote Copyright © 1978, American Musicological Society Inc. Used by permission. Permission to quote from Ganassi's *Regola rubertina* was graciously given by Patrice Connelly of Saraband Music, Australia. My gratitude to Indiana University Press for permission to quote from *Georg Muffat on Performance Practice.*

My gratitude to the University of Nebraska Press for permission to quote from Dietrich Bartel's *"Musica Poetica."* My gratitude to Princeton University Press for allowing me to quote from Frederick Neumann's *Ornamentation in Baroque and Post-Baroque Music, with Special Emphasis on J. S. Bach.*

My thanks to Pendragon Press for allowing me to quote from *The Harmonic Orator. The Phrasing and Rhetoric of the Melody in French Baroque Airs* by Patricia M. Ranum.

I am grateful to Schott Music, London, for permission to show the opening bars of Bach arranged by Kreisler: © SCHOTT MUSIC, Mainz, Germany, for all countries except USA, Canada, and Mexico. © Carl Fischer LLC for USA, Canada, and Mexico. Reproduced by permission. All rights reserved.

My gratitude to my friend and colleague Oliver Webber for permission to quote from his book *Rethinking Gut Strings*. Permission to quote from Quintilian's *Institutes of Oratory* was granted by Curtis Dozier. Toronto University Press kindly permitted me to quote from *Roger North on Music*.

My thanks to Scarecrow Press for allowing to quote from *A History of Performing Pitch, the Story of "A,"* by my late friend and colleague Bruce Haynes.

My thanks to Christian Lloyd, managing editor of the *Strad*, for supplying me with the 1908 quote on vibrato from the *Strad* and graciously permitting me to quote it. I am most grateful to Katharina Malecki of Bärenreiter, for all quotes by Tartini.

Dover Publications gave generous permission to quote from Leopold Auer's *Violin Playing as I Teach It*.

Judy Tarling graciously gave permission to quote from two of her works, *Baroque String Playing for the Ingenious Learner* and *The Weapons of Rhetoric: A Guide for Musicians and Audiences*, this permission also being accorded by Ian Gammie of Corda Music Publications, St. Albans, UK.

☙ ☙ ☙

My thanks go first to Suzanne Ryan, editor in chief, Humanities, at Oxford University Press USA, for her guidance and support over the many years I have spent writing this book. Initially a response to the needs of my students, it is they who have helped me the most, with or without realizing it, in the crafting of this course of lessons: my debt to them is incalculable.

I am most grateful to Elaine Harriss, PhD, of the University of Tennessee at Martin for allowing, nay encouraging, me to quote at length from her late husband's translation of Mattheson's *Der Vollkommene Capellmeister*. Jessica Ranft deserves more gratitude than I can express for decoding my handwritten musical examples and producing in their stead excellent computerized transcriptions: she also cleaned up the facsimiles and, with endless patience, made corrections of what were mostly my mistakes. Louise Jameson compiled the index for me and was meticulous in checking and correcting the spelling of names and titles. Alessandra Testai helped me with the Italian translations and recorded the audio clips with consummate artistry. Dr. Martina Lehner of the Österreichische Provinz der Gesellschaft Jesu patiently tracked down a Jesuit symbol relevant to the lessons on Biber. The Royal Conservatoire of The Hague helped and supported me in diverse ways, not least in the making of the videos, for which special thanks are due to Lex van den Broek and Siamak Anvari.

Brian Clark, of Prima la Musica, was the first musicologist to read extracts of the book in its early stages and to offer encouragement and advice. Bruce Dickey, cornettist and director of Concerto Palatino, helped me with my many questions regarding the early Italian repertoire, in addition to allowing me to quote from his writings. It was also of great benefit to discuss that repertoire with Philip Thorby.

My thanks also go to harpsichordists Patrick Ayrton and Nicholas Parle, my omniscient figured bass gurus, and to Amanda Babington and Lynda Sayce for their help. I am forever in debt to my teacher, Ramy Shevelov, for the wisdom of his thoughts, his way of teaching and, in this book, for the exercises on which Lesson 14 is based.

Last, without the constant encouragement, patience, advice, and dedication (call it love) of my wife Linda, this book would never have seen the light of day, nor could its author have survived the long years of toil.

The Baroque Violin & Viola:
A Fifty-Lesson Course

PART I

The Basics

NOTE

Throughout the book, I use the Helmholtz system of pitch notation to identify notes. For convenience, I reproduce the complete range of violin notes here. From the open G string to the B a third above, the notes are simply written g, a and b. From Middle C to the B a seventh higher, the notes are written with a single′ (c′ – b′). The following octave has a double″ (c″-b″) and above that the notes have a triple‴ (c‴ – e‴).

Lesson 1

Prelude

Our first concern is to find you a violin or viola and a bow with which you will be able to work your way through this course of Lessons.

Video 1.1

"But wait," I am occasionally asked, "do I really need a Baroque instrument to learn about Baroque style? Can I not learn from this book using my modern instrument?"

As you proceed in your studies, it will become clear that the Baroque violin and viola are rather different instruments from the ones you have been playing until now. The more we seek to emulate our colleagues from the seventeenth and eighteenth centuries, the more we will inevitably find ourselves straying from the comfort zone to which the well marked out path of modern-day pedagogy has hitherto led us.

If you find this thought too daunting, at least at this initial stage, and cannot commit to studying this new instrument, there will of course still be plenty for you to benefit from in this book. The problem is that style, aesthetics, sound, technique, and instrument are so inextricably bound up that were you to persist in working through the lessons with an instrument in a modern setup you would, I fear, be sacrificing much that is wonderful and unique about the experiences we shall be enjoying in the course of our Baroque journey.

Students and teachers are often heard to voice the fear that studying the Baroque violin or viola will in some insidious way interfere with and degrade their painstakingly developed "modern" technique. My experience of working with "modern" students has shown that, on the contrary, the study of Baroque repertoire and Baroque techniques has a beneficial effect on one's approach to later repertoire. Far from corrupting modern orthodox technique, such a study complements it, freeing up both the body and the imagination and leading to an altogether more thoughtful approach to music making.

Choosing a Violin or Viola

There are several options open to you. The first is to buy a "modern Baroque" instrument, one that is newly made but built as closely as possible to the way an Amati, Guarnerius, or Stradivarius was originally constructed. One can argue that playing on such an instrument is more historically correct because musicians in the Baroque period were themselves playing on new instruments, not on ones already hundreds of years old. There are many fine violinmakers today making excellent reproductions of Baroque instruments.

The second option is to find a seventeenth- or eighteenth-century instrument still in its original condition, one that has never been modified or converted to a modern setup. Such instruments are becoming ever harder to find, although they do occasionally turn up at auctions. For many musicians, including myself, the thought that one's instrument has already played the music one is studying or performing at the time it was composed is a source of great inspiration: will it in some mysterious way be able to guide one back into the ways of the past?

For those unable to find an affordable instrument in its original condition, the next option is to buy one that was built as a Baroque instrument but was later converted to a modern setup. Most instruments built before 1800 will be suitable for such a restoration. Once purchased, it can then be restored to its original condition by an expert luthier, preferably one who has experience of building "modern" Baroque instruments.

One advantage of this approach is that there is usually a plentiful supply on the market of instruments that fall into this category. Another advantage is that you can take your time before proceeding to the restoration, thus staggering the cost over as long a period of time as you need.

Everything that was done to the original instrument at some time in the nineteenth century would have to be undone, the whole process of modernization, where possible, reversed. The cost of converting is not inconsiderable, and I have known colleagues who have had such a conversion done in stages for this reason.

The first stage of this gradual restoration could be to have a luthier fit a Baroque bridge and tailpiece, and then simply to put on gut strings. It's a pragmatic beginning, not ideal because the instrument would still feel, behave, and sound like a modern one.

The second step would involve more carpentry: detaching the scroll, removing the neck and fingerboard and building new ones, and then reattaching the scroll. The bridge may have to be replaced once more to fit with the neck, which would now be entering the body of the instrument at an angle of 90 degrees. The sound post and bass bar might need replacing also, but that could be delayed and carried out as the final stage in the conversion.

The problem with this solution is that one can never truly predict what the newly "re-Baroqued" instrument will sound like once the process is completed. Interestingly, Stradivarius violins were not as sought after in the Baroque period as they came to be later on, once they had been converted into 'modern' violins. Heinrich Ignaz Franz von Biber, Pietro Antonio Locatelli, Antonio Veracini, and J. S. Bach all owned violins by Jacob Stainer, while Arcangelo Corelli preferred his Andrea Amati. The instruments of Stradivarius came to be preferred only later, when a more powerful sound had become a priority.[1]

The last and least satisfactory solution to the problem of finding an instrument for this course of lessons is very much a compromise one. If you have a spare instrument that you could use as your 'Baroque' one but you do not wish to have it fully converted, you can put on gut strings and have a Baroque bridge fitted. Again, what you will have is very far from being a Baroque instrument in either feel or sound. However, as long as the chin and shoulder rests are carefully put away in a cupboard, you could still learn much from working through this book with a setup of this kind.

Choosing a Bow

No study of the Baroque repertoire taking into account even the most basic aspects of historically informed performance practice can be considered serious if undertaken with a modern bow. The two species of bows behave in radically different ways and produce radically different sounds. The Baroque bow was conceived for the repertoire we shall be studying and there is much to be learned merely from using the same kind of bow with which our ancestral colleagues wooed their audiences. The modern bow was designed as a response to the demands of later composers working in a very different sound world and is therefore more suitable for that repertoire and less for ours.

The problem with choosing a Baroque bow is that the size, weight, and character of bows changed continuously throughout the Baroque period: one really needs at least three different models in order to tackle with any degree of historical accuracy the repertoire to be studied in this book!

If you can only buy one bow, I would advise buying a copy of a late seventeenth- or early eighteenth-century bow, the kind suitable for playing both the repertoire of the high Baroque composers such as Handel and Bach and, though not ideal, the earlier repertoire also. Such a bow could be around 65 cms. long, although there is absolutely no standard length or weight.

If you were able to buy a second bow, I would recommend one suitable for the repertoire covered mainly in Lessons 24 to 29 of this book, the music of roughly the first half of the seventeenth century. Such a short, light, and nimble bow, affectionately known nowadays as a "twig," will make playing this repertoire so much more rewarding than a heavier bow. Very few such bows survive, so modern bow makers tend to copy paintings or make their own designs. Such bows are usually around 60 cms. in length.

If you are able to add to your collection a longer mid-eighteenth-century bow, you could use that for late Baroque and early classical music as well—Haydn and Mozart, for example. It is important to realize that the evolution of the bow and the actual usage of bows by musicians were never synchronized or ordained. Some players were still using short bows while others were using longer ones; similarly, some were experimenting what we now call 'transitional' or 'classical' bows while their colleagues still clung to their much-loved 'Baroque' ones. There never was a date when a certain type of bow was declared obsolete and only more recent models permitted: we can only speculate as to the variety of bows used at the debut performance of Beethoven's First Symphony on April 2, 1800.

Bows in the Baroque period had detachable frogs that were clipped into place and held firm by the hair when in use: the first screw mechanisms only became available around 1740 but most bows, even of the transitional and classical variety being built in the last decades of the eighteenth century, still had clip-in frogs.

Many modern bow makers reproduce bows with clip-in frogs, and players who prefer such bows do so not just for reasons of historical correctness. The fact that the hair connects with the stick at both ends (instead of being attached inside the frog) helps the stick to vibrate better and therefore enhances the sound and the clarity of articulation.

One possible downside of the clip-in bows is that the tension of the hair cannot be adjusted quickly. To increase the tension, some material (usually pieces of paper or cardboard) must be wedged in between the hair and the frog. For the traveling musician playing in a damp church one night and in a dry concert hall the next, a more easily adjustable hair tension might be seen as advantageous. Your decision as to which type of bow to buy will be one of many you will have to make as you balance historicity on the one hand with pragmatism and personal preference on the other.

Strings

> Is it not strange that sheep's guts should hale souls out of men's bodies?
> William Shakespeare, Much Ado About Nothing, Act 2, Scene 3

Strings throughout the Baroque period were made principally with sheep gut. There are many makers of gut strings today, from quite small enterprises to large, almost industrial ones. Strings come in many different gauges, from very thin to very thick. Which strings you use will need to be the subject of a certain amount of experimentation on your part, as different instruments have different stringing needs. Personal taste is also a factor: some people favor heavy strings, while others prefer lighter ones. *"The choice of strings,"* writes Leopold Mozart (Introduction, 1, §4) *"must be made with the greatest care and not merely at random."*

"If the violin be a large model," he continues (Introduction, 1, §7), *"thicker strings will undoubtedly have a better effect; whereas if the body be small it will need thin strings."* Another factor is pitch. *"Just as the thicker strings give a better result with the flat pitch, so the thinner strings will serve better with the sharp pitch."*

As a Baroque musician, you will be playing in several different pitches (see below) and styles so you may find your stringing needs changing from one project to another. François Raguenet (1702) in his *Comparison between French and Italian Music* reports that the *"Italian violins are mounted with strings much larger than ours . . . and they can make their instruments sound as loud again as we do ours."*[2]

There are many kinds of G string available, from pure gut to gut covered in silver and/or brass. It is clearly important that the gauges of the strings you choose are suitably related to each other. When you press down the strings with your fingers, the resistance of each string should feel as equal as possible to all the others. Too great a difference in gauge and tension between strings will result in unnecessary complications for both the left hand and the bow. Mary Burwell (c 1670) wrote about this in relation to the lute.

"When you stroke all the strings with your thumbe," she says, *"you must feel an even stiffnes which proceeds from the size of the stringes."*[3]

A century and a half later, Leopold Mozart (Introduction, § 4) admonishes those who take not enough care in this matter. *"The violin is strung with four strings, each of which must be of the right thickness in relation to the other. I say 'the right thickness,' for if one string be a little too thick in proportion to another it is impossible to obtain an even or a good tone. It is true that violinists and violin-makers frequently judge these thicknesses by the eye, but it cannot be denied that the result is often very bad."*

Those who advocate a system known as "equal tension" argue that all strings should have the same amount of tension and that having the E string extremely tense and a covered G much less so is not only unhistorical and illogical but tonally disadvantageous. Aficionados of this system argue that instruments strung in equal tension sound *"fuller and richer, because the relatively high tension of the lower strings gives more depth and volume, and there is a wider range of both tone-colour and articulation available."*[4]

Using an equal tension setup will take some getting used to, especially with the use of a pure gut G that needs to be rather thick in order to have sufficient tension: some tailpieces and pegs might even need to have thicker holes drilled to accommodate them.

That wound G strings existed, however, is beyond doubt: Sébastien de Brossard (c. 1712) tells us of one *"entirely wound with silver"* that is thinner than a pure gut one, although he neglects to say by how much or how much silver was used. He also claims that D strings too are *"at present almost always partially wound with silver."* There is no evidence of how widespread this practice was.[5]

Johann Joachim Quantz (VII, 2, § 28) also mentions wound strings. *"Gut strings,"* he writes, *"are made from the little gut of sheep, and never with any other kind of animal."* However, to enhance the sound of the gut G strings, he adds, they are covered with a mixture of silver and brass, either entirely (filée) or with strands wound around the gut at intervals (demi-filée).[6]

Note: An explanation of the referencing method of both Quantz and Leopold Mozart is to be found at the start of the Bibliography.

℘ ℘ ℘

Historical gut strings cannot be used with adjusters, so tuning is done with the pegs alone. In a performance you may have only a few bars rest in the middle of a movement for a discreet emergency tweaking of a string. For this reason it is important that your pegs be maintained in optimum condition.

There are several methods of putting a new string on your violin: here are three to consider.

Method 1

- Pass the string downwards through the hole in the tailpiece.
- Attach the string by tying a simple knot as near as possible to the tailpiece.
- Thread the other end through the peg.

The disadvantage of this method is that you might need a pair of scissors to remove a broken string. In an emergency situation—for example, just as you are about to go on stage—this might take up valuable time.

Method 2

If the holes in your tailpiece are very small,

- Tie a knot at one end, too big to slip through the hole; thread the other end through the hole from underneath.
- Pull the string through and thread into the peg as normal.

Method 3

Some tailpieces have holes too large for Method 2. If that is the case, try this:

- Take an old gut E or A and cut off about four inches.
- Tie as many knots in this piece as you need to make a wedge that is too big to slip through the hole.
- Thread your new string through that wedge and attach it with a knot.
- Tidy the wedge carefully with a small pair of scissors.
- Thread the string through the hole from underneath and into the peg.

If you decide on Method 2 or 3, it can be useful to prepare a few strings in advance. This will save time when you need to put the string on; it will also allow you to pass through airport security without scissors!

Players accustomed to metal, plastic, and wound gut strings may voice the fear that pure gut strings are unreliable and likely to snap without warning. They forget, perhaps, that gut strings were the norm for all string players from ancient times until the mid-twentieth century and that if they could survive the great Romantic concertos of Mendelssohn and Brahms, the symphonies of Mahler, and the works of Stravinsky and Bartók, they must be perfectly suitable to our needs! It is true, however, that a gut E will not last for anything like as long as a pure metal one and that therefore we need to be vigilant regarding their state.

Tuning a string up to the desired pitch gradually should lengthen its life. If there is time, I tune a new E string up to an A′; I then tune it up a semitone every ten minutes until I reach E′. I always carry a pre-stretched, emergency string with me, one that will take less time to settle down if it is suddenly needed.

Do not worry if a string starts to fray a little, or if it sprouts a small whisker-like growth. This does not mean that it is about to snap, especially if it is an A or D string. However, you might want to prune such a growth with some fine scissors so that your fingers do not aggravate it further. I usually change an E string in this condition before a concert to avoid unnecessary anxiety, and if the condition of the string is not too bad, I keep it for periods of practice.

An old string or a frayed one might have become false. Pluck it and listen carefully: if the sound is pure and you hear just a single note, it means the string is true. If you hear something that sounds like several notes, a little like an out-of-tune honky-tonk piano, then the string is false. Playing with a false string will make intonation difficult, especially in double stops, so spare yourself a great deal of frustration and change the string!

Before putting on a new string, take a fine pencil lead and rub it well into the groove on the bridge and also into the groove leading into the peg box. This will allow the string to pass smoothly when tuning and will avoid the constant pulling forward of the bridge.

In spite of this precaution, the angle of the bridge should be checked frequently: its feet must be in total contact with the belly of the violin if the sound is to be healthy. If the bridge is leaning forward you will need to straighten it. Place the violin on your lap, the scroll pointing forward. Take hold of the bridge firmly on both sides, with your first and second fingers in front of it and your thumbs behind. Pull the top of the bridge gently toward you. Check that the angle is correct: if it is not, repeat the process. If moving the bridge requires too much effort you may need to wind the strings down a semi-tone to loosen the tension.

Sometimes, strings will break near the groove by the peg box, due to some roughness that has developed inside the groove. If this seems to be the case, ask your luthier to smooth the inside of the groove with a fine file.

Gut strings were not without their critics in the Baroque period: Michael Praetorius wrote in his *Syntagma Musicum* (1620) that in his opinion wire strings have a more *"gentle and pleasing sound"* than gut: Praetorius's strings would have sounded less strident than the higher tension metal E strings in use today. Covered strings were also being used in the seventeenth century, John Playford (1664) claiming that they *"sound much better and lowder than the common Gut string."* He favored silk covered with wire which, he reports, *"hold best and give as good a sound"* as wire on gut.[7] Appendix II describes the polemic caused by the transition from gut to metal strings in the twentieth century.

Pitch

"The diversity of pitches used for tuning is most detrimental to music in general," complained Quantz in 1752 (XVII, VII, §7) *"For this reason it is much to be hoped that a single pitch for tuning may be introduced at all places."*

This diversity of pitch was, in different places and at different times, of a range of around six semitones, from A = 388 Hz to A = 489 Hz, making the history of pitch extremely complicated.

"It is undeniable," continues Quantz, *"that the high pitch is much more penetrating than the low one; on the other hand, it is much less pleasing, moving, and majestic. I do not wish to argue for the very low French chamber pitch . . . but neither can I approve of the very high Venetian pitch. . . . Therefore I conclude the best pitch to be the so-called German A chamber pitch. . . . It*

is neither too low nor too high, but the mean between the French and the Venetian; and in it both the stringed and the wind instruments can produce their proper effect."

Quantz's appeal for an international standard pitch was not to be satisfied until a century and a half after his death when, in 1939, the International Standardizing Organization met in London and ordained that A = 440 Hz. Many modern symphony orchestras tune to this pitch, but others tune as high as A = 444 Hz.

The German chamber pitch, or *Cammerton,* that so pleased Quantz was around A = 416 Hz, but because A = 415 Hz is exactly a semitone lower than A = 440 Hz, this pitch was adopted as "standard" for today's international Early Music scene. I would recommend you therefore to tune to this pitch for now. However, as Bruce Haynes writes in his wonderfully comprehensive survey of pitch, *A History of Performing Pitch: The Story of "A,"* "*If we are interested in original sonorities, if we want our instruments to act and feel as they did when they were first played and our voices to function as they did for the composers who conceived their parts, it seems we have no choice but to renounce the luxury of a single hard-earned pitch standard."*[8]

I shall be suggesting pitches for each piece where appropriate.

There is one further issue to mention here, that of tuning your strings according to historical temperaments. For now it will be sufficient, if playing with a keyboard instrument, to tune each string separately, observing that the fifths are very slightly narrower than the perfect fifths you are used to. In Lesson 11 I shall address the question of tuning, intonation, and temperaments in detail.

❧ ❧ ❧

If you are now equipped with a violin, a bow and four suitable strings, you are ready to proceed to Lesson 2.

Notes

1. See Boyden, *The History of Violin Playing,* p. 195.
2. For the full text of Raguenet's "Comparison," see Strunk, *Source Readings in Music History,* p. 126.
3. The Mary Burwell Lute Tutor (c 1670) Folio 7v.
4. Webber, *Rethinking Gut Strings: A Guide for Players of Baroque Instruments,* p. 6.
5. Brossard, *Dictionary.* Quoted in Boyden, *The History of Violin Playing,* p. 321.
6. Garsault, F.A.P de, *Notionnaire, ou mémorial raisonné, Fuzeau* Facsimiles, France 1600–1800, Volume I, p. 223.
7. Playford, *A Brief Introduction to the Playing on the Treble-Violin.* Extract from "An Introduction to the skill of Musick." This appears only in the 1664 edition: *"There is a late Invention of Strings for the Basses, Viols and Violins, or Lutes, which sound much better and lowder than the common Gut String, either under the Bow or Finger. It is small wire twisted or gimp'd upon a gut string or upon Silk. I have made Tryal of both, but those upon Silk do hold best and give as good a Sound."*
8. Bruce Haynes, *A History of Performing Pitch, the Story of "A,"* p. xxi.

Lesson 2

Holding the Violin

In this lesson we learn about the many ways in which the violin was held during the Baroque period and then search for a way that reconciles complex and often conflicting historical evidence with our need to be technically secure and physically comfortable.

Some may ask why we cannot hold our 'Baroque' violin in the same way that we have always held our 'modern' violin? What difference can the way we hold our instrument possibly make to the music? To me, the answer is clear: our physical relationship to the violin impacts on just about every aspect of our playing; by adapting our hold to one based on the evidence of the many historical treatises available to us, we move one step nearer to those musicians whom, across the chasm of the centuries, we seek to emulate. Thus, casting ourselves adrift from our old ways of playing, we set ourselves free to embark on our journey into the past.

So let us not be afraid to change: after all, we change whenever we learn and we learn whenever we change.

The great advantage of the old kind of hold, or non-hold, is the physical freedom it gives to the left side of our body as well as to the bow arm, the head, and the neck. The modern hold, with its reliance on the molded chinrest and the often thick shoulder pad as well, is restrictive by contrast: the violin is virtually clamped between the player's chin and shoulder.

With the abandonment of these impediments, the violin will feel more integrated into our physical system, an extension of our body rather than an appendix to it, thus making it easier to express the physical gestures that play so important a role in Baroque music.

Let us read what David Mannes, a former concertmaster of the New York Symphony Orchestra and founder of what is today Mannes College, the New School for Music in New York, said in 1919:

> I absolutely disapprove, in theory, of chin rest, cushion or pad. . . . The more close and direct a contact with his instrument the player can develop, the more intimately expressive his playing becomes. . . . A thin pad may be used without much danger, yet I feel that the thicker and higher the "chin rest," the greater the loss in expressive rendering.[1]

The combination of body contact, shoulder pad, and chinrest also impacts on the way the wood of the violin vibrates, stifling a certain amount of the sound. Try for yourself the experiment in Exercise 1.

Exercise 1: Observing the violin's natural resonance

1. Hold the violin without touching it with your chin.
2. Tap gently on its back with the knuckles of your fingers and listen to the resonance produced.
3. Grip the violin between your chin and your shoulder and repeat. All you hear now is a stifled thud!

As we seek to draw closer to the ways we understand the violin was played in the seventeenth and eighteenth centuries, we must move away from the techniques of today and explore alternative paths, opening ourselves up to new experiences. Clearly, the sound of the instrument is related to the techniques used, and that includes the hold. The hold effects the organization of the whole bodily machine as well as the relationship between bow and violin.

You may object that there are some disadvantages: less security in shifts, for example, or more difficulty with vibrato. But that's how it was for Arcangelo Corelli, Giuseppe Tartini, and Heinrich Ignaz Franz von Biber! Supposing we discover, for example, that the vibrato we have been trained to use on our modern violin is physically impossible to produce without the chin gripping firmly on the violin: does that not prove that such a vibrato would have been impossible to produce in the period under discussion?

The way of holding I shall advocate later in this lesson allows the bow and violin to move freely in a kind of benignly fruitful opposition to each other, leaving the head and neck free, and releasing the shoulders and back.

As a student of this course, you will require a certain amount of patience as you enter into this initial period of experimentation. You may find it frustrating at first, but take courage: all modern players find the Baroque violin difficult at the beginning, and yet in time we all grow into it, finding our own ways of being comfortable and of feeling free. I am often impressed by how much quicker some of my students adapt than I did! When I was a beginner on the Baroque violin, I used to practice over a bed, in case I dropped the violin. I never did, nor, for that matter, have any of my students. I gradually became more comfortable playing in the new way. Now I find violins with chinrests and shoulder pads unspeakably clumsy, restrictive, and difficult to play!

❧ ❧ ❧

Let us be clear: there never was a standard universal way of holding the violin at any time in the period 1600 to around 1830, or for that matter even later, and therefore there can be no single 'right' or 'authentic' way to do so. From the tavern fiddler to the gentleman amateur, from the professional orchestral musician who rarely needed to venture beyond third position to the virtuoso soloist who reached dizzy heights at the top of the fingerboard, violinists found their own solutions according to their skill, their anatomy, and the demands of the music.

The sheer variety of holds shown in the paintings of the seventeenth and eighteenth centuries is as bewildering as the diversity of written descriptions outlined below. Iconographic evidence, although a valuable source of information, especially in the depiction of instruments and bows, is not wholly to be trusted even, as we shall see, within pedagogical treatises. Many painters from the Renaissance to the present time chose to depict musical instruments as objects of beauty, without the specific aim of portraying the way they were played with a degree of accuracy worthy of being considered instructive.

The *Oude Vioolspeler* by Adriaen Matham (1620–1660), now in the Rijksmuseum in Amsterdam, is clearly enjoying having his portrait sketched: the country scene in the background and the bagpipe hanging from his back, as well as his unorthodox way of bowing with his left hand, identify him as an "Old Fiddler" who plays in taverns and at fairs. *The Violin Player*, painted in 1626 by Gerard van Honthorst (1592–1656) and now in the Mauritshuis in The Hague, is probably neither a violinist nor a fiddler, for the same model appears in other paintings by Honthorst holding a lute, a guitar, and a viola da gamba. Although her bow hold is convincing (note that the thumb is placed under the hair, not the stick) the artist's remit is surely to portray the beauty of the young woman and the instrument, rather than to record for posterity an exemplary way of holding the violin (Figure a).

Figure a
Some violinists depicted in Baroque paintings are no more reliable as sources of pedagogic information than are the angels and cherubs of a Renaissance painting. These two portraits are by the Dutch painters Adriaen Matham and Gerard van Honthorst.

A more modern example of this phenomenon is the golden statue (1921) of Johann Strauss in Vienna (Figure b). His head is shown well clear of his violin, yet it is extremely unlikely that this is an accurate depiction of the way Strauss played in the second half of the nineteenth century. A more likely explanation is that the artist wished to show both Strauss's head and his violin in their entireties, without merging them into one another.

Figure b
A statue of Johann Strauss (1825–1899) in the Stadtpark, Vienna, appears to show him playing 'chinless.' The statue was unveiled in 1921.

The earliest description of how the violin was held comes from Philibert Jambe de Fer's *Epitome muscial* (Lyon, 1556). *"The Italian calls it 'Violon da braccia,'"* de Fer tells us, *"because it is held upon the arms, some with a scarf, cord, or other thing."*[2]

Some Baroque violinists today use this method very successfully, slipping a scarf between the belly of the violin and the tailpiece and then tying it round their necks. This certainly provides a measure of stability and security, without restricting freedom of movement.

From Matteis, whom Roger North[3] tells us *"held his instrument almost against his girdle,"* via those who recommend holding it *"below the left breast"* (Merck, 1695), *"on your left breast"* (Crome, 1735 (?)), *"somewhat higher than your breast"* (Lenton, 1693), *"below the shoulder"* (Playford, 1674), *"just below the left cheek"* (Montéclair, 1711), to *"just below the collar bone"* (Geminiani, 1751), the principle seems to emerge that violinists had to find a way to be comfortable so they could do what matters . . . play the music. As Leopold Mozart (Chapter II, §4) was to remark, *"We see daily examples of such clumsy players who find everything difficult because they restrict themselves by an awkward position of the violin and the bow."*

Controversy among Early Music revivalists has long raged over the use of the chin for holding the violin. Some schools insist that the chin *never* touch the instrument, basing their principle on Francesco Geminiani and others. This necessitates a technique of creeping along the neck of the violin with the help of an active wrist and thumb in order to change position downward. Some find this fairly easy to master, while others struggle with it for years. It became, in the early days of the Baroque revival, almost a defining issue for proponents of the 'Strictly Chinless' school, the acid test as to whether or not one was a true 'Baroque' violinist.

In today's competitive professional world, many Baroque violinists claim the right to a level playing field, in terms of technical security, with their modern counterparts. They also point to the convincing body of historical evidence that counters the exclusively 'chinless' or 'chin-off' argument. As a result, a greater degree of diversity in the manner of holding the Baroque violin has developed.

There is much iconographic and textual evidence to suggest that, for the most part, seventeenth- and eighteenth-century violinists held their instruments without keeping a permanent grip on them with their chins, although I know of no source that specifically forbids doing so; indeed, it is difficult to imagine why such an instruction should be indicated. Bornet (1786) comes close when he states that one should *"place the violin under the chin so that the button is more or less at the middle of the neck,"* adding that the head should be held straight and that *"the chin should not lean on the violin (que le menton n'appuye pas sur le violon)."* Whether "not leaning" and "never touching" are the same thing is not clear.[4]

Antonio Lolli (1784) states that *"the head of the instrument should be at the height of the chin"* but fails to expand on the subject, while Aurelio Signoretti (1777) advocates holding the violin *"under the chin, on the left side"* but then adds only that the chin *"should not touch the tailpiece,"* possibly because he was aware of the possibility of the tail gut snapping under pressure.

A few sources fail to mention the position of the chin at all, but some specifically advise holding on with the chin, especially when shifting. Johann Jacob Prinner (1624–1694) who knew both Heinrich Ignaz Franz von Biber and Johann Heinrich Schmelzer, writes in his *Musicalischer Schlissl* (Musical Key, 1677) that the violin must be held so firmly with the chin that the left hand can be totally free. Otherwise, he writes, it will be *"impossible to shift downward rapidly while playing in tune."* Furthermore, he suggests that those who rest the violin on their chests do so out of a kind of vanity, *"thinking it looks pretty and decorative, like a picture of an angel playing to St Francis."*[5] The conflict between practicality and appearance referred to by Prinner has already been discussed and will be further referred to.

Robert Crome, in his book *The Fiddle new Model'd* (London, c. 1735) clearly aimed at the amateur violinist, similarly advocates using the chin:

> *Take the Fiddle and hold it in your Left Hand. Let the Neck lie between your fore Finger and Thumb, turning your Wrist, that your Fingers may lie over the Finger Board to be in readyness when you want them: then let the back part rest on your left Breast, the best way is to stay it with your Chin, that it may remain steady.*[6]

At about the same time (1738), Michel Corrette's minimal information in *L'Ecole d'Orphée* on how to hold the instrument states: *"One must necessarily put the chin on the violin . . . especially when shifting downwards."*[7]

A portrait of Corrette (Figure c) shows the violin within grasp of his chin should he need to steady it; as is so often the case with such portraits, the violin is pictured sloping downward to allow the instrument to be clearly visible, a position that is unlikely to have yielded the optimal tonal results for this celebrated violinist.

Figure c
Michel Corrette: *L'Ecole d'Orphée. Methode pour Apprendre facilement à joüer du Violon*, Paris, 1738. Reproduced by kind permission of Anne Fuzeau Productions.

Puzzlingly, the Frontispiece to Corrette's later anthology of far more technically advanced pieces, *L'Art de se perfectionner dans le violon* (1782), depicts a more idealized view of the entranced violinist (Figure d).

Figure d

Frontispiece to Michel Corrette's *L'Art de se perfectionner dans le violon* (1782). Reproduced by kind permission of Anne Fuzeau Productions.

Although Geminiani (1751) writes, *"The Violin must be rested just below the Collarbone,"* the engraving in the French translation of his book, published just a year later, appears to show the violin held rather higher than that (Figure e). This portrait was, it seems, 'lifted' from the as yet unpublished treatise *Arte y puntual explicación del modo de tocar el violín* by the greatest Spanish violinist of the eighteenth century, José Herrando, Geminiani's head being placed onto the body of Herrando! Herrando's book was eventually published in Paris in 1756.

Figure e

Detail of the frontispiece of José Herrando's *Arte y puntual explicación del modo de tocar el violín* (Paris, 1756). The picture had been pirated and used in the French translation of Francesco Geminiani's book *L'art du Violon* four years earlier, Herrano's head having been removed and Geminiani's head substituted. The violin is clearly not being held according to Geminiani's written instruction of "under the collar-bone."

The two men knew each other well: Herrando was a colleague of Geminiani's brother Miguel, in Madrid. *"The stringholder* [tailpiece] *must come under the chin,"* Herrando writes, *"being secured by it, the face turned a bit toward the right hand."*[8]

The French version of Geminiani's book differs significantly on the key issue of the role of the chin. While the violin still should rest *"below the collar-bone,"* the use of the chin is advocated to steady the violin, especially when shifting:

The chin must lean a little on . . . the right side (of the violin) *so that when necessary it can be pressed down whenever the hand that holds the neck is obliged to move from position to position. Without the help of this gentle leaning, it could happen that the violin fall or lose the horizontal line that it must describe with the part resting against the chest."*[9]

This is confusing: anyone with an average length of neck will find it impossible to reach the violin while holding it so low (try it yourself!). If you wish to use your chin, you must hold the violin above the collarbone. Was the anonymous translator offering his own pragmatic solution to the problem of shifting?

In the German edition of Geminiani's book, published in 1782, the violin is described as being placed *"between the collarbone and the jawbone."*[10]

Leopold Mozart (1756) details two ways of holding the violin. The frontispiece picture of his book (Figure f) shows him holding the violin in a rather studio-posed way *"held chest-high (and) slanting,"* as he himself (II, §2) describes it. But he goes on to say of this picture that *"this position is undoubtedly natural and pleasant to the eyes of the onlookers but somewhat difficult and inconvenient to the player as, during quick movements of the hand in the high position, the violin has no support and must therefore necessarily fall unless by long practice the advantage of being able to hold it between the thumb and index finger has been acquired."*

Figure f
Frontispiece to Leopold Mozart's *Versuch*, showing the *"undoubtedly natural and pleasant"* way to hold the violin.

In Leopold's Fig. II (our Figure g, below) he shows how the violin *should* be held in what he says (§3) is a *"comfortable method."* Here, the violin is *"placed against the neck so that it lies somewhat in front of the shoulder and the side on which the E string lies comes under the chin, whereby the violin remains unmoved even during the strongest movements of the ascending and descending hand."*

Although Leopold does not specifically say so, the implication is that by holding the violin *"against the neck"* so that it *"remains unmoved"* he is arguably advocating steadying it with his chin.

Figure g
Leopold Mozart's
"comfortable method"
of holding the violin.

The first French translation of Leopold Mozart (1770) contradicts the original in one important detail: *"The second way of holding the violin is more comfortable for the player. One rests it on the collar-bone so that the chin is on the side of the fourth (G) string."*[11]

A portrait of Francesco Maria Veracini, reputed to have been a pupil of Corelli, clearly shows him in a 'chin-off' position (Figure h), although he too seems to be posing, rather than playing: notice, for example, the curious angle of his bow in relation to the violin.

Figure h
Francesco Maria Veracini
(1690–1768). Engraving
by J. June after a portrait
by F. F. Richter.

By the third quarter of the eighteenth century, experiments were being made to hold the violin on the left (G string) side. The treatise of L'Abbé le fils (1772) has the instruction to place the violin *"on the collar bone, so that the chin is on the side of the fourth (G) string.* By the end of the century the use of the chin is more frequently indicated, Bartolomeo Campagnoli (1797) writing that *"one puts the end of the violin on the collar bone and one leans the chin lightly on the table (couvert) on the side of the G string (bourdon.)"*

Eventually, a small chinrest would be used to prevent the violin from falling, but this did not become standard practice until the nineteenth century.

∾ ∾ ∾

Although holding in a permanently "chinless" way carries no technical dangers as long as the music barely leaves the first position, I personally do not consider it necessary or wise to establish this principle as a defining rule. Like many of my colleagues, I enjoy the freedom of playing chinless when I do not feel the need to steady the violin, but I have no qualms about steadying the violin with my chin when I consider it advantageous, for example, when shifting downward. Shifting upward is not a problem, as one is pushing the violin against one's body, but shifting down is more dangerous, more of a leap of faith!

Using different holds for different styles at different periods can work up to a point, but I feel we should avoid becoming too pedantic about a subject where evidence is both ambiguous and contradictory.

❧ ❧ ❧

How to Hold the Baroque Violin: A Beginner's Guide

Having read the above information, you may well find yourself perplexed and confused, so may I now recommend a starting point for finding your personal and ideal way of holding the violin? Naturally, every student has a different physiological and psychological makeup as well as different priorities. But in my experience, having learned this basic hold, each one seems to adapt and experiment, gradually arriving at a hold that is natural and workable for him or her.

Rest the right (E string) side of the instrument on your left clavicle (collarbone), the scroll pointing at a comfortable angle, not too far out to the left, not too far in to the right, at a height where you can place your chin on the violin easily should you eventually need to, while keeping your head free when you do not.

Leopold Mozart (II, §6) states: *"The violin must be held neither too low nor too high. The medium height is best. The scroll of the violin is then held on the level of the mouth, or at the highest, level with the eyes, but it must not be allowed to sink lower than the level of the chest."* Geminiani, in his 'The Art of playing on the Violin' (1751) agrees *"that the Head of the Violin must be nearly Horizontal with that Part which rests against the Breast, that the Hand may be shifted with Facility and without any Danger of dropping the Instrument."*

The advantage of holding the violin on the E string side of the tailpiece is simple: if it rests on the left shoulder, the violin has nowhere to fall and feels both secure and free. The violin should be slanted, the E string side being lower than the G string side so that, as Geminiani says, *"There may be no Necessity of raising the Bow very high, when the fourth String is to be struck."*

It is sensible to follow the advice Montéclair gives us in his "Simple Method" (1711). *"To hold the violin securely so that it will not move, one must press the button that holds the strings well against the neck under the left cheek."*[12]

Note that as you are now holding the violin with your chin on the right-hand side of the tailpiece, it will automatically be pointing more or less out in front of you, no longer away to your left. You will therefore find you are working in a more convenient and comfortable space, and this will make many aspects of bowing feel far more natural.

As to the left hand, hold the neck between the bottom joint of the index (first) finger and the thumb, with the least amount of tension possible. Leopold Mozart advises us (Chapter II, §4) that the neck of the violin must be *"held in such a manner between thumb and index-finger that it rests on one side on the ball at the base of the index-finger, and on the other side against the upper part of the thumb-joint, but in no way touching the skin which joins the thumb and index-finger together,"*

The sources are scanty on any additional advice, so you will need to experiment, letting *"your own discretion be your tutor,"* as Shakespeare puts it (*Hamlet*, act 3, scene 2). Be patient: you will find your own way eventually. I have had students with necks too long to be able to steady the violin with their chin: the choice for them is between using a lot of padding and playing totally chinless.

One certain advantage in playing 'chin off' is that it enables you to hear differently. Having a slightly greater distance between the violin and your ear enhances your ability to be objective about your own sound, as well as making it easier to hear the total sound when playing in a group. We can relate this to the painter stepping back to evaluate more accurately the most recent strokes of his brush.

All this is going to feel strange at the beginning, so courage and patience will be needed! We have all gone through the difficult process of learning to hold the violin in a different way from the one we have been used to for so many years. Remember, we are seeking to find a new freedom for the body, not additional restrictions. As we will not be playing Bach fugues or Tartini sonatas for a while, we will not need the extra steadying of the chin for the moment: perhaps we never will.

Leopold Mozart suggests (Chapter II, § 8) that *"if at first the beginner does not succeed in holding the violin freely in the prescribed manner . . . let him hold the scroll against a wall."* This will certainly help you achieve a greater sense of security and, magically, when you come away from the wall, a kind of 'wall-ness' will follow you, that secure feeling remaining—for a while! *"Let him repeat this exercise alternately 'free' and against the wall,"* continues Leopold, *"until he is finally able to play freely without it."* Remember to place a cloth over the scroll so as not to scratch the varnish.

Leopold's book is a rich source of advice and his somewhat pompous style is often amusing too. For example, among actions to be avoided he lists (II, § 6) *"the twisting of the mouth or wrinkling of the nose . . . the hissing, whistling or any too audible blowing with the breath from the mouth, throat or nose when playing a difficult note."* Student: take heed!

Another tip for feeling more secure while holding the violin in this way is to use a piece of chamois leather to help keep the violin steady and to protect it from the perils of perspiration. Cut off a strip about six inches long and four inches wide and then cut a small hole in the center. Stretch the hole so that the cloth fits tightly over the button of the violin and will stay on even when you are not playing. Many people find this more comfortable than having to hold just the bare wood.

One last detail is worth mentioning here: the so-called Geminiani grip (Figure i), a method prescribed by Geminiani of *"acquiring the true Position of the Hand, which is this: To place the first finger on the first String upon F; the second Finger on the second String upon C; the third finger on the third String upon G; and the fourth finger on the fourth String upon D."*

Being able to achieve this grip comfortably will ensure that your way of holding the instrument is likewise comfortable. Leopold Mozart, in the later (1787 and 1806) editions of his *Versuch,* copies Geminiani's advice wholesale.

Figure i
The "Geminiani grip," the perfect position for the left hand.

Postlude

As we begin to build our identities as Baroque violinists, absorbing information from the many disparate sources available to us, as well as from the instruments and repertoire, we will need to make choices and compromises that seem right for us. The aesthetic and technical makeup of the modern Baroque violinist is therefore more complex than would have been that of a Parisian violinist drafted into Lully's orchestra or one who worked all his life in San Petronio in Bologna.

The Baroque violinist of today is quite unlike any of these historical personalities. Playing music from a vast variety of periods and places, each one in a stylistically appropriate manner, is certainly not an activity that an eighteenth-century violinist would ever have dreamed of indulging in and is only possible now after a great deal of research and with a fair amount of guesswork.

Clearly, a Venetian violinist in 1620 could not have imagined what his instrument was to sound like in the hands of Veracini! But neither would Geminiani or Leopold Mozart have been likely to play Marini or Fontana in a historically informed way if indeed, as is almost inconceivable, they would have considered playing them at all. True, certain composers such as Corelli managed to glide through history without his fame ever being obscured but, as we shall learn when we study the tradition of playing Bach (Lesson 40), the concept that it is better to play music from previous periods in the way it was played when it was composed is a purely modern one.

Quantz, in his autobiography, tells us that as a young man he had studied the violin and had played works by Biber: we can only conjecture how the master of the 'Style Galant' sounded as he played works by the master of the 'Stylus Phantasticus.'

Notes

1. David Mannes, quoted in Frederick H. Martens, *Violin Mastery, Talks with Master Violinists and Teachers*.
2. Jambe de Fer, *Epitome musical*, p. 63, "L'Italien l'appelle Violon da Braccia ou violone, par ce qu'il se soutient sus les bras, les uns avec escharpe, cordons ou autre chose . . ."
3. Quoted in Boyden, *The History of Violin Playing*, p. 248, note 6.
4. Bornet, *Nouvelle Méthode de Violon*, 1786.
5. Prinner, *Musicalischer Schlissl*.
6. Crome, *The Fiddle New Model'd*, p. 34.
7. Corrette, *L'Ecole d'Orphée*, p. 7.
8. Herrando, *Arte y puntual explicación del modo de tocar el violin*, quoted in Boyden, p. 368.
9. Geminiani, *The Art of Playing on the Violin*.
10. Quoted in Boyden, *The History of Violin Playing*, p. 368.
11. Fuzeau facsimile violin treatises, France 1600–1800, Vol. 1, p. 233.
12. Montéclair, *Méthode Facile pour apprendre a jouer du Violon*, p. 2.

Lesson 3

The Bow, Creator of Sound

It is often said that the violin is the closest instrument to the human voice, but it is the bow, born from the human voice, a physical extension of that which is intangible, that creates, nourishes, and sustains its sound. The strings of the violin can merely alter pitch, but it is the bow that sings, speaks, exclaims, laughs, and dances. It can cry out in alarm, horrify, beat like a drum, but it can also soothe and seduce: without it, the violin is silent. Thus Bartolomeo Bismantova, in his *Compendio* of 1677 states that *"the entire art of playing the violin consists in knowing how to manage the bow well, to make good bowings, to make long bow strokes, and to play now loud, now soft, sweet and cantabile."* [1]

Throughout the period, the sources echo this principle: *"The Tone of the Violin,"* writes Francesco Geminiani (1751), *"principally Depends on the right Management of the Bow."* Leopold Mozart (1756) writes that *"the bowing gives life to the notes,"* while L'Abbé le fils (1761) is more poetic: *"One may call the bow "The Soul of the Instrument,"* he says *". . . because it is used to give expression to the sounds."*

> The bow is to the string what the brush is to the canvas. Sometimes, bold strokes with a thick-bristled brush are required; at other times a gentle dabbing with the tip of a fine brush adds just the right amount of paint. From the fluent perfection of Giotto's circle to the tiniest dot of the pointillist master, the brush manipulates color as the bow manipulates sound.

Holding the Bow

One way of holding the bow, used throughout the seventeenth and into the eighteenth centuries, was to place the thumb under the hair, with the other fingers on top of the wood. This hold is clearly illustrated in the 1665 painting by the Dutch artist, Gerard Dou, shown in Figure a, and is sometimes referred to nowadays as the "French grip." However, it was by no means confined to that country: Georg Muffat (1698) tells us that *"most Germans agree with the Lullists* (the followers of Jean-Baptiste Lully, 'founder' of the French style) *on the holding of the bow for the violins and violas; that is, pressing the thumb against the hair and laying the other fingers on the back of the bow."* [2]

John Playford, in his *Rules for the Treble Violin* (1674) echoes Muffat. The bow should be held with *"the Thumb being staid upon the Hair at the Nut, and the three Fingers resting upon the Wood."*[3]

Figure a
The 'thumb under' bow hold. Gerard Dou (1613–75), violinist, 1665, detail.

According to Roger North, it was Nicola Matteis who, early in the 1670s *"taught ye English to hold ye bow by ye wood only & not to touch ye hair which was no small reformation."*[4]

The hold Muffat and others describe gradually became obsolete, with one more closely resembling the "modern" way being universally adopted. Michel Corrette, in his *L'Ecole d'Orphée* (1738), writes that the French use the method described above while the Italians have their thumbs under the wood. *"Both methods,"* he says, *"are equally good— it depends on the Master who is teaching."*[5]

We will take time later in this book to practice the 'thumb under' technique, observing in what way it affects the sound and the articulation. I have my students try this both in seventeenth-century repertoire and in French music such as that of François Couperin (see Lesson 34). It is important to remember, however, that in the seventeenth century bows were much smaller and lighter than the kind of mid-eighteenth-century model you may well be using. The heavier the bow, the harder it is to control when using this hold. Therefore, while I encourage experimentation at all stages, I recommend starting with the more familiar bow hold, the thumb placed beneath the stick.

"The Bow," writes Geminiani, *"is to be held at a small Distance from the Nut, between the Thumb and Fingers, the Hair being turned inward against the Back or Outside of the Thumb, in which Position it is to be held free and easy, and not stiff. The Motion is to proceed from the Joints of the Wrist and Elbow in playing quick Notes, and very little or not at all from the Joints of the Shoulder. . . . The Bow must always be drawn parallel with the Bridge (which can't be done if it is held stiff) and must be pressed upon the Strings with the Fore-finger only, and not with the whole Weight of the Hand. The best Performers are least sparing of their Bow; and make Use of the whole of it, from the Point to that part of it under, and even beyond their Fingers."*[6]

As a teacher, I don't try and get my students to change the shape of their usual hold as long as there is no physical problem with it. You should be comfortable, aware that the stick has different qualities from the one you are used to. Try shifting the hand up a little from the frog, and experiment with balance, maneuverability, and ease of articulation.

Leopold Mozart (Figure b) shows us a "wrong way" and a "correct way" to hold the bow: he advocates holding it *"at its lowest extremity."*

Giuseppe Tartini advises us that the bow *"should be held firmly between the thumb and forefinger and lightly by the other three fingers, in order to produce a strong, sustained tone. To increase the tone,"* he says, *"press harder on the bow with the fingers and also press down the strings more firmly with the fingers of the other hand."*[7]

Leopold Mozart (Chapter II) insists that the elbow be not too high: he doesn't say why, but clearly the weight of the arm "hanging," as it were, from the string, will help produce the *"honest and virile tone"* he encourages us to aim for. *"One must,* he adds *"watch the right arm of the pupil unremittingly; that the elbow, while drawing the bow, be not raised too high, but remains always somewhat near to the body."* Figure c illustrates the faulty elbow position.

Figure c
"Der Fehler" (The Error) shows the elbow raised too high. Note that here too, unlike in the Frontispiece, the violin is being held close to the chin. Note also the lion's head scroll, possibly identifying the instrument as a Stainer, with the protruding ends of the strings. Leopold Mozart, Chapter 2.

The raising of the elbow is more relevant to modern violin technique. With the chin over the G string and the violin pointing away to the left, a complicated 'lever technology,' involving the pronating (revolving toward the body) of the arm is used. But with the chin now on the E string side and the work zone more immediately in front of the body, the raised elbow serves no purpose. The lower you hold the violin, the more you can drop the shoulders, free the neck, and, by keeping the elbow low, sink comfortably into the string.

One intrinsic quality of the Baroque bow is that it is heavier at the frog and lighter at the tip. Thus the bow has its own built-in dynamic system as well as the natural hierarchy of a strong down-bow versus a weaker up-bow. The modern bow (actually being pioneered in the second half of the eighteenth century) was partly designed to iron out this quality, and its suitability for the repertoire must therefore be called into serious question. However skilled we may become at imitating the qualities of the Baroque bow on its modern equivalent, an in-depth exploration of what the old bow can and cannot do is absolutely the key to unlocking the secrets of the music for which it was designed (see Exercise 2).

Exercise 2: Discovering the natural dynamics of the Baroque bow

Draw the bow slowly from frog to tip, without adding any weight or pressure: you will hear a distinct diminuendo. Coming back, you will notice a natural crescendo.

In order to take full advantage of this quality, we will need to be able to travel from one part of the bow to another part swiftly but without causing unwanted accents. I shall be giving you some exercises for that in Lesson 7.

Baroque music is extremely fragile: if a weak note is played too strong, or a strong one played too weak, the entire phrase is perverted and destroyed. Phrases need to be clearly structured and the hierarchy of important notes and less important notes meticulously respected. The responsibility for good phrasing lies with the intellect, the ear and the bow. Our bowing therefore needs to be highly organized if it is to produce the infinite subtleties that the music demands!

Having absorbed much information on how to hold the violin and the bow, we can proceed to the next lesson where we learn to make our first real sounds.

Video 3.1

Notes

1. Carter, *Performer's Guide to Seventeenth Century Music*, p. 467.
2. Muffat, Preface *to Florilegium secundum*, 1698, in *GMPP*, p. 33.
3. John Playford: *An Introduction to the skill of Musick*. London, 1674. p. 114.
4. Roger North, quoted in *The History of Violin Playing from Its Origins to 1761*, p 249, n7.
5. Corrette, *L'Ecole d'Orphée*, p. 7.
6. Geminiani, *The Art of Playing on the Violin*, p. 2.
7. Tartini, *Regole* (Rules for Bowing). Hermann Moeck edition p. 57.

Lesson 4

First Sounds
Celebrating Our Vocal Heritage

In this lesson we prepare to make our first sounds. After a brief discussion on how the Baroque violin and bow will by themselves lead us closer to the musical intentions of the composers who wrote for them, we consider why the very nature of Baroque music is incompatible with certain aspects of modern technique.

Having arrived at a fundamental truth concerning the elements that make up Baroque music, we discuss the vocal origins of instrumental music and decide that copying the human voice will provide us with a perfect inroad into the rediscovery of the old ways of playing.

We begin this task by exploring the spoken word, demonstrating how the imitation of language translates into the art of bowing. To this aim we consider a brief exposé on the importance of articulation, for which the Baroque bow is the perfect instrument, and we investigate the true nature of rhythm. We end the lesson by declaiming speeches from Shakespeare, speaking not with our voice but with our bow.

Video 4.1

৺৺ ৺৺ ৺৺

Just as the harpsichord is thought of by some as the quaint forerunner of the modern piano and the viol as the benign old grandfather of the cello, the Baroque violin is regarded in some circles as a somewhat primitive version of its modern counterpart (the "real" or "normal" violin, as I have often heard it described!).

Yet these instruments were the living voices of the music of their time. They became obsolete because styles of composition changed and sound worlds were conjured up for which they were no longer suitable. Today, as we travel back in time, we turn to them for help in bringing that lost sound world back to life.

The Baroque bow, that indispensable guide to the techniques for which it was designed, will reveal its secrets if we investigate comprehensively its intrinsic qualities, not only what it can do but also what it seems unable or reluctant to do. As we do so we will discover that it is perfectly designed to convey the infinite subtleties, inflexions, and colors that the music itself demands.

৺৺ ৺৺ ৺৺

Modern violin technique focuses on an essentially legato ideal inherited largely from the long singing phrases of the Romantic tradition. How many hours of effort did we as students invest in the quest for that mythical seamless bow-change at frog and point, coating over the inevitable crack with a constant vibrato that flows inexorably from note to note? Such ideals and techniques will be shown to be not only stylistically inappropriate but positively counterproductive to a convincing interpretation of Baroque music.

One of the misconceptions that can be said frequently to mar the performance of Baroque music when played in what I respectfully call a "less than informed" manner is that it is the performer's duty to employ such techniques to help imbue lyricism into a piece, even where there is in fact no real melody, or where the melodic element is secondary.

I am referring not only to dances or dance-based pieces, such as we find in Bach's E Major Partita, nor to the more rhetorical compositions such as the meandering, pensive Double of the Sarabande from his B Minor Partita, but also to music such as the opening of the third Brandenburg Concerto (Figure a) with its implied dialogue between an upper and a lower voice, its crisp rhythms and its varied articulations. To impose a lyrical 'melodicism' on such obviously non-melodic writing is surely to misunderstand the nature of the musical language in which the piece is written.

Figure a
Violin part of Bach's
Brandenburg Concerto
No. 3, opening.

Although melodic elements are clearly present in Baroque music, much of it is made up of elements derived from speech and dance, with little or nothing of what we may call "a good tune." This fundamental truth should be uppermost in our minds as we begin our study: we will refer to the links between speech, rhetoric, dance, and music throughout this book.

The key to a more fitting approach to all three of the above musical examples, and to the interpretation of so much of seventeenth- and eighteenth-century repertoire, is the concept, art, and technique of articulation. Articulation may be defined as *the quality of each bow stroke:* whether the stroke is long or short, attached to or detached from the notes on either side of it, whether it is attacked strongly or gently, has a sound that is constant, or that grows or diminishes, or that has time to do both. The Baroque bow will help us rediscover these unspecified nuances, these subtleties so long hidden under layers of legato and coatings of vibrato.

The farther back we go in musical history, the fewer specific written indications we find as to expression, tempo, dynamics, and the general ebb and flow of the music. Articulations, for example, were never specified until late in the Baroque period, and even then often ambiguously. In the course of this book we will learn how to choose and execute the maximum variety of articulations that we can use to make non-melodic music endlessly varied and fascinating for our audience.

જી જી જી

Searching for Our Vocal Roots

In order to uncover clues as to how the violin was played in its infant years, we need to remind ourselves of how the instrumental idiom was born. Just as the primitive proto-musical grunts and moans of our prehistoric ancestors were eventually to develop into formalized language, so in turn did our Western instrumental music evolve back out of language, seeking independence from its vocal roots and the dominance of text.

This 'emancipation' of instrumental music was made possible by the realization that music did not need to have words to have meaning and relevance to its listeners. This was a revolutionary concept, and it changed forever the story of music, reaching fruition with the outpouring of the utterly original, experimental (one could add "avant-garde") sonatas that heralded in the Baroque era.

Almost every source I know, from the mid-sixteenth century to the end of the Baroque period and indeed beyond, bids the instrumentalist imitate the human voice. Indeed, from Sylvestro Ganassi (Venice, 1535) onward, copying the human voice is seen as the key to good instrumental playing. In the mere eleven lines that make up Chapter 1 of Ganassi's *Fontegara*, "Defining the aim of the recorder player," he states this no fewer than four times:

1) *"Be it known that all musical instruments, in comparison to the human voice, are inferior to it. For this reason, we should endeavour to learn from it and imitate it."*
2) *"You can imitate the expression of the human voice on a wind or stringed instrument."*
3) *"An instrument can imitate the expression of the human voice by varying the pressure of the breath"* (for us, that relates to the bow!).
4) *"The aim of the recorder player is to imitate as closely as possible all the capabilities of the human voice. For this it is able to do."*

In Chapters 23 and 24, Ganassi reaffirms this belief, adding that *"in imitating the human voice, it must be an expert and experienced singer that you should imitate intelligently."*

In the Baroque period, musicians were not as specialized as they are today: one could say they were far better trained, for they were taught to play several instruments and to sing and compose as well. As Quantz (X, §18) was to write, *"If (the beginner) has the opportunity to study the art of singing, I strongly recommend that he do so."*

I frequently ask students to imagine how a phrase would sound if their favorite countertenor were standing beside them in the studio. It is clear that many of the answers students seek from their teachers (or at any rate from me) could be perfectly well resolved if only they would sing the passage through to themselves and observe what their natural musicality is telling them: more on that later.

The scarcity of specific technical instruction in many of the treatises may also be due to the conviction on the part of the writers that if, as so many of them point out, the source of all inspiration is the human voice, that is where we must turn for even the most detailed aspect of instruction. Much

| of what we call 'interpretation' is the observation of what the voice does naturally. Similarly, much of what we call 'technique' is the physical means of realizing those observations in sound. |

C. P. E. Bach agrees: *"It is a good practice,"* he writes, *"to sing instrumental melodies in order to reach an understanding of their correct performance. This way of learning is of far greater value than the reading of voluminous tomes or listening to learned discourses."*[1]

❧ ❧ ❧

"Listen to my bow," Arcangelo Corelli used to say, *"can you hear it speaking?"*[2] Teaching our bow to speak clearly and expressively will be our first major task; but what exactly does the human voice do? Exercise 3 is designed to demonstrate how different texts necessitate changes in more than one aspect of our bow technique.

Exercise 3: Relating bow articulation to textual variation

Figure b shows four equal quarter notes on the A string: sing the four notes to the following words, and observe the differences in articulation that the words demand. Once you have sung an example and observed its nuances, imitate your voice with your bow.

1) **Ah**: all four notes slurred in one slow bow, legato.
2) **Amen:** played with two notes per bow. It is probably best to start on an up-bow, with a gentle accent on the M of "men."
3) **Ah! I'm dying!** Three bows are needed here: one for "ah," one for "I'm" and one for "dying." "Ah!" is cut short to about an eighth note to make the exclamation more dramatic, so quite a fast bow is needed. "I'm" calls for a slower bow with a crescendo, the d of "dying" is well accented, but without too fast a bow, slurred to a softer "ing."

Figure b

Four notes articulated in three different ways, according to different texts.

Having played each of these examples as written, play them again, this time on a single note, such as an open string. Be sure to reproduce the articulations and nuances of sound in the same way as before. Try using pressure rather than speed of bow to bring out the nuances.

Exploring the Rhythm of Words

The rhythm of music comes from the rhythm of language: that is why the rhythm in, say, Hungarian folk music is utterly different from that of English folk music. The true rhythm of a word or phrase is very difficult to write down accurately, as the transcription (Figure c) that Béla Bartók made of a folk melody he had recorded clearly shows:

Figure c
Béla Bartók: folk music transcription.

Most of us have been trained to play music "in time," meaning in a theoretically and mathematically accurate way. Yet reducing rhythms to their easiest-to-write and simplest-to-play form, as computer programs frustratingly do, runs contrary to the art of imitating language. We need to avoid a bland, mechanical way of playing, one that puts theory or rules above practice and expression. When we attempt to play the natural, as opposed to the literal, length of each syllable, with all the subtle rhythmic and dynamic inflexions that are inherent in spoken or sung language, we realize that the written dots can represent little more than an approximation of what the living result should be.

> The process of learning is sometimes also a process of 'unlearning.' We need not feel we are abandoning techniques we have hitherto acquired; but we will be laying many of them aside in order to achieve our new aesthetic and stylistic goals. How long have we toiled to control our bows, seeking to play with total rhythmic precision! It will take some time before we are comfortable with this new concept of what is "rhythmic." First, we need to free ourselves from the idea that rhythm is an exact science and embrace the "art of rhythm" as one of our newly rediscovered expressive devices. In short, we need to train ourselves to be less servile and more creative with those black dots on the page.

As a Baroque violinist, you will be spending much of your time working with singers. Sometimes you will be playing in unison with them, so you will need to play with exactly the same inflections, accentuations, rhythms, etc., that they use. You will also need to be constantly aware of the words and their meaning, as well as what the character whom the singer is portraying is feeling and expressing at any one time, so that you can color your sound accordingly. Elsewhere, for instance in the introduction to an aria or a chorus, it is you who will first play the melody that the singer will take over, so prepare it well: play words! (Exercise 4).

Exercise 4: Investigating the *real* rhythm of a word

Listen to the recording of the words listed below and repeat them aloud, reciting them exactly as you hear them. Once you have spoken a word at the normal speed, it will be helpful to repeat it in slow motion, observing its rhythmic complexities.

- Corelli
- Frescobaldi

Audio 4.1

- Michelangelo
- Beautiful
- Kyrie Eleison

Now play each word on an open string. Imitate the exact rhythm of your voice, copying the stresses and inflections as closely as you can. Be careful not to control your bowing arm in a manner that impedes the free flowing of the word. If this occurs, try putting down your bow and practicing the rhythm with your arm alone, observing and eliminating any tightness.

Did you find that you tended to simplify the rhythm of these words when playing them, distilling them into clear but inaccurate formulae? Most people do this at the beginning, not yet able to reproduce the rhythmic complexities or the dynamic nuances present within the words they themselves speak. When I give a class to beginners on the Baroque violin, I often ask the students to introduce themselves by playing their names in this way: only rarely do I manage to decode them! I have also come to classes with the menu from an Italian restaurant and challenged the students to order their choice of dishes by speaking with their bows.

Let us now analyze the five words of Exercise 4 in detail:

- In "Corelli," the three syllables are not equal either in length or stress: "Co" is accented with an immediate diminuendo leading into the rolled "r." There is a Messa di voce (<>) through the "e," the climax of which is the strongest part of the word, and there is a little extra bounce on the "lli." An Italian speaker would pronounce both "l"s, with a barely perceptible break in the sound between the "e" and the "lli."

  I would regard the "Co" as an anacrusis to be played up-bow.

- The first two syllables in "Frescobaldi" are unequal: "Fres" is longer than "co," but in an indeterminate proportion, more like two parts to one part of a triplet than a dotted rhythm. The "ba" is longer than the other syllables and has a Messa di voce within it. The "di" bounces lightly off the end of the "bal."

- "Michelangelo" is a word with an elusive *actual* rhythm. "Michel" is a kind of rapid double anacrusis, or upbeat, to the "an," which is the climax of the word in terms of stress. The "an" is the longest syllable and has a <> shape, while "gelo" is about the same speed as "Michel."

- In "Beautiful," the "Beau" has two syllables, "bee" and "yoo": it is not a dipthong. The "bee" is not too short and crescendos into the "y" of "yoo" which is accented. The "yoo" sound is long and shaped, another Messa di voce, and the last two syllables, "ti" and "ful" are shorter but not equal either in strength or length: "ti" is shorter and weaker.

- In "Kyrie Eleison," the "kee" sound has a strong consonant followed by a Messa di voce. The "ree" occurs as the Messa di voce weakens: although it is much shorter than the "kee," it too has a Messa di voce embedded within it. The "ay" sound is slightly accented but even it has a hint of the <> shape. The rhythm of the syllables "ri" and "e" has a lilt difficult to notate accurately. There is the slightest of commas between the two words. In "Eleison" the "e" appears to crescendo into the "lei," but on closer analysis it too turns out to be more of a Messa di voce. The "lei" is the strongest syllable of the two words, a slow, clear Messa di voce, with the "son" at the end of it. Here again there is a lilt that it would be wrong to iron out into any easy-to-notate rhythmic formula.

As we will have observed, the swelling of the sound known as the Messa di voce, the "putting forth of the voice," is an important expressive device, ubiquitous in the Baroque period and indeed long after. This is not a 'rule': it is simply that the internal shaping of a note, however short, keeps the sound alive. We shall have more to say of this effect, along with other factors governing the transferral of vocal characteristics into our bowing technique, in the next lesson. In Lesson 9 there are detailed exercises explaining how to execute one to perfection.

> The great singer and pedagogue Pier Francesco Tosi writes in 1723 that the teacher should *"teach the art to put forth the Voice, which consists of letting it swell by Degrees from the softest Piano to the loudest Forte, and from thence with the same Art return from the Forte to the Piano. A beautiful Messa di voce, from a singer that uses it sparingly . . . can never fail of having an exquisite Effect."*[3]

In Exercise 5, we move on from playing single words to playing whole speeches by Shakespeare, declaiming them like actors on a stage. You may find it inspiring to listen to these speeches on recordings, or watch them on YouTube. Naturally, these are only suggestions: I encourage my students to recite their favorite poems in this way, in whatever language they are most comfortable.

Exercise 5: Playing words

1. Recite each of the three speeches of Shakespeare below, declaiming the words as if you were a great actor or actress on the stage of a theater.
2. Recite it again, this time playing the words on an open string; at the same time. make sure your voice is guiding your bow and NOT the other way round!
3. Play the speech without speaking, still on a single note: try to play it so clearly that Ganassi, could have been referring to you when he writes in his *Fontegara*, "It is possible with some players to perceive, as it were, words to their music."

The first speech is a classic piece of rhetoric from Julius Caesar in which the speaker, Mark Anthony, attempts to win over the crowd at Caesar's funeral. The opening two lines require a stirring tone, but the more philosophical sentiments that follow suggest a different dynamic. Take time between thoughts: the crowd needs this to understand and digest the information.

> Friends, Romans, countrymen, lend me your ears;
> I come to bury Caesar, not to praise him.
> The evil that men do lives after them;
> The good is oft interred with their bones;
> So let it be with Caesar. The noble Brutus
> Hath told you Caesar was ambitious:
> If it were so, it was a grievous fault,
> And grievously hath Caesar answer'd it.
> *Julius Caesar* **(1623), act 3, scene 2**

In the next one, Hamlet's famous soliloquy on existence, we are privy to his most private thoughts and reflections: unlike in the previous extract, the speaker is not attempting to persuade others.

> To be, or not to be, that is the question:
> Whether 'tis Nobler in the mind to suffer
> The Slings and Arrows of outrageous Fortune,
> Or to take Arms against a Sea of troubles,
> And by opposing end them: to die, to sleep
> No more; and by a sleep, to say we end
> The Heart-ache, and the thousand Natural shocks
> That Flesh is heir to? 'Tis a consummation
> Devoutly to be wished.
> *Hamlet* **(1603), act 3, scene 1**

And last, Juliet speaking about love to her "gentle Romeo."

> Dost thou love me? I know thou wilt say "Ay";
> And I will take thy word. Yet, if thou swear'st,
> Thou mayst prove false. At lovers' perjuries,
> They say Jove laughs. O gentle Romeo,
> If thou dost love, pronounce it faithfully.
> *Romeo and Juliet* **(1597), act 2, scene 2**

Postscript

There are certain assumptions made about violin playing today, deeply influencing the way it is taught from the earliest years. An 'ideal' sound, one produced by a rich and continuous vibrato, is brought to life by a singing bow and seamless bow-changes. There are bow strokes, neatly categorized and practiced according to clear pedagogical methods, and there are aspects of interpretation that have somehow found their way onto the pedagogical statute books with little or no historical justification. I call this way of playing 'instrumentalism,' born of an overriding vision of how the violin should sound and, to some extent, regardless of repertoire or style.

Instrumentalism has its virtues, no doubt, but when applied to music of the Baroque culture it fails to convince. How can one justify inflexible rules about rhythm and the duration of notes, with the professorial eyebrow ever ready to rise if a note is mathematically too long or too short, or if a string of equal notes is not absolutely metronomic, when such conventions never existed at the time?

Throughout this book, we will strive to return to an older, more natural and less stringent view of how the instrument should sound, determined neither by an abstract, all-embracing ideal of an omnipresent 'beauty' of sound, nor by applying post Baroque conventions and principles, but by interpreting music in specific styles according to what is historically known or can be intelligently surmised from the sources, the repertoire, and the instruments we use.

I am often questioned about Baroque music and the supposed 'Rules' that apparently have to be learned for a performance to qualify as 'authentic.' I hope this book will reveal that the way of making music in a historically informed manner obeys the dictates of nature, logic, imagination, and taste.

Notes

1. C. P. E Bach, *Essay*, Chapter 3, Performance, § 12.
2. Quoted in *Roger North on Music*, p. 359 "Some say England hath dispeopled Italy of viollins. And no wonder after the Great Master made that instrument speak as it were with humane voice, saying to his scollars—*Non udite lo parlare?*"
   A similar quote is found on p. 111. "And if it be sayd that it is impossible to produce speech out of inanimate sounds, or give an idea of thought, as speech doth, I answer that whenever a strong genius with due application hath attempted it, the success hath been wonderfull; as when the great Corelli used to say *Non l'intendite parlare?*"
3. Tosi, *Opinioni de' Cantori Antichie* Modern, Chapter 1 , § 29.

Lesson 5

Copying the Human Voice

Sweelinck's Garrulous Little
Swallow (1612)

> Known as the "Orpheus of Amsterdam," Jan Pieterszoon Sweelinck (1562–1621) spent most of his life as organist of the Oude Kerk in Amsterdam. He was celebrated both as a composer and teacher, attracting pupils from all over North Germany, and he can be said to be the founder of the North German school of organ playing which was to culminate in J. S. Bach.

In this lesson, we continue our quest for a more rhetorical approach to playing by investigating not merely the rhythms but the actual sounds of words, their vowels and consonants, and by exploring ways of replicating these sounds on the violin.

To achieve this, we will need to lay aside certain cherished concepts of sound that we have hitherto considered 'violinistic' and 'expressive' in a general, tonal sense. Our task is to teach our bow to speak, so that we may pursue in ever-greater detail our stated principle: that the key to true expression lies in copying the human voice.

Seventeenth-century vocal music is essentially text-oriented. The words and the sentiments they evoke are of paramount importance, the role of the music being to serve, portray, enhance, and express them. The music is not an end in itself: indeed, much of it is more like 'speech-music' than melody.

The singer, acknowledging this hierarchy, retraces the steps of the composer's creative process. His initial task is to understand the text, not only in terms of language but also in its historical and cultural context, taking into account any dramatic, theological, psychological, or emotional implications he may discern.

Correct pronunciation (this should ideally include historically correct pronunciation) and clear enunciation is vital because the text must be intelligible to the audience: to give priority to the beauty of the voice itself, to risk smothering the subtle details of the text under a golden blanket of exquisite sounds, would be to renounce one's role as a purveyor of words and meaning.

Today's jazz singers, whispering and cooing into their microphones, can color their voices in any number of ways, including vibrato; their words will always be crystal clear because volume and projection are issues to be dealt with by their sound engineers.

Opera singers, on the other hand, to whom being heard above a large orchestra in a great hall is a primary concern, may be prepared to sacrifice some diction for the sake of extra volume and to ensure that their voices will be heard in all their glory, for it is their glorious voices that entice the public into the opera house or concert hall. If the words are none too distinct, surtitles are on hand to help the audience understand them: Ella Fitzgerald had no need for such a device!

Something of the same predicament faces the modern-day instrumentalist. The focus on a specific sound ideal including a continuous vibrato—which became standard only in the first decades of the twentieth century, in part to increase the carrying power of the instrument—may be considered legitimate for certain repertoire in certain acoustical conditions. For our purposes, however, this ideal of sound production cannot help but dissipate and obscure the refined details of our 'speech-music.'

౼ఌ ౼ఌ ౼ఌ

It is important to apply oneself patiently and methodically to the minutiae detailed below, constantly making the transition back and forth between intellectual understanding and practical experiment on the violin. *"Such dissembling,"* Quantz (XI, § 16) assures us, *"is most necessary in music."*

As we mold the myriad details that have emerged from our dissembling of speech into a coherent whole, we shall find that our style of playing has been transformed into one quite distinct from the modern ideal and infinitely more fitting to our needs. More specifically, we shall have a clearer notion of how the bow was used at the beginning of the seventeenth century, at the very moment the first violinists stepped out on stage to proclaim the advent of a new art form, the Baroque sonata.

౼ఌ ౼ఌ ౼ఌ

"Garrula rondinella" is a song about a little swallow who awakens the lovesick singer at break of day, thus re-awakening his pain! It comes from Sweelinck's collection of *Rimes françoises et italiennes,* published in Amsterdam in 1612, and described as *"suitable as much to instruments as to the voice."* These pieces can thus be sung by two voices, played by two instruments, or performed by a single voice with an instrument playing the other part.

Scores 5.1–5.4

In the introduction, Sweelinck makes it clear that *"when performing with instruments without voice it is absolutely necessary to be acquainted with the texts in order to achieve appropriate articulation."* They are therefore ideal material for the purpose I have outlined above.

The text in Italian is below: listen to it on the recording. The English translation follows.

Audio 5.1

Garrula rondinella,	Garrulous little swallow
Che nel spuntar del die	Who at the break of day
Mi svegli ancor le pene mie.	Awakes once more my pain
Che dici'n tua favella	What say'st thou in thy language
Con tante parolette e dolci accenti?	With so many little words and sweet accents?

Duolti del tu'Amor forse e t'en lamenti?	Does thy love perhaps pain thee and dost thou lament?
Ben n'ho pietà, deh cara ospite amica	Well do I pity thee, my dear visiting friend
Canta à la mia nemica;	Sing to my enemy;
Farai più con tai note	Thou willst do more with such notes
Ch'eloquenza d'Amor unqua non pote.	Than love's eloquence could ever do.

Text 5.1

Audio 5.2

Having listened to the poem in its entirety, download the word-by-word version of the text and the second recording and practice speaking the words separately after the speaker.

"Garrula rondinella" is in two equal parts: on the website you will find parts for solo violin, violin duet, solo viola and viola duet.

Let us start by exploring the rhythm. If we declaim the first two words, "Garrula rondinella," in an absolutely metronomic way, meticulously obeying the notated rhythm, they will sound wooden, pedantic, and unnatural. That is because, as we discovered in the previous lesson, each word has its own rhythm (which can itself vary when used in different contexts) and we cannot reduce rhythmic complexities into simplistic formulae without losing the flavor of the words and with it the expression of the music to which those words are set.

Also missing when speaking, singing, or playing in this unnatural and rather bland manner is the aspect of communication, for our objective must always be to share with our audience that which we seek to accomplish. This "rhetorical" element, the part of a performer's art that seeks to convince, sway, influence, and stir the emotions of an audience, is a central, fundamental component in the interpretation of Baroque music (see Exercise 6). We will refer frequently to this important subject and learn about it in detail in Lesson 23.

Exercise 6: Copying the rhythm of the speaking voice

1. Listen carefully to the recording: observe the rhythm of each word, and then imitate it with your own speaking voice. Try to catch that subtle lilt which is the natural rhythm of these words.
2. When you can speak each word as rhetorically as our singer, speak the entire piece through. It might help if you imagine you are onstage in a theater, projecting your voice to the back of the hall, perhaps with the help of some histrionic physical gestures.
3. Now listen again, this time imitating each word in turn on the violin. Use just one note (an open string is probably best).
4. Play the whole piece through, still on an open string.
5. Still on one note, play and speak at the same time. Make sure your bow is perfectly synchronized with your voice, ensuring that your speaking voice is controlling your speaking bow, and not the other way round! It often helps students to move around, even to dance, while doing this, rather than standing stiffly.
6. Play the piece with the notes as written.

It is not only the rhythm of the words that we must attempt to reproduce: the consonants and vowels must also be faithfully copied. The techniques we use to re-create the sounds of the human voice with our bows are varied and subtle, and it is not my intention to give exact instructions for each syllable. While we should not consider that speaking words with our bow is an exact science, it is nevertheless worth attempting some kind of methodology that will be helpful as a starting point.

Vowels

In Italian, the word for a vowel is "vocale." The significance of this should not be lost on us, for it is in the vowels, formed by the position of the tongue and lips (nasal vowels exist too, but not in Italian) that we hear the true beauty of a voice, whether in a long, dazzling coloratura passage or in a simple but expressive word like "amore" (love). In most words, more time is spent in the singing of vowels than of consonants.

Long vowel sounds will almost always have a dynamic shape to them; otherwise they will sound bland and inexpressive. We have already mentioned the Messa di voce and will learn about it in greater detail in Lesson 9. But we can add mini-Messa di voces to shorter vowels too, to give them life and bounce.

There are seven vowels, investigated in Exercises 7 and 8: fortunately, in Italian these are mostly pronounced in a single way, unlike in English, where there are many possible variations.

- A: bright and open, as in "apple."
- E: as in "met," alternatively as in "may."
- I: as in the word "teen."
- O: as in OK, alternatively as in "bought."
- U: as in "blue."

Exercise 7: Investigating vowels

1. Sing through each of the vowel sounds listed above, observing the different timbres each one produces. "Aaa," for example, has an open sound and is sung with an open mouth. "Ooo" and "Eee" each produce a distinct sound, simply because the shape of the mouth is different.
2. On an open string, experiment with reproducing these vowel sounds. It is possible to make rounder sounds and more strained or pinched sounds by varying the old formula "bow speed, bow pressure, point of contact" and, by rolling the stick with the fingers to alter its angle, controlling the amount of hair making contact with the string.

Exercise 8: Keeping the vowel sounds alive

1. Sing the first word, "Garrula" on one note, in very slow motion, with each syllable of equal length and with absolutely no added expression: how dead and robotic it sounds!

2. Now take the first syllable "Ga" and implant a Messa di voce into it (<>). The second syllable "ru" is weaker, and the "la" is weaker still, although it does lead through to the next word, so implant a mini-crescendo into it.

3. In "rondinella," the first two syllables each have a small Messa di voce and crescendo to the climax of the word, the "e" of "ella," which has the longest vowel sound enhanced by a substantial Messa di voce. The final vowel rebounds off the "ll" and is weak.

4. Slowly sing both words again with these added details, noticing how much more interesting it sounds now. Repeat several times, gradually speeding up: even at a fast tempo, you can clearly distinguish the enlivened version from the original bland one.

5. Repeat 1 to 3, this time playing on an open string with your bow while singing. Imitate your voice as closely as possible, using mainly finger pressure on the bow for the three Messa di voces.

6. Play without singing out loud, but continue to sing through your bow, transferring all the nuances into pure string sound.

Diphthongs

A diphthong is defined in the *Oxford Dictionary* as a "sound formed by the combination of two vowels in a single syllable, in which the sound begins as one vowel and moves toward another." In English, the two vowels are not pronounced separately, but melt into each other: the words "owl" and "loud" are examples of this.

But in Italian, both vowels are pronounced: a subtle, portato-like impulse by the bow to replicate the second vowel will serve to distinguish a diphthong from a single vowel sound. The two vowels of a diphthong cannot be equal in duration, for that would sound wooden, lacking in grace. In English, the longer one, known as the syllabic vowel, is always the first, but in Italian it can be either the first or the second. The stronger vowel should last longer than the weak one.

Note: all bar numbers marked in this lesson refer to the top voice, although the remarks apply equally to both parts. The fact that the texts of the two parts overlap makes the total effect more complex.

Listen carefully to the following sounds on the recording: In Bar 5, the "gli" of "svegli" is complicated to pronounce: a good way of learning to do so is to say "all Ye," dropping the "a" of "all" and saying the remainder with your tongue tucked behind your bottom teeth. The "i" sound is thus the lyrical, shaped one.

Of the other double vowels, "duol" in Bar 23, the "pie" of "pietà" in Bar 30 and "più" in Bar 38 are diphthongs. The "quen" in Bar 39 and the "qua" of Bar 40 are not: a "u" routinely follows a "q" and has no sound of its own. Neither is the "ai" of "tai:" these are two separate syllables (a-i) because "tai" is a poetic form of "tali."

The sound of a word is also determined by its meaning. For example, as "mi svegli" (Bar 5) means "awakens me," a bright and airy sound may be seen as appropriate: this can be achieved by using a fairly fast bow speed. Later on, the persistent repetition of the words suggests a different emotion as we realize that the awakening is not a happy one. When the reason for this is stated ("Awakes once more my pain") the note values become longer and the Messa di voce more painful, achieved by a slower bow. In "pietà" (Bar 30), which means "pity," a similarly slow Messa di voce will produce a more poignant sound (the accent on "à" means that the final syllable is stressed).

Further complex sounds:

- Bar 8: in "gli, e" and "gli an" the "e" and "an" need to be heard. I would suggest a subtle portato stroke of the kind indicated above.
- Bars 9–10: in "mie" the stress is on the first vowel, made clear by the composer's florid ornamentation.
- In Bar 17, "te e" is an example of a diphthong where two vowels belonging to different words share a single syllable. One can express this phenomenon by insinuating a two-note portato stroke within the single note, a subtle wave-like motion of the bow. The "ci ac" in Bars 18 and 19 are further examples of this.
- Bar 24: "tu'A" (a condensed form of "tu" and "Amor,") can also be achieved in this way; here the "A" should be given more time within the syllable than the less important tu.'
- Bar 36: in "mia" the first syllable is the stressed one.

Single and Double Consonants

Let us now turn our attention to consonants (Exercise 9). Some single consonants, such as "t" and "p," are produced by blocking the flow of breath with the tongue, lips, or teeth, after which the air is expelled into a vowel. These consonants can have no pitch of their own. Others, such as "n," "v," "m," or "l." are formed by only partially blocking the flow of breath. These consonants can therefore be sung to a pitch without the use of a vowel.

On the violin, pressing the bow into the string and then releasing it, causing a clear, clicking sound, can express 'hard' consonants, such as "t" and "k". This may be compared with a modern Martelé or Collé stroke, a kind of 'bow pizzicato.'

"Soft" consonants, such a "b" and "p" can be expressed by gently striking the string from above, rather like in a modern Spiccato, or by placing the bow on the string but not clicking the sound.

For softer consonants like "n," "v," "m," or "l," the string may be gently stroked with the bow, applying a sensitive pressure with the fingers to produce a humming kind of sound.

Double consonants in Italian are pronounced quite literally, thereby lasting twice as long as single ones. Clearly, this affects the rhythm of the syllable that contains them. The double "l" in "rondinella" therefore demands a springing quality to the "ella," with a little extra energy on the "la."

In singing, this springing quality is enhanced by interrupting the flow of breath very slightly before the double consonant: not to do this would produce the effect of a single consonant and a less interesting rhythm. It is easy to simulate this effect with the bow by temporarily releasing the pressure.

It should be noted that some double consonants, such as "mm" and "rr" cannot be articulated in the same way: instead, they are sustained for twice as long as with a single consonant.

Now, try to emulate single and double consonants with the violin.

Exercise 9: Exploring Consonants

A. Exploring single consonants

Work your way through the alphabet, speaking each consonant and then singing it. Explore how each sound is produced, whether with the lips, tongue, teeth, or palate.

Find a way to play each consonant with the bow. Investigate bow pressure, bow speed, point of contact, whether the stroke starts silently on the string, or with a click on the string, or from the air (with varied speeds and a more or less percussive sound)

B. Exploring double consonants

1. Sing the word "spaghetti" on one continuous note: the "tt" will sound like a single "t."
2. Now sing it again, with a break in sound between the "ghe" and the "tt." You will notice that little feeling of 'bounce,' which is the hallmark of a double consonant.
3. Repeat the process, using the word "rondinella."

The final vowel of "rondinella" must be shortened so it doesn't run into the next word. There is a comma in the text, where singers will naturally take a breath. As instrumentalists, we too must learn to clarify phrases, observe punctuation, and breathe. This may involve taking decisions that contradict the literal, mathematical value of a note: we must learn not to be pedantic about note values.

Bowings

Although no composer of the time would have dreamed of marking in bowings, I have added some to the printed part. This is to enable you to incorporate a basic truth intrinsic both to Baroque music and to the bow designed to serve it: syllables are either strong or weak, and strong ones are best played with a down-bow. We shall have much to add to this later on.

Now listen to the other words on the recording:

- Bar 4: "die." There is a Messa di voce on "di" and a little impulse on "e." Try playing the Messa di voce using extra pressure on the bow rather than extra speed. Extra speed produces an empty, breathy kind of sound, whereas extra pressure gives the sound more body and texture. We shall study this technique in detail in Lesson 9.
- Bar 7: between each repeated "mi svegli" there should be a comma, as there is in the text: we can best achieve this by playing both eighth notes on up bows. The "mi" should be joined to "svegli," but the "gli" should not be joined to the following "mi." Therefore, the second eighth note must be longer than the first and a little delayed.
- Bar 9: "pene" (pain). The meaning of a word has a direct bearing on the way the composer sets it and must also be a crucial factor in the way we sing or play it. The word "pene" is 'painted' by the long "pe" which swells till it becomes a dissonance with the bass note C (Bar 11). It then resolves with the "ne,"

> Here we meet a fundamental principle for the first time: a dissonance is always stronger in expression than the consonance that follows it. A suspension, being by definition dissonant, is thus always stronger than its resolution.

The word "stronger" usually implies "louder," but there is clearly more to upholding this principle than merely turning up the volume. Dissonance can express pain, conflict, and suffering in varying degrees; but it can also represent a sweeter kind of anguish, an ecstatic or mystical state of mind, for example. The consonance that follows implies some form of relief or closure, but its exact nature will be dependent on that of the dissonance. We will learn more, in the course of this book, about how to be alert to the nuances of harmony and the relationship of harmony to emotions.

- Bar 13: in "dici" the first syllable is stronger and longer than the second. There must be separation between the eighth notes, corresponding to the comma in the text, to make the text clear.

Bars 15 and 16: "con tante parolette" means "with so many little words." The rapid succession of syllables with a predominance of consonants is onomatopoeic, evocative of the chattering swallow.

- The "let" of "parolette" (words) is strong, the climax of the bar, but the "te" that follows is weak. "Tante paro" has no particular nuance, but the rhythmic intensity of the motive needs to be assured. Don't forget, the sound must be slightly interrupted before the double consonant; otherwise it will sound as a single consonant only.
- Bars 16–17: "dolci accenti" means "sweet strains" so make the sound sweet too!
- Bar 22: "duol" (pains) has a slow <> within the "o" sound.

- Bar 23: the e″♭ after the e″♮ implies a dark sound, matching the meaning of "duolti."
- Bar 31: the word "deh" is an exclamation meaning "woe" or "ah!" It should have a strong gesture, or accent, on the "d."
- Bars 39–41: the long melisma on "po" must have shape. Try following the contour of the line dynamically, so that when the notes rise the sound grows, and when they fall, it drops. The lower part will do the same, so the shapes will be quite independent, making for a more interesting whole. There can be a small comma between the rising fifths in Bars 39 and 40 to make clearer phrases, although the lower part will not allow us to take any actual time here.

Postscript

As stated in the title, Sweelinck's *Rimes françoises et italiennes* contains songs in French as well as Italian. We would do well to work on one of the French songs, taking into account the different sounds and conventions of that language, for each spoken language differs in the way it is sung. If English is your first language, or if you wish to explore its idiosyncrasies, you will derive great benefit by studying songs by John Dowland or Henry Purcell, 'transcribed' for violin in the manner outlined in this lesson.

As Baroque violinists, we spend much of our time playing with singers, working mainly in Italian, Latin, English, German, or French. Whatever language we are working in, we need to be aware of its peculiarities and nuances by listening carefully to the singers who have been working with their vocal coaches in much the same way we have been working in this lesson.

Lesson 6

Five Exercises to Help Accustom You to 'Chinless' Playing

The more we study the Baroque violin, the more aware we become of how different a creature it is to its modern descendant. Only time will tell whether you personally will emerge from this course of lessons as a 'chin-off' player, but I can assure you that you will find this very different physical approach both enriching and liberating.

In the early stages of 'chinless' playing we must patiently re-program the head's memory, convincing it that its role as a vice for holding the violin firmly in place is passé. We spoke in Lesson 2 of the advantages of using a wall to help us feel more stable: we should continually return to the wall whenever we feel the need to free our head, drop our shoulders, and eliminate any tension in our back.

Much of the basic information presented in this lesson could apply equally well to playing the 'modern' violin or viola. Yet it takes on a special significance for us at this stage of our study because taking our chin off the violin has consequences not just for the upper body but also for the whole physical machine.

The role of the back is in essence a negative one, for it can have no will of its own. For the two hands to be able to function freely, the back must be neutral. Just as we cannot run freely with our legs shackled together, so we cannot play freely if the back is in any way interfering with or hampering the movement of the hands. Exercise 10 will illustrate what this neutral will-less back looks like.

Exercise 10: Visualizing the ideal back

1. To illustrate the state of neutrality described above, take a coat or jacket and hang it on a peg, its back toward you.
2. Hold the cuff of the right sleeve and shake it about as if it were your bow arm. Observe how the shoulders are free and how the ripples caused by your shaking spread right down the back.
3. Now do the same with the other cuff, as if your left hand is playing a difficult scale passage.

---

4. This jacket is your ideal back: there are no 'brakes' at the shoulders, where your arms merge into your back, and the back itself is without a trace of resistance.

5. While you are playing, focus your mind on your back and visualize it as that neutral, rippling jacket.

Next are some simple but very effective exercises that I frequently resort to with students whose physical machine needs some basic reorganization. In the hierarchy of the body, the hands reign supreme, for it is they who activate the bow, control the sound, and play the notes. In the previous exercise we visualized the ideal back, one that in no way restrains the hands or hampers their intricate tasks. In the exercises that follow, beginning with Exercise 11, we explore how the hands can be trained to do their work without involving the back.

Exercise 11: Training the hands to be active but independent

1. Stand just behind a high-backed chair, close enough to be able to touch it.
2. Grasp the top of the chair with both hands and squeeze it moderately hard. At the same time, ensure that there is no automatic physical reaction, effort, or tension in any other part of your body. While continuing to squeeze, check your shoulders, your back, your neck, and head and release any tension you find.
3. It should feel as if the signal to squeeze the chair comes straight from your brain into your hands, bypassing every other part of your body.
4. Practice this exercise many times a day in different situations: squeeze the table, this book, the door handle, until you can do it without the least reaction anywhere else in your body.

If you have mastered Exercise 11, we can move on to a more advanced version, one based on the same principle but that involves motion (Exercise 12). For this, you will need the help of another person whom, for the sake of the exercise, I shall call K, of male gender.

Exercise 12: Training the hands to be active while all else remains passive

1. With your right hand, hold K's right hand.
2. Ask K to squeeze your hand quite tightly. Observe what other actions and reactions that causes: does he tighten the muscles to the left of his right shoulder, under his clavicle? Does he stiffen his back and neck? Does he stop breathing? (Some people do!) Using the information you gained in Exercise 11, teach K to squeeze using only the muscles of his hand.

3. Once he can do this, get K to squeeze your hand again. This time, move his hand around, up and down, sideways, in a circular motion, as if his arm were a scarf you were gently twirling, all the time making sure there is no resistance from any part of his body.

4. If there is resistance, show him the exemplary back with the jacket from Exercise 10 and ask him to emulate that, or show him a real scarf twirling around, and then try again. If he still finds this exercise too difficult, try 5 below.

5. Hold K's hand without him squeezing, and play with it as before, twirling it around gently (remember, there are some movements the arm is not designed to do!). When his body is totally neutral and passive, ask him to start squeezing gently without sacrificing that neutrality. If he succeeds, he should squeeze harder.

6. Do the same with the other hand: it may be easier, but it could also be harder.

7. Now try both hands at once. You can do this best if both of you cross your arms.

8. Finally, manipulate both of K's hands while he squeezes yours in such a way that he feels he is playing the violin.

9. Having thus taught K, you now need to swap roles so that you too will rightfully benefit from this exercise!

Exercise 12 is one we should constantly be revising. Not only does it teach us more about freeing the back, it actually helps us solve specific technical problems, particularly with regard to difficult bowing patterns. Let us take, as an example, the two Allegro passages from the opening of Arcangelo Corelli's Sonata 1 (Figure a). In order to manage the complicated bariolage patterns, the back must be neutral and the shoulder similarly void of tension. The right hand must be free from any constraint and must have absolute priority. Any attempt by the shoulder and elbow to make their own set of movements must be considered a harmful distraction, for it is the *hand* that holds the bow, not either of them. They can assist the hand only by being passive and by not interfering. Exercise 13 will help you find a perfect working relationship between the hands and the rest of the body.

Figure a

Two Allegro passages from the opening of Corelli's sonata Op. V No. I.

Exercise 13: Letting go of your back

1. Lie down on a table, your right shoulder a few inches from the edge. The table needs to be long enough to carry your entire body. A platform or step could also be used, but not the floor, as there will be no room for your bow.
2. Adjust your torso so that the small of your back is lying flat on the table. If your head is not comfortable, you may need to support it with a book or books. Allow your body to sink into the table and scan it for any tension there may be, releasing it as much as you can.
3. When you are perfectly relaxed, take your violin and bow (someone may have to be charged with handing them to you.) Play the first Allegro passage through, fairly slowly: the sound will not be your best (in fact it will probably sound quite awful!) but persevere anyway. When you have played it several times and brought it up to tempo, swing your legs gently over the edge of the table and slowly sit up.
4. Still perched on the table, play the passage again. Your body should feel quite different in terms of organization and the passage should feel much easier to play.
5. Now play the passage again, standing up.

Students who practice this exercise frequently, on any passage difficult for the bow, will derive constant benefit from it. Visually, there is often a definite and positive change from 'before' to 'after.' Be careful to observe the 'after' position so you can replicate it whenever you experience stiffness or feel the need for a swift 'pit-stop' reorganization of the body.

Although the use of a table is far more beneficial, you can remind yourself of the sensation of 'letting go' by occasionally leaning against the wall while playing. A similar "spot check" that can be carried out is described in Exercise 14.

Exercise 14: Carrying out a spot check while playing

1. While you are playing, lean your body, from the waist up, slowly over to the right.
2. Still playing, release any feeling of grip in the muscles around the right shoulder, allowing your bow arm to feel it is dangling in space.
3. Ensure that the fingers of the right hand continue to feel a healthy contact with the strings.
4. Still maintaining this feeling of contact with the strings and of no grip around the shoulder, resume your normal upright position.

❧ ❧ ❧

Recalling These Exercises in a Performance Situation

Now that we have mastered these exercises in a theoretical way, we need to put them to the test in real-life situations. For just as the swimmer, having practiced his strokes to perfection while standing or lying on the floor, encounters many new challenges on entering the choppy water, so the violinist on the concert platform may perform less competently than in the sheltered environment of his or her practice studio.

The factors that may threaten our ideally organized and tension-free body are

1. Technical factors
2. Emotional factors
3. Nerves

Technical Factors

Difficult passages can cause us to stiffen at precisely the moment when the body needs to be most tension-free. We can condition our body to react in a healthy way to such passages by taking exercises such as those by Ševčík, for which little or no emotional input is needed, and practicing letting go in all the ways mentioned above while playing them. Figures b and c are examples of these exercises for the right and left hands. Start slowly and gradually build up the speed until the maximum possible speed is reached.

Figure b
Ševčík, op. 2, part 4, no. 32.

Figure c
Ševčík, op. 1, part 1. no. 5.

Emotional Factors

The desire to express the emotional content of the music can cause the body to imagine itself part of that expression. The result is not only physical tension but also a loss in the actual expressive quality of the sound, for it becomes difficult for the player to distinguish between the emotion he or she feels and the emotion he or she hears in the sound itself. It goes without saying that it is the latter that reaches the audience.

Channeling the expression from the imagination through the physical body and into the sound without having it diverted into gestures and grimaces, however expressive these may be and however satisfying to the player, is one of the hardest aspects of playing the violin.

To combat this diversion and to drive a wedge between the real and imagined sound, I get students to understand that they can achieve any kind of expression in the sound with no expression on their faces or in their bodies at all, or even with an expression totally inappropriate to the affect. Try playing the profound first movement of the Bach C-minor obbligato sonata with total conviction and a broad grin on your face, or the joyous opening of the G-major sonata with an expression of tragic sorrow on your face and a lively, sparkling sound and you will see what I mean!

Nerves

Playing in front of our public can cause symptoms of fear resulting in, among other things, harmful physical tension. Much has been written on the subject of stage fright and its effects. In the present context, I will limit myself to two pieces of advice.

First, having understood the principles formulated in this lesson and having worked on the exercises, condition yourself to letting go the instant you become aware of tension. Release any tension you may feel before playing, between the movements of a piece, and when you have even a single bar's rest. At first, releasing will be an act of will, but with time it will become a conditioned reflex, an activity that your body will perform without conscious thought.

Second, remember to breathe! One symptom of fear is a shortage or a suspension of breath: stage nerves can cause this too, as we contract the diaphragm and block our breathing. Taking several deep breaths before coming on stage, breathing in and out slowly, certainly helps to calm the nerves. In our practice, we should remember to monitor the diaphragm, ensuring it is free and that we are breathing normally. This awareness of breath, practiced in our studio, can be transferred to the onstage situation.

In Appendix VIII, I give some exercises for relieving back pain and stiffness, while in Appendix VII I discuss mental stress and offer some advice on how to deal with it.

Lesson 7

More Basic Concepts and Techniques

"A Division on a Ground" by
Mr. Faronell, from *The Division Violin*,
London, 1684

The French violinist and composer Michel Farinel (also known as Faronell, 1649–1726), studied with Carissimi in Rome, became court musician to the Spanish Queen, and was later a violinist in Louis XIV's court at Versailles. This is his best-known piece, a set of variations (Divisions) on "La Follia," a very popular tune from the sixteenth to the eighteenth centuries and beyond, and the subject of many sets of variations by composers including Arcangelo Corelli, Antonio Vivaldi, and Jean-Baptiste Lully. Farinel's composition first appeared in John Playford's 'The Division Violin' (1684), the frontispiece of which is reproduced below (Figure a).

Figure a
*The Division Violin
(1684) was a
Choice Collection of
Divisions for the Treble
Violin . . . being of great
benefit and delight for
all Practitioners on the
violin* by John Playford,
the leading English music
publisher of his day.

In this lesson we study our first complete piece of music written specifically for the violin and introduce several basic concepts and techniques:

1. The melody and bass lines are inseparable: we cannot consider one without the other.
2. The link between phrasing and bowing is direct and crucial, far more so than with a 'modern' bow.

3. Rhythm, articulation, the retaking (or not) of the bow, punctuation, tessitura, the differentiation between 'Good' and 'Bad' notes, awareness of impulses and rebounds, causes and effects: these are just some of the ingredients to be found in our expressive cookbook.

Score 7.1 The title of our piece, "A Division on a Ground," means that the violin part is a series of divisions, or variations, composed over a constantly repeated ground bass that, in this case, is eight bars long. You can download a violin and a viola version from the book's Score 7.2 website.

52

The Importance of the Bass Line

The first thing we notice when glancing through a facsimile (or a good, unedited, modern transcription) of a Baroque piece is that the melody and the bass line are printed together. This was true from the early 1600s right up to the end of the Baroque period. The continuo player, usually a harpsichordist, theorbist, or organist, possibly joined by a single line bass instrument such as a cello or a bassoon, played the bass line with his left hand and improvised a suitable part in his right hand. Knowing what the melody instrument was playing was clearly essential to this realization, whether the composer had figured the bass to mark the harmonies or not.

Conversely, keeping in close touch with the bass line was vital for the player of the top part, not only in order to understand the harmony but because much of the information concerning character, phrasing, dynamics, articulation, and other elements is embedded in it.

Modern editions that print the violin part separately may be considered disingenuous for they risk promoting the myth that music is somehow divided into two parts, melody and accompaniment. This concept of 'accompaniment' in music, certainly in Baroque music, is misleading. It is vital that the music be considered as a whole, a unity we must not fragment if we are to understand it in all its intriguing complexity.

> Studying the violin part without relating it to the bass can be compared to the actor who learns his lines without understanding how his character interacts with the rest of the cast: woe to the Romeo who knoweth not the utterances of his Juliet!

Another point of interest to observe on the pages of this piece is that there is a complete absence of dynamic markings; so it is with most music of the period. Adding dynamic nuances was one aspect of the performer's art, based not merely on his whim (although spontaneity was a hallmark of musicians of the time) but on his harmonic awareness and his skill in observing and bringing to life the subtle twists and turns of the music. Later composers, writing more complex scores, were to use dynamic markings partly in order to spell out such hidden nuances.

Different harmonies express different emotions: some may be characterized as plain, perhaps representing the more straightforward human feelings, while others are more complex, suggesting conflict, yearning, ecstasy, or rage. The more intense harmonies are called "strong," the less emotive ones "weak," and we can take this relationship as one starting point in our quest for a legitimate dynamic system.

In terms of a single line, notes that rise may be said to represent emotional strengthening, while those that fall appear to weaken; thus the dynamic line may follow the visual contour of the notes. Again, such a basic principle is merely a starting point and is by no means immutable.

Let us start to interpret Farinel's piece by examining the ground bass. At first sight, it may appear to be a fairly ordinary progression of notes; starting on the tonic, it descends to the dominant (its lowest point), then returns, moves one step lower, and so on.

But if we can train ourselves to experience each step not as perfunctory but as an emotionally transformative event, our perception of the line will be radically enhanced. For example, the second note is not merely lower than the first; it is by its nature weaker, on a subjective level perhaps darker. Similarly, notes three to four may suggest uncertainty, while the F is not merely the highest note but the most powerful, suggesting something on the lines of momentary triumph.

The emotional messages we receive from the transition between one note and another combine to shape the dynamic scheme (Figure b) that we need to acknowledge and be guided by throughout the piece.

Figure b

The notes and dynamic scheme of Michel Farinel's Ground Bass.

Tempo and Rhythm

The tempo of the ground bass should, in theory, remain constant throughout. However, some minor fluctuations, unmarked by the composer, are inevitable if the character of a particular variation seems to demand it. Such license is granted by contemporary sources, though not in the specific context of a ground bass: Thomas Mace, in his *Musick's Monument* of 1676, tells us that we can find the right character of a piece *"by Playing some Sentences Loud, and others again Soft, according as they best please your own Fancy, some very Briskly, and Courageously, and some again Gently, Lovingly, Tenderly and Smoothly."*[1]

The rhythm here is that of a saraband or a chacony, although there is no marking to that effect. Two of the most popular dances of the Baroque period, they are characterized by a second beat that often has a clear, individual character of its own, although it is not necessarily stronger than the first. This is in contrast to a minuet, for example, in which the first beat of the bar is clearly the strongest of the three.

In addition to the overall dynamic and emotional hierarchy described above, each bar has its own internal hierarchy. The first note is always strong, in varying degrees, but the second can be anything from very weak to even stronger, depending on the musical context.

The suggested internal hierarchy for the first and second beats in Bars 1–8 is roughly as follows:

- Bar 1: strong/strong.
- Bar 2: strong/weak.
- Bar 3: strong/strong, the second beat growing toward Bar 4.
- Bar 4: strong/weak.
- Bar 5: strong/strong.
- Bar 6: strong/weak, the third beat weaker.
- Bar 7: strong/strong.
- Bar 8: strong/weak, the third beat weaker.

Were the harmony to change on the second beat of a bar, the second beat could well be stronger than the first, but this never happens in Farinel's piece.

The Hierarchies and the Bow Impulses

It is the task of the bow to ensure that these hierarchies are clearly discernible. In this context, we may think of the action of the bow in terms of impulses, each sound being the result of either an active or a passive impulse from the arm. If the hierarchy is strong/strong, both strokes will require similarly active impulses; but if the hierarchy is strong/weak, an active impulse of the bow arm on the down-bow is followed by a more passive rebound. In this case, it might be helpful to think of the up-bow as bouncing back after colliding with a large rubber ball.

The principle of playing strong notes on down-bows and weak ones on up-bows is based partly on the natural phenomenon of gravity, coincidentally under investigation by Sir Isaac Newton at the time Farinel's piece was written (his theory was to be published three years after Playford's book, in 1687).

The design of the Baroque bow further facilitates the audible differentiation between strong or "Good" notes and weak or "Bad" ones. Developing an awareness of this dichotomy is central to our art: choosing the right bowing may occasionally demand a certain amount of ingenuity, but choosing the wrong one could well muddle a phrase.

This trinity (of natural law, bow technology, and phrasing) is to be cherished and cultivated throughout our studies.

The practice, sometimes encountered today, of playing the first two beats in a French sarabande or chaconne with down-bows is not a bowing specifically mentioned in any French text. Georg Muffat, our principal source of information on Lully's rules of bowing, gives us no instruction specifically relating to a sarabande, although he does tell us that strong beats should always be played down-bow, and gives us some examples of double down-bows in other contexts. In his Preface to *Florilegium secundum*, written around the same time as Farinel's piece, Muffat writes: *"Of the three notes which make up a whole measure in triple time, the first would be played down-bow, the second up-bow, and the third down-bow, when played slowly."*[2] The reader is invited to explore the physical and aesthetic sensations that Muffat's bowing, illustrated in Figure c, engenders.

The application of this bowing to bars with three quarter notes in our Farinel piece, such as Bar 6, gives us an interesting result: it eliminates any sense of anacrusis to the following bar and gives the music an extra lilt. As Farinel had been a violinist in Louis XIV's court, we are justified in experimenting with Lully's bowings here. We must be wary of giving the third note too much strength, however, for as Muffat informs us, *"The greatest skill of the Lullists lies in the fact that even with so many repeated down-bows, nothing unpleasant is heard,"* adding that their playing had *"an extraordinarily delicate beauty."*[3]

The time signature here is a complicated one, being also a tempo indication. The **C** with the dot inside is an old Mensural sign for triple time. The 3 underneath complements that and the 1 means we should feel the music in 1, the tempo therefore being brisker than if we were to feel it in 3. "Mensural" refers to the system of musical notation in use from the late 1200s until around 1600, although various legacies of the system lingered until well into the seventeenth century. The word "mensural" means "measured," and is used because this system could define rhythmic values in terms of numerical proportions, something that in the earlier Gregorian plainchant had not been possible.

Observations

Theme

Bars 1–8: our first task is to integrate each bar, complete with its internal hierarchy, into the overall dynamic scheme outlined in Figure b.

Bar 1: as we need to be on a down-bow for the first note of Bar 2, the previous note, which is weak, will be on an up-bow. Such corrections will become second nature with experience, but they may need to be pointed out at this stage.

As with the rhythm of words, the rhythm of dance is often elusive; we should therefore adopt an informed and creative attitude to note values, rather than adhering to a mathematically literal one. For example, if the first notes of our piece are played with their literal length, it will create a melodic, lyrical effect; but if we cut the first note short, so that there is an articulation between it and the next one, we will achieve a livelier, more dance-like feel. If we then lengthen the second note and shorten the third a little, briefly stopping the bow in between, the feeling of noble dance will be well established.

Bar 2: a slight caesura, or comma, placed between the notes will create an elegant sense of poise.

Bars 2–3: to assure clear phrasing, we need another caesura over the bar line between Bars 2 and 3. The caesura is like the pause we take between poetic phrases to avoid muddling the meaning. However, we do not want to lose the pulse, so instead of taking time, we will slightly shorten the second note of Bar 2.

Music, like speech, needs punctuation. The Baroque composer may infer it, but he rarely marks it. It is for the performer to clarify what is embedded in the composer's score.

Bar 3: we need another articulation after the first note.

We now have a choice of options as to how to play the sixteenth notes:

1. We could slur them to the second note.
2. We could slur them to the second note, adding a trill to the long note.
3. We could slur just the two sixteenth notes, on an up-bow, with or without adding a trill.
4. We could play them detached, with or without adding a trill.

The less exact the instructions of the composer are, the more the performer is called upon to make decisions.

If we decide on an option that includes a trill, I would start the trill on the note itself, not from the note above. Playing an appoggiatura e″ would predict and therefore detract from the e″ in Bar 4. As there is also a D in the bass, it would sound better if the trill grows out of the d″. Trills at this time can start from either note, depending also on the harmony.

Option 3 would more accurately mirror the eighth note in Bar 1. We would need to shorten the second note of the bar and articulate a little before the sixteenth notes.

Option 4 might add more panache to the moment: lengthening the second note as much as you feel you can, then lifting the bow off the string and finally bunching the sixteenth notes together as tightly as possible would be dramatic.

Whatever you decide, you can do something different in Bar 11. If you do trill, you will need to stop it and leave just the d″ sounding before proceeding.

In Baroque music, it is vital that the phrasing be as clear as it is in a poem where, if the lines mingle and the phrases run into one another, we are unable to grasp the poet's meaning. Moreover, the internal architecture of a Baroque phrase is perilously fragile, far more so than a Romantic one. If one note of a Baroque phrase is given too much or too little importance, the whole structure will come toppling to the ground.

Bar 4: lead through to Bar 5, but still with a slight caesura over the bar line.

Bar 5: in view of the climactic nature of this bar, we can give even the eighth note a slightly pompous character. Detach it from the previous note and make it heavier than the corresponding eighth note in Bar 1.

Bars 6 and 8: it is important that the third quarter note in these bars does not have the quality of an upbeat to the following bars. If there had been an upbeat to Bar 1, we would have been able to justify an upbeat here, but that was not the case. One way to avoid this, whatever bowing you use, is to play the whole bar within a diminuendo, and by playing each note shorter than the previous one.

Bars 8–9: clarify the phrasing with a comma between these bars. The following bars could be played *piano*, but that will set a precedent for the rest of the piece, so it may be better to avoid this.

Bars 14–15 form a hemiola in the top part, although not in the bass. To understand how the phrasing changes in a hemiola, think of these two bars as being a single bar in $\frac{3}{2}$ time. The last beat of Bar 14 would normally be weak, but as it is now the second beat of a hemiola, it is strong. The first beat of Bar 15 would normally be strong, but in a hemiola it is merely the second half of a half note beat, and is thus weak.

In Bar 15, we can put a trill on the c″♯. Here, the effect will be stronger if we begin on the upper note (d″) because in the context of the A major chord that will create a dissonance before being resolved. Cadential trills were considered so normal that they are rarely marked.

The dots on the page are not 'the music': they are an approximate representation of the music. The music is the sound we hear.

In the Baroque period, theory and practice were far from identical. The exact length of a note was not necessarily equal to its literal value but could be decided on by the performer according to various musical criteria as well as by individual taste. The spirit, emotional quality and character of the piece dictated myriad details that were unwritten by the composer.

The theory we learned in the course of our training is not valid for all historical periods, nor is the rigorous and pedantic way in which such theory is sometimes applied.

We must not assume that each note is to be played to its exact full length, or that notes of equal value should be rhythmically identical.

The relationship between written and played ones was to be clearly described by Marie Dominic Joseph Engramelle (1727–1805), a French Augustinian friar, mathematician, and acoustician. In his *Tonotechnie* (1775) Engramelle distinguishes between the notation as written and the actual sounds as played. *"The notes in the music,"* he writes, *"indicate very precisely the total value of each note; but their real lengths ('tenues') and the value of the silences ('silences') which . . . serve to detach one from the other, are not indicated by any sign.*

All notes . . . are part 'tenue' and part 'silence.' The part which I call 'tenue' or 'son' (sound) always occupies the beginning of the note; and the part which I call 'silence' ends it. The 'tenue' is more or less long according to the character of the note; and the length of the 'silence' depends on the length of the 'tenue. . . . [T]hese 'silences' at the end of each note decide . . .their articulation and are as necessary as the 'tenues' themselves."

Engramelle was the inventor of a mechanical recording technique, the eighteenth-century equivalent of the piano roll. Aware of the inherent inadequacies of musical notation and in order to program his mechanical music box so that it would reproduce more accurately the way great musicians of the time actually played, he devised a system of charting all aspects of the music including tempi (often exceedingly variable), articulation, and the exact ratio of *"notes inégales"* (see Lesson 34).

Variation 1: Dotted Notes

The pulsating sound of dotted notes is to be heard throughout the Baroque period. In this variation we encounter them for the first time and learn how to tackle the challenges they pose.

The very nature of this rhythm is dance-like. The second of each pair of dotted notes should always be weaker than the first, but to play it, the bow must travel faster, potentially producing an accent. One way of avoiding this is for the bow not to remain on the string all the time. Exercise 15 is designed to meet this first challenge.

Exercise 15: Practicing the dotted rhythms

1. Practice the dotted rhythm on an open string in the following way:
   - Play a down-bow, using about four inches of bow, in the middle of the bow.
   - Take the bow off the string and return it to the string about two inches lower than where you started.
   - Play a sixteenth note with a quick flick of the wrist and connect it to the next down-bow.
   - Practice this slowly at first, speeding up very gradually until you have reached the tempo you have set.
2. When you are comfortable in the middle of the bow, continue to practice the bowing while moving gradually a little higher up toward the frog. When you reach the frog, return to the middle and move down toward the tip. There will come a point where you can no longer take the bow off the string. Nevertheless, work down to the tip, keeping the bow on the string.
3. Travel back again toward the frog while continuing to play the same rhythm, always with the up/down bowing. Notice where in the bow it sounds best and is most comfortable.

It is the ability to take a simple formula and make each repetition thereof sound unique and convincing that marks out the imaginative player from the less adventurous one. If our imagination is not constantly active, our playing will sink into routines that will prove tedious to the audience; indeed, becoming enslaved to well-practiced physical movements may be considered one of the greatest threats to artistry.

Here, the relationship between the long and short notes does not need to be consistent: the rhythm can vary from literal to extreme (very long/very short) depending on the context. The articulation can also vary, the gap between the notes ranging from very long to non-existent, the latter implying a more cantabile sound.

The next challenges are also musical ones, to which our technical ingenuity must supply the answer.

1. How do we avoid making each unit of two notes equally stressed?
2. How do we conform to the dynamic scheme of Figure b?

The simplest answer to the first question is that we should travel down the bow through each bar without retaking, returning to where we started before the last sixteenth note of each bar.

But if we do that, we fail to meet the requirements of the overall phrasing. The answer to the second question is that we need to be far subtler in our retakes, retaking only to the extent that the phrasing demands: the following is a guide to the extent of retaking needed for the first five bars of Variation 1:

- Bar 1: a slight retake before the final sixteenth note (we do not need to come back all the way because Bar 2 is weaker than Bar 1).
- Bar 2: a bigger retake before the final sixteenth note, taking us back to where we started in Bar 1.
- Bar 3: an even greater retake before the final sixteenth note, because this bar is stronger and grows toward Bar 4.
- Bar 4: the biggest retake before the final sixteenth note, taking us nearer to the frog, where the sound is strongest.

Exercise 16 is designed to help you travel quickly from one part of the bow to the other, facilitating the retaking process.

Exercise 16: Learning to travel through the bow while playing the dotted rhythm

1. On an open string, play the dotted-rhythm formula three times at the frog. Before the last sixteenth note and without interrupting the rhythm, travel through the air to the middle of the bow and continue. Repeat this procedure back and forth, as illustrated in the example below, until you are comfortable with it. Ensure that the hand travels easily through the air, unimpeded by any 'brakes' in the shoulder or back.

2. Repeat No 1, traveling between the middle and the point.
3. Repeat between the frog and the point.

> 4. Play the formula once only, then travel from the frog to the middle, on to the point, then back via the middle to the frog.
> 5. Repeat at all parts of the bow, in no particular order.

Make sure that *not all strong beats are equally strong,* and that the dotted rhythms are not distorting the basic dynamic scheme we have agreed on.

In Bars 8, 10, 12, and 14, the composer varies the hierarchy by shifting interest onto the third beat of the bar. Treat the group of sixteenth notes as a re-energizing flurry, the notes not necessarily equal either in rhythm or in sound.

In the penultimate bar, there should be another trill on the long e″: this time it could be more interesting to begin on the upper note.

Variation 2: Good Notes and Bad Notes

> All notes are important, but some notes are more important than others.

We have probably all been implored at some time by a teacher or conductor to "sing every note!" But what if the music is not melodic? What if there is no real 'tune'? Here, for example, the music has rhythm and shape but no actual melody as such, so an instruction to "sing every note" seems irrelevant. What, then, are we to do with it?

The answer becomes clear when we cease to give chase to non-existent melody and examine instead the elements of which this music is made up. Clearly, dance is one important ingredient here. If one were to choreograph this variation, the number of steps would not be equal to the number of notes: one would have to decide which notes needed an individual step and which did not.

Similarly, as we know from previous lessons, the rhythms and nuances of language make up another important element in Baroque music. When we speak, we stress certain syllables and merely whisper others: if we did not, our speech would be monotonous and dull, and we could never hope to hold the attention of those with whom we wish to communicate.

In music, exactly the same principle applies: we must learn to distinguish the important notes from the less important ones, those that need to be stressed and those of lesser importance that can remain in the background. Without this perspective there can be no phrase.

With this in mind, Quantz (XI, § 12) was to urge us to *"make a distinction in execution between the principle notes, ordinarily called accented or in the Italian manner 'good' notes and those that 'pass,' which some foreigners call 'bad' notes. Where it is possible, the principle notes always must be emphasised more than the passing."* It should be noted that he is primarily referring here to the length of the notes, although he adds that important notes should both be *"heard a little longer, and with a stronger tone"* than the others.

> If every note is important, no note is important.

In each bar of this variation, the first note is "good," so we should play it strongly. The second note is always "bad," so we can let it go: it still needs to be heard, of course, but it is as if it bounces passively off the first one. It should also be shortened and detached from both the note before and the note after. The last note of each bar leads into the following bar and can therefore be quite strong.

There is oftentimes a clear link between dynamics and articulation: a forte note will thus not only be louder than a piano one, it will also be longer. Here, we can vary the length of the first notes of every bar, following the basic dynamic scheme referred to in Figure b.

Similarly, the sixteenth notes can lengthen as we crescendo toward the climax of the variation and be shortened thereafter.

Bar 5: the low note (f′) is weak and short. The following three step-wise notes can be long and cantabile. This pattern can be repeated until Bar 7, but in Bar 8 the pattern changes: here, the first two eighth notes can be long, the last two short.

Once again there is a hemiola at the end of the variation (last three bars) with a trill (starting on the upper note) on the long e″ of the penultimate bar. Similar trills can be played at the end of all subsequent variations: this is a convention, not a rule.

The overall dynamic scheme on which we decided at the start of this lesson should be respected throughout.

Variation 3: Varying the Articulation

The same principles apply here as in Variation 2:

- Lose the bad notes in order to clarify the perspective and achieve interesting and convincing shapes and patterns.
- Shape the dynamic line to coincide with the visual contour.

Varying the articulation is one of the most important means of expression at our disposal and is essential for keeping the music alive and interesting. The length and dynamic quality of each note determines its role in the overall scheme, while the amount of attachment or detachment from the notes on either side determine its relationship to its immediate neighbors. In Exercise 17 we explore the vast spectrum of articulations available to us.

Exercise 17: Exploring the vast spectrum of articulations

In this exercise, we go through a whole cycle of articulations from the very shortest stroke to the longest possible one. In theory, every single note will be fractionally longer than the one before it. When we have reached the longest one, we complete the cycle by returning from the longest back to the shortest. Do not stop playing during the cycle and keep the tempo constant at around 3–4 notes per second.

1. At the middle of the bow, bounce the bow vertically up and down on the string as if it's playing on a trampoline, making no sound. Use a 'see-saw' movement (pronation) of your upper arm to achieve this.
2. Start moving the upper arm horizontally to produce a very short spiccato. This is your shortest stroke!
3. Without stopping to play, gradually lengthen your stroke: the movement of the bow will become less vertical and more horizontal as you do this.
4. After a while the bow will be spending more time on the string than off it, until the stroke is 100% horizontal and you are playing a "detaché" stroke.
5. After a while, start reversing the process by lifting the bow very slightly at each end of the detaché. Gradually make the stroke shorter until you have returned to the original noiseless vertical trampoline bounce.

When you have completed the above Exercise 17, work through Variation 3 again, using the maximum possible variety of articulations. Play it slowly, striving for an ideal that no two consecutive notes have the same length, sound or quality.

Most established principles may be contradicted, and such contradictions may be helpful in avoiding routine sameness. For example, while it may be true in principle that the stronger the dynamic the longer the note, a flagrant deviation from this may be exactly what is needed to rejuvenate our audience's attention!

The first four notes of Bar 1 decline both dynamically and in length. The last two could lengthen and grow into the next bar. However, in order to reflect the dynamic scheme to which we have vowed allegiance at the start of this lesson, we should group the bars into pairs, in which case the last two notes of Bar 1 remain short, as are all the notes in Bar 2 except the last one which can be considered an anacrusis to Bar 3.

Variation 4: The Singing Bow

The melody returns in the form of a descant, a minor third above the original pitch: this suggests a more cantabile style.

Bars 6–7: we can regard this as a hemiola, the adjacent eighth notes an opportunity for a more cantabile stroke.

Notice the hemiola in the last three bars: to make this clear we need to slightly stress the f″ in the third last bar but avoid stressing the f″ in the penultimate bar. The first two eighth notes in the third last bar should both be played with up-bows.

Variation 5

In this variation, the second beat again bounces off the first, but in a more complex, ornamented way. The first four notes are therefore to be played within a diminuendo.

There should normally be a slight comma before the last three eighth notes, which can be played with anything from short, detached strokes to broad, more lyrical ones. Try to get as much variety in the strokes as possible: again, the challenge is to play no two bars with the same articulation.

Bar 5: where the tessitura sinks, there is a natural drop in dynamic level, giving the music something of a mumbling quality.

Bars 9–15: the three-note dactyl motive we had in the opening bars now occurs on every beat, re-energizing the music.

Variation 6

A long sequence of equal notes in triple time, such as we have in the first eight bars, can sound better if we bow it out rather than playing the third beat with another up-bow; in this way we avoid too many accents. As the second bar is anyway weak, starting it on an up-bow makes good musical sense: indeed the whole phrase works very well thus. However, if the third note of a bar is to be played on a down-bow, we must make sure to lighten it!

When the variation breaks into eighth notes, make sure you shape them well. Your bow should speak, telling a story in sound which is constantly fascinating and will hold the attention of your audience. In Lesson 13, we will investigate more thoroughly how to play equal notes in a flexible and subtle way

Variation 7: Our First Double Stops and Our First Shift

With the Baroque bow, the nearer to the frog one is, the more space there is between the hair and the stick: this is where the bow is at its most active and where the sound is loudest. Try not to get cornered, as many beginners do, down at the tip: that is the least active part of our bow.

Make sure both fingers in a double stop are pressed down enough so the sound is equally wholesome in both notes and there is no whistling. If not, frustration with the sound could lead to an unproductive over-activity of the bow. Once again, bowing this variation out works well musically (you will need to take an extra down-bow in Bar 9).

Bar 12: here we make our first foray, albeit brief, out of first position! If your hand is big enough, simply hoist your fingers into second position, leaving your thumb behind, and bring your fingers down again for the next bar. If your hand is too small to do this successfully, shift up with the whole hand, including the thumb, then draw your hand back for the next bar and normalize the thumb position when it is convenient to do so.

Variation 8: A Ricochet with Separate Bows

Our aim here is to make the first five notes sound like a single unit, rather than five separate notes. To achieve this, we need to give a strong, active impulse to the first note, the remaining four being a kind of passive reaction to it within a diminuendo. We must avoid the temptation to work too hard with the bow on the passive notes, especially the last one.

The technique involved is comparable to that of a *ricochet* bowing, in which the bow is first thrown onto the string and then allowed to bounce along by itself. You can practice this on a single note, perhaps an open string, to get the feel of it. Later, you can practice the first five notes of Bar 1, first in *ricochet* and then with separate bows, a kind of 'bowed out *ricochet.*'

Finally add the last three notes, but still without any additional impulse.

Bar 5: because of the surprise drop in tessitura, this bar appears to contradict the basic dynamic scheme we agreed on in Figure b.

Variation 9: Written Slurs and High Tessitura

Tessitura is an important factor in our interpretative detective work. The first three variations, like the Theme, began on the tonic note, d″, the next five on an f″ a minor third higher. This variation is the only one to begin on an a″, the highest beginning of all.

It is also unique in that the composer has added detailed slurs, characterizing the section more clearly than any other.

These two observations are major clues as to the character of this variation. It is certainly more lyrical: one could say that the first eight bars contain more pathos and passion than we have encountered in any other variation. This might impact on the rhythm and articulation of Bar 1, where the eighth note could achieve its literal value and the bar could be void of any commas.

Bar 2 could be bowed out to eliminate any dance feel.

Bar 6: the dotted rhythm is in contrast with the more mellifluous Bar 2.

Bars 13–15: it will be better to play the last note of Bar 13 on an up-bow, so that we can start the hemiola on a down-bow. The two eighth notes in Bar 15 can both be up-bows.

Variation 10

Here again, the tessitura is significant. Dropping down an octave in Bars 5 and 13 indicates more than mere dynamic contrasts: the feel of the music changes to something more intimate, and we should color our sound accordingly. A lighter, more feathery kind of stroke will achieve this.

Bar 9 to the end: the final statement of the theme is not maintained to the end. We again drop down the octave, finishing the piece not in an atmosphere of bravura but with hushed tones.

Notes

1. Thomas Mace, *Musick's Monument*, p. 130.
2. *Georg Muffat on Performance Practice*, p. 35.
3. Idem, p. 106.

Lesson 8

Learning to Feel

Developing a Heightened
Awareness of the Emotional
Power of Sound and the Intervals

In this lesson we explore how sounds elicit emotions and how, having heightened our awareness of the effect of sounds, we can better communicate these emotions to our public.

The extraordinary power of music has been recognized since ancient times: witness the biblical David soothing the bitter torment of King Saul, or Orpheus who not only calmed the barbarous minds of men but even charmed wild beasts and caused woods and rocks to move.

In 1649, the French Philosopher René Descartes published *Les Passions de l'âme* (The Passions of the Soul) in which he claimed to have identified a tiny gland in the center of the brain known as the "pineal gland" which, when agitated by "the spirits" causes us to feel emotions. Nowadays, concepts of the soul and the heart as the seats of feeling and love have been expelled from the terminological nest by the rapidly developing literature of cognitive neuroscience, providing a more scientific explanation as to how sounds and other stimuli cause us to feel certain emotions. It is not a subject we need to dwell on here: as M Jourdain's Music Master says in Molière's *Le Bourgeois gentilhomme*: "*La philosophie est quelque chose; mais la musique, monsieur, la musique . . .*"[1]

Johann Mattheson, in *Der Vollkommene Capellmeister* (1739), acknowledges the work of Descartes and advises us to read it "*since it teaches one to distinguish well between the feelings of the listeners and how the forces of sound affect them.*"[2] That the phenomenology of emotion is of supreme relevance to the performing musician is to state the obvious, for the performer's primary mission is to create the sounds that the composer has imagined in such a way that they will "affect" the listener. Of the many sources that define this task, none is as clear or as eloquent as that of Francesco Geminiani. The opening words of his preface to *The Art of Playing on the Violin* (1751) are as follows: "*The Intention of Musick is not only to please the Ear, but to express Sentiments, strike the Imagination, affect the Mind, and command the Passions.*"[3]

One of the very first tasks I perform with new students is to refresh and heighten their awareness of the emotional impact that even the simplest sounds can engender (see

Exercise 18). The second step is to consider ways of communicating that heightened emotional awareness to their future public, for everything we play, every sound we make, must be with the aim of *"striking the Imagination and affecting the Minds"* of our listeners.

▶
Video 8.1

Exercise 18: Heightening our awareness of sound and its effect

1. Let us begin at the beginning, with what we could call the very essence of music! Imagine one single note played in succession by a variety of instruments: first by a bell, then by a harp, a horn, a piano, a viol, and a flute. The effect that each sound has on us is different, because the timbre or quality of each sound is different, even though the actual note is the same.

2. Next, let's imagine a violin playing that same note, but with an additional element: dynamics. It starts softly, gradually grows louder, and then dies away to silence. We have still heard just that one note, yet within it we have experienced, if we have allowed ourselves to be open to it, an entire journey, a micro-spectrum of experience.

Each one of the sounds imagined in Exercise 18 is meaningful to us because it relates to some aspect of our consciousness, mirroring our experience, echoing our feelings, and recalling memories. Perhaps that is why we use so many music-related phrases in our everyday speech: for example, "her words touched a chord deep within him" when we mean finding empathy, or we talk about an idea "finding resonance" within a section of the population, or of communities living "in harmony" with one another.

The poet William Cowper (1731–1800) puts it thus:

> *There is in souls a sympathy with sounds,*
> *And as the mind is pitch'd, the ear is pleased*
> *With melting airs, or martial, brisk or grave.*
> *Some chord in unison with what we hear*
> *Is touched within us, and the heart replies.*[4]

When two notes are sounded, either one after the other or simultaneously, our emotional response becomes significantly more complex.

Emotional Information: What Sound Tells Us

Music is often referred to as a language. If it is, it is certainly not one in which intellectual communication between two or more people is achievable. Yet there is undeniably a more abstract meaningfulness in the relationship between one sound and another. What that meaning is, in terms of words, lies very much within the realm of subjectivity—if we could put precisely into words the message a piece of music seems to be conveying, we wouldn't need music at all.

Exercise 19 is one I use with students to intensify their awareness of just how much feeling can be contained in two simple notes coming into contact with each other. If we wanted to use more contemporary terminology we could replace the term 'message' with 'emotional information.'

Exercise 19: Exploring emotional information

1. On any keyboard instrument play, slowly, a rising semitone, say D' to E♭.

2. Savor the emotion you feel, with all the care and intensity of a wine connoisseur savoring a rare vintage. Some may say this interval speaks to them of foreboding or fear, others that it represents awakening or doubt— words are not important!

3. Next, play the same two notes backward: E♭ to D'. The message now means something completely different, does it not? Perhaps it conveys a sense of release or of setting down. Such reactions are, of course, personal and subjective: if a simple interval could indeed express an unambiguous and specific emotion, music would be a quite different phenomenon! So let us for now not try to relate our intervals to specific emotions: let us abandon words and allow feeling a free rein!

4. Next, play a whole tone, d'—e"—a mere semitone in difference, yet in feeling it conjures up very different emotions.

5. Continue exploring the intervals, taking time to savor the emotional information special to each one, relishing the utterly different emotion each one communicates.

6. Go through all the intervals in Figure a in this way. Take your time, allowing each interval in turn to "*strike the Imagination, affect the Mind, and command the Passions.*"

7. Try doing the same thing in a lower or a higher octave, and observe what difference tessitura can make to the way you feel.

Figure a

Each interval, played forward or backward, elicits a different emotional response.

When we listen to more than two notes played in succession, the emotional information we receive becomes more complex. (Figure b).

Figure b

Groups of more than two notes contain more complex emotional information.

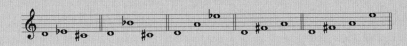

The aim of these exercises is to open our minds in order to receive emotional information directly from the sounds themselves. This requires a mindset very different from the one required in selecting emotions from one's own acquired 'collection' and projecting them onto the music, of daubing the music with colors from one's own personal emotional palette. The first involves deep awareness and, to the extent that it is possible, the laying aside of one's own cherished store of feelings in order to explore the path the composer has mapped out. The other involves using the composer's notes more as a convenient vehicle to express emotions that owe their origins to sources outside the particular music in question but that may not necessarily be appropriate to it.

> The more I have taught young musicians, the more I have understood that learning to play well includes learning to feel more intensely, and that the musical and expressive development of a musician, which requires constant nourishment, is alas too often neglected in favor of pure 'instrumentalism.' By 'instrumentalism' I mean the systematic study of an instrument from a predominantly abstract technical standpoint, learning to play the instrument rather than learning to play music (assuming the basics have been learned and are functioning well). This acquired "technique" is then evident no matter what repertoire is being studied, so that what we may hear is, alas, more technique than music.

Let us now progress from gleaning emotional information from a mere handful of notes to applying our intensification of feeling to a whole movement (Exercise 20). We will take as our example the Preludio to Corelli's Sonata 7, the first of the Chamber Sonatas of his opus 5 set (Figure c).

Figure c
Preludio of Corelli's Sonata op. 5, no. 7.

Exercise 20: Heightening awareness of the emotional impact of intervals in Corelli's Preludio

1. Ignoring both rhythm and tempo, without any preconceived idea as to how this movement should sound, forgetting even that it is by Corelli or that it is written for the violin and taking no heed of the bass line, play each interval in Figure d in turn, savoring to the full its unique quality and energy: some intervals may soar, evoking elation, while others plunge or sink, evoking doubt or despair.

   It is best to do this on a keyboard instrument first and then by singing, so that you will not be tempted to think in 'violin' terms. Work through the movement one phrase at a time.

Figure d
Single intervals from the opening phrase of Corelli's Sonata op. 5, no. 7.

While you sing, you can enhance your experience of the intervals through physical gesture, expressing each one in turn so that its essence is felt throughout your entire being. As playing the violin involves the channeling of emotional and spiritual elements into sound via physical movements, feeling the intervals physically will help your playing when the time comes. Gesture is an essential aspect of Baroque expression, whether in painting or sculpture, in the theater or in ballet; it is an important part of our study also.

2. Next, do the same with a small group of Corelli's notes, still feeling each interval as intensely as before but also being aware of the complexity of emotions elicited by the group (Figure e).

Figure e
Groups of intervals from the opening of Corelli's Sonata op. 5, no. 7.

3. Finally, sing through the entire movement in the same way.

We cannot express that which we do not feel. Quantz (X, §22) articulates this idea as follows: *"Inner feeling—the singing of the soul: if the beginner is not himself moved by what he plays, he cannot hope for any profit from his efforts, and he will never move others through his playing, which should be his real aim."*

Our audience will never be able to feel that which we are not convincingly expressing. We have to find appropriate ways of successfully delivering the passions contained in the music to our audience, to persuade *them* of what *we* have learned to feel. The next stage for us will be to learn how to communicate, with the sounds of our violin, our deepening awareness of the emotions contained in the most basic musical 'cells' to our public (Exercise 21).

Exercise 21: Communicating emotional information in sound

Repeat Exercises 19 and 20, this time on the violin, expressing in sound the same emotions in each interval that you have discovered from the previous exercises. Remember, your bow is your voice and the movement of the bow corresponds to the physical gestures you have been making. Work methodically, singing, gesturing and then reproducing in sound those elements. Try asking yourself this: "on a scale of one to ten, how close is the emotion caused by the sound I am making to the emotion I experienced before?"

C. P. E. Bach goes further than Quantz, stressing the need to manipulate one's emotions in order to be convincing. *"A musician cannot move others unless he too is moved. He must of necessity feel all of the affects that he hopes to arouse in his audience . . . in languishing, sad passages, the performer must languish and grow sad. Thus will the expression of the piece be more clearly perceived by the audience. . . . [S]imilarly, in lively, joyous passages, the executant must again put himself into the appropriate mood."*[5]

It is interesting to compare the quotes from Quantz and C. P. E. Bach with that of the Roman rhetorician Quintilian, who in his *Institutes of Oratory* (c. 95 ce) writes that *"the chief requisite, then, for moving the feelings of others is, as far as I can judge, that we ourselves be moved, for the assumption of grief, anger, and indignation will be often ridiculous if we adapt merely our words and looks, and not our minds, to those passions."*[6] Lesson 23 will deal more fully with Quintilian, rhetoric, and the links between rhetoric and Baroque music.

The identification and subsequent expression and communication of emotion was, together with the related art of rhetoric, absolutely central to music making in the Baroque period, for performers and composers alike. *"All musical expression"* writes Friedrich Wilhelm Marpurg in 1749 *"has as its basis an affect or feeling."* Indeed, "affect" was a key component of Baroque aesthetics in all artistic fields, from painting and sculpture to dance and theater. *"A Philosopher,"* continues Marpurg *". . . seeks to bring light to our understanding. . . . But the orator, poet, musician seek more to enflame than enlighten."*[7]

Contemporary writings on the subject went under such titles as the "Theory" or "Doctrine" of the Affects or Passions or, to use the best-known German term, the "Affektenlehre."

Johann Mattheson (1739), as we shall see in Lesson 39, uses the *Affektenlehre* to form almost a pseudo-scientific method of composition. One aspect of this is his exploration of the relation between feelings and intervals. *"Since for example joy is an **expansion** of our souls,"* he writes, *"thus it follows . . . that I could best express this affect by **large** and **expanded** intervals."*[8]

On the other hand, *"If one knows that sadness is a **contraction** of these subtle parts of our body, then it is easy to see that the **small** and **smallest** intervals are the most suitable for this passion."*[9]

Johann Philipp Kirnberger, a student of J. S. Bach and the inventor of two tuning systems known as Kirnberger I and Kirnberger II, attempts a more specific table of the affects of intervals. In the second part of his *Die Kunst des reinen Satzes* (The Art of Strict Musical Composition) published in Berlin in 1776, the rising semitone is described as "sad and anxious," the falling one as "very sad." The rising major second is "pleasant," the falling one "serious and peaceful." The rising minor third is "sad and painful" but the descending one is "calm." The rising major third is "joyful," while the descending one is "melancholy." The ascending octave is "happy, courageous, encouraging," and the descending one is "very soothing."[10]

ॐ ॐ ॐ

How to Prepare: Manipulating Our Emotions

I occasionally observe students preparing to play a piece simply by organizing their bodies into a perfect textbook position; but inwardly they do not prepare at all, so what we hear may be perfect and textbook but is not expressive. The question therefore arises, "how do I prepare myself inwardly for the task of conveying the emotions inherent in the music?"

For part of the answer we may take the analogy of an organist: before beginning to play, he or she must decide which stops to pull out in order to make the kinds of sounds appropriate for that piece: perhaps the organist will choose only string sounds, or he might include an oboe or a flute, or maybe the Vox Humana. So we too, before we begin to play, must pull out certain imaginary stops, deciding which colors we wish to draw from our instrument, which affect or affects inherent in the music we must strive to convey.

Preparation means asking ourselves "What is the affect of this piece?" and "What must I do in order to make my audience feel that affect?" To achieve this goal, we need to train ourselves to 'switch on' emotions that are possibly not relevant to our actual mood.

Consider the actor who, ecstatically happy in his personal life, steps onto the stage to play King Lear, or the actress who, in the midst of a deep personal crisis must play proud Queen Titania. The performing musician, just like the actor, must be able to 'set up' his state of mind, tampering with the chemistry of his personal feelings, deciding on which affects and sounds will serve his purpose. Shakespeare recognizes the need for this self-manipulation in these famous lines from Hamlet, who observes (act 2, scene 2),

> *Is it not monstrous that this player here,*
> *But in a fiction, in a dream of passion,*
> *Could force his soul so to his own conceit*
> *That from her working all his visage wann'd,*
> *Tears in his eyes, distraction in's aspect,*
> *A broken voice, and his whole function suiting*
> *With forms to his conceit?*

To help students manipulate their feelings in the way Hamlet suggests, I find the following mental image helpful: we carry within us an 'emotional keypad' containing all the emotions that a human being is capable of feeling. As we cannot convey emotions we are not feeling, we need to click on that keypad before we play in order to activate the appropriate emotions—for example, joy, anger, sorrow, exuberance, or regret.

In Exercise 22, we practice activating these emotions.

Exercise 22: Activating emotions on demand

1. Play the following notes with a minimum of emotional input.

2. On your "emotional keypad," switch on each of the emotions listed below in turn. When you are satisfied that you are intensely feeling the selected emotion, play the

extract again. Observe to what extent the different emotions you are experiencing influence tempo, dynamics, bow speed, articulations, etc.

- Joy
- Anger
- Sorrow
- Pity
- Love
- Doubt
- Exuberance
- Anxiety
- Regret

3. Apply each of these emotions in turn the following extract, the opening bars of Handel's F-major sonata.

Notes

1. Molière, *Le Bourgeois gentilhomme*, act I, scene 2. "Philosophy is one thing, but Music, Sire, Music . . ."
2. Johann Mattheson, *DVC*, Part 1, Chapter 3, § 51 (p 104).
3. Francesco Geminiani, Preface to *The Art of Playing on the Violin*.
4. William Cowper, *The Task*. Book VI, lines 1-5, 1785.
5. C. P. E Bach, *Essay*, Chapter 3, § 13.
6. Quintilian, *Institutes of Oratory*, p. 427; Chapter II, 26.
7. Marpurg, *Der Critischer Musicus an der Spree*, September 2, 1749. Quoted in the Eulenburg edition of C. P. E. Bach's *Essay*, pp. 80–81, note 3.
8. Mattheson, *DVC*, Part 1, Chapter 3, §56, p. 104.
9. Mattheson, *DVC*, Part 1, Chapter 3, §57, p. 105.
10. Kirnberger, *The Art of Strict Musical Composition*, pp. 373–374.

Lesson 9

The Inner Life of Sound

"Messa di voce"

In this Lesson we learn how to execute one of our most important expressive devices, the Messa di voce, referred to in almost every treatise of the Baroque period, although not necessarily by that name. We also explore related ways of keeping our sound alive, expressive, and interesting in a slow movement for, as Quantz says (XIV, §1) *"a true musician may distinguish himself by the way he plays the Adagio."*

Before we begin, let us read an extract from a letter that Tartini wrote to a young pupil of his, Maddalena Lombardini, in 1760. Tartini had established his Scuola delle Nazioni violin school in Padua in 1728, attracting pupils from all over Europe, and this letter allows us a unique glimpse into his way of teaching; in it, he advises Maddalena on a few aspects of technique that she should work on. Maddalena was later to achieve fame as an international violin virtuoso and as a composer.

Padua, March 5, 1760.

My Very Much Esteemed Signora Maddalena,

Your principal practice and study should, at present, be confined to the use and power of the bow, in order to make yourself entirely mistress in the execution and expression of whatever can be played or sung, within the compass and ability of your instrument. Your first study, therefore, should be the true manner of holding, balancing and pressing the bow lightly, but steadily, upon the strings; in such a manner as that it shall seem to breathe the first tone it gives, which must proceed from the friction of the string, and not from percussion, as by a blow given with a hammer upon it. This depends on laying the bow lightly upon the strings, at the first contact, and on gently pressing it afterwards, which, if done gradually, can scarce have too much force given to it, because, if the tone is begun with delicacy, there is little danger of rendering it afterwards either coarse or harsh.

Of this first contact, and delicate manner of beginning a tone, you should make yourself a perfect mistress in every situation and part of the bow, as well in the middle as at the extremities; and in moving it up, as well as in drawing it down. To unite all these laborious particulars into one lesson, my advice is, that you first exercise yourself in a swell upon an open string, for example, upon the second or a-la-mi re: that you begin pianissimo, and increase the tone by slow degrees to its fortissimo; and this study should be equally made, with the motion of the bow up, and down, in which exercise you should spend at least an hour every day, though at different times, a little in the morning, and a little in the evening; having constantly in mind, that this practice is, of all others, the most difficult, and the most essential to playing well on the violin. When you are a perfect mistress of this part of a good performer, a swell will be very easy to you; beginning with the most minute softness, increasing the tone to its loudest degree, and diminishing it to the same point of softness with which you began, and all this in the same stroke of the bow. Every degree of pressure upon the string, which the expression of a note or passage shall require, will by this means be easy and certain; and you will be able to execute with your bow whatever you please.

Your obedient and most humble servant,
Giuseppe Tartini

It is important to observe that Tartini's first priority is the "*use and power of the bow*" and that he is primarily concerned with its *expressive* power. "*To play well,*" he would tell his pupils "*it is necessary to sing well.*" Although he does discuss a more articulated stroke later on, he offers no technical information on what we would today call "bow strokes." However, a comprehensive overview of his bowing patterns is to be found in his *L'arte del arco*.

The "swelling" Tartini speaks of, and which he advises Maddalena to practice three times a day for twenty minutes, is the Messa di voce, literally meaning "the placing of the voice." "*To draw a beautiful sound from the instrument,*" Tartini writes in his *Regole*, "*place the bow on the strings gently at first and then increase the pressure.*" But, he warns us, "*If the full pressure is applied immediately, a harsh, scraping sound will result.*"[1]

Throughout the seventeenth and eighteenth centuries there are numerous references to the Messa di voce as an expressive vocal device. From Giulio Caccini, who, in the introduction to his *Nuove Musiche* (1602) talks of the *"swelling and abating of the voice"* as one of *"the foundation(s) of passion,"* to Johann Adam Hiller, creator of the German singspiel and kantor of the Thomaskirche in Leipzig; in 1780, Hiller writes of *"another beautiful quality—a gradual crescendo and diminuendo of the sound—the so-called Messa di voce. This can be performed from pianissimo up to fortissimo and then be brought back down again."*[2]

In his book *The Present State of Music in France and Italy* (1771) Charles Burney writes of the great castrato Farinelli: *"The first note he sung was taken with such delicacy, swelled by minute degrees to such an amazing volume, and afterwards diminished in the same manner, that it was applauded for full five minutes."*[3]

Tartini does not tell us exactly how to execute the Messa di voce, but fortunately Geminiani is a little more informative. "*One of the principal Beauties of the Violin,*" he writes, "*is the swelling or encreasing and softening the Sound; which is done by Pressing the Bow upon the Strings with the Fore-finger more or less. In playing all long Notes the Sound should be begun soft, and gradually swelled till the Middle, and from thence gradually softened till the End.*"[4]

For Leopold Mozart "*Every tone, even the strongest attack, has a small, even if barely audible, softness at the beginning of each stroke. . . . [T]his same softness must be heard also at the end of each stroke*" (Chapter V, § 3). Although he does not employ the term Messa di voce, his dynamically divided bow (Figure a) is a clear, graphic illustration of its use, to be applied equally to up-bows and down-bows.

"*Begin the down stroke or up stroke with a pleasant softness,*" he writes; "*increase the tone by means of an imperceptible increase of pressure; let the greatest volume of tone occur in the middle of the bow, after which, moderate it by degrees by relaxing the pressure of the bow until at the end of the bow the tone dies completely away*" (Chapter V, § 4).

Figure a

Leopold Mozart's dynamically divided bow. "Foible" means "soft" and "Fort" means "strong." Extract from the first French edition. Reproduced by kind permission of Anne Fuzeau Productions.

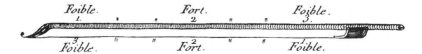

Using pressure as a principal means of execution in a slow, expressive Messa di voce ensures that the sound has texture and body. Too much use of speed will produce an empty, breathy sound. However, some variation of bow speed is essential if we are to avoid strangling the sound.

Exercise 23 will teach us the first step in acquiring a good Messa di voce, gathering together the information we have acquired until now.

Exercise 23: Learning to play a Messa di Voce (1)

The open string

1. Place the bow on an open string, at the middle. Let it rest with only its natural weight, applying zero pressure. It is important to slant the bow so that not all the hair is in contact with the string; a vertical bow, using full hair, is less supple than a slanting one.

2. With your forefinger, gently and slowly press the bow into the string until the stick is almost on the string. While doing this, do not move the bow along the string.

3. Slowly release the pressure until the bow has returned to its initial state, resting on the string. Regulate this release well: do not allow the bow to leap back in an uncontrolled way and try to prevent it from shuddering.

4. Repeat No. 2, this time while moving the bow slowly up and down for a few inches. Start with zero pressure; then add pressure until the sound is at cracking point before releasing slowly. You will need to increase the bow speed a little to prevent the cracking of the sound, but do not increase it more than is absolutely necessary.

5. Repeat this many times, gradually using more bow. You should by now be avoiding, but only just, the cracking of the sound. The more bow you use, the slower you should add the pressure. Remember to start and finish with zero pressure, in order to obtain the maximum dynamic range.

6. Follow Tartini's advice by practicing this for twenty minutes three times a day!

In the same paragraph as his diagram (Figure a) Leopold Mozart mentions two further technical devices, to be practiced in conjunction with one another. The first refers to the "point of contact," as it is called today. *"In the soft tone . . . the bow should be placed a little farther from the bridge or saddle; whereas in loud tone . . . the bow [should be] placed nearer to the bridge."*

The other device involves the pressure of the fingers of the left hand. This should be altered according to the dynamics: *"In the soft tone,"* Leopold writes, *"relax the pressure somewhat . . . whereas in loud tone the fingers of the left hand should be pressed down strongly."* The variation in finger pressure does indeed alter the dynamics, but care should be taken not to cause the pitch to fluctuate as well.

In the following paragraph (Chapter V, § 5) Leopold adds further information with reference to Figure a, this time regarding vibrato. *"The finger of the left hand,"* he writes, *". . . must move forward towards the bridge and backward again towards the scroll."* In a rare mention of the speed of vibrato as a means of expression he continues with an instruction to do this *"in soft tone quite slowly, but in loud rather faster."*

In Exercise 24 we merge this additional information with the technique studied in the previous exercise. We also learn to vary the amount of hair that comes into contact with the string, a further means of achieving our perfect Messa di voce: I should add that, to my knowledge, this latter technique does not feature in any eighteenth-century source.

Exercise 24: Learning to play a Messa di Voce (2)

A) Altering the point of contact

1. Place the bow on any string at the frog, near the top of the fingerboard, with zero pressure on the stick.
2. Draw the bow toward the middle, adding pressure on the stick to produce a crescendo, while steering the bow ever closer to the bridge.
3. Having reached the climax point close to the bridge, diminish the pressure on the stick and allow the bow to drift back toward the fingerboard.

B) Altering the finger pressure in the left hand

1. Place any finger on any string, using just enough pressure to make a passable sound with the bow.
2. Slowly increase the pressure until you reach the optimum sound; when you have held the optimum sound for a while, diminish the pressure and return to the original sound.

C) Altering the amount of hair in contact with the string

1. Tilt the bow forward so that the minimum of hair is in contact with the string.
2. Using a rolling movement with your fingers, rotate the bow until the hair is at 90 degrees with the string and the maximum amount of hair is in contact with it (you can practice this movement by rolling a pencil between fingers and thumb).
3. Practice this while playing a Messa di voce: the fuller the hair, the fuller the sound.

D) Combining A, B, and C

1. Play the Messa di voce as studied in **A**, with the first finger on any string. Combine this with the fluctuation of finger pressure described in **B** and with the technique described in **C**.

2. Repeat with each finger in turn.

3. Play a scale combining all these elements.

E) Adding vibrato

Repeat D, adding some vibrato toward the climax point. Ensure that it begins slowly and imperceptibly, gradually speeding up until it reaches its maximum intensity at the loudest moment of the Messa di voce. The speed of the vibrato should correspond in intensity to the volume produced by the bow.

Adding vibrato to a Messa di voce was by no means Leopold's idea: half a century before, Roger North had penned a most poetic description of the Messa di voce, writing that *"a long note should be filled and softened imperceptibly, so as to be like also a gust of wind, which begins with a soft air, and fills by degrees to a strength as makes all bend, and then softens away againe into a temper, and so vanish."*[5]

The sound of the Messa di voce, North added, was to be warmed with a *"gentle and slow wavering"* vibrato.[6]

Today, vibrato is clearly no longer the *"gentle and slow wavering"* motion North describes, used occasionally for the purpose of warming the sound. Its constant use has, alas, not only devalued it but has led to far less emphasis being placed on the expressive power of the bow. I find that it is only when vibrato is entirely eliminated that many students realize how much they have been relying on it for expression and, to their amazement, what an empty sound their bows make without it! It is as if the blood has ceased to flow through the veins of the music. What the collective sources tell us is that every sound, like every human being, has an interior life, and that if this is not constantly nurtured by the bow, the music will cease to live. We discuss the question of vibrato in Lesson 21.

❦ ❦ ❦

We have noted Geminiani's instruction that all long notes should include a Messa di voce. But short notes too, he insists, should have shape, even when they are played fast. His Example XX is reproduced in Figure b (below). *"This Example,"* he writes *"shows the Manner of Bowing proper to the Minim, Crotchet-quaver and Semiquaver both in slow and quick Time. For it is not sufficient alone to give them their true Duration, but also the Expression proper to each of these Notes."*

There should always be some *"swelling of the sound,"* Geminiani insists; if there is not, it is either "mediocre" or just plain bad: *"cattivo."*

- The filled-in triangles over the notes in No. 1 indicate the *"swelling of the sound"*: he calls this "Buono" (good).
- The lines in No. 2 mean that *"the Notes are to be play'd plain and the Bow is not to be taken off the Strings."* He calls this "Mediocre" or even, in No. 4, "Cattivo."
- The vertical wedges in No. 5 indicate a *"Staccato, where the Bow is taken off the Strings at every Note,"* which Geminiani judges to be either "Cattivo o Particolare" (Bad or a Special Case). Presumably, he is saying that even though they lose their expressive shapes, some off the string bowings are occasionally permissible. It is important to work through Geminiani's Example XX in detail: Exercise 25 will help you breathe life into your sound.

Exercise 25: Breathing life into the sound

Geminiani's Example XX

1. In the slow notes, apply pressure with the forefinger to mold the dynamics: do not use too fast a bow.
2. Gradually speed up, maintaining as much of the above technique as possible.
3. Play the plain notes as well—for example, the ones marked "Cattivo" in No. 4—so that you can contrast these rather lifeless sounds with the expressively shaped sounds that you are achieving elsewhere.

Quantz, writing as a celebrated flute virtuoso, is equally clear about the nature and ubiquitous role of the Messa di voce. *"If you must hold a long note for either a whole or a half bar, which the Italians call messa di voce,"* he writes (Chapter XIV, § 10) *"you must first tip it gently with the tongue, scarcely exhaling."* In violin terms, this translates as beginning the stroke with a minimum of attack. *"Then,"* he continues, *"you begin pianissimo, allow the strength of the tone to swell to the middle of the note, and then from there diminish it to the end of the note in the same fashion, making a vibrato with the finger on the nearest open hole."*

Quantz agrees with Geminiani on the importance of keeping the sound alive and expressive even in short notes. *"Each note, whether it is a crotchet, quaver, or semiquaver,"* he writes (Chapter XIV, § 11) *"must have its own Piano and Forte, to the extent that the time permits."*

Figure b
Francesco Geminiani, Example XX from *The Art of Playing on the Violin* (1751).

Composers rarely specified dynamic fluctuations in their published works. One composer who did was Giovanni Antonio Piani. In his opus 1 sonatas, published in Paris in 1712, Piani provides an unusually large amount of instruction for the performer, including fingerings, bowings, and dynamic markings. Figure c shows the opening of Piani's Sonata VIII. The shaped line over the first notes of Bars 1 and 2, in the middle of Bar 3 and at the end of Bar 4, denotes a Messa di voce. The line at the start of Bar 3 denotes a crescendo; Piani has a corresponding marking for a diminuendo. In his explanation of the symbols, Piani writes that the dynamic changes should happen "imperceptibly," [insensiblement] implying that there should never be a point in a crescendo or a diminuendo when the dynamic changes suddenly become apparent.

Figure c
The opening of Sonata 0 by Giovanni Antonio Piani (1678–1760). Note the contrasting indications regarding the character of each part, "Affetuoso" for the violin and "Staccato" for the bass.

Another composer to indicate dynamics within single sounds was Francesco Maria Veracini (Figure d). In his opus 2 Sonatas (1744) entitled "Sonate accademiche," Veracini uses three symbols. He explains their meaning in an introductory "Intentions of the Author." The first symbol, as in Bars 1 and 3 of Figure d, signifies "a Bow started Piano, strengthened until Fortissimo and diminished until Piano." The second, as in Bar 1 of our second line, signifies "a Bow started Piano and finished Forte," while the third, on the half note A″ in the next bar, signifies "a Bow started Forte and finished Piano."

Figure d
Opening of the Sonata op. 2, no. 5 by Francesco Maria Veracini (1690–1768). "Come Sta" means it is to be played "as it is," i.e., without ornamentation. The "S" markings in the bass indicate "Solo," meaning without any harmonization until the Figures in the following bar. The movement is to be played "With the Greatest Gravity."

Exercise 26 aims to provide the technical means necessary for the tonal and dynamic inflections needed to bring rhetorical fragments to life and to maintain constant interest within melodic lines. It is based on the last of Leopold Mozart's four diagrams on bow division (Chapter V, § 8). In this (Figure e) he advocates practicing *"with loud and soft twice in one stroke,"* adding that *"this can be performed four, five, and six times; yes, often even more in one stroke. One learns through pratice of this . . . to apply strength and weakness in all parts of the bow; consequently it is of great use."*

Every nuance, every inflection, must be achieved by the bow: what Leopold is here acknowledging is that even within a single bow there can be more than one inflection, and that the duty of the bow is constantly to feed the sound that the music demands. Exercise 26 provides information on how to achieve a living, breathing sound.

Figure e
Leopold's fourth bow division. "Foible" means "soft" and "Fort" means "strong." Extract from the first French edition. Reproduced by kind permission of Anne Fuzeau Productions.

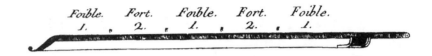

Foible. *Fort.* *Foible.* *Fort.* *Foible.*
1. *2.* *1.* *2.* *1.*

Exercise 26: Keeping the sound consistently alive

A. Pressure

1. Place the bow on the string at the middle.
2. Using mostly the forefinger, squeeze the bow gently but firmly into the string and release it again.
3. Repeat No. 2 many times, at a suggested rate of 200 squeezes per minute.
4. While continuing to squeeze in this way, move the bow at a moderate speed up and down the string, causing a constant fluctuation of dynamics.
5. Gradually reduce the speed to 100 squeezes per minute. The number of fluctuations should now be 10 per bow.
6. Gradually reduce this number until there is only a single Messa di voce per bow.

B. Speed

1. Play a slow bow, starting at the frog. When you reach the middle, change to a sudden fast bow that takes you straight to the point. Do not slow down after the fast part.
2. Repeat this on an up-bow.
3. Where S = slow and F = fast, continue the exercise with an ever-increasing number of speed changes. Repeat each of the following formulae many times.

   FS; SFS; SFSF; SFSFS; SFSFSF.

Video 9.1

In the next lesson, we will apply our knowledge of the Messa di voce and the technical skills we have learned to a single movement of Corelli, the Adagio from his Sonata, op. 5, no, 3.

Postscript: Additional Study Material

The Messa di voce continued to be an important expressive device long after the Baroque period: many books of nineteenth-century études begin with a study for the expressive control of the slow bow, including those by Rodolphe Kreutzer, Pierre Rode, and Federigo Fiorillo. Figure f shows the opening of the first étude, op. 36, by Jacques-Féréol Mazas, published in 1843, with no fewer than ten printed examples of a Messa di voce in the first sixteen bars. A note with a crescendo is known in French as a "Son enflé" (swollen sound) while one with a diminuendo was a "Son diminué." One that did both, as in a Messa di voce, was called a "Son filé" or spun sound.

Figure f
Jacques-Féréol Mazas (1782–1849), opening of Étude no. 1, book 1, op. 36 (1843).

The bowing exercises of Otakar Ševčik, particularly Parts 3–6 of his opus 2 (1893) are ideal for focusing attention on the intricacies of string crossings that are such an important part of the Baroque violinist's technique; equally useful are the exercises for controlled dynamic fluctuation, such as those in Figure g.

Figure g
Otakar Ševčik (1852–1934), *School of Bowing Technique*, op. 2, part 1, no. 5, Variations 253–54.

I also advise my students to practice the following étude (Figure h) of Kreutzer: it has different numberings according to the edition (Exercise 27).

Figure h
Rodolphe Kreutzer (1766–1831), Étude.

Exercise 27: Learning to "feed" the sound by varying bow pressure and speed using the Étude by Kreutzer.

1. Start by playing half a bar per bow; exaggerate the phrasing using bow pressure to feed the sound of the most lyrical notes (you need not maintain a steady rhythm).
2. Repeat, varying the sound by using only bow speed.
3. Using a combination of pressure and speed, aim for the most singing sound imaginable.
4. Gradually adjust the tempo until you can play one bar per bow.

Notes

1. Tartini, *Regole* (Rules for Bowing). Hermann Moeck Edition, p. 56.
2. Suzanne J. Beicken, *Treatise on Vocal Performance and Ornamentation*, p. 64, § 9.
3. Burney, *The Present State of Music in France and Italy*, 1771 edition, p. 216. Quoted in *The Gentleman's Monthly Intellegencer* 40 (May 1771), p. 272.
4. Geminiani, *The Art of Playing on the Violin*, Example 1 (B) (2), p. 2.
5. North, *Notes of Me*, p. 149.
6. Boyden, *The History of Violin Playing*, p. 255.

Lesson 10

Applying the Messa di voce

Arcangelo Corelli: Adagio from Sonata, op. 5, no. 3

In this lesson, we learn how to integrate the Messa di voce into our playing, using the Corelli Adagio (Exercise 28), tempering it according to the demands of the music, and we practice synchronizing the gestures of the bow with our breathing, another step toward connecting the outer artist with the inner one. We consider how dissonances and consonances relate and, embedded in the 'Observations' section, we find discussions on the various functions of the trill, on the importance of being at ease in second position, and on the topics of hemiolas and chromatic fingerings. There is a section on "Sound and Expression" and, to end the lesson, we set ourselves the task of replicating Corelli's exercise to produce long, sustained sounds.

Score 10.1

Score 10.2

Exercise 28: An initial application of the Messa di voce technique

1. Play through the Adagio by Corelli, consciously adding a Messa di voce to every single note. There should be much variety in the degree of swelling and decaying of the sound, according to the importance of the note in the phrase, but no note should, for the moment, be allowed to remain bland or lifeless.

2. Begin at a moderate tempo, but gradually decrease it. The slower the tempo, the more alert you need be to the living sound, the slow but constant dynamic fluctuations occurring organically within each note.

3. Listen carefully to the sound, eliminating any flaws you notice: the key to controlling the sound is active listening. There should be no surprises, such as sudden, uncontrolled increases or decreases in volume or the shuddering of the bow.

4. Remember Tartini's advice on the importance of practicing this exercise for twenty minutes, three times per day.

"Playing in good Taste," Geminiani reminds us in his notes to Example XVIII of *The Art of Playing on the Violin*, is about *"expressing with Strength and Delicacy the Intention of the Composer."* Having practiced the Messa di voce technique on the whole movement, you will surely have noticed that whereas some notes sound appropriately expressive as a result, others seem over-blown, perhaps even a touch grotesque.

Careful to avoid the notoriously ubiquitous 'Baroque Bulge' that provoked so much censure in the early days of the Baroque revival, we shall place our trust in our own inherent good taste, determining which harmonies seem to call forth a strong Messa di voce and in which a more delicately nuanced approach seems more fitting. We should be vigilant in detecting sounds that are shapeless, empty of expression, and devoid of inner life and meaning, so that we may imbue them with a suitable color and personality, thereby bringing them back from the dead.

Some sounds, however, do need to be sustained, their powerfully expressive nature characterized by consistency rather than by nuanced shape. Robert Bremner (1777), while acknowledging that *"the practice of the swell* (Messa di voce) *. . . is of the utmost consequence to those who wish to send a melodious Adagio, or any air home to the heart,"* nevertheless points out the validity of *"a steady equal pressure of bow. A daily practice of this manner of bowing is of equal importance with that of the swell, if not more so."* Bremner, a Scottish pupil of Geminiani, proclaims that *"the swell and Sostenuto . . . may be said to be the roots from whence all the other powers of the bow spring."*[1]

When an outpouring of emotion calls for strong and passionate sounds, make use of the freedom that chinless playing offers by moving the violin creatively in the opposite direction to the bow. This will add an extra dimension to the Messa di voce, for as it flows through your physical body, the resonance of the violin will be enhanced.

Dissonances and Consonances

The ready supply of dissonances for spicing up the harmony in Baroque music is one of its chief expressive delights. *"To excite the different passions,"* Quantz (XVII,VI, § 12) writes, *"the dissonances must be struck more strongly than the consonances."* Here is one clue as to how our sound should grow and diminish. *"Consonances,"* he continues *"make the spirit peaceful and tranquil; dissonances, on the other hand, disturb it."* This leads us to a triple dynamic truth:

1. A suspension will always be stronger than its resolution.
2. We should grow into dissonances, savor their expressive quality, and then die away from them.
3. A note that starts out as a consonance but ends up as a dissonance will need to grow in order to arrive strongly at the dissonance.

It should be emphasized once more that "stronger" here implies more than a mere increase in decibels; a convincing Messa di voce is wrought from its shifting colors, from the subtle thickening and dilution of its timbre, the intangible guiding of the sound toward its expressive goal. Thus "stronger" may well imply the diminishing of volume, for just as spiritual anguish is as affecting as physical pain, its outward expression may be more contained, even stifled (Exercise 29).

Exercise 29: Observing the dissonances and establishing a hierarchy among them

1. Go through the Corelli Adagio again, marking all the dissonances that occur between the violin and the bass.
2. Distinguish between strong, powerful dissonances and more gentle, intimate ones.
3. Decide to what extent each dissonance impacts the dynamics, according to our stated principles.

Let us take Bars 4 and 5 as an example: here, the e″ that links them in the violin part starts out as a consonance but becomes dissonant when the bass changes to an F. As we need to lean into this dissonance, we will crescendo through the e″ using the techniques learned in the previous lesson. The e″ climaxes when it clashes with the F in the bass; we can wallow in this dissonance for a while, after which we must release the pressure.

The following note, a′, is a consonance and may be considered as being of lesser importance, a note that requires no special care and can even be shortened. We then crescendo again through the following d″ until it clashes with the bass note G♯ in Bar 6 (the chord here is an E7 and is thus still dissonant).

Remember that the use of the Messa di voce is not limited to loud notes. It can equally bring to life soft sounds and should therefore be practiced at all dynamic levels.

Authentic emotional intensification through the medium of a Messa di voce cannot be convincingly achieved merely by the dutiful application of practiced techniques, however useful these may be as a first step. The muscles and nerves that apply these techniques must be activated by the inner voice coursing through the medium of our physical body as it transforms our artistic intention into sound. Exercise 30 is designed to help you feel the Messa di voce in this way, not merely as a technical procedure but as an emotional experience resulting from a specific harmonic truth.

৵ড় ৵ড় ৵ড়

Exercise 30: Breathing the Messa di voce

1. Without your violin, imagine the tempo of Corelli's adagio.
2. Count the first two beats of an imaginary preliminary bar; on the third beat, take a deep breath, in tempo.

3. Bar 1: exhale on Beat 1; your breath should take the form of a Messa di voce, lasting for one quarter note.
4. Follow the exhalation with a short, shallow inhalation of breath: this is Beat 2.
5. Beat 3 is another, deeper inhalation, corresponding to the anacrusis to Bar 2.
6. Bar 2: Beat 1 is a fairly rapid exhalation. Beats 2 and 3 are formed of a single, slow inhalation in the form of a Messa di voce.
7. Repeat the entire exercise, this time coordinating your breathing with expressive gestures in your right arm. The speed and shape of the gestures should be entirely at one with your breath.
8. Repeat the entire exercise playing on an open string, the gestures of your arm entirely at one with your breathing, guiding your bow.

The observations that follow are intended to help you work through the movement bar by bar, keeping the sound alive and expressive in a well thought-out way.

Observations

- Bar 1 may be considered an anacrusis to Bar 2: we should crescendo through the bar to greet the bass entry. The first note (e″) will sound more engaging on an open string and needs an elegant, majestic Messa di voce. The a′, also an open string, is weak. The third note grows till it plunges into Bar 2.
- Bar 2: the g♯ has a slow Messa di voce; the a′ is weak, but with a hint of crescendo, following the line of the bass.
- Bar 3 can be seen as an anacrusis to Bar 4; the b′ is therefore not very strong, but has a Messa di voce. The c″ crescendos: keep the eighth note alive with a mini Messa di voce.
- Bar 4: the first note is strong, with an active Messa di voce, while the second is a re-action to it, and is thus weak; take care that the e″ nevertheless remains alive, a 'sound' as opposed to a mere note. Caring for the sound of even the weakest note is important: this one may have just a hint of a Messa di voce. Before the last note there is an unwritten rest, or comma, enabling us to give a gentle but confident gesture at the beginning of the long e″. Think of this comma as a 'silent crescendo,' during which you bring the bow through the air back to the frog. The e″ will be more poignant if we use an open string.
- Bars 4–5: as discussed above, grow through the e″ into the beginning of Bar 5 so that the dissonance with the F in the bass is clearly and poignantly expressed.
- Toward the end of Beat 1 in Bar 5, the sound will abate a little.
- The a′ in Bar 5 is a resolution and is therefore weak: be careful not to accent it simply because you need to get back to the frog! A better idea is to bring the bow back through the air, producing a smaller comma than in Bar 4.

- Bars 5–6: The d″ is a Messa di voce: grow through it into the beginning of Bar 6, so that the dissonance with the G♯ in the bass is clearly and poignantly expressed, after which the sound will abate a little.
- Bar 6: the c″ is weak, but the b′ is the start of a hemiola and is therefore a little stronger.
- Bar 7: Even though we are not ornamenting the movement at this time, we should at least put a cadential trill (+) on the b′. Start the trill not from the upper note (c″) but from the b′ itself, as the b′ will clash with the A in the harmony, producing a spicier effect. (For a contemporary harmonic realization of Bars 7–8, see Figure a, below.) C² rescendo on the b′ to enjoy this dissonance before beginning the trill: in this case a wistful trill will be appropriate, starting slowly and gently accelerating. Stop trilling just after the A in the harmony resolves onto the G♯, leaving the b′ as a plain note with a diminuendo. You could add a sixteenth note a′ as an anacrusis to the next bar.

Figure a
Harmonic realization of Bars 7–8, by Antonio Tonelli (1686–1765).

On Trills

A trill gives life and expression to a note but, as with every ornament, it should not contradict the affect of the moment: that is not its role. Ornaments should enhance, not undermine or challenge, and must therefore be crafted so as to blend in with each individual aesthetic situation.

Trills fall into two main categories. Some, mostly on short notes, serve to add sparkle and energy to *"pieces which are very lively and full of spirit and movement,"* as Leopold Mozart puts it (X, § 7). Such trills do not really enhance the music's deeper emotional impact: they are normally fast and have very short, perhaps even inaudible, appoggiaturas, the fingers nimbly rising and falling with 'electric' energy.

The other kind of trill contributes to the expressive power of a note, mainly through the appoggiatura that, as its name suggests, leans on the main note in a way that expresses anything from wistfulness to heartfelt grief. In this category, the speed of the trill is likely to be slower, possibly speeding up or slowing down during its course, the fingers rising and falling in a gentle and controlled singing motion, without a trace of automatism. *"The slow (trill)"* comments Leopold Mozart (X, § 7) *"is used in sad and slow pieces."*

- The first phrase ends in Bar 8, and we can clarify that with some punctuation, putting a comma before the second note. The bass, however, pushes though the bar, as if it wishes to connect the end of the phrase with the beginning of the next one. If the bass is to be played by a cello, it will need to use an expressive Messa di voce much as the violin has done in Bars 4–6. The violin too, crescendos at the end of Bar 8 into the dissonance at the start of Bar 9.
- Bar 9 begins with a dissonance, expressed with a Messa di voce, the sound relaxing when the Bass resolves onto the G♯. The three eighth notes crescendo into Bar 10: put an individual crescendo onto the last of them (e″) for extra poignancy.
- Bar 10: the dissonant ninth chord on the first beat needs a strong Messa di voce. The weakest note is the a′: we could put a tiny comma after it, even though it flows with the Bass into the next bar. The e″ crescendos into Bar 11.

Dissonances can be used to express myriad emotions, from anguish and yearning to ecstasy or horror. We need to learn how to identify the appropriate emotion and how technically to convey it.

- Bar 11: take advantage of the open string to shift into second position on the a″ (see below.) The dissonant seventh chord suggests a less tormented, possibly ecstatic affect, expressed with an appropriate Messa di voce. The three eighth notes form an expressive and lyrical link to the resolution in Bar 12. On the way, however, the harmony changes, making the c‴ dissonant with the new D in the harmony. For this reason, the c‴ should be prolonged and its own Messa di voce added. (See Figure b for Tonelli's realization.)

Figure b
Bar 11, realized by Tonelli.

- Bar 12: the music settles on the dominant major chord of E major. A serene Messa di voce would express the relief of leaving behind so much dissonance. You might want to add some more expression by adding a trill to the g″♯: in this case, it will be the appoggiatura a″ that has the Messa di voce, the following trill slow and lingering. As there is a rest in this bar, we can take our time over this.

The term 'rest' is misleading, for the music does not stop. Silence is a suspension of time and can be very meaningful and intense if handled well. Communicate the silence to your audience by acting it out—listen to it without moving, then breathe slowly and bring your bow back to be ready for the next note at a speed corresponding to your breath. In other words, breathe with your bow!

> As breath gives life to the voice, so our bow breathes, in silence and in sound, now inhaling, now exhaling, now quick, now slow, in suspension, inspired, inspiring, alive to every atom of the music: the bow is our voice.

❧ ❧ ❧

In Praise of the Second Position

Violinists the world over can be divided into two categories: those who are comfortable playing in second position and those who, merely in order to avoid doing so, are ready to undertake the most virtuosic feats! For the Baroque violinist, learning to be fluent in the use of the "half position," as it was sometimes known, is essential: besides being useful for preserving the tone color and avoiding awkwardly brief string crossings, whole passages can sometimes be made to work best in second position. Being the shortest of shifts, it is the easiest to execute when playing chinless.

Tartini, in his letter to Maddalena Lombardini quoted in Lesson 9, is very firm on the importance of playing in the second position [a mezza smanicatura.] *With regard to the finger-board,"* he writes, *"I have one thing strongly to recommend to you . . . the taking of a violin part . . . and playing it upon the half shift . . . and constantly keeping upon this shift, playing the whole piece without moving the hand from this situation. . . . This practice should be continued till you can execute with facility upon the half-shift any violin part . . . at sight."*

Leopold Mozart devotes a whole section (VIII, II) to what he calls the "Half Position," [halben Applikatur] recommending us to *"practise it diligently"* (§ 1) and giving many examples of its use *"for the sake of convenience,"* (§ 9) *"not from necessity but for the sake of equality of tone and therefore for the sake of elegance,"* (§ 10) and in double stopping *"partly from necessity but also partly from convenience"* (§ 11).

He also mentions extending the fourth finger to reach up to the second position without actually shifting (§ 13) and reminds us that it is *"much easier to descend from this position than from the whole* [third position] *because it is nearer to the finger position of the natural manner* [first position] *of playing"* (§ 14). Shifting down must be done so as *"to deceive the ear of the listeners; that is, so that they may not perceive the change and swift descent of the hand"* (§ 14). As always, Leopold Mozart refrains from providing us with information about the technical aspects of shifting.

This instruction to use the second position is taken from the Preface (Avertissement) to the opus 1 sonatas of G. A. Piani (1712), illustrated below. The "Chanterelle" is the E string and the "Seconde" is the A string.

Quantz, who had trained as a violinist in his youth, also advocates (XVII, II, § 33) the use of the second position ("*mezzo manico*"), particularly *"in avoiding the open strings, which sound differently than when stopped with the fingers."* In the same paragraph he advocates going into position to avoid fourth-finger trills because trills are *"generally better made with the third rather than the little finger."* I personally beg to differ: trills with all fingers should be part of our regular study!

୨୯ ୨୯ ୨୯

- Bars 13–20 are as Bars 1–8. We may return to the first position in Bar 13, extending the fourth finger at the end of the bar, or we may remain there until the start of Bar 15.
- In Bar 20, the bass makes the end of its phrase clear by cutting out on the last beat. This time it is the violin that begins the next phrase, but the low E in the bass gives us no time to pause. All we can do to make the new phrase clear is to snatch a breath between the first and second notes, best achieved by taking an extra down-bow on the g″.
- Bar 21: the c″ does not lead to a dissonance, unlike the long notes earlier on (e.g,. Bars 4–5); therefore the Messa di voce does not need to stretch to the following bar and should be gentle: simply following the bass line, which unfolds before returning to the original note, will give us the shape of a Messa di voce! Likewise the d″ in Bar 23.
- Bar 22: place a short comma after the first beat, corresponding to the one in Bar 20. This time there is no need to take an extra down-bow, although you may prefer to do so. The same applies to Bar 24.
- Bar 25: the f″ does crescendo through to the dissonance at the start of Bar 26.
- Bars 26–27: there is a hemiola here. Some hemiolas are easy to spot, while others are less obvious. Sometimes there is ambiguity, and we need to decide whether or not to treat a passage as a hemiola at all. The strongest harmony here is on Beat 2 of Bar 27 (there is a dissonant C in the harmony) after which it resolves, the phrase ending on a weak C-major chord in Bar 28 (see Tonelli's realization in Figure c).

Bar 27 needs a trill on the d″: yes, with your fourth finger, one you might need to put into training! Here we should begin on the lower note, so as not to negate the dissonance: in any case, the previous note e″ has already served as an upper appoggiatura.

Hemiolas: To Be Heard as Well as Seen?

The practical difference between hemiola and non-hemiola lies in the positioning of the stresses, the good and bad notes, and the consequent implications for the bowing. In Figure c, the hemiola will be clarified if the bowing starts down and does not adjust; the good beats (1, 3, and 5) will all be played with down-bows. If there were no hemiola, the start of the second bar would be strong and the third note should therefore be taken on an up-bow.

We should anyway be wary of 'preaching' hemiolas, pointing them out too blatantly as if bringing to light some hidden secret that the audience at all costs must be made aware of. Sometimes hemiolas do need to be obvious; at other times they are just part of the fabric of the music. Anyway, when improvising ornamentation in a movement such as this, clarity of stress may be lost.

Figure c
Bars 26–28 in Tonelli's realization.

- In Bars 28–29 and 30–31 the bass phrases are two bars long. The continuo should make this clear by taking a fraction of time before the second beats of Bars 28 and 30, before which there is in any case a large leap upward. The chromatic rise in the violin part indicates an increase in intensity and dynamics. We have arrived on a quiet up-bow in Bar 28, and we are able to crescendo toward the hemiola in Bars 32–33; we can keep the tension here with a slight Messa di voce on each note.

  More importantly, a Messa di voce encompassing two bars (Bars 28–29 and again Bars 30–31) introduces a secondary ebb and flow within the overall crescendo.

ৎ৵ ৎ৵ ৎ৵

A Note on Chromatic Fingering

To the modern ear accustomed to equal temperament, in which all semitones are equal, it may have come as a surprise to learn in Lesson 11 that in 'pure' intonation there are in fact major and minor semitones. It appears that not everyone knew that in Geminiani's time either. *"Many may, perhaps, imagine that these scales are merely Cromatic,"* he writes (Example II) *"as they may not know that the Cromatic scale must be composed only of the greater and lesser Semitones; and that the Octave also must be divided into 12 Semitones, that is, 7 of the greater and 5 of the lesser."*

Geminiani's chromatic fingerings therefore, are surprising; he insists (Figure d) that a different finger play each note *"for two Notes cannot be stopped successfully by the same Finger without difficulty, especially in quick Time."* It is unclear what his reasoning is, except possibly to make the transition between one note and the next clearer. However, it is surely easier to adjust the subtle intonation of semitones with a single finger than with two.

Figure d

Extract from Francesco Geminiani's Essempio II.

Leopold Mozart's fingerings (Figure e) appear to be based on the principle that notes with the same name are played with the same finger.

Figure e

Leopold Mozart, chromatic fingering chart (Chapter III, § 6) in the French edition. Reproduced by kind permission of Anne Fuzeau Productions.

- Bars 32–33 form a hemiola. This time, Corelli's bowings allow no ambiguity or doubt. If we have arrived in Bar 32 on an up-bow we will need to play another up-bow on the f‴♯.

   In such impassioned moments, the lower note of the trill itself takes on the role of appoggiatura. Lean on the f‴♯ and play a Messa di voce, beginning the trill just after its dynamic climax. As the Messa di voce dies away, stop the trill so we hear a brief moment of plain f‴♯ before the following note.

- Bar 34: The hemiola ends here, but the bass quotes the opening motive again, so a new section overlaps with the old; the bass crescendos into the dissonance in Bar 35.

- Bars 35 and 36: The violin part picks up the motive the bass started in Bar 34 and uses it in both these bars. The b′ in Bar 35 is an unprepared dissonance: to emphasize the effect of this, it needs to be played with a strong gesture. The affect becomes more turbulent as a result, with further dissonances occurring in Bars 36 and 37 on Beat 1, and on Beat 2 of Bar 38. Shaping each quarter note will help to express this turbulent passion, combined with an overall crescendo and perhaps a slight increase in the tempo.

- Bars 37–38 are a hemiola, although the first slur, over three notes, slightly confuses it. A crescendo on each f″ will heighten the emotional tension. In Bar 38, trill on the e″ from the lower note.

- Bar 39. No sooner has the hemiola ended than the bass eighth notes re-energize the music. Snatching a breath for the f″ by taking another down-bow will help dramatize this: the f″ crescendos into the dissonance in Bar 40, relaxing just before it resolves onto the e″.

- Bars 41–42: The chromatic and syncopated bass line increases the intensity of the music. Taking a new down-bow on the second beat of each bar will enhance the implied sense of urgency. However, such a passage will eventually demand an intensification of improvised ornamentation, in the heat of which such calculated bowings will cease to be a priority.
- Bars 43–44: possibly the most impassioned hemiola. In Bar 43, a frenzied trill on the g‴♯ will add to the intensity: it could start on the upper note, but a prolonged a″ appoggiatura will detract from the more climactic a″ on Beat 3. In any case, the upper note a″ has already been sounded at the end of Bar 42.
- Bar 44: a cadential trill on the b′ starting on the note to enhance the dissonance.
- Bars 45–47: we have returned to the tonic key of A minor, so we may regard the remaining bars as a coda. A long Messa di voce over two bars leads us gently into the rather surprising B♭-major chord in Bar 47. The bass phrase starts on the second beat of Bar 45, so the continuo will put a comma before it, and another, smaller, comma after the first beat of Bar 46.
- Bars 48–49 are a hemiola. The affect here contrasts with the more passionate hemiolas recently encountered: we could describe this one as 'yearning' or 'regretful.' Use a slow bow for the Messa di voce on the g″♯, allowing the sound slowly to unfurl. This is the emotional climax of the hemiola, after which we can proceed more purposefully toward Bar 50. In Bar 49, trill on the b′, starting on the lower note.
- Bars 50–51: this is a written-out hemiola, not uncommon in Corelli's music. A not too extravagant cadenza would definitely be in order here (see Figure f for a suggestion). An in-depth study of Corellian ornamentation will be given in Lesson 21.

Figure f
A possible cadenza for the last two bars. Like all cadenzas, it should sound spontaneous, not measured.

Sound and Expression

Last, in this lesson I want to add some words about sound and expression. There exists something of an urban myth that playing the Baroque violin with a full-blooded sound is in some way a regrettable relic of the Romantic aesthetic with which all twenty-first-century musicians have sadly but inevitably been tainted. Baroque violin playing in the early stages of the Historically Informed Performance (HIP) 'movement' incorporated a necessary reaction to what it saw as an anachronistic aesthetic and a view of interpretation that took little, if any, account of historical realities. This 'anti-romantic' element resulted in some aspects of playing being clearly divided into 'right' and 'wrong' in the unwritten constitution of the HIP movement.

One of the defining characteristics of the emerging HIP violin school was a sound purged of any trace of 'modern' style. Emotion was understated, articulation was overstated and often unnatural, and perhaps too much emphasis was placed on whether the violin was being 'correctly' held. Today, with HIP being widely adopted and absorbed into the musical mainstream, this marking of stylistic territory is in itself an anachronism. Information from the sources can now be taken on board free of consideration as to whether it contradicts any cherished precepts of the Baroque revival.

The relatively colorless sound of the Baroque violin espoused by some musicians in the early stages of its revival does not correspond accurately to information gleaned from the sources. The impression that Baroque superstars such as Heinrich Ignaz Franz von Biber and Arcangelo Corelli, often playing in large spaces (Salzburg Cathedral or the Palazzo della Cancelleria in Rome) made on their audiences is difficult to imagine if their sounds were not powerful, intensely expressive, and highly colorful.

It is worth quoting here more words of Robert Bremner, who informs us that *"Corelli judged no performer fit to play in his band, who could not, with one stroke of his bow, give a steady and powerful sound, like that of an organ, from two strings at once, and continue it for ten seconds; and yet it is said, the length of their bow at that time did not exceed twenty inches."*[3]

Corelli's exercise is replicated in our Exercise 31, below.

Corelli's acoustical world, as revealed in all the genres in which he worked, from his solo sonatas to his concerti grossi, was one of gloriously rich sounds, in which he clearly loved to wallow, and we should not be inhibited in our expression when playing his music. Muffat, who studied with Corelli in Rome, tells us that the Italians were extremists with regard to dynamics and tempi: slow was very slow, fast very fast; *piano* was very soft and *forte* very loud.[4]

François Raguenet, in his oft-quoted *Parallèle des italiens et des françois* of 1702, describes how the Italian artist, when performing music of a stormy nature *"is seized with an unavoidable agony; he tortures the violin; he racks his body; he is no longer master of himself, but is agitated like one possessed with an irresistible motion."*[5]

Perhaps Raguenet was referring to Corelli when he wrote these somewhat satirical words. When his text was translated into English in 1709, the following was added to it by the anonymous translator: *"I never met with any man that suffered his passions to hurry him away so much whilst he was playing on the violin as the famous Arcangelo Corelli, whose eyes will sometimes turn as red as fire; his countenance will be distorted, his eyeballs roll as in an agony, and he gives in so much to what he is doing that he doth not look like the same man."*[6]

Corelli's influence as both composer and teacher was unique in his time. His music was printed, reprinted, distributed and imitated everywhere, causing Roger North to exclaim that it was *"wonderfull to observe what a scratching of Correlli there is every where— nothing will relish but Corelli."*[7]

Bach transcribed him, Couperin emulated him, Tartini used his theme as the basis for his *L'arte del arco*, pupils came to him from all over Europe, disseminating his style and technique. There is even evidence that copies of the opus 5 sonatas were owned by the Emperor of China!

Exercise 31: Replicating Corelli's exercise for increasing the power of sound

1. Set your metronome to 60 quarter notes per minute.
2. On two open strings, play four bows of four metronome beats each. Play as loudly as possible.
3. Play four bows of five beats each, then four bows of six beats.
4. Carry on slowing the bow down in this way until you reach your absolute maximum without cracking the sound. Remember to make a *"steady and powerful sound, like that of an organ."*
5. Without pausing to take a rest, gradually decrease the number of beats until you return to four beats per bow. Then continue all the way to one beat per bow: by this time, the sound you make should be very powerful indeed!

Leopold Mozart endorses the principle of this Exercise. In Chapter V, § 9 he encourages us to carry out a *"very useful experiment."* The idea is *"to produce a perfectly even tone with a slow stroke. Draw the bow from one end to the other whilst sustaining throughout an even strength of tone. But hold the bow well back, for the longer and more even the stroke can be made, the more you will become master of your bow."*

Summary

Strong emotions need to be communicated through the sound we draw from our violin. This must be constantly alive and expressive, with as broad a palette of colors as possible. Extreme dynamic variation, based on the recognition of the harmonies, especially the relation between dissonances and consonances, helps keep the sound alive and interesting. Using vibrato only rarely, the expression comes mostly from the bow, with its constant changes of pressure and speed varying the dynamics even within a single note.

Notes

1. Bremner's article "Some Thoughts on the Performance of Concert Music" appears as an introduction to Six Quarttetos for two Violins, a Tenor and Violincello (op. 6) by J. G. C. Schetky, published in London in 1777, British Library. Schetky was a German composer and cellist who settled in Edinburgh and became a friend of Robert Burns.

2. Antonio Tonelli (1686–1765): harmonic realisations of Corelli sonatas. MS in the Biblioteca Estense Universitaria, Modena (I-MOe): Mus.F.1174. Available on IMSLP

3. Quoted in Boyden, p 256.

4. GMPP, pp 75–6.

5. Quoted in Strunk, SRMH, p 118.

6. Sir John Hawkins, *A General History of the Science and Practice of Music, Volume the Fifth* (1776), Book III, p. 310. Quoted in Allsop, Arcangelo Corelli: `New Orpheus of Our Times,' p 53.

7. Quoted in 'Roger North on Music,' p XX

Lesson 11

Temperament and "Historical" Intonation: An Outline

In this lesson we investigate temperament and 'historical' intonation, a vastly complicated subject and one which it is impossible, and I think unnecessary for our purpose, to give a fully scientific account of here.

The first thing to realize is that what we have hitherto considered to be 'in tune' may not in fact be so from a historical perspective. If we base our intonation on that of the modern grand piano, we will unfortunately be quite badly out of tune when playing with a harpsichord tuned to a 'historical' tuning system of which, to make matters more complicated, there are several! But let us not panic: we shall always have our ears to help us.

Let me briefly outline the problem. Supposing you were to tune an imaginary piano in a series of perfect fifths starting right down at the bottom, let's say with a C, and ending at the top when you get to the next C in the cycle, seven octaves later. For mathematical reasons, those two Cs will be out of tune with each other: the top one will be about an eighth of a tone sharp, enough to be uncomfortably noticeable. The thing to do, therefore, is to tamper with, or "temper" the intervals, so that the frequencies of the leftover bit (known as the "comma") are distributed almost imperceptibly within some of the octaves (no instrument before the modern piano having such a wide range). There are many ways of doing this, and the resultant systems are known as "temperaments."

In fact, we violinists encounter similar problems in other situations without even thinking about it: if we tune an orchestra in perfect fifths from the bottom string of the double bass to the top string of the violin, the violin e″ will sound sharp. When we practice intonation in a string orchestra or a quartet, we constantly have to adjust to make the harmonies sound convincing. When string players adjust their intonation, they are in fact carrying out their own "tempering," and many are the arguments in such situations because, to a degree, intonation is a personal and variable aspect of string playing, part of a string player's expressive freedom.

Other instruments do not have this freedom, at least not to the same degree. Harpsichords and organs, for instance, cannot normally adjust their intonation except by retuning, so they need to be tuned to a set system.

From the mid-sixteenth century, builders of keyboard instruments had attempted to solve this problem by "splitting" the keys into a front and back part, each part plucking a separate string. The composer and theorist Nicola Vincentino (1511–1572) had built a four-octave harpsichord (the archicembalo) with seventy-seven keys, thirty-six per octave, in 1561. But it was Friedrich Suppig who published perhaps the most extreme work for enharmonic keyboard: the aptly named *Labyrinthus musicus* (1722) contains a "Fantasia" that passes through all twenty-four keys: it was composed for a keyboard with thirty-one notes per octave!

⁊ ⁊ ⁊

In the sixth century BC, Pythagoras had based his tuning system on perfect (pure) fifths that made the major third, if it was also pure (see below) sound sharp. This system was still considered practical in the Middle Ages but in the Renaissance, when more intervals were coming into common usage, it needed to be modified. Fifths were very slightly narrowed, so that they would still sound in tune with the pure major third: this is the fundamental characteristic of what we call 'meantone' temperaments.

The most common meantone tuning, quarter-comma meantone, was first described in Pietro Aaron's book *Thoscanello de la musica* (Venice, 1523), and it was used throughout the seventeenth century and into the eighteenth. The fifths are narrowed by a tiny amount, a quarter of a syntonic comma (which is itself a barely perceptible difference in frequency). The exact mathematics of this system are quite beyond me, so if you are intrigued, look it up elsewhere! Here is one of the formulae you may come across:

$$5\frac{1}{4} \approx 1.495349 = 1200 \lg 5\frac{1}{4} \text{ cents} \approx 696.578 \text{ cents}$$

The meantone tuning systems (there are several variants) are the systems that we who play Baroque music now use. A kind of modified meantone tuning was in use right up until the late 1800s in some places: as with many aspects of Baroque performance practice, the change to what we consider 'modern' practice came only very recently, not at all at the end of the Baroque period!

⁊ ⁊ ⁊

The intonation system that we grow up with today is very different. Our modern piano divides the octave into twelve mathematically equal semitones, or half steps, and this system of tuning is therefore known as equal temperament. It's a very handy system, because you can play in all major and minor keys, but like all compromises, it comes at a price: if every scale you play has exactly the same intervals, the individual flavor of each and every key is lost.

> Just as the ancient Greeks chose their modes according to the mood required, individual tonalities can, especially in meantone temperaments, be said to possess their own individual flavors or "affects." Assigning a specific affect to a key must inevitably have a strong subjective slant, as Quantz (XIV, § 6) recognizes when he tells us that some people *"assert that each passion can be expressed as well in one key as in the others,"* although he personally

disagrees with them. The individual qualities of each key are arguably more elusive under the system of equal temperament. Appendix III, which you will find on the website, reproduces Marc-Antoine Charpentier's "Tableau des Energies des Modes," a list of tonalities and the emotions they evoke.

Musicians in the Baroque period valued 'pure' intonation and would have considered this equal temperament system dull and, to their ears, out of tune. In the same way, people today who have the sound of equal temperament in their aural memory might consider the historical tuning system(s) to be out of tune—it just depends on what you are used to. Once you are more familiar with 'pure' intonation, you will most probably find the compromise of equal temperament lacking in character.

How Do We Learn "Pure" Intonation?

One easy way to begin to investigate historical temperaments is simply to play with a well-tuned harpsichord and explore its tuning. Harpsichordists have to study how to tune their instruments in several temperaments, so they will be able to guide you safely through the labyrinth.

If this is not practical for you, there are some electronic harpsichords on the market that are tuned to a choice of half a dozen historical temperaments. A good electronic tuner, one that has several historical temperaments programmed into it, is another very useful tool for exploring various meantone systems. Some can even be downloaded onto your mobile phone.

Most musical cultures from ancient times have recognized the phenomenon of the octave, the apparent 'sameness' of two notes, the higher one of which has a frequency double that of the lower one. Octaves have always been mathematically pure in every tuning system. This is not a decision someone has made in a moment of enlightenment: it is a mathematical truth, an acoustical fact. Perhaps it was discovered thousands of years ago by our hunting ancestors strumming on their bows while waiting to shoot arrows at their supper.

If, within a pure octave, we have the slightly narrow fifth already mentioned, we will need to enlarge the fourth to compensate for it. Both these 'tamperings,' however, are barely perceptible. The more problematic intervals are the thirds and, as we will discover, there are even many different sizes of tones and semitones too!

"Everyone knows not," writes Tosi *"that there is a Semitone Major and Minor, because the difference cannot be known by an Organ or Harpsichord, if the keys of the instrument are not split. A Tone . . . is divided into nine almost imperceptible Intervals, which are called Commas, five of which constitute the Semitone Major, and four the Minor."*[1]

As we violinists can adjust our intonation, I propose that we explore our new intonation system further by taking up our violin. First, we must tune the strings so that the fifths are slightly narrower than perfect, in C. P. E Bach's words, taking away a *"barely noticeable amount of their absolute purity."* [2]

Quantz instructs us clearly on how to tune to the keyboard. *"To tune the violin quite accurately,"* he writes (XVII,VII, § 4) *"I think you will not do badly to follow the rule that must be observed in tuning the keyboard, namely, that the fifths must be tuned a little on the flat side rather than quite truly or a little sharp, as is usually the case, so that the open strings will all agree with the keyboard. For if all the strings are tuned sharp and truly, it naturally follows that only one of the four strings will be in tune with the keyboard. If the A is tuned truly with the keyboard, the E a little flat in relation to the A, the D a little sharp to the A, and the G likewise to the D, the two instruments will agree with each other. This suggestion is not presented as an absolute rule, however, but only as a matter for further reflection."*

Leopold Mozart on Overtones

When we play a note on any instrument, the vibrations from that note (which we call the 'fundamental note') set off a series of other notes, or 'overtones.' We call the series of overtones the 'harmonic series,' and the intervals of a fifth, fourth, third, and so on are to be found in that series. These intervals are therefore, like the octave, natural phenomena, as much a part of nature as the structure of a snowflake!

Leopold Mozart (VIII, III, §20) recognizes this phenomenon and makes use of it to explain clearly how to tell if an interval is "in tune," that is, "pure":

> *I have proved that on the violin, when playing two notes simultaneously, the third, now the fifth, now even the octave, and so on, make themselves heard of their own accord in addition thereto and on the same instrument. This serves as undeniable proof, which everyone can test for himself, if he be able to play the notes in tune and correctly.*

In other words, an interval is in tune when a kind of 'ghost bass note' is audible underneath and is in tune. This extra note, says Leopold, shows *"how powerful is the harmonic triad."* He then gives the examples listed below in "A Summary of Leopold's Examples."

Leopold had not discovered this phenomenon himself. In his *Trattato di musica secondo la vera scienza dell'armonia*, published in 1754, two years before Mozart's *Versuch*, Tartini writes that he had discovered this "terzo suono" or "third sound" in 1714 (see Exercise 32). Believing that the origin of all truth lay in nature, Tartini, a deeply philosophical writer, considered this discovery a revelation, a glimpse into how the mysteries of nature and music were interwoven. Leopold helped himself to much material from the *Trattato*, never acknowledging Tartini as his source.

A Summary of Leopold's Examples

- Play a minor third and you will hear an additional note of a major third (or tenth) below the lower note:-

- Play a major third and you will hear an additional note of an octave below the lower note:

- Play a perfect fourth and you will hear an additional note of a fifth below the lower note:

- Play a minor sixth and you will hear an additional note of a major third (or tenth) below the lower note:

- Play a major sixth and you will hear an additional note of fifth below the lower note:

Finally, Leopold suggests moving between intervals *"for then the interchange of these droning tones strikes the ear more sharply."* He gives the following examples:

Exercise 32: Learning to hear the "terzo suono"

1. Play through all of Leopold Mozart's examples, adjusting each interval until the undertone comes into focus and is clearly audible.
2. Although the Baroque violin is generally richer in overtones than its modern equivalent, some violins do produce brighter undertones than others, so you may find the "terzo suono" difficult to hear at first. It helps to play the double stops with a healthy, strong sound.
3. If all you hear is a vague mumbling sound, it most likely means that your interval is not pure. Experiment with the intonation until the *"muffled and droning sound,"* as Mozart describes it, comes into focus.
4. Remember to heed Leopold's advice to pass back and forth between intervals: this will help you to perceive the undertones more clearly.

In Exercise 33, we compare 'pure' intervals to the intervals we find in equal temperament on our piano.

Exercise 33: Comparing pure intonation with equal temperament

1. Tune the A and D strings on your violin carefully to your piano (yes, to your piano!) and then tune the other strings as you normally do.
2. Play your open A and D strings; then play a fourth (e' and a'), and then a major third (f♯ and a'). Tune the f♯ according to the "ghost bass note" (that will be a D sounding a third or a tenth below the f♯). Be patient, experimenting with the intonation until you can hear it clearly.
3. When you have found the "pure" f♯, compare it to the piano's f♯: you will hear that the "pure" one is **flatter** than that of the piano.
4. Go back to your new 'pure' f♯, and this time play a d″ a minor sixth above, on the A string. The sixth will seem bigger than the one you are used to. Holding that d″ (which will be a pure octave with the D string) find a b♭, a minor sixth above it, on the E string. Adjust the b♭ until you hear your "ghost bass note," which should be also a B, probably a tenth below the d″.
5. When you have done this, compare the b♭ you have found on the E string with the piano's b♭—you will notice that the violin is now **sharper** than the piano.

We have discovered that the flats in 'historic' tuning will be sharper than modern flats, and that the sharps will be flatter than modern sharps. And this in turn means that, in Leopold Mozart's words (III, §6, note 1), *"for example, D flat is higher than C sharp, A flat higher than G sharp, G flat than F sharp etc."* But do not despair, for Leopold adds encouragingly that *"the good ear must be the judge."* He uncharacteristically forsook the opportunity to further mock those who play with a continuous vibrato, which he disliked so intensely, leaving the present writer with the onerous responsibility of pointing out that such vibrato as is practiced by many of our contemporaries will more than likely eradicate any trace of such subtle tonal distinctions!

In our modern system of tuning, coming back to the piano, an A♭ and a G♯, for example, are the same note, because they are played by the same key. If we wish to play with a piano we need to use equal temperament in order to be in tune with it, although some flexibility is possible. Other instruments that have fixed intonation must also be accommodated in this way. In Baroque music, composers stay within the tonal boundaries that 'pure' intonation allows, so we rarely encounter enharmonic problems within a single piece. However, if we choose a program of pieces in very different keys, we might well be in trouble.

Just as our two notes on a single violin produce our phantom bass note, all instruments, and the voice too, produce not a single note but a series of harmonic overtones around the main or fundamental note. When we play with other instruments, our common overtones need to gel in order that the harmony will sound in tune. When this happens, the full effect of the harmony is heard just as the composer would have intended.

Peter Prelleur's Fingerboard

Peter Prelleur, organist of Christ Church Spitalfields in London and, in the evenings, Master of Musick in the Angel and Crown tavern in Whitechapel, wrote a guide for musicians entitled *The Modern Musick-Master* (1730) including a section titled "Art of Playing on the Violin." Figure a reproduces the fingering chart from this book that perfectly illustrates meantone temperament tuning on the violin. Notice the enharmonic distinctions he marks between, for example, a g″♯ and an a″♭ on the E string, the former played with a second finger, the latter with a third.

Figure a

Fingering chart from Peter
Prelleur's *The Modern
Musick-Master* (1730).

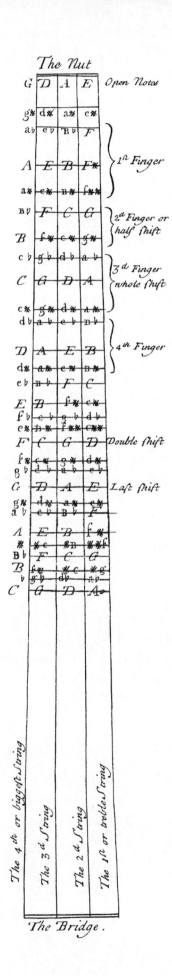

The concept of the inherent qualities of tonalities was still controversial in the nineteenth century. Thus Christian Schubart could write in his *Ideas to an Aesthetic of Tonality* (1806) that the "dreadful" key of D♯ minor represented the soul's "deepest distress and blackest depression," F minor suggested "deep depression and a longing for the grave," and that both B♭ major and B♭ minor "prepared one for suicide." (No hint of subjectivity here!) By comparison, Charpentier (1682) had described B♭ major as "magnificent and joyful" although he did call B♭ minor "obscure and terrible."

Hermann von Helmholtz in his *On the Sensations of Tone as a Physiological Basis for the Theory of Music* (1863) described C major as being "Pure, certain, decisive; expressive of innocence, powerful resolve, manly earnestness and deep religious feeling" where Charpentier had written "gay and warlike."

Notes

1. Tosi, *Opinioni de' Cantori Antichie Moderni*, Chapter 1, 15.
2. C. P. E. Bach, *Essay,* Introduction to Part 1, § 14.

Lesson 12

Chinless Shifting: Technique and Application

Section One: Toward a Methodology of Shifting

Although in his teaching the author by no means insists on unremittingly chinless playing, he recognises that some students do feel it brings them closer to their authentic ideal and that others, for reasons of physiology, have little choice. Unfortunately, most of the venerable authors of the historical sources provide little if any specific information on the techniques of shifting. Many violinists today base their shifting techniques on Geminiani's book, partly because it is forthcoming on the subject. Leopold Mozart, although he devotes almost the whole of Chapter VIII to the positions, offers us no technical information at all on the mechanics of shifting, while Tartini is at the same time uninformative and enlightening when he writes: *"As regards changing position, it is impossible to give any hard and fast rules. The student should adopt whatever method he finds most comfortable in each case, and he therefore should practise the hand shifts in every possible way so that he is prepared for any situation that might arise."*[1]

In Section One of this lesson I attempt to remedy this dearth of information by positing detailed guidance on how to shift without using the chin, based very loosely on the sparse clues Francesco Geminiani and others have left us. The information I provide may be perceived as lacking historical justification, but I hope it will prove useful nevertheless. I am in no position to say whether the many great teachers of the Baroque era chose to remain almost universally silent on this matter because they did not wish to reveal their secrets in writing or because, like Tartini, they did not insist on their students adopting any 'one-method-fits-all' technique, wisely knowing that they would anyway evolve their own ways of shifting based on instinct, idiosyncratic talent, preference and physiology, much as students do today.

Section Two of the lesson combines the techniques learned in Section One with our understanding of pure intonation, as we study Geminiani's scales.

Conscious that everyone has different priorities and that every hand is unique, I will begin with a quote from Pierre Dupont's 1718 violin method *Principes de violon.*

Although the context is entirely other, the logic of the argument is relevant: it is best, Dupont is sensibly advocating, to begin with the prescribed ways and then to search for your own.

> Q. Is one obliged to observe all the rules of bowing?
> A. Yes, when learning them, because this helps you acquire the style of the [different] airs; but once you are acquainted with the style, you can take whatever licence and liberty you judge to be appropriate. [2]

🙠 🙠 🙠

Shifting without clutching the violin with our chin is a skill that demands patience and application to acquire, just like any skill we have ever practiced. Although chinless shifting, particularly in a downward direction, can initially feel like trying to climb down a rope ladder in a hurricane, the techniques do share much common ground with modern shifting techniques, so we need not feel we are starting from zero. Indeed, we should consider the practicing of our 'chinless scale book' as a work in progress, noting that for most of this book, indeed for much of the Baroque repertoire, shifting into high positions is rarely required.

The Four Springs

We can identify four physiological springs involved in the mechanics of shifting: that of the wrist, the forearm, the elbow, and the thumb. Having explored them individually, we will learn to harness their natural energy for our purpose.

A: *The Wrist Spring*

1. Hold the palm of your left hand up in front of you, a little to the left of your face. The forearm and hand should be perfectly aligned, your elbow hanging loose. Release any tension with a quick check of your head, neck, elbow, and shoulders. The armpit must not be clasped shut: there should be enough space to fit a tennis ball inside.
2. Close your fingers to make a fist: do not clench!
3. Bend your wrist away from you as far as it will go.
4. Release the wrist, allowing it to spring back by itself.

B: *The Forearm Spring*

1. Repeat Nos. 1, 2, and 3 (above).
2. Instead of letting the wrist spring back, release the forearm so that it moves forward to align itself with the wrist. To do that, the elbow will open and the upper arm will move automatically.
3. Each time you repeat this, your hand will move farther away from you. However, after about four times this will no longer happen naturally.

C: *The Elbow Spring*

1. Return to the original position of No. 2 in A (above).
2. Bring your elbow inward, to the right, a few inches.
3. Let the elbow spring back by itself.
4. Push your elbow outward, to the left, a few inches.
5. Notice: it will not spring back!

D: *The Thumb Spring*

1. Return to the original position of No. 1 in A (above).
2. Move your thumb back as far as it will comfortably go.
3. Allow it to spring back.
4. Move your thumb toward you as far as it will comfortably go.
5. Allow it to spring back.

110

❧ ❧ ❧

Techniques of Displacement

Exercises 34 through 48 work on shifting and displacement. Our first step in shifting is learning how to "creep" up and down the fingerboard, starting with the smallest interval, that of the unison (Figure a).

Figure a

Basic displacement techniques.

Exercise 34: The basic technique of displacement

Bar 1: Ascending

1. At letter "a," lighten the pressure of the first finger on the string.
2. At letter "b," the first finger displaces the second, leaving the thumb behind.
   The displaced second finger leaves the string with the lightness of rising smoke. There should be no abrupt movements, the first finger floating gently up the string to its new place. Aim for a seamless join, listening carefully to eliminate unwanted sounds or gaps in the sound.
3. At letter "c," the thumb spring brings it gently back to its natural position and the hand position returns to normal.

Bar 2: Descending

1. At letter "a," the second finger displaces the first, leaving the thumb behind.
2. At letter "b," the thumb's spring brings it gently back to its natural position and the hand position returns to normal.

When descending, the displaced finger may leave the string for a fraction of a second before settling again, ready for the next note.

Exercise 35: Achieving seamless displacement

The key to a seamless shift is listening, our ears constantly monitoring the sound.

1. Play the f' with the second finger using long, slow bows. Listen intently to the sound.
2. Repeat, switching fingers as written. Listen carefully, aiming for a sound as close as possible to that in No 1.
3. Repeat, switching fingers ever faster.
4. Do the same with Bars 2 and 3.

Exercise 36: Winding and releasing the elbow spring

The elbow spring will help power the hand as it shifts up and down. Support the violin against the wall. Place the fingers on the notes of the first chord (below) and, without leaving the strings, slide lightly up to the second chord, drawing your elbow inward as you slide: this should feel like winding up the spring of your elbow.

1. Release the elbow and return to the first chord.
2. The wrist must be kept loose at all times.

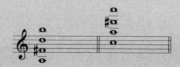

Exercise 37: Displacement scales

Using the techniques learned in Exercises 34 and 35, practice 'creeping up and down the fingerboard on these scales. As you become more secure with the mechanics, ensure that the sound sings beautifully: there is no point perfecting a sound you will never want to use! Practice on all strings, both legato and detached.

1. Practice with the scroll of the violin against a wall or curtain, covering the scroll with a cloth for protection if necessary. Before playing, drop your shoulders and release any tension you may find.
2. Move away from the wall and play the scales again. Return to it for help whenever needed: you will gradually be able to wean yourself away from using it.
3. Practice each scale slowly; at every step, repeat the processes learned in Exercise 34.
4. Practice both the upper and lower fingerings in the first stave.
5. As you ascend, steer the hand by winding up the elbow spring. Releasing the spring will help drag the hand down.

Playing ascending scales is never as difficult as coming back down again. Having become used to the idea of 'creeping and adjusting,' let us tackle the mechanics of descending scales.

Exercise 38: The mechanics of shifting down

1. Place the violin on your collarbone, steadying it with your right hand.
2. Place all four fingers on any string in the sixth position.
3. Move the fingers hand down one position, without moving your forearm.
4. Realign the forearm with the wrist using the movement learned in the second bar of Exercise 34 (above). The thumb adjusts naturally.
5. As you shift down further, the overall movement resembles a caterpillar climbing down the stem of a flower.
6. Repeat, this time steadying the violin by placing your bow on the string, without moving it. Using the bow to steady the violin might be a novel concept, but it is a fact of chinless life!

Exercise 39: Adjusting the hand when shifting down two positions

1. Practice the following line (starting in the sixth position on the A string) using the first finger only. Shifting down two positions will magnify and clarify the movements involved. Practice initially without the bow, focusing on the action of the left hand. Play at a moderate tempo, resting the scroll against a wall or curtain and using the wrist movement we practiced above. The letter "A" in Bar 2 means "adjust." Here, you can give yourself time to bring your arm back to its optimum position. Once the movements have become automatic, repeat using the bow.

2. Repeat No. 1 away from the wall. Practise slurred and with single bows, remembering always to make a beautiful sound with the bow: never train yourself to play like a robot!

3. Practice the following lines in the same way. Each one uses a different finger.

Geminiani's technique is not to be confused with the more modern method, advocated by Carl Flesch and others, whereby the thumb is sent ahead of the fingers in any downward shift of one or two positions: it then acts as a stabilizer while the hand is drawn back. Sol Babitz [3] proposes this as a solution to chinless shifting, without quoting any historical source, and many Baroque violinists today, finding this method more comfortable and secure, have likewise adopted it.

Exercise 40: Adjusting the hand when shifting down by single positions

Work through the following lines in the same way as in Exercise 39. Continue to use the wall for support if needed.

ళ ళ ళ

Exercise 41: Preparatory exercises to scales in broken thirds

Practice this scale pattern with each of the three fingerings marked. Practice first without the bow, then play it both slurred and detached, on all strings.

ళ ళ ళ

Exercise 42: Rising and descending scales in broken thirds

Practice each of the following scales on all strings, both slurred and detached. Always make a singing sound.

1. At each step when ascending, leave your thumb in position and, using the wrist movement hoist your finger gently upward. On the second tied quarter note, at the letter "A," allow your thumb to move to its natural position.

2. When descending on the same finger, leave your thumb behind. On the second tied quarter note, at the letter "A," allow your thumb to spring gently down.

Exercise 43: Shifting between consecutive positions using Ševčík, op. 8, nos. 1–7

We are now ready to begin a more advanced study of shifting, consolidating the techniques we have learned so far. The most comprehensive exercises for shifting were compiled by Ševčík; his opus 8, of which an extract appears below (Figure b) serves our purpose perfectly. It is important to play these exercises expressively and perfectly in tune: never lose the flow between the inner musician and the sound: that is a dangerous path to tread!

Figure b
Ševčík, op. 8, no. 1 (detail).

1. Practise Bar 1 slowly, legato and detached. Play with a singing sound, as if you are working on an extract from a concerto by Vivaldi or Locatelli.

2. Gradually increase tempo until your maximum speed is reached.

3. Practice each of the six bars on the G string separately, then play through Bars 1–6 complete.
4. Having practiced Ševčík's exercise No. 1 on the G string, change the formulae by practicing his exercise 2 on the D, exercise 3 on the A, and exercise 4 on the E. That way you will keep your mind fresh and your listening alert.

❦ ❦ ❦

Exercise 44: Shifting over two strings

Shifting over two strings is achieved using the same principles as for a single string. Ševčík, op. 1, no. 5, Book 2 (Figure c) provides many examples to work on. If your hand is big enough you should be able to play most of these leaving the thumb behind in the first position. For purposes of practice, however, I would also recommend you to shift into position, normalizing the hand position as soon as possible. As a first step, you may need to prolong the note after the shift to give yourself time for this.

Figure c
Ševčík, op. 1, book 2, no. 5 (detail).

❦ ❦ ❦

Exercise 45: Shifting by displacement over two positions

Note: if your hand is too small to reach up or down a third, especially in the lower positions, additional adjustments with your thumb will be necessary.

1. Slur each bar in a single bow.
2. Bar 1, Beat 3: the first finger displaces the third, the thumb remaining behind. The thumb adjusts ("A") on Beat 4.

3. Bar 2, Beat 2: the third finger displaces the first, the thumb remaining behind. The thumb adjusts in Beat 3.

4. Bar 3, Beat 1: on the first eighth note, the first finger moves up, the thumb remaining behind. The thumb adjusts on the eighth note.

The same principle applies to Exercise 46.

117

Exercise 46: Shifting over two positions

In the examples below, the basic principles of shifting in the 'modern' way are appropriate: the notes marked with an asterisk are guiding notes. Their function is to guide the hand to the new position. Slur every bar in one bow.

In the following three examples, we shorten the guiding notes used in the previous example until they disappear. altogether. However, they remain as a 'ghost note' in the hand's memory, indicated by the brackets in the last two bars (3).

If there is no time to adjust the hand on the note that has shifted, adjust it on the following note.

Exercise 47: Scales on one string

Practice the following scales on a single string with each of the three marked fingerings. Start with no sharps or flats, adding one sharp each time: when you run out of sharps, start again, this time adding a flat each time. Practice on all strings and with a variety of bowings.

For downward shifts with larger intervals Geminiani states (The Art of Playing on the Violin, p. 3) that *"in drawing back the hand from the 5th, 4th and 3d Order [Position] to go to the first, the Thumb cannot, for Want of Time, be replaced in its natural Position; but it is necessary it should be replaced at the second Note."* In other words, the fingers descend first, after which the thumb follows.

Some of the fingerings Geminiani suggests, such as those in Figure d, may surprise us, especially now that we are making a determined effort to play chinless. Upward shifts of a whole tone from a fourth to a first finger (Bar 1) are not difficult to negotiate, but downward shifts of the same interval with the same fingers (Bar 2) are risky. Geminiani either assumes his reader has very large hands capable of carrying out his instructions or realizes that it is up to each of us to find a way of negotiating such leaps.

Figure d
Geminiani, *Essempio* 14, no. 10a (D minor).

Exercise 48: Kreutzer shifting Etude

This Étude contains ideal material for consolidating the techniques learned in this lesson. It should be practiced daily, legato and detached, until you feel completely comfortable with it.

Many of the standard books of Études were composed in the eighteenth or early nineteenth centuries. Rodolphe Kreutzer (1766–1831) composed his *Études or Caprices* in around 1796. Although it can be argued that his Études are designed with the Tourte bow in mind, his aim was also to consolidate techniques already in existence. As different editions have different numbers, I am quoting the opening bars of this Étude in Figure e.

Figure e
Kreutzer, Étude.

Shifting and Expression

Leopold Mozart (VIII, § 16) advises us to *"await a good and easy opportunity to descend in such a fashion that the listener does not perceive the change,"* while Tartini, upon whose work Leopold drew heavily, seems more concerned that no gaps are to be heard.

As we shall observe, however, the sources are not entirely consistent about the necessity for shifting in an absolutely inaudible manner and it is possible to argue that such seamless, sterilized shifting has become an unwarranted obsession of the modern HIP performer. What about the ubiquitous advice to copy the human voice: do singers actively suppress any audible connection between notes?

Michel Pignolet de Montéclair, in his "Principes de Musique" (1736), mentions an ornament he calls the "son glissé" (slid sound). Likening this to the dancer who, rather than lifting his foot to a new position, gently slides it along the ground, he describes how the singer glides up or down a semitone or a tone with no clear break. To imitate this, he continues, viol players gently slide their finger up or down from one note to the other. Clearly, this ornament is used for special effect in specific emotional contexts; nevertheless, it is worth recognizing that such portamento effects are not the unique tools of the Romantic composers to be universally shunned by purists.[4]

"The human voice glides quite easily from one note to another," writes Leopold Mozart (5, § 14) going on to remind us that *"singing is at all times the aim of every instrumentalist."* The implication is clear: some form of audible slide is natural and permitted. Indeed, Leopold gives us examples of both upward shifts (Figure f) and downward shifts (Figure g) using the same finger within a slur.

Figure f
Leopold Mozart (Chapter 8, § 6, N.4).

Figure g
Leopold Mozart (Chapter 11, § 7). The "u" signs above the first note (the first two bigger than the others) indicate vibrato, starting slowly and gradually speeding up.

The question is not, therefore, whether slides should be rooted out as unhistorical in the middle of the eighteenth century but whether they may be legitimately exploited as an expressive device. For this there is no evidence in any source from the Baroque period. Nevertheless, Charles Burney does give us indisputable evidence in his "General History" that such portamenti were being used for expression at the time of writing (1776.) *"Beautiful expressions and effects,"* he writes, *"are produced by great players in shifting, suddenly from a low note to a high, with the same finger on the same string."* At what point *"great players"* began to produce such *"beautiful expressions and effects"* is a matter for speculation.[5]

In conclusion, I believe that although shifting as a significant means of expression, for example with a deliberately cultivated portamento slide, should be considered an aesthetic anachronism, a relic of a more modern style of violin playing, an audible shift used either as a technical expedient or as an emotional tool can nevertheless be justified in the right context; indeed, an approach that seeks to sterilize what happens naturally may itself be considered unhistorical.

Video 12.1

Section Two: Applying Pure Intonation to Geminiani's Scale Studies from His *The Art of Playing the Violin* (1751)

Section Two contains exercises for applying pure intonation to Geminiani's scale studies from his *The Art of Playing the Violin* (1751). In this part of Lesson 12 we will refresh and consolidate our understanding of pure intonation, having made our first forays into that subject in the previous two lessons. This section consists entirely of exercises (Exercises 49–58) and contains little new information. The reader is advised to work through the exercises over an extended period of time and to return to them periodically, as with any form of scale practice.

It is important to play these exercises with a clear, strong sound to assure the audibility of the harmonic overtones, and we should recall what Quantz (X, § 22) tells us: *"A beginner must be constantly attentive when he plays, and must take great care that he hears each note as he sees it with his eyes."*

Practice Exercises 49–58 in C major; then return to Exercise 49, adding one sharp or one flat, and practice all the exercises again, this time in G or F major. Work through all the major keys in this manner.

Although in the early stages of this practice you will become aware of the need to tune notes a little differently to the way you are used to, you will quickly adapt, especially when you start to play with well-tuned keyboard instruments. Much of what you are struggling to learn now you will pick up instinctively through the experience of playing with others, so there is no need to become frustrated: in Baroque orchestras and ensembles we always need to spend time at rehearsals making sure we understand the quirks of whichever temperament is being used. A question to the keyboard player such as "Can I hear your E flat" is quite normal, as is the answer "Don't use mine, it's a D sharp!"

Before working on these exercises, I advise you to tune your strings individually with the help of an electronic tuner that uses historic tuning systems. If you have a choice of systems, choose Young I or Vallotti to begin with: later, you can experiment with other temperaments.

Exercise 49: Investigating "pure" intonation (1)

In this exercise, we investigate "pure" intonation, training our ear to hear, recognize and assimilate it. We do this by building up our scale from the initial fifth to a succession of perfect fourths and major or minor thirds.

1. Play the first double stop with a strong sound until you hear the harmonic overtone clearly; then proceed to the next one, again listening for the harmonic overtone. When you are satisfied that both are in tune, play the pair of double stops backward and forward until you have understood and assimilated the relation between them.

2. Now play only the voice containing the moving notes (in the first pair this is the lower voice with the notes a' and b' backward and forward, studying carefully the relation between them.

3. Having established the intonation of the second double stop, proceed to the third one and repeat the processes detailed above.

4. Play the whole exercise through, carefully listening out for the harmonic overtones.

Now repeat the entire exercise on the D and A strings.

Finally, repeat the exercise on the G and D strings.

Exercise 50: Investigating "pure" intonation (2)

Now that we have enhanced our perception of pure intonation, we can practice it on the following scale of perfect fourths:

Exercise 51: Investigating "pure" intonation (3)

The next scale exercise incorporates the perfect fourths you have just practiced while at the same time highlighting the intervals between single notes. If you are in any doubt about a note, go back to the relevant double stops.

You can vary the exercises and make them more interesting by adding bowings and rhythms to the basic patterns. This will keep your interest alive and your mind alert, as well as sharpening your awareness and intensifying your powers of listening.

Such variations also bring our basic intonation exercise into the realm of virtual repertoire. Always remember to avoid practicing such exercises in too dull or mechanical a way: once you are convinced about the intonation, play them again with artistry, as you would if you were playing a sonata or a concerto.

Exercise 52: Investigating "pure" intonation (4)

The next exercise is in triplets; as there are no repeated notes here, there is no place for the ear to rest, so our listening faculty must be even more finely tuned: the faster we play, the faster we have to listen.

Again, remember that there is little value in practicing such an exercise in a dull, robotic way. Once we have understood and practiced the basics of pure intonation, we need to assimilate and apply what we have learned. We can only do that by integrating our awareness of that intonation into the totality of our listening. Let us remind ourselves of Leopold's pertinent comment (VI, § 2) that *"charming as these triplets are when played well, they are equally insipid when not executed in the right and proper manner."*

Exercise 53: Investigating "pure" intonation (5)

The next example shows our scale in broken fourths in its most basic form.

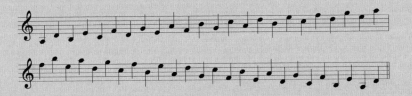

Exercise 54: Investigating "pure" intonation (6)

In this exercise, we apply what we have learned from our scale studies in fourths to scale studies in broken thirds. As in Exercise 1, you can vary these exercises by inventing combinations of bowing and rhythmic variations.

Exercise 55: Investigating "pure" intonation (7)

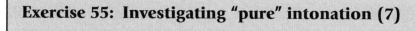

Exercise 56: Investigating "pure" intonation (8)

Exercise 57: Investigating "pure" intonation (9)

Exercise 58: Investigating "pure" intonation (10)

Last, a two-octave scale, to be practiced according to the pure intonation which the above exercises and the information at the start of this lesson have helped us discover:

Applying Pure Intonation and Chinless Shifting to Geminiani's Scale Studies

Geminiani's *The Art of Playing the Violin* includes a graded scale system complete with fingerings and a bass line. It also contains what we would today call 'études', also with a written bass part and with the addition of bowings. Such a gold mine of information must delight any modern student of the Baroque violin and will repay a detailed and ongoing study.

Concurrently with our basic work on Exercises 49–58, we can now apply what we are learning there to the scales in Geminiani's book.

Exercise 59: Playing in tune with the bass in Geminiani's Essempio XIV

A note is only in tune in relation to other notes, either those one is playing oneself or those being played by others. Good intonation, like intelligent phrasing, depends to a great degree on how aware of and responsive we are to the bass as well as to the overall harmony. Exercises 59–62 are designed to train the ear to respond to the bass line. Quantz (X, § 15) writes that the beginner *"must constantly direct his ear to those who play with him, particularly to the bass; in this fashion he will be able to learn harmony, time, and purity of intonation so much the more easily."*

Ask a colleague to play the tonic or the dominant note of the first scale as a continuous long note. If you can't find anyone with enough patience to do this with you, use an electronic tuner or keyboard to provide the bass note.

Listening carefully to this 'drone,' play the notes of the scale very slowly. Do not "assume" you are in tune, based on past habits, but find the purest intonation in relation to the bass note. You will probably be able to hear the occasional "ghost bass note" that we learned about earlier, caused by the two notes being perfectly in tune, even when played by two separate instruments.

Exercise 60: Playing in tune with the bass in Geminiani's Essempio XII

This exercise requires the help of a second person to play the simple bass line of Geminiani's Essempio XII while you play the top part. It is an excellent lesson in learning to hear yourself in relation to a bass line: you may find that hearing both parts at once is easier when you are playing chinless, as this gives you some distance from your own sound.

Practice slowly at first, listening carefully to the bass and ensuring that you are using pure intonation based on what you hear.

Practice the shifts over and over again: as Geminiani himself advises (p. 5) *"'tis necessary to examine very frequently the Transpositions of the Hand in (Example XII), until they are entirely impressed on the Mind."*

In all shifts, it is important to hear the note you are aiming for in your mind before shifting. In this way the ear learns to guide the hand.

I recommend stopping before each downward shift to give yourself time to remember the "drill": the fingers move down first, then the thumb descends and the hand normalizes its shape. When practicing slowly, do not continue until the shape of your hand after a shift is normal.

It is a useful additional exercise to swap parts with the other person in this and the following exercises. This will heighten your awareness of the relationship between treble and bass. Remember also that, in spite of your concentrating predominantly on issues of intonation, no exercise need ever sound dull: always aim to play in an expressive, artistic way!

Exercise 61: Playing in tune with the bass in Geminiani's Essempio VIII

Geminiani's Essempio VIII offers a way of developing a singing way of playing that is not only perfectly in tune with the bass but also reflects the artistic nuances that such an interesting bass line suggests. *"In this are contained 20 Scales in different Keys,"* Geminiani writes, *"very useful for acquiring time and the stopping in Tune."*

Exercise 62: Playing in tune with the bass in Geminiani's Essempios IX, X, XI, and XV

Essempios IX, X, XI, and XV are further studies for intonation, as well as for shifting. At this point I would recommend moving on from playing with just one bass note to playing with a keyboard instrument so you can hear not just the bass line but the complete harmony. Many people find the sound of the harpsichord difficult to play with at first: it takes some time before you can hear the notes as clearly as you can on the more *sostenuto* sound of the organ. If this is the case, try practicing with an organ first and only later with a harpsichord.

Exercise 63 covers an essential skill for all kinds of playing.

Exercise 63: Playing in tune when your strings are out of tune

Gut strings are sensitive to climate and temperature: when you play in a cold hall, you will find the pitch rising, whereas in a hot theater the pitch will tend to drop. Moreover, the harpsichord, organ, and the wind and brass instruments will also be affected by temperature, and not always in the same way as your strings!

A constant awareness of the pitch of your strings is obviously essential, so practicing with your strings perfectly in tune, or stopping every few minutes to check them, is to live a cloistered life that will fail to prepare you for the reality "out there." You should therefore practice the exercises in this lesson with your E string deliberately tuned slightly flat, or your A slightly sharp or both. A flat string can be slightly sharpened with the first finger if a long open string is needed, but you may have to abandon open strings altogether if the situation becomes extreme. Practicing with your strings out of tune is fun and will certainly pay off when you find yourself in a difficult concert situation.

ༀ ༀ ༀ

Finally, in this lesson, here are some words of wisdom and consolation from Johann Mattheson. In his *Der Vollkommene Capellmeister* of 1739 he writes:

> *One can easily imagine that every clavier, organ or harp tuner adjusts this temperament his own way, perhaps as to how his hearing is accustomed to this or that: for very few among these people can give either reason and cause, report or answer, on how or why they do something. . . . The most common type of temperament, finally, stating it quite grossly, rests on the following three statements:*
>
> 1. *Octaves, minor sixths and minor thirds must everywhere be pure.*
> 2. *One must raise major sixths and fourths somewhat.*
> 3. *One must however lower fifths and major thirds somewhat.*
>
> *How much this somewhat should be is another question, about which very few instrument teachers know anything."* [6]

Notes

1. Tartini, *Regole* (Rules for Bowing). Hermann Moeck Edition, p. 56
2. Quoted in Tarling, WOR, p.129.
3. See Donnington, p. 155.
4. Montéclair, *Principes de Musique,* pp. 88–9.
5. Charles Burney, *General History* (Vol II, p 992, note "n"), quoted in Boyden, p. 381.
6. Mattheson, *DVC,* Part 1, Chapter 7, § 88, p. 168.

Lesson 13

Bringing Fast Notes to Life

The Inequality of the Equal. Albinoni:
Sonata, op. 6, no. 2, Allegro

The Venetian Tomaso Albinoni (1671–1750) has the dubious distinction of being most celebrated for a piece of music he did not actually compose, the famous Adagio in G minor for violin, strings, and organ. He was a prolific composer, ranked in his time with Corelli and Vivaldi, and is known to have written about eighty operas. Bach based four keyboard fugues on subjects taken from his opus 1 and thought his bass lines sufficiently interesting to be used as harmony exercises. Although much of his work was lost during the bombing of Dresden in World War II, one hundred sonatas and fifty-nine concertos still exist. The opus 6 Sonatas were published in about 1712 by Estienne Roger and Michel-Charles Le Cène in Amsterdam, under the title "Trattenimenti Armonici (loosely translatable as Harmonic Entertainments) per camera a violino, violone e cembalo."

How to Play Equal Notes in a Flexible and Subtle Way

Score 13.1

Score 13.2

In this lesson we shall consolidate some of the information we learned from Michel Farinel's "Divisions on a Ground" in Lesson 7. We shall also consider some further aspects of interpretation useful for bringing to life passages that, on the face of it, may seem straightforward and simple.

First, let us explore ways of playing notes of theoretically equal value in a flexible and subtle way. We are speaking here of passages consisting entirely of, for example, eighth or sixteenth notes. Such passages are extremely common in Baroque music: if they are played too rapidly, as a mere vehicle for displaying the performer's dazzling facility, the musical content will be obscured. More impressive will be a tempo that allows us to shape the music in a way that will hold the attention of our audience, fascinating them by means of artistry rather than by mere velocity. As Quantz (XII, §27) puts it, *"The listener is moved not so much by the skill of the performer as by the beauty which he knows how to express with his skill."*

A whole movement, a few bars, or even just a few notes executed in an absolutely uniform manner with an identical bow stroke and sound is rarely necessary or justifiable and could sound very dull indeed. Even in a complex score where tight ensemble is essential—for example, in the third movement of Bach's third Brandenburg Concerto—there is no justification for rigidly mechanical playing, and we should constantly be on guard against it. On principle, such playing runs contrary to the spirit of rhetorical music making.

Inside any string of sixteenth notes there is an inner musical world that is alive and constantly fascinating, if only we can discern it and bring it to life: vivid colors, shifting patterns and shapes sparkle and pulsate within the living sound in which no two notes sound exactly alike, so that our audience's attention, like our own, never wanders.

Precisely what these patterns and shapes are must be determined by our own observation, imagination, and judgment. Some are visually obvious: leaps look and will sound different from stepwise notes. Rising notes often suggest a crescendo, descending notes a diminuendo, the dynamics following the visual contour of the notes.

> One guiding principle is that not all notes are equal in importance: some are clearly of more consequence than others and therefore need to be stressed to create a sense of perspective within the line. *"Where it is possible,"* Quantz writes (XI, § 12) *"the principal notes must be emphasized more than the passing (ones)."* However, creating perspective is not only about stressing notes: it is also about underplaying the less important ones.

The Three Flexibilities

Notes equal in value can be played flexibly by varying any or all of the following three elements:

1. Rhythm.
2. Dynamics.
3. Articulation.

Rhythmic Flexibility

We need to be clear about the distinction between beat (pulse or tactus) and the actual rhythm of the notes within that beat. For the music to be intelligible and coherent, the beat needs to be steady, although there are special moments when it can be more flexible—for example, when one phrase ends and a new one begins, or when the music needs to breathe more.

In Albinoni's Allegro, we can make the music more interesting and expressive by elongating important notes and speeding up less important ones, for as Quantz writes (XII, § 5), *"The principal notes should always be heard a little longer than the passing ones."* Tosi refers to such rubato, *"the stealing of Time"* as an *"honourable Theft."*[1]

Accentuating a note by stretching it produces what is known as an "agogic" accent. It is important to exaggerate these when playing slowly so that when the tempo is stepped up they will still be discernible. In any case, exaggeration at this stage is better than producing a rigid, unyielding, and incessant flow of notes. Gradually we will learn to scale down the 'pulling around' of the rhythm until it sounds more natural and less mannered. Remember, the point is to make the music more subtle, interesting and expressive: what is exaggeration to some is legitimate and tasteful to others! Exercises 64, 65, and 66 explore the flexibilities of rhythm, dynamics, and articulation.

Exercise 64: Exploring rhythmic flexibility

1. On an open string, play a bar of equal sixteenth notes with a time signature of ⁴⁄₄. Begin with a moderately fast tempo (60 quarter notes to a minute).

2. Keeping the pulse steady (it will be useful to use a metronome), lengthen the notes marked L (Long), compensating for this by hurrying the subsequent notes, marked s (short). Do not deliberately accent the "L" notes; merely lengthen them. Repeat each example many times.
   - Lsss ssss Lsss ssss
   - Lsss Lsss Lsss Lsss
   - Lsss LsLs Lsss LsLs
   - LLss LLss LsLs LLss
   - Ssss LLLL ssss LLLL
   - ssLL ssLL ssLs ssLs

3. Now do the same with a time signature of ³⁄₄:
   - Lsss Lsss Lsss
   - ssLs ssLs ssLs
   - LsLs ssLs Lsss
   - Lsss LsLs Lsss
   - ssLs ssLs Lsss

4. Invent your own 'composition' on one note, using the maximum variety of Long/short notes to make it as interesting and complex as possible. Let there be no limit to your fantasy in this! For example,
   - Lss Lss LLL sss LLLL ssss L ss LLL ss LLL etc.

5. Finally, play Bars 5–14 of our piece, keeping the pulse steady but lengthening any notes that you feel have a little extra importance and need a little extra time.

Dynamic Flexibility

The perspective between notes of more and less importance, so necessary for bringing this music to life, can also be achieved in terms of dynamics. We must take care, however, not merely to turn down the volume switch for the less important (piano) notes but to engage with them as actively as with the more important (forte) ones. "*For piano does not consist in simply letting the bow leave the violin and merely slipping it loosely about the strings,*" writes Leopold Mozart (V, § 12); on the contrary, "*the weak must have the same tone quality as the strong, save that it should not sound so loudly to the ear.*" In the next lesson we will explore how to adapt the contact of the bow with the string, thus ensuring that all notes, regardless of volume, are played with a living sound.

Exercise 65: Exploring dynamic flexibility

1. On an open string, play a bar of equal sixteenth notes with a time signature of $\frac{4}{4}$. Begin with a moderately fast tempo (60 quarter notes to a minute).

2. Keeping the pulse steady (it will be useful to use a metronome) emphasize the notes marked L (Loud) distinguishing them from those marked s (soft). Do not deliberately lengthen the "L" notes; merely stress them. Using extra bow speed for the "L" notes will produce more of a sharp accent whereas using pressure, applied mostly with the first finger, will produce a gentler, more integrated sound; try both options. Repeat each example many times.

   • Lsss ssss Lsss ssss
   • Lsss Lsss Lsss Lsss
   • Lsss LsLs Lsss LsLs
   • LLss LLss LsLs LLss
   • Ssss LLLL ssss LLLL
   • ssLL ssLL ssLs ssLs

3. Now do the same with a time signature of $\frac{3}{4}$:

   • Lsss Lsss Lsss
   • ssLs ssLs ssLs
   • LsLs ssLs Lsss
   • Lsss LsLs Lsss
   • ssLs ssLs Lsss

4. Invent your own 'composition' on one note, using the maximum variety of loud/soft notes to make it as interesting and complex as possible. Let there be no limit to your fantasy in this! For example:

   • Lss Lss LLL sss LLLL ssss L ss LLL ss LLL etc.

5. Finally, play Bars 5–14 of our piece, keeping the pulse steady but stressing any notes that you feel have a little extra importance.

Flexibility of Articulation

The third way of varying the sound of passages of equal notes is through articulation. In the following exercise, articulation implies the extent to which the bow is on or off the string. As we have seen previously, there are many subtle variations of "off" and "on." In Lesson 7, Exercise 17, we explored the vast spectrum of articulations available to us, from the shortest off-the-string note to the longest on-the-string one. With this exercise we hope to achieve a greater flexibility to move rapidly and spontaneously from one articulation to the other, thereby improving the quality of perspective and interest in a single line of notes.

Exercise 66: Exploring flexibility of articulation

1. On an open string, play a bar of equal sixteenth notes with a time signature of $\frac{4}{4}$. Begin with a moderately fast tempo (60 quarter notes to a minute).
2. Keeping the pulse steady (it will be useful to use a metronome) play the notes marked L (Legato) on the string and those marked s (Spiccato) off the string. Repeat each example many times. Remember that "on" the string can mean totally on, mostly on, or scarcely on, just as "off" can mean very slightly off or touching the string only for a microsecond.
   - Lsss ssss Lsss ssss
   - Lsss Lsss Lsss Lsss
   - Lsss LsLs Lsss LsLs
   - LLss LLss LsLs LLss
   - Ssss LLLL ssss LLLL
   - ssLL ssLL ssLs ssLs
3. Now do the same with a time signature of $\frac{3}{4}$:
   - Lsss Lsss Lsss
   - ssLs ssLs ssLs
   - LsLs ssLs Lsss
   - Lsss LsLs Lsss
   - ssLs ssLs Lsss
4. Once again, invent your own 'composition' on one note, using the maximum variety of articulations to make it as interesting and complex as possible. Let there be no limit to your fantasy in this! For example:
   - Lss Lss LLL sss LLLL ssss L ss LLL ss LLL etc.
5. Finally, play Bars 5–14 of our piece, keeping the pulse steady but varying the articulation according to the importance of each note. Lift the less important notes and play the more important ones with a more singing stroke. Remember, there are infinite varieties of "on" and "off." The challenge is that no two consecutive notes have exactly the same articulation!

Having worked on your three flexibility studies, try to combine them into a single performance. I often find that students who are not used to such freedom are inhibited, as if fearsome of breaking some deeply engrained rules. My answer is this: "Exaggerate wildly, create a caricature of an outrageously undisciplined performer: I will tell you if you overdo it!" Rarely has such a student succeeded in shocking me: on the contrary, they frequently give their most convincing performance ever!

꿍 꿍 꿍

Before exploring this movement in detail, let us seek out some technical advice from Tartini on the playing of Allegros. In his letter to Maddalena Lombardini, he advocates practicing the Allegros of Corelli every day, starting slowly and gradually speeding up *"until you arrive at the greatest degree of swiftness possible: but two precautions are necessary in this exercise; the first is, that you play the notes staccato, that is separate and detached, with a little space between every two: for though they are written thus,*

they should be played as if there was a rest after every note, in this manner."

Practicing certain passages of our Allegro in this way, Bars 68–75, for example, is surely beneficial to the clarity of the sound, but not to the variety of articulations we are hoping to achieve. Fortunately, in his *Regole*, Tartini is more forthcoming, indicating an important distinction between what he calls "cantabile" and "allegro" passages.

"If the melody moves by step," he writes, *"the passage is cantabile and should be performed legato."* By "cantabile" he means that *"the transition from one note to the next must be made so perfectly that no interval of silence is perceptible between them."* On the other hand, *"if . . . the melody moves by leap, the passage is allegro and a detached style of playing is required."*[2]

On the basis of this information alone we can achieve a significant amount of variety of stroke in our Allegro, articulating the leaps while playing stepwise notes in a more legato manner. In the interests of a more thorough pedagogical exploration, however, we will need a more detailed approach.

Observations

Our tempo must be lively, as indicated; however we should heed Quantz when he comments (XII, § 11) that *"everything that is hurriedly played causes your listeners anxiety rather than satisfaction. Your principal goal,"* he continues, *"must always be the expression of the sentiment, not quick playing."*

Bar 1: the first note is strong, possibly a little stretched, but not played with too fast a bow (that would create an unseemly accent.)

The three subsequent notes become both weaker and shorter. From the third note to the end of the bar the bow can be allowed to come slightly off the string; this should happen naturally, without deliberately deciding on any kind of clearly identifiable spiccato stroke. Remember that bow strokes as such did not exist until the early nineteenth century: what *did* exist was a vast plethora of expressive articulations to which we have recourse. Let us exploit that rich variety of sounds and avoid becoming trapped in the limited uniformity of studied spiccatos and détachés!

Bar 2 links the two strong bars on either side, but is itself weak. Over-accentuation of the first note would destroy this strong/weak relationship. Notice that the bass remains on the tonic G, not rising to the dominant until the second beat, so the first two notes can be seen as a continuation of Bar 1.

Slurring the first two notes would facilitate the necessary crescendo into Bar 3, arriving there on a down-bow and thus avoiding the necessity of taking two up-bows at the start of the bar.

We can trill on the third note, slurring it to the two termination notes at the end of the bar, although for greater energy these could be played detached.

Bar 3 is a strong bar, weakening as it diminuendos into Bar 4: over the first four notes the bow stroke becomes progressively shorter so that the last two notes are slightly off the string.

Bar 4: shaping the note according to the bass line produces a Messa di voce. The bass is also the start of the first sequence of the piece, ending in Bar 11.

ॐ ॐ ॐ

Adding Slurs: A Misdemeanor?

If the human voice is the legato instrument par excellence and if it is our aim to "*rival the most perfect human voice,*" as Geminiani writes in the second sentence of his Preface, it follows that legato must be among the most cherished attributes of our instrument: after all, with our bows we can create glorious legatos such as few instruments can dream of!

There are no printed slurs in this movement, but does that mean we are not 'allowed' to add them? Purists there are who believe we should not meddle with bowings not indicated by the composer, but the historical evidence is clearly in contradiction to that view.

In Essempio XVI of the same book, Geminiani shows us "*in how many different Manners of bowing you may play 2, 3, 4, 5 and 6 notes . . . for it is to be held as a certain Principle that he who does not possess, in a perfect degree, the Art of Bowing, will never be able to render the melody agreeable nor arrive at a Facility in the Execution.*"

Leopold Mozart provides another unequivocal answer. As "*it is to be seen how greatly the slurring and detaching distinguishes a melody . . . not only must the written and prescribed slurs be observed with the greatest exactitude,*" he writes (XII, § 11), "*but when, as in many a composition, nothing at all is indicated, the player must himself know how to apply the slurring and detaching tastefully and in the right place.*"

Tartini gives us only one specific rule for adding slurs: "*Notes ascending or descending by semitones,*" he writes, "*should always be played in a single bow.*"[3]

Composers and treatises from the sixteenth century onward either talk about slurs or write them in. One reason a composer such as Albinoni might have refrained from writing bowings was that in not writing any, he is giving the performer freedom to put them in when he or she feels they are tasteful. Furthermore, the performer might not want to put in the same slurs on the repeat time: having the composer's suggestions on the page would be too restricting.

Bowings, then, are part of the performer's right of ornamentation in this kind of music. Where slurs are written in, we should play them, but where no slurs are written we should not feel we are committing a misdemeanor by adding some!

Figure a

Extract from Francesco Maria Veracini's Sonata 12 (1744). The sign over the b♭ in the second bar indicates an up-bow.

Francesco Maria Veracini (1744) was one of the few composers to use symbols for up-bows and down-bows (Figure a).

Sequences

A sequence is defined in the *Oxford Dictionary of Music* as "the more or less exact repetition of a passage at a higher or lower level of pitch." But if we listen carefully, we will observe that a phrase or fragment changes its emotional impact when repeated on different tonal platforms, just as our feelings about a landscape or a building can change when viewed at different moments in the day: at noon, a mountain may evoke uplifting and noble feelings but at night, or in the moonlight, it may stir up very different emotions.

As with our concept of "emotional information" (see Lesson 8) each repetition of even the simplest passage played in sequence must be quite distinct in content and meaning and needs to be communicated as such, using variations in dynamics, articulation, and intent. By "intent," I mean the subtle alteration of one's state of mind, required to feel and communicate a new emotion or affect.

Exercise 67: Increasing awareness of the individuality of repetitions within a sequence

In the following sequence, each repetition has a distinct emotional flavor, even without harmonization. Play each bar separately, savoring its unique essence. Then play the whole sequence, observing the shift in emotion between bars.

The differences are less obvious in the top line of our next sequence, in which no dynamic scheme is clearly implied. The sequence could be equally effective with an overall diminuendo or an overall crescendo. Alternatively, each bar could have its own strong/weak or weak/strong dynamic scheme.

I have harmonized these two bars in two different ways: play each fragment in turn with its bass note, exploring the individual feel of each one. Note the difference between the feel in the two harmonized versions. Then play each sequence in full, monitoring the constantly shifting affect. Note also that in these examples, the dynamic implications are less ambiguous.

Sequence 1: Bars 4–11

Each unit of the sequence is two bars long, starting (for the violin) in Bar 5. The temptation in the violin part may be to crescendo into the second of the two-bar unit, but in the bass line the hierarchy is clearly strong/weak, so we should phrase accordingly.

Each repetition of the sequence can be said to be weaker than the previous one, and each has a different feel about it. The weak bars will either lead us back via a crescendo to the next strong bar or continue in diminuendo, necessitating a stronger gesture at the start of the next strong bar. We do not need to use the same solution each time, for predictability will never hold the attention of our audience!

Although Bars 5, 7, 9, and 11 are strong, we could give the impression of four-bar units by underplaying Bars 7 and 11 and making a special point of energizing Bar 9.

The first note of the strong bars could be stretched to produce an agogic accent, but again, we should strive to avoid too rigidly consistent an approach.

Sequence 2: Bars 12–14

Here, the units are of single bars. A crescendo through the entire sequence is clearly indicated by the rising of both parts.

Because of the intervals separating the bars, the sequence has a jagged, urgent quality. A slight comma between each bar will help express this. A dynamic (agogic) accent on each first note is followed by the others scurrying to get to the next bar line on time.

Bars 15–16 form a hemiola, with the highest notes of the movement. The first note (c''') comes after a dramatic leap of a seventh, so it merits a strong gesture with the bow: hover on it a little before heading right through to the end of the hemiola with a singing bow stroke and without accents. The last note of Bar 16 will have a cadential trill on it, starting on the upper note (b''♭.)

Bar 17: a comma between the notes will mark the end of the phrase.

Bars 18–20: Bar 18 is in D major and is sandwiched between two bars of G minor: we should reflect this in the sound, stretching the first note (a'') and using a stronger, brighter bow stroke. The last note (a'') can change color so that Bar 19 has a more yearning, lyrical quality.

The dynamics in Bars 19–20 follow the graphic line. As the diminuendo progresses, the strokes diminish in size and the articulation becomes more detached. There can be a sense of easing into Bar 21 by means of a subtle slowing down before the bar line.

Sequence 3: Bars 21–24

This sequence starts softly and grows, the bass rising by step: the octave displacement in the bass in Bar 23 could be a signal to drop the dynamic level in order to build it up again in the following bars, or it could serve to enrich the texture.

The units begin on the second note of each bar: lengthen the first note of each bar and put a comma after it to clarify this. As the sequence intensifies we can abandon this phrasing.

There are two types of crescendo possible here:

1. Each unit crescendos to the first note of the following bar.
2. Each unit starts a little louder than the previous one.

> Some musicians in the early days of the Baroque music revival, noting that Baroque composers had indicated neither crescendos nor diminuendos, assumed that such dynamic subtleties could not have existed in those far-off times. As it was also seen as evident that the harpsichord was not able to achieve such changes in dynamics (a fact entirely and consistently disproved by all great harpsichordists today) the misguided doctrine of only playing sudden fortes or pianos was widely adopted and the term "terraced dynamics" coined. This term is not a historical one and is not found in any source.

Sequence 4: Bars 26–28

This sequence is a diminuendo, following the falling graphic line of the notes.

Each tied note crescendos into a dissonance (not with the bass note, but with the root of the $^6_5$ chord).

The three notes following the tied ones could be articulated differently as the diminuendo progresses. For example:

- In Bar 26 they could all be lyrical.
- In Bar 27 the first note could be a little shorter, the others lyrical.
- In Bar 28 they could all be a trifle lifted.

As always, varying the articulation makes for a more interesting listening experience.

Sequence 5: Bars 30–33

In Bars 31 and 33, we can add a trill to the second note (see note to Bar 2). Starting them on the upper note creates a fleeting dissonance with the bass.

Each two-bar unit in the violin part forms a hemiola, although the bass contradicts this. To ensure that this cross-rhythm is well enunciated, use pressure from the first finger to bite into the string, producing tiny accents on each beat. This will also help the trills to sound more brilliant.

Bars 34–37: each two-bar unit is a hemiola, so take care not to accent the start of Bars 35 and 37.

Put a comma over the bar line into Bar 36: a new down-bow after the bar line will achieve this naturally.

You could add trills to the last notes of Bars 35 and 37, but this might be seen to clutter the line.

Bars 39–49 contain no new material.

Sequence 6: Bars 50–52

The accent shifts onto the second beat, ambiguously in Bar 50, clearly in the next bar and forcefully in Bar 52 as the intervals become more extreme. Bar 52 is both the end of a sequence and the start of a new one, beginning on the second beat.

Sequence 7: Bars 52–58

The first beats of Bars 53, 55, and 57 are strong; the first beats of Bars 54 and 56 are weak. The whole sequence lies within a diminuendo.

Vary the stroke and color of the sixteenth notes in Bars 52, 54, and 56. Think of the five sixteenth notes after the tied notes in Bars 53, 55, and 57 as weaker: play them with a less active bow and perhaps a more articulated stroke.

Bar 59: after sixteen bars with just one bass note in each, the bass is now reactivated, indicating an increasing sense of urgency.

Bars 59–60: we could slur the first three notes in one bow, possibly on the repeat time: it would certainly give some refreshing new life to our performance! If we do this, however, we must be careful not to sustain the bow all the way through the slur, but to give it an impulse at the start of the slur and then let it glide along 'by itself,' a little like free-wheeling on a bicycle. If we maintain pressure on the bow throughout the slur, the sound will lose its lightness and clarity and become thick and stodgy.

The sources recognize this danger. The first note of a slur *"must be somewhat more strongly accented and sustained longer,"* says Leopold Mozart (XII, § 10), and the others, *"on the contrary, being slurred on to it in the same stroke with a diminishing of the tone, even more and more quietly and without the slightest accent."*

Bars 61–63: another hemiola. Be careful when playing hemiolas not to leave the bow on the string, especially in a fast tempo: you will be in danger of pushing the up-bows too hard and accenting them. Hemiolas in this tempo need to dance, so take the bow slightly off the string after the first notes of Bars 61 and 62. Put a trill on the last note of Bar 62. Bar 63 will be on an up-bow, which is appropriate as anyway it is a weak bar.

Bar 67: the bass, having risen and fallen twice (Bars 63–54 and 65–56) now descends, returning in Bar 68 to a one note per bar pattern.

Sequence 8: Bars 64–67

This sequence begins in the bass. Shape the first notes of Bars 65 and 67 to give them expression. In Bar 65 the following notes will diminish, but in Bar 67 we can grow through the bar to start the following sequence *forte*.

Sequence 9: Bars 68–73

There are three units of two bars each, the first bar stronger than the second, the whole sequence being within a diminuendo.

Vary the articulation: for instance, the last three notes of Bars 69, 71, and 73 can change from broad to short. In Bars 68, 70, and 72, the first note can be stretched, the next three rebounding passively off it, perhaps even slightly off the string.

Sequence 10: Bars 74–75

Bars 74–75 make up a two-bar sequence within a crescendo. This crescendo can either be 'terraced' or consistent. In a 'terraced' crescendo, Bar 75 would have the same internal shape as Bar 74, but it would start louder. The first note could be agogic, and the descending notes would be in a diminuendo. The start of the hemiola in Bar 76 would be the loudest point of the three bars.

A consistent crescendo would mean that each note of Bars 74 and 75 would be a little louder than the previous one.

Another possible scheme for these two bars would be a combination of the above options: a diminuendo in Bar 74 and a consistent crescendo from Bar 75 into Bar 76.

Sequence 11: Bars 79–end

Bars 67–78 are repeated, possibly as an echo. Alternatively, we could vary the articulation, adding slurs where we feel they enhance the expression.

Summary

In this lesson we have once more underlined how observing and maximizing the potential of what is written down in both parts is the key to a successful interpretive stance. One conclusion we arrive at, which I still enjoy proclaiming even after many years of repeating it, paraphrases the great George Orwell:

> All notes are equal, but some notes are more equal than others.

Notes

1. Tosi, chapter IX, 42.
2. Tartini, *Regole* (Rules for Bowing). Hermann Moeck Edition p. 55.
3. Tartini, *Regole* (Rules for Bowing). Hermann Moeck Edition p. 57.

Lesson 14

Learning to Feel Comfortable on Gut Strings: The Bow

It takes a while to become comfortable playing on gut strings: the way they feel both under the bow and under the fingers is very different from how modern metal or plastic strings feel. In this lesson and the next you will find exercises that help you better to acquaint yourself with the sensation, the sound, and the joy of gut.

The much-quoted triad of basic components used in sound production on modern strings holds true for gut strings also:

1. Bow speed.
2. Pressure.
3. Point of contact.

For the Baroque bow, however, with its built-in dynamic scheme (see Lesson 4) we must add a fourth component:

4. Location, the place along the bow where the desired sound is most naturally to be found.

In addition to this formula there are a number of variables:

1. The length of the string, which is constantly being altered by the action of the fingers: it can be anything from its full length (an open string) to a very short length (when we play a note high up on the fingerboard).
2. The resistance of each string (being of different gauges) both to the fingers and to the bow.
3. The color and dynamic of the sound required (which is constantly changing).

These variables are, of course, equally important when using modern strings, but the specifics with gut are very different. These specifics cannot be quantified because there are too many combinations of variables for that to be possible. As we cannot hope to memorize the infinite combinations of these constantly fluctuating factors, we need a different approach in order to monitor and control our sound. That approach can best be summed up by the word "awareness."

Awareness means not only constantly listening to the sound; there must also be physical awareness of the quality of the contact between bow and string, the means by which that sound is produced, controlled, and regulated. The object of Exercises 68–74 in this lesson is to heighten awareness of the complex relationship between ear, hand, bow, and string, *"for what,"* asks Leopold Mozart (V § 2) *"can be more insipid than the playing of one . . . who scarce touches the strings with the bow."*

❦ ❦ ❦

The area of activity in the right hand with which we are primarily concerned here is centered on the joints under the knuckles that are nearest to the tips of the fingers. This is where the fingers are wrapped around or in close contact with the stick. It is here (one of the most sensitive parts of the body) that the center of our tactile, physical awareness lies.

The ear, constantly monitoring the sound, transmits and receives a continuous flow of information messages to and from the point of contact via this part of the hand, which can then control the ever-fluctuating contact of the bow-hair with the string. Similarly, the string, being itself in a constant state of flux, sends messages via the bow and the hand back to the ear.

To maintain this constant two-way flow of information between the ear and the hand, both must be in a state of total awareness. For the hand, this means not merely the absence of stiffness, which would block the flow, but a constantly shifting equilibrium that allows the fingers to maintain a healthy contact with the string via the stick and the hair throughout the entire length of the bow. The hand must be free and supple, a living organism in a constant state of flux adapting to the changing demands of the sound.

We use the terms "bow-hold" or "grip" but in fact we do not really *hold* the bow at all, much less *grip* it. The bow is balanced within the hand, as effortlessly as possible, until it feels almost weightless. Only if it is not comfortably balanced will there be a perceived need to grip it.

Before starting the exercises, perform a quick 'body scan.' This involves checking every part of your body from head to foot for any possible tension. If you become aware of a muscle that is tense, release that muscle and continue your scan. While practicing these exercises, you need constantly to ensure that your entire body is free from tension and is in a 'neutral' state.

The task here is to investigate how much pressure is needed to obtain a good, clear, 'basic' *forte* sound: more subtle varieties of sound will be sought later on. In order to succeed, your hand will need to feel comfortable, with no hint of stiffness. Ensure that the bottom knuckle, the lowest joint, is supple, springy, and not raised up, and that the thumb is not squeezing the stick.

This exercise has two parts, the Experimental Phase and the Evaluation Phase.

Exercise 68: Cultivating a dynamic awareness of gut strings

A: The Experimental Phase

This is equivalent to the archer taking aim at a target.

1. Place the middle of your bow on the E string.
2. Adjust the angle of the hand and the position of the fingers until there is no tension at all and the hand feels perfectly at ease and well balanced. The fingers will now be free to feel the living contact with the string unimpeded.

Finding a comfortable hand position is similar to what you do naturally when you sit on a chair: you shift around, adjusting and modifying your position until you feel totally balanced and comfortable.

3. With your fingers, feel and test the resistance of the string as transmitted via the stick and hair. Experiment with the amount of pressure you estimate will be needed to achieve the good, basic sound you have in mind. Take as much time as you need to do this, much as you would when aiming at a target with a bow and arrow. When you are convinced that you have found the healthy contact with the string that you need, proceed to the Evaluation Phase.

B. The Evaluation Phase

This is equivalent to the archer letting fly his arrow and assessing the result.

Play a short stroke from the middle to the point. The sound must be as quick and short as a martelé, but to avoid confusion we will call it a 'trial note.' Use your listening to evaluate and judge the result: if the sound was too crushed, you will have used too much pressure; if it whistled, you will have underestimated the amount of pressure required. If the sound was clear, short, loud, and healthy just as you imagined it, your Experimental Phase will have been successful!

"It is true," writes Leopold Mozart (II, § 11) encouragingly "that at first, the rough character of a strong but as yet unpurified stroke greatly offends the ears. But with time and patience the roughness of sound will lessen, and with the strength of tone the purity thereof will be retained."

Now, without taking the bow off the string, begin the process over again at the tip of the bow. Once more, adjust the angle of the hand and the position of the fingers until there is no tension at all and the fingers are able to feel the resistance of the string as comfortably as they did before. Once you feel the hand is in an optimal position (it will of course look and feel very different from when you were at the middle of the bow), test your judgment by making another short martelé-like 'trial note' back to the middle of the bow. Once again, listen carefully to the sound and evaluate it.

It is important to be patient, not proceeding to the Evaluation Phase until you are confident that your preparations are complete. Regard the Experimental Phase as a kind of meditation, an investigation with no pre-conceived ideas, as the archer does when he patiently calculates the future trajectory of his arrow, factoring in the speed and direction of the wind.

Remember that only the fingers are active, constantly testing the contact with the string, as a person crossing a stream on stepping stones carefully tests each stone to evaluate its stability and resistance.

Make as many attempts as you need to obtain your ideal sound, remembering that the trial note must be short and martelé-like, producing, as it were, a single sound rather than a longer, more complex one.

When you feel that you have become thoroughly acquainted with the E string, repeat the entire process on the A, D, and G strings. Each string will feel different, according

141

to its flexibility and resistance, but you do not need to quantify the differences: you need only to feel, experiment, and listen.

When you have completed your investigation of all four strings and are comfortable with the results, you can move on to playing pairs of open strings as follows:

- G D
- DG
- DA
- AD
- AE
- EA

Here there is still only one Experimental Phase. Take time to feel the contact with the first string and, when you are satisfied, play the two strings one after the other, without pausing to experiment with the second string. The feeling of contact passes quickly from one string to the next, and the ear judges the resultant sound of both notes.

Playing the second note of a pair in this way is like scooping up an object from the ground while running. Instead of stopping, picking it up, and then continuing, you gather it up while in motion, in one single action.

If the first note sounds healthy but the second note is too weak or too strong, your instant appraisal of the resistance of the second string will have been faulty. Repeat until you regularly hear both notes sounding equally loud and equally clear. Only then should you proceed to the next pair. However, if the second note is repeatedly too weak or too strong, you may want to work on it separately first, returning to the pair once you have established a healthy contact with it.

When you have completed all these pairs, proceed to the next stage which is to play groups of four notes:

- DAEA
- ADAE
- GDAD
- DGDA

The same principle applies: feel comfortable and well balanced, release all tension, assess what seems to be a healthy contact with the first string in the group, then transfer that feeling onto the other strings in turn, evaluating the quality of all four short 'trial notes.' Once all four notes are clear and loud, proceed to the next group.

The last two groups of notes in this exercise are as follows:

- GDAE / EADG
- GDGAGE / EAEDEG

Pause at the halfway point for a rapid, fleeting Experimental Phase.

Exercise 69: Practicing Exercise 68 between the nut and the middle of the bow

It is clear that such a demanding routine as the one explained in Exercise 68 necessitates demands the highest degree of mental alertness if it is to be beneficial. It must therefore never be attempted when the mind is tired. It is equally true that, like the Intonation Exercises of Lesson 12, these exercises must be practiced over a period of considerable time if they are to bear fruit.

Exercise 69 follows an identical routine to Exercise 68, but it is practiced between the nut and the middle of the bow. At the nut, the distance between the stick and the hair is at its maximum, so you might well find it more difficult to feel the contact with the string. However, as the lower half of the Baroque bow is where the sound is naturally loudest, you will be spending much of your playing time there. Exercise 69 will help you feel as comfortable here as Exercise 68 did in the upper half.

At the nut, the third and middle fingers are the ones with the most important roles in the feeling process. The little finger's role is to balance the bow: as only its tip touches the stick, it cannot feel contact with the string in the way the other fingers do. Leopold Mozart (II, § 5) insists that the *"little finger must lie at all times on the bow . . . for it contributes greatly to (its) control."* As a sensitive assessor of the string, the index finger is also redundant here, as well as being irrelevant to the balancing process: indeed, some modern violin schools advocate unwrapping it from the stick altogether at the upper part of the bow, thus shifting the balance back toward the other fingers.

Pay attention that the shoulder muscles do not act as 'brakes' to the hand as it moves from nut to middle. You might find it useful to close your right eye when practicing this exercise: in this way, you cannot see your right arm so you will be able to visualize your hand as an independent projectile flying unimpeded through space.

Remember always to use a short trial note: a single sound, not a longer, more complex one.

Exercise 70: Dividing the bow into two parts

This exercise combines the Exercises 68 and 69 and uses the whole bow divided into two parts: in a down-bow from the nut to the middle and then another from the middle to the point, and in an up-bow from the point to the middle and then another from the middle to the nut.

For the single notes at the start of the routine there is always a full Experimental Phase at the nut and the point. At the middle of the bow there is only a short pause for a fleeting Experimental Phase, just long enough for the hand to adapt and to feel the string afresh before moving on.

For the pairs and groups of notes there is just one Experimental Phase, before the first sound.

Exercise 71: Using the whole bow

This exercise is identical to Exercise 68 but uses the whole bow for each note.

Exercise 72: Using a detaché-like stroke

We now move on from the single, short 'trial note' we have been using thus far to a longer, detaché-like stroke. Repeat each step of Exercises 68-71, feeling the string as carefully as before in the Experimental Phases but this time, having produced a clear, loud, and singing trial note at the Evaluation Stage, follow this with a more sustained detaché-like stroke, still feeling the resistance of the string as before.

෴ ෴ ෴

Leaving behind the routine hitherto followed in this lesson, we move on to the next step—feeling the differences in contact between bow and string caused by the shortening and lengthening of the string by the fingers of the left hand. Exercise 73 illustrates the need for this in an extreme way!

Exercise 73: Understanding the principle of adapting bow pressure

1. Play a 'trial note' on an open string: the sound must be clear and pure.
2. Place a finger two octaves higher on the same string and, without altering the pressure used in (1) play that note: it will screech!
3. Adapt the pressure on the high note until the sound is clear and pure.
4. Now play the open string again, without altering the pressure used in (3): the sound whistles!
5. Adapt the pressure on the open string until the sound is clear and pure.
6. When you can play both notes with a pure sound, one after the other, change the top note to a seventh above the open string; then a sixth, a fifth, etc.
7. Repeat on all strings.

Exercise 74: Monitoring bow pressure while playing scales

When the string is less radically shortened, the pressure will still need to be adjusted. Remember: it is the ear that is the judge. Be relentlessly aware of the contact, because it will forever be changing, from note to note, string to string, position to position and phrase to phrase. Constantly evaluate the sound quality: as always, your ears are your best teachers!

Practice the following scale in the six ways described below.

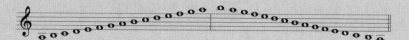

1. Practice each note a number of times using the short, martelé-like 'trial' stroke we used before. Take time, as in the Experimental Phase, to feel the string carefully before sounding and evaluating. Each note will feel subtly different because of the difference in string length.
2. Play the whole scale, pausing briefly before each note to feel the changing resistance of the string.
3. Repeat No. 1, playing each note four times: two short 'trial notes' and two longer detaché-like strokes. Test the resistance of the string before playing.
4. Play the whole scale with the longer detaché-like strokes, stopping to feel before each note.
5. Play the whole scale with the longer detaché-like strokes, this time without stopping to feel before each note, but continuing to feel the contact while playing.
6. Transpose the scale into the higher positions, Second to Seventh, and repeat Nos. 1–5.

Lesson 15

Learning to Feel Comfortable on Gut Strings: The Left Hand

Gut strings are less smooth, less 'perfect' in some ways, less predictable than modern ones, and they feel very different under the fingers. Their tactile qualities can be compared to the sensations you feel while stroking the surface of an antique oak table, the grain of the wood in living contact with your skin, as opposed to that of a perfect, shiny, plastic tabletop.

In the previous lesson we focused on the bow's complex relationship with the ever-changing conditions of the strings. Now we will learn to gauge how much pressure we need apply with the fingers to achieve the clear sound we want and, following this, we shall explore the expressive role of the fingers and their connection to our inner voice.

The sources are not too forthcoming on these issues. Georg Muffat, in his *Florilegium secundum*, warns that *"the ear will be offended whenever the string is not pressed firmly enough to the fingerboard, as a nasty, scraping sound will result."* [1]

Geminiani makes it *"a constant Rule to keep the Fingers as firm as possible"* while Leopold Mozart (II, § 6) contents himself with saying, *"If the strings are not pressed well down they will not sound pure."* Let us explore, in Exercises 75 and 76, a more subtle approach to this question.

Exercise 75: Investigating the optimal amount of finger pressure

1. While playing a continuous open string with your bow, lower any finger lightly onto it. The sound, of course, will whistle.
2. Continue to play, gradually increasing the pressure on the string with the finger until the sound has become clear, wholesome, and in tune: you have now found the optimal finger pressure for that note.
3. As an experiment, continue to press harder. Observe that the sound no longer changes: more pressure than the optimal amount you discovered before is therefore wasted energy and will lead only to stiffness.
4. Reduce the pressure again until you have returned to the optimal pressure for that note.

Co-ordinating the ear with the fingers becomes more complex as conditions change: the constant fluctuation of the resistance of the string as we shift higher up the fingerboard or move from one string to another calls for a constant state of tactile awareness matched with an unceasing awareness of the sound.

Exercise 76 is designed to expand our tactile understanding of the strings by exploring the resistance encountered when playing scales. Geminiani suggests (*The Art of Playing on The Violin*) page 3 (C)), that, as fingering *"requires an earnest Application . . . it would be most prudent to undertake it without the Use of the Bow."* In our exercise, the finger indeed feels the pressure first, but the ear immediately evaluates it through the sound produced by the bow.

Exercise 76: Exploring the tactile relationship of the left hand with gut strings

1. Repeat Exercise 75, determining the optimal amount of pressure needed to play an f″ with your first finger on the E string.
2. Release the pressure and glide up to a g″. Repeat Exercise 75.
3. Continue up the scale of F major in this way, testing the pressure at each step of the way.
4. Repeat steps 1–3, using the other fingers.
5. Repeat the entire exercise on the other strings.

When the sound is unsatisfactory, there may be a temptation to rectify it by working harder with the bow. Although this could possibly be the correct reaction, the fault could also lie with the failure of the fingers of the left hand to hold the string down with the correct amount of pressure. This is particularly true when we play double stops or chords. In such a case, each finger involved must individually apply the right pressure for the sound to be pure: if there is one finger out of four that lacks a healthy contact with the fingerboard, the chord will whistle.

ক্ট ক্ট ক্ট

The Fingers: Slaves of Our Inner Voice

Now that the fingers are aware of how it feels to have a healthy contact with the strings, we can move on to the next question, that of the relationship between our inner voice and the movement of our fingers.

One could say that gut strings are less 'naïve' in character than their modern substitutes. Playing on gut strings, I find, demands a more direct commitment from the fingers than playing on modern strings, which are less subtle in touch and thus simpler to sound. By commitment, I mean that the complex tactile activity that the living gut string demands enhances and stimulates the process of expression from its source, the imagination, to its realization in sound.

The manner in which we put our fingers down onto the strings and take them up again directly affects the musical phrasing. Although it is the bow that makes and shapes the sound, we nevertheless must be watchful that the action of the fingers is never automatic, never independent of our musical intention.

The fingerboard of the violin may be said to be 'touch sensitive' in a similar way to the keyboard of a piano, as opposed to that of a harpsichord or an organ, for on these latter instruments the action of the fingers does not impact the sound in any comparable way.

If our aim is, as J. S. Bach writes in the title page of his *Inventions and Sinfonias* (BWV 772-801), *"above all, to arrive at a singing style of playing,"* then we need to ensure that the fingers are the slaves of our inner voice, conveying to the string the intricate subtleties of phrasing and timing that spring from our artistry and our imagination.

Many aspects of technique first formulated in the pedagogic treatises of post-revolutionary France were derivative of earlier practices, so I find it hard to believe that a great artist such as Tartini would not have known and taught this aspect of left-hand technique, even if it seems not to have been written down until Pierre Baillot's *L'art du violon* of 1834. *"The movement (of the fingers),"* Baillot writes, *"happens in various ways and is always born from the nature of the passage from which one wishes to extract total expression. The fingers,"* he adds, confirming his awareness of the rhetorical traditions of earlier times, *"articulate as if pronouncing words, and sometimes seem to be speaking."*[2]

❧ ❧ ❧

The action of the fingers can be active or passive: there are therefore four categories of basic finger actions:-

1. Down, active: an energetic movement where the finger hits the string at speed, causing an accented change of note.
2. Down, passive: the finger is lowered onto the string with just enough speed to cause a clean change of note, but with no accent.
3. Up, active: an energetic movement where the finger springs up from the string at speed, causing the lower note to be accented.
4. Up, passive: the finger is raised from the string with just enough speed to cause a clean change of note, but with no accent.

There are, of course, myriad shades of both active and passive finger actions; furthermore, a finger may come down actively but be raised up passively, or vice versa. Consider the phrasing of the following fragment:

To make the crescendo convincing, we need to sing not only with the bow but with the fingers as well. The first finger will come down quite passively, but each successive finger will come down in a progressively more active way.

Similarly, in order to make the crescendo in the next fragment convincing, the fourth finger will need to come off the string passively, but each successive finger will come off in a progressively more active way.

When we combine the previous two fragments to form a longer phrase, the first finger should come down passively but each successive finger will come down in a more active way, climaxing with the accented e″. In the descent, each successive finger will come off in a more passive way.

In the following fragment, the accent is obtained by an active lifting off of the fourth finger.

Similarly, the accented c″# in the next fragment is obtained by a very active lifting off of the third finger.

We continue this cycle though the next five fragments (Ex 6 to Ex 10), shifting the accent onto a different note each time until we return to our starting point (Ex 1). In Ex 6 and Ex 7, the desired accent is produced by actively lifting the preceding finger. From then on, it is produced by actively striking the accented note.

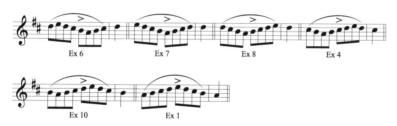

Exercise 77 is designed to synchronize your inner voice with your fingers.

Exercise 77: Phrasing by varying the finger action

Practice each of the above fragments in the following ways:

1. Sing the phrase: it must sound like a beautiful melody.
2. While singing, play with the left hand only. Ensure that the fingers move in total agreement with your voice, expressing every nuance of dynamic and being entirely at one with it.

3. Repeat No, 2 while simultaneously bowing an open e″ on the E string. The sound of the e″ must reflect the nuances of the notes you are playing on the A string.
4. Every finger will have a slightly different musical role in each phrase, either more active or more passive.
5. Experiment with different phrasings even within the same example: there may be more than one possibility.

We may conclude that, providing there is no actual physical problem in the hand or fingers, there is no such thing, when dealing with expression, as a 'right' or 'wrong' finger action. The movement of the fingers is either appropriate or inappropriate to the desired expression. As is so often the case, it is the musical demands that determine the physical, technical actions; just as the flowing stream catches the slats of the watermill wheel and turns it, so the voice activates the fingers.

> The more we focus on controlling our fingers and our bow in abstract, physical ways, devoid of artistry, the greater the danger that they will function independently of our artistic intent.

Let us now return to the Allegro of Albinoni's Sonata, op. 6, no. 2, that we studied in Lesson 13, applying to it what we have just discussed. The purpose of Exercise 78 is to ensure that your fingers are totally at one with your inner singing voice. The fingers have no technique of their own: their duty is to translate your inner voice into tactile terms that correspond exactly to every nuance of the music. Just as the lens of a camera organizes received light to produce an image, so are our fingers both the receivers and the transmitters of our musical intentions.

Exercise 78: Achieving total obedience of the fingers to the inner voice

1. Hold your violin as if it were a guitar.
2. Finger the notes of the Albinoni movement while singing in the most expressive and free manner possible.
3. Ensure that the fingers are totally synchronized with your singing voice in these two ways:
   i. Timing: your fingers neither precede your voice nor act after it.
   ii. Expression: the action of each finger comes onto the string or leaves it in total agreement with every nuance of your voice: dynamic, rhythmic, and in terms of articulation.

4. Be on guard against unilateral, mechanical actions by the fingers that do not obey your inner voice.

5. Repeat No 2, holding the violin normally.

Video 15.1

Notes

1. Georg Muffat, *Florilegium secundum*, in *GMPP*, p. 32.
2. Baillot, *L'art du violon*, p. 152.

PART II

Re-Examining the Familiar
Sonatas by Vivaldi and Corelli

Lesson 16

The Starting-Point of Interpretation: Learning to Observe

Arcangelo Corelli: Sonata, op. 5, no. 7

In this lesson and the next, we undergo a detailed examination of the first of Corelli's five chamber sonatas from Part Two of his opus 5, the sixth and final work of the set being his renowned set of variations with the title "Follia." The sonatas of Corelli constitute one of the mainstays of the Baroque violin repertory and we make no apology for returning to them several times during the course of this book.

Score 16.1

Score 16.2

The five sonatas *da camera* are technically easier than the six sonatas *da chiesa* (Corelli himself does not use these titles) that make up Part One, with virtually no chordal writing or virtuosic passages to tax the performer; one may even wonder whether they could have been written partly with a didactic purpose in mind.

At first sight, this sonata may appear simple and straightforward; but as we investigate further it will reveal complexities we never suspected, raising many crucial and fundamental issues. Before we approach the sonata itself, however, I propose to discuss key questions concerning the nature and process of that we know of as "interpretation."

Interpretation: A Question of Taste?

As a veteran teacher of both the modern and the Baroque violin, I have come to realize how much of my work has to do with helping students think clearly and discerningly about what is printed on the page of even the most basic piece of music. The twin acts of perception and processing of the musical text form the key to two questions many advanced students seem never seriously to have considered:

1. What do we mean by 'interpretation'?
2. What does the process of interpretation actually involve?

One frequently heard answer to the first question relegates the process of interpretation to almost a mere matter of taste. Such an answer goes something like this: "Interpretation is the way *I* feel about the music." I would describe that definition as egocentric, not in a judgmental sense, I hasten to add, but because it highlights the purely subjective element of interpretation, placing the 'I' at the center of the process. Although that 'I' is inevitably a major factor, and to an extent an immovable one, it is by no means the only one.

A more objective definition, one similar to what an actor might offer in interpreting the role of Hamlet, for example, goes like this.

"First and foremost, I need to study the text in great detail. This will raise many questions—for example, the meaning, at the turn of the seventeenth century, of words that might have fallen into disuse or changed meaning since Shakespeare wrote them. I will begin to build up my understanding of what each phrase means, how it contributes to the significance of the speech, and the impact of the speech on the other characters. Gradually, the character and psychology of Hamlet will reveal itself to me; the deeper I immerse myself in his words, the more I will understand his feelings at any given moment, his fears and torments, his humor and his indecisive mindset. Of course, I have to do similar work with the lines of the other characters in the play, especially as they relate to mine."

"In the next stage of my interpretive journey, I will have to practice speaking each fragment of the speech, so that the meanings I have discovered can be successfully communicated to the audience through the undulating quality of my voice, the rhythm of the words, the poignancy of the silences, and the movements of my body, face, and eyes. I have to learn to feel as Hamlet feels, as if I myself am metamorphosing into Hamlet."

Thus, the process of interpretation for the actor is more about identifying with his character and laying aside, to the extent that it is possible, his own 'I.' This is a radically different definition from the subjective one quoted above. Oscar Wilde was unequivocal in endorsing our actor's view of the artist's role. In the second sentence of his *The Picture of Dorian Grey* he writes: *"To reveal art and conceal the artist is art's aim."*

> Our mission is not to express ourselves but to reveal the music.

For the musician too, the starting point of the interpretative process involves a detailed observation and analysis of the text, on the basis of which evidence musical decisions can legitimately be made. The "Observations" sections in this book seek to do just that, demonstrating how much detail is embedded in the text and how a thorough examination of this detail will reveal the clues that will allow us faithfully to *"reveal art."*

Working through the intricate details of the "Observations" sections will be a painstaking but enriching task, demanding from the student at least as much patience as the author needed to write them. To fortify us in our task, let us adopt the following mantra:

The Starting-Point of Interpretation Is Observation.

Editions or Facsimiles?

The process of interpretation and those freedoms that our colleagues of yesteryear enjoyed form part of the legacy with which we are now entrusted. Some editions add so many instructions to the composer's original that there is little left for the performer to do other than blindly follow the editor's preferences. Such editions deprive the musician of the essence of interpretation, that of observing exactly what the composer wrote and, using intelligence, information, and imagination, bringing those symbols on the page into the world of sound. Let us avoid the use of such editions: most music in our repertoire is now available either in facsimile or in faithful transcriptions by responsible historically informed editors.

Instrumentation in Corelli's op. 5 Sonatas

One striking feature of the Preludio, in common with many other movements of these sonatas, is the equality of parts, the bass almost entirely imitating the violin part. Although the bass is figured, the movement is ideally suited to be played by a violin and a cello without a harpsichord, as indicated on Corelli's title page: "Sonate a Violino e Violone o Cimbalo" (sonatas for violin and violone *or* harpsichord.)

Of the other movements, only the Giga contains a significant amount of material shared by both parts. In the Corrente, which has much in common with the 'Moto Perpetuo' movements of Sonatas 1–4 and Sonata 6, the violin predominates. In the Sarabanda too, the bass, though arguably equal in expression to the violin part, nevertheless has more of a supportive role.

We may remind ourselves that, by contrast, the instrumentation of the Albinoni sonata movement we examined in Lesson 13 was marked as "violino, violone e cembalo" (violin, cello *and* harpsichord). In both Corelli's op. 1 and op. 3 sets of Trio Sonatas, the title page reads "Sonatas for Two Violins, and Violone or Archlute, with a Bass for the Organ."

Corelli does not indicate a preference for the "violone" over the harpsichord out of some kind of expediency. Sonatas for violin and a bass string instrument were in vogue during the latter part of the seventeenth century. Thus Giovanni Maria Bononcini, in his *Arie . . . a violino e violone o spinetta* (1671) insists that *"one should bear in mind that the violone will produce a better effect than the spinet since the basses are more appropriate to the former than to the latter instrument."*[1]

So which instrument is meant by "violone"? David Watkin makes a convincing case for the cello, an instrument that, as Bach was shortly to prove, was *"a self-accompanying chordal instrument capable both of cleverly hinting at, and of realizing fully, the complex harmonies and polyphonic textures of his music."* This argument certainly reconciles the instrumentation question with the existence of the figured bass. *"Furthermore,"* Watkin adds, *"Bach did not write his unaccompanied works for cello . . . in a vacuum. A school of unaccompanied*

157

writing for this 'single-line bass instrument' had sprung up in Northern Italy during the last two decades of the 17th century."[2]

Means of Expression

In Lesson 8 we used this Preludio to heighten our awareness of the emotional impact of the intervals contained within it. As a result, what may have appeared on the surface to be a series of disjointed and angular fragments came to be experienced as a fast-flowing stream of vivid and constantly shifting sensations, teeming with emotional information.

This information must now be transformed into sound in order successfully to communicate it to our audience. The technical devices required to realize our musical intentions are the following:

1. A constant fluctuation of dynamics, colors, and nuances. This is achieved by varying the bow pressure, bow speed, point of contact, and location along the bow where the desired sound is to be found.
2. A wide variety of articulations.
3. The stressing of important notes.
4. The understating of less important notes.
5. The lengthening or shortening of notes according to their importance.
6. Rhythmic subtlety and flexibility in notes of equal value.
7. The attribution of consonants to certain notes and vowels to others.
8. The inner shape of notes (crescendos, decrescendos or both).

Choosing a Convincing Tempo

The opening movements of Corelli's chamber sonatas are all marked "Preludio." Two are marked "Largo" and two "Adagio": the one under consideration in this lesson, marked "Vivace," is thus the only one that does not conform to the slow–fast–slow–fast pattern. Vivace, we should recall, translates as "lively," a description of character rather than tempo: playing the Prelude too fast risks devaluing the effect of the exhilarant Corrente that follows.

The choice of a convincing tempo can sometimes be made with reference to the sonata as a whole. I am not implying that we should necessarily seek out a direct mathematical proportion between all movements: such decisions are perilous, restrictive, and of dubious historicity for the period under discussion. Certainly, the use of a regular pulse or tactus to provide cohesion to a work was a feature of pre-Baroque music and, as we shall learn in Lesson 27, one that was carried over into the early seventeenth-century sonatas that paved the way for the genius of Corelli to emerge.

But the idea that greater unity in this short four-movement sonata will be achieved by maintaining a consistent pulse is certainly worth exploring. Setting our metronome to around 54 beats per minute as a basic tactus, the four movements would thus be played as follows:

1. Preludio: tactus = one half bar.

2. Corrente: tactus = one bar.
3. Sarabanda: tactus = one quarter note.
4. Giga: tactus = one bar.

ॐ ॐ ॐ

Preludio

The title Preludio defines this movement as an introduction to the three dances that follow, the Corrente, Sarabanda, and Giga. All Corelli's op. 5 chamber sonatas, except "Follia," follow this pattern. Sonata 11 is a little different, having a Preludio at the start and a movement entitled Gavotte at the end, but no other dance titles.

It is interesting to observe that J. S. Bach's F Major Partita, which we shall explore at the end of this book, also consists of a suite of dances introduced by a Preludio: since this word is the only Italian title in that Partita, we may infer that Bach, writing not long after, was following the Corellian example.

We observe first that there are no dynamic markings in the entire movement: we shall therefore have to glean the dynamics from within the text. This is normal practice in the interpretation of works from the Baroque period—composers generally mark dynamics only when they want an effect that could be considered unpredictable. For example, at the end of both halves of the Giga movement of this sonata, Corelli writes *piano;* if he had not written this, it probably would not have occurred to us to end softly.

We have already remarked on the equality of parts in the Preludio. As the bass part 'trails' the violin part, there is a resultant displacement and overlapping of strong beats. We should therefore take care to identify our strong beats, for we cannot assume that they will fall on the first or third beat of a bar. For example, in Bars 8–12 the bass part has stresses on the first and third beats, whereas the violin part, which begins this sequence on the last beat of Bar 7, has its stresses on the second and fourth beats. The first beat of Bar 8 is therefore weak for the violin but strong for the bass. Note that the concept of a strong/weak hierarchy does not imply that a 'strong' beat is necessarily an accented one.

Bars 1–3: the first phrase carries us right through to the start of Bar 3. Within this single graphic arch lie a host of details that must be understood so that their energy may be released, and their meaning expressed. At the same time, their place and importance within the whole must be clear and proportionate.

Notice that, apart from three descending semitones, there is no step-wise motion in this phrase. Indeed, the entire movement is dominated by leaps, suggesting a certain agitation or bustle.

Broadly speaking, the dynamics follow the graphic curve.

Bar 1: the quality of the anacrusis, even if we have chosen to play in a soft or secretive manner, must 'invite' the following sounds, predicting the energy of what is to come.

> An anacrusis does not 'precede' the music: it is *part* of the music.

Avoid accenting the first note, d'. This will prejudice the flow of the musical line, as stresses tend to beget other stresses.

Vary the articulation of the eighth notes, according to your fantasy. Avoid the stereotypes of long/short or heavy/light: they may come in useful on occasion but could also arrest the flow of the music. In any case, we need to shun playing by formulae!

We should be wary of becoming trapped in the illusory safety of a well-practiced spiccato, martelé, or any stroke that sounds like something learned in the abstract—a studied, technical feat with no specific musical application. We are in 1700, a whole century before the categorization of bow strokes. Challenge yourself to ensure that no two notes should sound the same and remember what we learned about the true nature of rhythm: that it is alive and fanciful rather than mechanized or mathematical.

The rising sixth to the syncopated d″ is the most striking event in the phrase and needs careful consideration to express its rhythmic and melodic significance.

> There are two basic categories of syncopations, with various determining factors, including harmony, natural dynamic flow, the behavior of the other part or parts, and the rhythm of dance.
>
> 1. In the first, the syncopated note is weaker than the preceding note, bouncing passively off it or emerging from it in a more *cantabile* way. The strong note may be long or short and the second one sprightly or lyrical. The bowing for this may be down/up, or down/down (almost slurred, with little or no retaking of the bow).
> 2. The syncopated note is stronger than the preceding note, evoking defiance or surprise. In this case, the first note is likely to be shortened and the second accented, although it may also be sustained. The bowing may be down/down with either a small or a larger retake, or it could be up/down (perhaps tucking in an extra up-bow for the first note).

In the case under consideration, stressing and lengthening the f′ would be absurd, so I would choose option 2, shortening the f′ and playing the d″ with another down-bow. Note that the d″ begins over an F in the bass and ends over an E: we must therefore shape it, growing stronger in order to peak at the point of dissonance, for dissonance is emotionally stronger than consonance; furthermore, the syncopation may be seen as a re-energizing of the phrase as it continues its journey toward Bar 3.

According to Georg Muffat, who studied in Rome and who knew Corelli well, referring to him as "the Italian Orpheus," the resolution note, too, must be clear. "*Sincopi and ligature* (slurs)," he writes in the preface to his *Auserlesene Instrumental-Musik*, "one *must rather play forte and staccato, so that which begins the ligatura and that which sounds the dissonance against the other part, as well as that which resolves it are not weakened by timid and languid bows.*"[3]

Certainly, the c″♯ here cannot be "*timid and languid.*" True, it is a resolution and should therefore be weaker than the d″, but even if it does not have the energy of the original anacrusis, it must have enough personality to lead us convincingly into the next bar.

Bar 2: the third note (e″) creates a dissonance with the bass. We can lengthen it to make it more expressive; in that case, to avoid ungainliness, we need also to lengthen the previous note a little.

The length of the first five notes of Bar 2 will therefore be longer than those in Bar 1, enhancing the sense of flow through the long phrase.

The bass, having imitated the violin, now sinks step-wise toward the cadence. This further suggests a smoother bow stroke on the part of the cellist to which the violin needs to adapt.

Bar 3: the harmony, having moved from D minor to G minor in Bar 2, now reaches A major. As both parts have descended chromatically into the bar, the cadence is weak. We should therefore take care to diminuendo and not to accentuate the c″♯. For the bass line, however, having dropped more than an octave, the start of this bar feels as much like a new beginning as the ending of a phrase.

Bars 3 and 4: the two parts of the sequence feel quite distinct, so they should be expressed with different sounds. The first part starts in D minor and cadences in G minor, whereas the second one goes from C major to F major. Try leading into Bar 4 with an earnest crescendo, playing the rest of the bar rather more simply and nonchalantly, with no corresponding crescendo into Bar 5.

The two sixteenth notes in Bar 4 merely form an ornamented version of the single eighth note anacrusis (a″) in Bar 3. They could be played lightly, with the rhythm gently 'swung,' the g″ longer than the f″.

Bars 5–6: each part divides into two, an upper and a lower.

- The two higher notes are more assertive than the lower ones and should be played louder. They could also be long, the second one probably longer than the first.
- The lower ones are reactive and can be put into imaginary parentheses. They can be shorter.
- The rhythm should reflect this perspective: stretch the second assertive note and rush the lower part, while keeping the beat steady.
- In the second half of Bar 6, the violin part breaks this pattern, with single higher (assertive) notes and lower (reactive) notes alternating.

My annotated version below (Figure a) will make this clear.

Figure a
Annotated version of Bars 5–6.

161

At the very end of each line of the facsimile, in both parts, you will notice a symbol that starts as a small "w" on a line or space, before straightening out. This symbol, known in Latin as a "custos," is a cursor, used from the eleventh century onward to help guide the eye from one line to the next and to tell us in advance what the next note will be. In Italian it is called a "guida," in French a "guidon," and in German a "Wächter."

Bar 7: after six bars of intense movement and interest, the section ends with a fairly clichéd cadence in F major. This is to allow the music, and the listener, a moment of rest. A cadential trill may be added to the g″: however, the figured bass indicates (by the numbers 4 and 3) that there are two harmonies under this note. The first includes an f, which is dissonant to it: moreover, owing to the close spacing of the parts here, there is nowhere for the continuo player to play the f other than just under the violin's g′.

I would therefore start my trill on the g′ itself, not on the upper note, enforcing, rather than obscuring, the dissonance. For the second chord, the dissonant f′ resolves to an e′ (see Figure b).

Figure b

Bar 7, Beats 2–3.

Do not be in a hurry to start the next phrase: after the f′, do what is natural to any singer or actor—breathe! Notice that the bass here is inactive, allowing you the freedom to take the time necessary to distinguish the new phrase from the old.

Notice that instead of being four eighth notes behind the top voice, as at the beginning, the bass is now only two eighth notes behind. The effect is an intensification of the interplay between the two parts.

Bars 7–12: there are five fragments here, separated by eighth note rests. For each fragment or motive, ask yourself the following questions:

1. What is the structure, meaning, and character of this fragment?
2. What can I do to ensure it does not have the same feel as the others?
3. How can I make it sound more characterful?
4. Which technical means should I use to express the meaning in sound?

Let me give sample answers to these questions.

Fragment 1, Bars 7–8

There is an overall rise of a perfect fifth from the first note to the last, suggesting exaltation or joy. Internally, the fragment consists of two ascending fourths separated by an ornamented descending minor third.

The first of the sixteenth notes is dissonant with the bass. The rhythm has an energetic feel to it.

This fragment is unique in that the overall direction is upward, so its character is the most optimistic. The others differ in tessitura, direction, energy, and in rhythm.

Adding a slur to the sixteenth notes could make the fragment sound quite banal. To avoid this, and to add swagger to the fragment, I will stretch the preceding eighth note (f″) a little, and then bunch the sixteenth notes together.

In addition, instead of playing the two d″s at the start of Bar 8 equally, I shall phrase them, shortening the first and re-energizing the second so that it has the character of a vigorous pickup to the following g″. Both d″s will be played up-bow.

This demands much energy in the bow: I shall take it off the string after the first note (c′) and hit the string from the air on the second. I shall also take the bow slightly off the string between the two d″s in Bar 8. I will not play the final note (g″) with too fast a bow: that could produce a wild accent. Instead, I will make the sound more assertive by shaping it with a mini Messa di voce.

Fragment 2, Bars 8–9

The overall pitch interval here is a descending second (g′ –f′), indicating a contrasting response to the previous fragment, with a less positive energy. Notice that the rhythm, too, is different from that of the previous fragment.

The dynamic scheme of the first two fragments combined forms a Messa di voce shape. Diminishing activity in the bow and a diminuendo in Bar 9 will achieve this.

The final note, f′, needs little, if any, energy or shape.

Fragment 3, Bars 9–10

The rhythm and shape are the same as the previous fragment, but the tessitura has sunk further. Whereas the three last notes of Bar 8 were in C major, described by theorists of the time as a joyful tonality, those in Bar 9 are in G minor, a sadder, sweeter key. I would therefore soften the articulation here, using a slightly longer, gentler stroke.

Instead of a descending perfect fifth over the bar line into Bar 10, we have a diminished fifth, an interval with an altogether different feel. The absence of an open string will automatically dampen the sound and lower the energy level and dynamic.

Fragment 4, Bars 10-11

This fragment stands out as defying the overall downward trend. The tessitura has risen dramatically, suggesting a more optimistic, lyrical sound, achieved by a broader, singing bow-stroke at a higher dynamic level. The disappearance of the usual sixteenth notes will facilitate this more sweeping feel.

Fragment 5, Bars 11–12

Bar 11: the bass line ceases to imitate the violin, its two descending diminished fifths defying the violin's optimism and drawing the music toward an eerie end to the first half.

Bar 12: the descending, chromatic tenths and long note values arrest the hitherto busy movement. A slight slowing up and the delaying of the second note will enhance the effect of this bar.

I would choose not to disturb the effect of this bar with a cadential trill, but if you opt for one (possibly only on the repeat?) it should start on the upper note, e'.

Take a breath before continuing, especially on the repeat time.

ক্ত ক্ত ক্ত

Second Half

If the rhythm in the first half of the Preludio has been simple and symmetrical, in the second half it is more complex and often intentionally ambiguous. Indeed, much of it seems to be in triple time: try beating in three from the beginning of Bar 13 to the middle of Bar 15 in the violin part, and you will see what I mean. For the bass part, which continues to imitate the violin, the same feeling of triple time starts from Beat 2 of Bar 13.

This is also true later on: taking Beat 4 of Bar 18 as our downbeat, we can comfortably beat three in a bar all the way to the middle of Bar 22. The slurs in Bars 21 and 22 reinforce the triple feel, although one could postulate that, by stressing the start of each slur, a time signature of $\frac{6}{8}$ is implied here!

Much of this additional rhythmic interest will be audible with little or no extra effort on our part, but some subtle highlighting of these rhythmic intricacies may be called for.

> There is often a fine line between clarifying a feature of the music and pointing it out in too emphatic a manner. We should be wary of playing as if our prime purpose is to 'educate' our audience, making them fully aware of every musical decision we make. When my students do this, I tell them: "Don't preach, express!"

Bar 13: we need to breathe before proceeding, as the rise in tessitura and the new energy of the music require time. Note the tenor clef in the bass, facilitating this higher tessitura. (As violinists, we can employ a cunning ruse to help us play in this clef: read it as a treble clef while transposing down one note.)

Bars 13–17: a predominant feature of these bars is the interval of the rising fourth, recalling perhaps the opening two notes of the piece. Among the eight occurrences of this interval in each voice, there is a variety of qualities and functions, some assertive, others more hesitant, requiring diverse attacks, gestures, and bow speeds. This applies to the first of the two notes as well as to the second.

As a rough guide, we can relate the quality of each rising fourth to its tessitura: Bar 13: the e″ to a″ fourth is stronger than the d″ to g″ one at the end of the bar and has a greater sense of forward motion. Contrasting gestures of the bow arm are necessary to achieve this difference: give the former a more positive, assertive gesture, using more bow and shaping the a″ clearly (<>); the g″, having less personality, suggests a more passive gesture, using less bow and minimal shape.

The lower notes of each rising fourth also have correspondingly differing energies: the anacrusis (e″) to Bar 13 is confident and strongly articulated, whereas the d″ has barely any discernible sense of anacrusis at all.

Bar 14: the three notes after the tie (g″–e″) emerge from the relatively passive gesture at the end of Bar 13. They are thus of little significance and can be played within a diminuendo. Shortening the e″ will enable you to give more impetus to the following g″, a longer anacrusis that grows in dynamic as it soars toward the c‴, the highest and most powerfully lyrical note of the movement. Crescendo through it, being careful not to use too fast a bow, and play the following eighth note equally lyrically, leading into Bar 15.

To reach the c‴ we can shift into second position while playing the open string. To return to the f″ in Bar 15 we can either stretch the first finger back and then normalize the hand position, or we can shift the whole hand back to the first position before normalizing.

Alternatively, we can stretch up to the c″, leaving the thumb behind in the first position until we normalize the hand while playing the f″ in Bar 15. Practice both methods before deciding which one works best for you, but do avoid the temptation to use the third position: that would be far too fussy. If you are one of the many violinists fearful of the second position, now is the time to face up to the challenge and overcome that fear!

Bar 15 begins by continuing the passionate lyricism of the previous bar. Shape the f″ (<>) but cut it a little short to give clarity to the next anacrusis (d″) that, though less powerful, can still be lyrical as it leads into a beautifully shaped g″ at the end of the bar.

Bar 16: a gradual diminuendo toward the middle of this bar is implied by the relatively static nature of the music between the two f″s in Bars 15 and 16. This diminuendo is also necessary to achieve the crescendo throughout Bar 17 implied by the rising sequence of rising fourths.

The c″ in Bar 16 is the least obvious anacrusis in the sequence. We could make it more anacrusis-like, but as this is a low point it is unnecessary to do so: it would anyway sound contrived and could detract from the d″ anacrusis at the end of the bar that starts the crescendo to the next high point in Bar 18.

Bar 17: the energy of this bar is intensified by both anacruses being formed of two sixteenth notes instead of a single eighth note.

Bar 18: the first bass note, an E♮, is the only dissonant note we have had under the second note of any of our rising fourths. It forms a diminished fifth with the violin's b″♭ and signals both the climax and the impending end of the section.

We expect to cadence in F major but Corelli, raising the bass by a major second (B♭–C) takes us first to a second inversion F-major chord and then, keeping the same bass note, on to C major. The slur in the violin part serves to guide us firmly toward this unexpected event. We could enhance this effect with a diminuendo and by slowing up a little toward the middle of the bar.

Play Beat 4 softly and a little late, although not without energy, for it heralds the start of two bars of crescendo.

Bars 18–21: there is another sequence of rising fourths here; in Bar 19 we have a′–d″ and in Bar 20 we have b′–e″, but in each of these cases Corelli adds a minor third to take on the role of anacrusis. This device will serve to highlight the climactic rising fourth into Bar 21. Shorten the c″♯ in Bar 20 and lengthen the e′ that follows, so as to arrive at the a″ in Bar 21 with a strong and positive gesture.

There are two further rising fourths: one into Beat 4 of Bar 21 and the other into Beat 3 of Bar 22. As a result of the slurs, however, these two do not have the quality of clear anacruses.

Bars 21–23: with the ambiguous feeling of triple versus compound time mentioned earlier and the sweeping legato bow strokes, the mood here contrasts with the tightness and intricacy of the detached strokes that have hitherto been a dominant feature. These slurs are the only real ones in the movement, so we must make the most of them. With the descending tessitura, the music subsides and the sound becomes darker.

Bars 23–24: the rhythmic element is very strong here, in both parts. The chromatic descent in the violin part adds to the drama. Mark the rhythm with high-energy bow strokes. Put an extra down-bow on the first beat of Bar 24 and add a trill, starting on the note itself (d″). Hear the d″ clearly before beginning the trill and cease to trill on the third eighth note beat of the bar.

જ઼ જ઼ જ઼

In Exercise 22, Lesson 8, we practiced manipulating our feelings and we observed the ways in which these self-imposed shifting emotions impacted the sound we made while playing just a few random notes.

Following our meticulous examination of Corelli's Preludio, I propose, as a welcome catharsis, carrying out a similar experiment with the notes of this movement (Exercise 79). First, we will imbue ourselves with one of the emotions listed in the exercise and then we will play the whole movement while feeling that emotion.

Second, we will speculate on which emotions the music itself suggests. We could mark our parts with as many emotions as we can identify before playing through the movement. At first, we may need to hesitate when we arrive at a new emotional point in order to give ourselves time to adapt, to feel that emotion; later, we should feel confident enough to switch emotions without stopping.

Exercise 79: Hearing the same music through different emotional filters; identifying appropriate emotions (affects) and practicing the transitions between them

The concept that specific tonalities relate to specific feelings is one expressed by many writers during the Baroque period. To describe the key of this sonata, D minor, Jean Rousseau (1691) and Marc-Antoine Charpentier (1692) both use the word "serious."

Charpentier and Johann Mattheson ascribe to it feelings of piety, the latter adding "doubt, calm and contentment" as well as "grand and agreeable feelings." Jean-Philippe Rameau (1722) considers the key "sweet and tender."[4]

1. Feel each affect mentioned above and investigate how this feeling changes the way you play the Preludio. Before playing, you may find it helpful to imagine the sound, to hear it in your inner ear.

Just as looking at an object through different colored glasses changes the way we see that object, so hearing the music through a variety of emotional filters will reveal to us different aspects of it. This will impact tempo, sound, dynamics, articulation, etc., and will unlock different elements contained within the music, enhancing our understanding and appreciation of it.

2. Take each phrase of the Preludio in turn and investigate how experiencing each of the following affects alters the way you play it. To do this, you will need to immerse yourself in each affect in turn, activating the appropriate emotional button on your 'Keypad of Affects,' just as actors are trained to do.
   • Seriousness
   • Piety
   • Doubt
   • Contentment
   • Grandeur
   • Agreeable feelings
   • Tenderness
   • Anger
   • Excited apprehension
3. Finally, take time to identify the emotions you associate with the Preludio on a bar-by-bar basis: you may wish to jot these down on your score. When you have done that, activate each of those emotions on your Emotional Keypad as you come to them. You may need to pause before each change of emotion to give yourself time to adjust your feelings, but you should also practice the myriad transitions without stopping.

Afterthought: What Happens Within

Reinforcing the bond between the inner artist and the physical world of movements and sensations known by the collective noun "technique" is a task to which we will constantly return. Many so-called technical problems encountered in the execution of a phrase can be sidestepped and overcome if the artistic intention is clear and that bond is healthy. Seeking to analyze what is physically wrong may not be the correct approach if the true fault lies deeper. I do not refer here to basic technical faults such as raised shoulders, stiff wrists, or faulty movements of the fingers of the left hand, but rather to the means of executing a phrase, a gesture, a healthy variety of articulations, etc. Such tasks depend on our imagination and inner artistry being allowed to permeate freely into the physical body and from there to pass unimpeded into the sound.

Notes

1. Allsop, *Arcangelo Corelli: "New Orpheus of Our Times,"* pp. 120–21.
2. David Watkin, "Corelli's op. 5 sonatas: 'Violino e violone o cimbalo?'" *Early Music* 24, no. 4 (November 1, 1996): 645–63.
3. Quoted in Allsop, *Arcangelo Corelli: "New Orpheus of Our Times,"* p. 37.
4. Tarling, *BSP*, p. 7.

Lesson 17

Corelli: Sonata, op. 5, no. 7

Corrente

The "corrente" (the word means "running") was originally a dance symbolizing courtship, in which the dancers zigzagged swiftly around each other. Its French counterpart, the courante, was rhythmically more sophisticated and developed into a slower, graceful, and more majestic dance.

While smooth, legato lines came to be considered an ideal of the romantic aesthetic, the interest and excitement achieved by constantly changing note patterns and intricate string crossings was a hallmark of eighteenth-century writing for the violin. Remaining in the first position (known in Italian as the "luogo naturale," the "natural place") would have been the optimal way to exploit such patterns to maximum effect. Staying in the first position also allows the violin to resonate more freely, avoiding the more muffled sounds produced by moving higher up the fingerboard, especially on the D and G strings.

Although changing positions to avoid unwanted differences in timbre, especially in *cantabile* passages, is encouraged in the sources, we should refrain from attempting to iron out string-crossing patterns that are idiomatic of a polyphonic writing style: on the contrary, rather than thinking of them as technical challenges, we should seek to realize their expressive potential.

We may think of each string as having its own distinct voice, somewhat like a soprano-alto-tenor-bass choir. That is why the strings were given individual names, some of which are still in use today. In Italian, the E was known as the *cantino,* the little singing string, while the A was the *canto*; the D was the *tenore* and the G the *basso*. In French the E was the *chanterelle,* while the G was the *bourdon*. In German, the E was known as the *Sangseite,* or "song-string."

In writing for their instrument, the violinist-composers of the time knew how to relate technique to emotion: a languid melody would be more likely to proceed step by step with occasional easily negotiable larger intervals. A series of extreme string crossings would be seen as formulae implying unrest or struggle, the effect enhanced by an inevitable element of rhythmic instability.

The interplay of timbre, articulation, dynamics, perspective, and rhythm meant that string-crossing patterns were a cherished resource of infinite fascination. The modern ideal of imperceptible changes of bow and inaudible string crossings, in pursuit of which students spend many long years of toil would, I believe, have surprised and bemused Corelli and his contemporaries.

ೞ ೞ ೞ

Observations

Bar 1: the anacrusis, a common feature of the Corrente, serves to launch the music forward. The two first notes thus form a single unit, or gesture, as opposed to two activities. To understand the difference, sing the word "away" as opposed to the words "stand still."

We cannot perfect this gesture without first deciding how to continue, for in our minds this 'launching' should take us right through to the perfect cadence in Bar 3. If there were three quarter notes in the bass in Bar 1, we would need immediately to slot into the rhythmic flow. But instead, Corelli writes a half note, giving the music a sense of rhythmic suspension. It is as if our first note in Bar 1 flies timelessly through the air before being gathered up by the bass at the end of the bar. Practically, we can think of it as a Messa di voce, with the f′ coming just before the end of the decrescendo.

Bar 2 is an example of the kind of string-crossing pattern mentioned above. Exercise 80 is designed to help you deconstruct it, perceiving and highlighting the different voices so as to make the bar as interesting as possible to your audience.

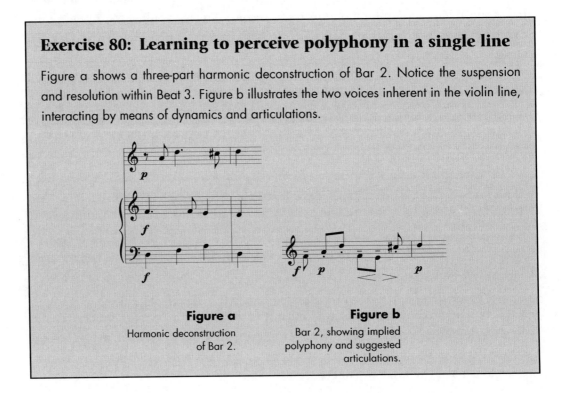

Exercise 80: Learning to perceive polyphony in a single line

Figure a shows a three-part harmonic deconstruction of Bar 2. Notice the suspension and resolution within Beat 3. Figure b illustrates the two voices inherent in the violin line, interacting by means of dynamics and articulations.

Figure a
Harmonic deconstruction of Bar 2.

Figure b
Bar 2, showing implied polyphony and suggested articulations.

1. Practice Figure b slowly, exaggerating articulations and dynamics.
2. Gradually speed up, until you reach your chosen tempo. You will lose many of the exaggerated features, but something of the 'three-dimensional' approach will still remain.
3. Wearing your newly acquired 'three-dimensional glasses,' deconstruct other bars in the movement, extracting from them the maximum interest and expression.

Bars 3–8: the first bass notes of each bar move downward in a stepwise motion, from a D in Bar 3 to a low F in Bar 8. We see a corresponding downward movement from d″ to a′ in the violin part, starting in Bar 3. This suggests a diminishing intensity over these bars, involving at least an element of diminuendo.

Within that diminuendo it is tempting, looking at the violin part alone, to suggest a possible hierarchy of strong and weak bars. Some may see Bars 3, 5, and 7 as weak, with the three eighth notes at the end of them leading into the following bars, making those bars stronger.

Others might prefer to make Bars 5 and 7 strong, which means that Bar 8 will be weak, a convenient situation because Bar 8 is also the start of an upward sequence with an implied crescendo toward Bar 12. It all depends, apparently, on how we see it.

Such decisions are rarely arbitrary: both proposed phrasings are based on the evidence of a single line, that of the violin, and we have already discussed the perils of taking such decisions. A close examination of the harmony will enlighten the single-line phrasemaker.

The harmony in Bar 3 is D minor; but at the start of each subsequent bar within our diminuendo there is a seventh chord, a dissonance that resolves on the second beat. This progression of 7 to 6 chords over a descending bass is one of the devices that Corelli's pupil, Francesco Gasparini, lists in his treatise *L'armonico pratico al cimbalo* (1708) as being a standard harmonic progression in Corelli's music.[1]

Figure c shows a realization of the harmony in Bars 3–8 by Antonio Tonelli (1686-1765). [2] Play the progression slowly on a keyboard to savor the dissonances and their resolutions to the full.

Figure c
Harmonic realization of Bars 3-8 by Antonio Tonelli (1686–1765).

Such strong, emotive dissonances at the start of every bar must lead us to rethink the phrasing, for the strong/weak hierarchy we postured above is at least partially flawed; yet it would be just as wrong to accent each bar.

What options do we have, then, to add fluidity to these bars, to give them shape and direction within the diminuendo we spoke of? My solution would be to stretch the first notes of Bars 4 and 6 a little, placing a barely audible comma after them, but without any clearly discernible accents. This will help create the impression of two-bar mini-phrases, as well as giving a charming lilt to the musical line.

Bars 5 and 7: executing the string crossings to and from the low notes requires some time. Corelli knew this, and he also knew that the rhythmic and dynamic inflections thus created would add interest to these bars. The stepwise notes in Bars 3, 5, and 7, on the other hand, can be smoother, a lyrical contrast to the leaping, more erratic formulae that prevail.

Bars 8–9: the ninth chords have their own poignancy, so a longer, more expressive bow stroke on the first note of these bars is appropriate. Lengthening a note in order to accentuate it, as we have already observed, is a common expressive device, known as an agogic accent. The speeding up of subsequent notes in order to preserve the overall pulse provides further rhythmical interest and flexibility to these bars.

Bar 10: the stepwise motion suggests a smoother, more cantabile bow stroke.

Bars 10–12: we can either crescendo right through to the start of Bar 12, or we can see the start of Bar 11 as the climax point, with a subsequent diminuendo into Bar 12. The silent bass at the start of Bar 12 could be said to vindicate the second option.

Bar 11: playing six equal notes will sound very dull. We can consider the g″s to be a mere ornamentation of the main note (f″) and for this reason we can play them lighter, perhaps even a little shorter. Whichever dynamic scheme is preferred, the bar should be played with a clear sense of direction.

Bar 12: to clarify the phrasing we can slightly delay the second eighth note. The articulation could be a little shorter than in Bar 10 to give a more 'tiptoe' effect.

Bar 13: an ornamented version of Bar 11, the triplet rhythm serves to relieve us from the constant eighth notes. They can be played in a playful manner, with a light bow and light finger action.

Bars 14–15: delay the second note of Bar 14 and drive through to the strong ninth at the start of Bar 15. The rest of Bar 15 is a more passive response to the assertive nature of Bar 14.

Bars 16–17: the rhythm of the bass suggests a hemiola; but on Beat 1 of Bar 17, both the strong harmony and the violin's slur suggest otherwise. Here, the interest lies more in the syncopated cross-rhythms implied by the three descending pairs of notes in the violin, and on their interaction with the hemiola-style rhythm of the bass. Practice the bar in a slower tempo, clarifying the cross-rhythms by accenting the first note of each pair and by articulating between the pairs. At speed, we will lose most of this detail, but an interesting residue will remain.

> Sometimes hemiolas can benefit from being clearly stated; at other times they are best left to speak for themselves or to be allowed to remain shrouded in ambiguity.

Bar 17: although no slur between the f′ and the e′ is marked, adding one can be justified by the notated note values, the $\frac{4}{3}$ harmony and the need to play the chord in Bar 18 on a down-bow.

Bar 18: the chord marks the end of the phrase and should neither be too loud nor sound snatched. Integrate it into the sound of the previous bar, rolling the bow slowly across the strings to produce maximum resonance. For the bass, the start of the bar is more of a new beginning as it strides decisively away from the cadence.

Bars 18–23: the bass initiates a sequence, passing from F to C major, then into G minor with the emotive intervals of Bar 20 and on to D and A minor before reaching E major in Bar 23, its highest note in the entire movement.

In the violin part, there is much step-wise movement now, so a more cantabile bow stroke can be used. We have already risen in tessitura in Bar 18, but as we soar ever higher the sound becomes more passionately lyrical.

Bars 22–23: there are a few possible fingerings for this passage.

1. Move the hand into the second position on the a″ at the start of Bar 22, leaving the thumb behind. Bring the hand back while playing the first open E string in Bar 23.
2. If your hand is too small for this or you cannot feel comfortable, shift the whole hand up to the a″. You can then shift the second finger down to the g″♯ at the start of Bar 23 and normalize the hand position during the first open E string.

   Alternatively or you can play the g″♯ with a first finger, catching the d″ with your third finger and normalizing the hand while playing the second open E string of the bar.
3. Stay in the first position the whole time, stretching your fourth finger up to the c‴ and immediately bringing it back for the b″.

Bars 23–26: to distinguish the lower, moving voice from the higher, static one, play these bars across two strings. The dynamic balance must favor the more interesting part, so highlight the lower part and lighten the bow on the open E String. Use your wrist for the string crossings.

The chromatically descending bass line from Bar 24 onward could indicate a diminuendo, but we clearly need the hemiola in Bars 27 and 28, with its jubilant double stops over a dancing bass line, to be climactic. It could therefore be more convincing if we decrescendo in Bar 23 to start Bar 24 a little less, and then crescendo into Bar 27.

Within this overall crescendo there is also an internal phrasing: you can see this phrasing most clearly in the bass, where the middle note of each bar appears to be the weakest.

The third eighth note of the violin part in Bars 23, 24 and 25 is always dissonant to the bass. We need to highlight this interesting second beat with a playful nudge of the bow.

Bars 27–28: ask your bass player to shorten the notes, so as to make the hemiola dance more. In Bar 28, add a lower-note trill to the b′, losing the e′ when you stop the trill one eighth note before the a′.

It is often stated that trills in Baroque music must start with an upper note appoggiatura. But an appoggiatura affects the harmony and therefore this 'rule' is not always appropriate. Take as an example Bars 33–34 (Figure d), again realized by Antonio Tonelli, which is the same as Bars 28–29. Here we have a Perfect Cadence with a $\frac{4}{3}$ harmonic progression within the dominant bass note. This means that the harmony contains the root (e) and the fifth (b) but instead of the third there is a fourth (a). The dissonance between the fourth and the fifth is then resolved by the fourth descending to a third (g sharp). An upper note (c) trill would confuse the harmony and negate the dissonance, so a lower note trill is to be preferred.

Figure d

Bars 33–34, realization by Antonio Tonelli.

Bars 27–29: it is not clear whether the *piano* marking, clearly written over the second bass note in Bar 29, implies a diminuendo from Bar 27, or whether we should maintain the *forte* until Bar 29 and change to *piano* on the second beat. There is no reason to doubt the accuracy of the printer, for Corelli himself oversaw and must have checked the first edition carefully.

If we adopt the latter solution, how do we explain why the violin does not have a chord at the start of Bar 29, as it does in Bar 34, even though the first half supposedly ends *piano*?

Looking ahead to the corresponding place in the second half (Bars 70–72) we see a unison d' in the violin part, just before the *piano* in Bar 72. Is this unison simply completing the harmony, or does it also indicate a strong first beat? (The last note of the piece also has that unison, but it is *piano*: echoes have to imitate exactly).

My own view is that after the resonant chord in Bar 27, there will be something of a de facto decrescendo toward Bar 29, but not enough to render the *piano* marking redundant.

Ending a section with a *piano* is one of Corelli's hallmarks, so I would resist the temptation to crescendo to another *forte* in Bar 32 and to finish the first half with a loud flourish. Although some crescendo toward Bar 32 is difficult to resist, I would keep it to a minimum and then diminuendo until the end of the section, using shorter bow strokes. The final chord would then be played as a blurred arpeggio, rolling the bow in a feather-light and leisurely manner from string to string as a lute player might, slowing up and lingering on the a' before returning to the fray.

Corrente: Second Half

Bar 35: we are now in A major, a tonality described as "playful and jesting" by Mattheson and "joyful" by Rameau and Charpentier (although Mattheson confusingly adds "lamenting and sad" to these qualities).[3] We are more than an octave higher than we were at the start, and playing an open E string: the feeling is surely one of elation! Note that there is only one harmony in this bar, unlike in Bar 1. The stepwise eighth notes here and in Bars 37 and 39 can be played with a singing bow.

Bars 36, 38, and 40: these bars have two voices, a moving lower one and a static upper one. Imagine these voices played by two hands on a keyboard: the left hand plays the moving part, phrasing toward the following bar, while the right hand touches the upper notes more lightly, creating a perspective between the interesting and the more functional.

Remember that although sequences are visually similar, each step is quite distinct emotionally. Thus Bar 36 (A major), Bar 38 (G major) and Bar 40 (F major) have particular emotional flavors within their alphabetic and dynamic descent.

Bars 36–41: the bass sequence takes a surprising turn in Bar 41, a B♭ usurping the place of the expected B♮. Bar 41 is also a low point dynamically, a distinct change in the figuration in both parts forming a new sequence that crescendos to Bar 45. A slight slowing up and diminuendo in Bar 40 will serve to highlight this notable turning point.

Bars 41–44: the gear change to triplets adds excitement and vitality to the music. Start softly but with high-energy bow strokes; each change of bow has a perceptible electric charge to it. As you crescendo, broaden out the stroke so it becomes more lyrical.

Bars 44–48: if you prefer the effect of crossing strings in Bars 46–47, shift into the third position in Bar 45. The time taken for this shift will provide the desired effect of a small comma before the new section.

Alternatively, if your hand permits it, this entire passage could be played in the first position by extending the fourth finger. If this is not feasible, shift up to the second position on the first note of Bar 44, then either stretch the first finger down for the f″s in Bar 47 or play that bar over two strings. Whatever your fingering, take advantage of the open E string in Bar 48 to return to the first position and normalize your hand.

Bars 48–49: we could regard these bars as a hemiola. However, the strong, dissonant $\frac{7}{5}$ harmony at the start of Bar 49, coming after the relatively weak F major harmony at the end of the previous bar, as well as the bowing pattern, suggests that the supposed hemiola is ambiguous and demands no special treatment on our part. Contrast these bars with Bars 70–71: here, the bass suggests that the strong beats are on the first and third beats of Bar 70 and the second beat of Bar 71, while the first beat of Bar 71 is weak. The bowing pattern confirms this hierarchy.

Bar 49: because of the $\frac{4}{3}$ harmony (see above) the trill in Beat 2 should start on the lower note (g″).

Bars 50–59: because of the predominantly stepwise motion and the lyrical nature of the music, as well as the rise in tessitura (the d‴ in Bar 51 being the highest note in the entire sonata) a more singing bow stroke is called for. Investigate the location along the bow where this is most naturally to be found.

Bars 52–53: another ambiguous hemiola. The $\frac{7}{5}$ harmony and the slur in Bar 53 make the start of that bar strong. Add a lower-note trill to the a″.

Bars 55, 57, and 59: our first notes are all dissonant, inviting heartfelt and lyrical Messas di voce. In the middle of these bars, the bass rises up a sixth to prolong this dissonant harmony. Ask your bass player not to take time to reach these notes, but rather to play them slightly early and then to hover on them, something akin to the famous anticipated second beat of an authentic Viennese Waltz.

If we react quickly to the early bass notes on Beat 2, we will have more time to enjoy these dissonances by slightly elongating the first of our three eighth notes, using a singing bow.

Bars 56, 58, and 60 are weak, which is why the bass cuts out on the first beats. However, they have a wistful quality, suggesting a tender, pastel sound, achieved with a minimum of bow pressure. We can elongate the first note of each bar and then hurry the remaining notes, but take care not to make each bar irregular in the same way: the irregular should not be allowed to become regular!

Bars 60–66: if the sequence from Bars 54–59 has implied something of a diminuendo (and we should certainly ease gently into Bar 60) the change from stepwise motion to an arpeggiated figuration in this new sequence suggests a change in affect from the lyrical to something more turbulent. This is emphasized by the strong second beats in the bass, coinciding with our highest notes. We can achieve this sense of turbulence by using a shorter, irregular bow stroke with plenty of flexibility in the rhythm.

Bars 67–72: the crescendo that has led us from Bar 60 to an expected climax in Bar 67 is frustrated at the last moment by the sudden drop in tessitura, a shorter version of the same sequence starting again an octave lower. Notice that the bass has returned to same tessitura as in Bar 60: this compression of parts dulls the sound for a while, but release comes with the upward gesture of the seventh chord in Bar 70, with its augmented fourth in the upper notes. Continue this *forte* until the start of Bar 72.

Bars 70–74: notice that the articulation of the hemiolas is different from that of Bars 27, 32, and 48. Put lower-note trills on the second beats of Bars 71 and the penultimate bar.

❧ ❧ ❧

We may have spent many hours of our lives struggling to achieve the perfect bow control, one that allows us to perform many functions within a precise, metronomic discipline. Such control is important, for we must indeed be masters and mistresses of the bow: however, in music of this kind, a flexible rhythm within a mostly steady pulse is, as we have learned, one of the means of bringing the music to life. Too much rigidity in the rhythm will impede expression and turn a lively and interesting movement into a dull exposition of one's technical prowess.

> Learning to play *with* a metronome can be revealing, but learning to play *like* a metronome is fraught with danger.

Exercise 81 is more like a game, taking rhythmic flexibility to an absurd extreme. I call it "Cheating the Metronome."

Exercise 81: Cheating the metronome

1. Set your metronome to 40 clicks per minute.
2. On an open string, play 4 notes to each bar in strict time.
3. Now play 4 notes completely out of time. You may rush, drag, delay—whatever you like, but there must be only four notes per bar and the first of each four must be in time with the metronome. Do this for about 30 seconds.
4. Repeat 3, but with 6 notes per bar.
5. Set the metronome to your chosen tempo for this movement (it will be somewhere around 60 clicks per minute) and repeat 3 and 4.
6. Play the movement with the metronome, playing as much out of time as you can, but with the first beat of each bar coinciding perfectly with the metronome.

Sarabanda

The *zarabanda* originated in Latin America and was imported into Spain, where it was danced to texts, mostly lewd, accompanied by guitars and castanets. Considered too erotic by the church, it was eventually banned in 1583! It reappeared in Italy in the early 1600s and for much of the seventeenth century remained a fairly fast dance. In France, the slower and more stately 'ballet du cour' version of the dance eventually served as a model for the later sarabandes of J. S. Bach and others. Corelli's *Largo* marking leaves us in no doubt about which category of sarabandes this one belongs to.

There is a widely circulating myth about the sarabande, according to which it has as a hallmark a second beat stronger than the first. While it is true that the second beat does often have a distinct character of its own and occasionally may indeed feel stronger than the first, something one could not say about a minuet, for example, such a characteristic is not mentioned in any source I know of. Aficionados of the obligatory strong second beat even advocate playing the first two beats with down-bows, a bowing similarly not referred to in the sources, although it could be effective on occasions.

The D minor Sarabanda from Bach's second Partita for solo violin, for example, has many bars with a strong first beat and a very distinct, if not stronger, second beat that in theory, for both musical and technical reasons, could be bowed in this way (Figure e).

Figure e

Opening of the Sarabanda from Bach's D Minor Partita, BWV 1004.

But consider one of the most famous vocal sarabandes, the aria "Lascia ch'io pianga, mia cruda sorte" (Let me weep, my cruel fate) from Handel's opera *Rinaldo* (Figure f. The emotional information contained in the second beats of Bars 1, 2, and 4 is far from negligible and is given additional potency by the emptiness of the silences that follow. Yet it is only in the third bar, on the "cru" of "cruda" (cruel) that the second beat actually carries more emotional power than the first.

Figure f

The opening bars of "Lascia qu'io pianga" from Handel's *Rinaldo* (1711).

Corelli's Sarabanda has two halves of eight bars each. Both halves have the same structure, being formed of two four-bar phrases, of which the first may be said to be sub-divided into two two-bar phrases. The movement ends with a hemiola.

It is mainly in the bass that the typical short/long sarabanda rhythm is in evidence: Bars 1, 5, 6, and 7 in the first half and Bars 10, 12, and 13 in the second half all contain this feature. The violin only has it in an ornamented form in Bars 9 and 11: in each of these two bars the second beat is dissonant and may therefore be considered stronger than the consonant first beat.

Observations

Note: Lesson 30 will deal with ornamentation in this movement.

In Baroque music, notes such as those at the end of Bars 2 and 4, in both parts, must not automatically be assumed to be anacruses, up-beats to the following bars. There is an analogy here with poetry, where a weak syllable at the end of a line should not automatically lead into the following line: this could distort both meter and meaning.

Such a note can be seen in one of three ways:

1. A clear anacrusis: one that flows inexorably through to the following bar.
2. A clear ending: one that has no obvious relation to the following bar.
3. An ambiguous ending: one that is technically an ending but nevertheless hints at a feeling of continuity with the following bar.

Here, the diminished fourth interval between Bars 2 and 3 in the bass part makes for an uneasy transition; the third beat of Bar 2 cannot aesthetically be considered an anacrusis. To ensure that it is not artificially manipulated into sounding like one, we can shorten it and place a comma after it. This comma must be present in the violin part too; thus the first four-bar phrase becomes subdivided into two two-bar phrases.

Likewise, the D in the bass in Bar 4 cannot be seen as an anacrusis to Bar 5, so another comma will be needed here. (A comma will also be needed at the end of Bars 10 and 12, for similar reasons.)

Bars 1–2: the direction of the music leans toward Bar 2, but there are two routes to achieving this. Both are valid, so we may consider playing the repeat differently from the first time.

- Option 1 is to crescendo into Bar 2. Bow division is important here: play the first note (a″) in the upper half of the bow, starting in the middle. Play the following two notes on up-bows, each one with its own crescendo and each one longer than the previous one.
- Option 2 is to play the first note with a full sound and diminuendo through the bar. Articulate slightly between the first three notes, without taking the bow off the string. Then, over the bar line, take the bow off the string and internalize what I call a 'silent crescendo,' a welling up of emotion in preparation for the b″ flat that follows (it will help to move the violin toward the bow while this is happening.) The bowing here can be down/up/up or down/up/down with another down at the start of Bar 2.

> The 'silent crescendo' is similar to the illusion a keyboard player might convey when, taking his hands off the keys in the rest after a soft chord, he prepares to play a stronger one.

Bar 2: the build-up of emotion during this 'silent crescendo' is released into the sound of the b″♭, which will have a slow, yearning Messa di voce. Having brought the violin toward the bow, we now help the projection of the sound by raising it and moving it back with a slow, expressive gesture to the left.

As the sound wanes, shift the point of contact away from the bridge and play the a″ as a passive release, with no impulse in the up-bow. Use the comma after the a″ (mentioned above) to take the bow slightly off the string and move toward the middle of the bow.

> The ability to move the violin freely in the opposite direction to the bow is one of the rewards for playing without chinrest or shoulder pad, especially when playing chinless, for it can greatly enhance the sound. However, it is best reserved for special moments: too much movement can distract an audience! Our dignity on stage is part of our rhetoric: as Leopold Mozart (II, § 6) was to put it, "you must not allow [the violin] to turn backward and forward with every stroke, making yourself laughable to the spectators."

If Bars 1–2 may be said to have constituted a forward-leaning statement, Bars 3–4 are by contrast more of a backward-leaning counterstatement. Bar 3: the $^6_5$ chord elicits a stronger emotion than the D minor chord that follows. The f″ therefore starts weakly but grows into the more dissonant $^7_5$ chord. Any temptation to nudge Beat 2 into a mythical Sarabanda-type accent would therefore be misguided.

Bar 4: the e″ is less emotionally potent than was the b″♭ in Bar 2. The bass line, having risen up a fourth into Bar 2, now rises a mere second into Bar 4, indicating a weaker gesture.

Bars 5–8: the second four-bar phrase is unified by a descending bass with its Sarabanda rhythm. A gradual diminuendo is implied.

Bar 5: at first glance, this bar is identical to Bar 1. However, whereas Bar 1 was made up of a single D minor harmony and the second note (f″) was therefore rather passive, the figuring of the second chord here indicates a change of harmony to B♭ major. This f″ is thus more potent and needs a little more texture, achieved by a gentle leaning on the stick.

Bar 6: the C-major seventh chord resolves to an A minor harmony on the second beat. The first chord is therefore more powerful than the second, causing us to squeeze the e″ and lighten the a″. The last note (a′) is heading toward the B♭-major seventh chord at the start of Bar 7, so it can crescendo into the bar line.

Bar 7: the d″ starts strong, with a Messa di voce; it then weakens as the harmony resolves to a G minor chord on the second beat. The c♯, being dissonant to all three notes of this harmony, can be extended so as to tease the ear with this delicious dissonance!

Bar 8: although weak, we still need to keep the sound alive through a discreet Messa di voce.

Sarabanda: Second Half

Bars 9–12 consist of two units of two bars, separated by a faint comma.

Bar 9: note the use of the ♭ symbol as a substitute for the ♮ sign, a common notational feature in this period.

The second chord, D7, may seem more interesting than the first, but the bass line certainly does not suggest that the D is any stronger than either of the F sharps. A gentle nudge of the bow in recognition of the seventh will give the c′ just enough personality, with the final eighth note played as a clear anacrusis.

Bar 10: the figure 4 in the bass indicates that although the harmony is G major, there is a fourth (C) in place of the third (B). The figure 3 with the natural sign indicates that the fourth descends to a third, which is a b♮.

The dissonant start of the bar suggests a strong emotion; a well-shaped, expressive Messa di voce with its climax on Beat 2 (where the bass drops the octave) prolongs the dissonant suspension. This is resolved only when the Messa di voce withers, a gentle up-bow fading out just before the bar line.

Bars 11–12: pictorially and expressively the same as the previous two bars, the lower tessitura implies darker, more intimate thoughts, expressed by a more hushed quality of sound.

Bars 13–14: a steep rise in tessitura in both parts indicates an awakening from these dark thoughts, the music moving forward with fresh resolve through a harmonic progression from D minor to E♭ major in Bar 13 and on to A major in Bar 14.

The notes f″/e″♭/g″/c″♯, possibly representing the sign of the cross, have a particular drama about them. The diminished fifth interval into Bar 14 has a sense of plunging slowly onto the c″♯, rather than hitting it.

Bars 14–15: Corelli ends the movement with a hemiola, clearly discernible in both voices, in which all three long notes contain a Messa di voce. Sink into the string with a slow bow on the first c″ sharp and allow the sound to grow toward the climax in Beat 2 of Bar 15: this note has an expressive trill, starting slowly on the dissonant lower note and speeding up, but only very slightly, before stopping completely before the eighth note.

Be careful not to accent the up-bow eighth notes. The function of the first one may appear to be merely rhythmic, requiring a light bow. However, the passing bass note (G) underneath does complicate the harmony, forming an augmented fourth with the violin: we therefore need to give our note a little more weight.

The second up-bow eighth note leads us to the climax and can be longer and more lyrical, while the third waits for the trill to cease before drawing the movement to a gentle close.

⁓ ⁓ ⁓

Giga

> The word *Giga* appears in Dante's *Paradiso* (xiv.110) where it means some kind of stringed instrument, possibly a fiddle: *"E come giga e arpa, in tempra tesadi molte corde, fa dolce tintinno . . ."* (And as a fiddle and harp, strung with many strings, a dulcet tinkling make . . .) The etymological link between the instrument and the dance is significant, existing also in German (the word *Geige* meaning violin.) The Jig was a dance popular in the British Isles from the 1400s: Shakespeare (*Much Ado about Nothing*, Act 2, Scene 1) referred to it as being "hot and hasty," but the word may well come from the French verb *giguer*, meaning 'to frolic.' By the late 1660s the dance had arrived in Italy and, still largely associated with the violin, was to be regularly included in sonatas by composers from Corelli to Tartini.

Of all the Gigas in Corelli's op. 5, this one may be said to be the least rustic in affect. In comparison to the last movements of Sonatas 5, 8, 9, or 10 (or that of Sonata 3, a Giga in all but name) this one is fleeting and mischievous. Figure g shows the Giga from Sonata IX, a rousing movement with an almost plodding bass, reminiscent perhaps of a country-dance.

Figure g
Opening of the Giga from Sonata 9 from Corelli's op. 5.

Observations

Bars 1–9: Corelli's Giga starts in the middle of a bar: this may leave us wondering where the good beats are and how we should phrase. Do we stress the start of Bars 2 and 3?

That would seem unnatural and clumsy. Do we stress nothing and merely crescendo to the start of Bar 3? That sounds plausible until we realize we will have to repeat that phrasing four times, which will sound tedious—or do we do nothing at all, keeping our cards close to our chests?

Over-active phrasing can disturb the flow of the music just as no phrasing at all can render it lifeless. Here, the subtlest of shapes (<>) over the first bar line should be adequate: if we remain aloof from any more clearly pronounced phrasing we can create a longer phrase that leads all the way to the obvious climax point at the start of Bar 9. We achieve this by placing a comma after the first note of Bars 3, 5, and 7, followed by a slight increase in volume.

If you are playing with a harpsichord and a cello, you might consider having the cello alone entering in Bar 3, with the harpsichord joining in Bar 5. Thus there will be a terraced dynamic build-up with an added crescendo leading to Bar 9. Although no bowings are specified, the cello should, when practical, use the same bowings as the violin.

Throughout this movement, the bowing formula changes little, but the sound we make should be varied. Sometimes, in the more passionate moments, we will need a more lyrical on-the-string version. At other times, such as when the sentiment is more playful, a more off-the-string version will be appropriate. Exercise 82 will help infuse energy and bounce into the stroke while varying the dynamics.

Exercise 82: Infusing more bounce into the stroke

1. Cast the bow onto an open string in a down-bow direction, allowing it to bounce twice, in the manner of a ricochet. After the second bounce, catch it and immediately throw it back onto the string in an up-bow direction so that it bounces once more. Hold the bow very lightly so that you can feel a tingling sensation in your fingers, the result of the vibrations from string, hair, and stick being communicated to them.
2. Repeat this procedure until you can play the following formula in a rhythmic manner.

3. Gradually speed up this formula: find the location along the stick where this bowing works best at the tempo you are in. When you have reached sixty dotted quarter notes per minute, play the whole movement in the same way.
4. Keep the body still and use very little bow.
5. As you speed up further toward your chosen tempo for this Giga, you will gradually lose the clear ricochet sound, but something of the bounce will remain. It is this bounce that will give clarity to your stroke.

Bars 9–11: the triplets cease for two bars in the bass, suggesting a broadening out of the sound. Allow the long notes to sing, enjoying the release from the confines of the previous bowing. According to the bass, the G-minor seventh chord at the start of Bar 10 is the climax point, but for the violin it would be unnatural not to consider the start of Bar 9 as a first climactic point that continues into Bar 10. Bar 11 is an ending for the violin but a new and energetic beginning, in A major, for the bass.

Bars 11–15: express each individual fragment in a convincing way. The dialogue between the two parts will be more interesting and vital if each part is true to itself, reflecting its own emotional information rather than making compromises to blend with the other. Playing the printed bowings as written, the two parts articulated in different ways, will also help achieve this:

- Bar 11 in the bass has a vigorous, A major quality, but the violin responds in the gentler D minor.
- Bar 13 in the bass is in G major and this time the violin responds in the more open C major.
- Bar 15 in the bass is in F major, but this time the violin ignores the bass and goes off on another tack altogether.

Bars 16–18: the bass ceases to dialogue with the violin and drops in tessitura. This suggests a less vigorous mood, a more lyrical sound.

Bar 19: we may be expecting to cadence quietly on the tonic of F major, but the leap in tessitura up to the third and fifth of that chord revitalizes the music.

Bars 19–25: this time it is the violin that leads the dialogue. Instead of the downward sequence we had in Bars 12–15, we now have an upward one, so we can start softer and more off-the-string and then crescendo, lengthening the notes as we go.

In the sequence from Bar 11 to Bar 15, the note patterns were the same in both voices. Here, this is not the case: in the violin part, the middle note of each set of three is higher than the other two, but in the bass the second note is lower than the two on either side. This suggests a more confrontational dialogue, to be expressed by a more intense sound.

Bars 25–30: at the passionate climax of this sequence, the lyrical, chromatic descent in the bass suggests a longer, more sweeping bow stroke for the violin, perhaps more in the upper half of the bow where bounce is not an option. From the middle of Bar 28, where the bass changes course, it can become shorter and more vigorous again.

Bar 35: be sure to give this note its true value, after which there is a silence at the beginning of Bar 1 or, on the repeat time, at the start of Bar 36.

Giga: Second Half

Bars 36–44: the bass leads, perhaps surprisingly in F major, and the violin enters with the inverted formula that it maintains until Bar 42, when the parts come together with the same note pattern as they crescendo into the subdominant climax (Bar 44).

Bar 44: this is the first bar where a single harmony (G minor) is maintained throughout. The beginning of the bar is strong, emphasizing its climactic significance and establishing a pattern for Bars 45 and 46. However, in the bass the second half is the start of a chromatic descent to Bar 47; we can acknowledge this new beginning by articulating half way through the bar, delaying and accenting the second beat a little. The two strong beats and the slight stretching will give this bar its special significance.

Bars 44–48: keep the bow on the string to produce longer strokes, bringing out the passionate, frenetic nature of these bars. When the cello switches from impassioned chromaticism to the more punchy bass line half way through Bar 47, we can revert to a more vigorous bowing.

Bars 49–52: the only legato section of the piece should be played with maximum lyricism.

Bars 49 and 51: the first note of each bar is the longest the violin plays in the entire movement, not counting the last note of each half. In both cases, play a Messa di voce and fractionally delay the second bass note that, rising up, gives the violin new impetus.

Bars 53–59: it is tempting to ornament so basic a part, but it is the virtuosic bass part that is predominant here and we should avoid trying to upstage it!

Bars 59-69: see Bars 44–47.

The *piano* section needs to contrast with the *forte* section, so I would maintain the *forte* right up to the start of Bar 64. We can take a tiny amount of time so as not to catapult head on into the *piano*. Instead of a 'bravura' ending, the movement slips charmingly into silence.

Notes

1. See Allsop, *Arcangelo Corelli: "New Orpheus of Our Times,"* p. 89.
2. Both harmonic realizations in this Lesson are by Antonio Tonelli (1686-1765). Tonelli's realization of the complete Op. 5 of Corelli is one of the major sources of information for continuo players, studied, it is said, by Handel himself
3. Tarling, *Baroque String Playing*, p. 7.

Lesson 18

Transforming Musical Decisions into Sound

In this Lesson, I offer more advice on how to navigate the complex but vital transition between that which we have intellectually understood and the sounds that will be emotionally convincing to our audience. Having demonstrated how the starting point of the interpretive process is a minute examination of the musical text in its historical context, our task now is to convey the results of our understanding into the world of sound.

I often ask students in their first lesson, much to their bemusement, what music is. As with the question "what is interpretation," discussed in Lesson 16, the answer is often subjective and personal: "music expresses emotions" or "music is what I love most in the world" are two typical responses. I try to lead them away from stating what music does or the extent of its importance in people's lives to defining what music actually *is*.

The answer we ultimately arrive at is encapsulated in a single word: 'sound.' *"In most books which deal with music,"* complains Johann Mattheson in 1739, *"a great deal is made of number, measures and weights; of sound, however, . . . scarcely a word is said, but sound is passed over as briefly as if it were of little or no importance."*[1]

Sound is the raw material of music: just as a chair is fashioned from wood and a statue from marble, music is made of sound. Dynamics, accents, phrasings, and articulations are all descriptions of what the living sound does. Words such as "serious, sad, graceful, tender, intensification," and phrases such as "Messa di voce" or "a dramatic momentary re-energizing of the phrase" remain mere intellectual constructs and poetic images that will only succeed in moving our audience if they are fashioned into vivid and convincing sound. As René Descartes, in his *Compendium musicae* of 1618, puts it: *"The basis of music is sound; its aim is to please and to arouse various emotions in us."*[2]

A dynamic indication is a written clue as to the quality of the intended sound. A *piano* marking does not instruct us simply to play quietly: it invites us to enter a sound world that can express emotions and plumb depths otherwise inaccessible to both performer and audience, a world, incidentally, that our Baroque instruments are ideally equipped to explore. Just as night is neither the absence nor the opposite of day, *piano* is neither the absence nor the opposite of *forte*, nor does it in any way imply the absence of sound or a deficiency of expression.

An accent may require a sudden, brusque movement of the bow or its slow sinking into the string: in both cases, it is the intended quality of the *sound* that determines the exact nature of that movement. Whatever sound seems appropriate to a particular accent must be the result of our imagining and searching. Evaluating and analyzing the precise and elusive formula involved in the resulting technique is not necessarily helpful to us: all that counts is the sound. *"Sound"* writes Mattheson *"is the sole subject . . . of music, just as hearing is its object."*[3]

> If we have found the right sound, we will have found the right technique.

Human beings are highly sensitive to sound and it is above all the *sound* of the violin that, throughout the centuries, has held audiences spellbound. This was recognized by Marin Mersenne who, in his *Harmonie universelle* of 1636 writes: *"The sounds (of the violin) have more effect on the spirit of the hearers than those of the Lute or other string instruments."*[4]

I emphasize this because, in my experience, there is a danger that practitioners of the early violin become more concerned with playing in a mythically 'correct' way than in an imaginative and expressive way within the parameters of what we understand to be historically acceptable. Their playing therefore falls short of realizing the goals formulated by Geminiani as *"The Intention of Musick."*

The fear of sounding too modern can be a disquieting issue facing the fledgling Baroque violinist. Entering into new sound worlds with unfamiliar aesthetic parameters and conventions will necessitate the adaptation or even the abandonment of techniques acquired during a long and painstaking modern training, as well as the re-examination and possible rejection of cherished inherited values. Learning how to replace such anachronistic techniques and values with others that better satisfy the emotional demands and historical truths associated with that glittering mosaic of musical styles grouped under the umbrella term 'Baroque' demands the acquisition of much new information and its gradual application through many hours of patient study and experiment.

It is perhaps worth mentioning here that there is a philosophy of interpretation, expounded by some HIP specialists today, that takes the objective/subjective debate we discussed in Lesson 16 to an extreme. Broadly, this view states that it is enough for the musician merely to play the notes correctly for the music to come alive on its own: to give of oneself is to impose on the music that which is not necessarily inherent in it.

I reject this viewpoint as being neither historical nor effective, for *"concealing the artist"* is not the same as suppressing or denying artistry. The emotional input of the player, if he or she has taste and discernment, does not distract from the music nor does it impose itself on it: on the contrary, the composer's wishes are fulfilled when his score is brought to life through the humanity, passion, and skill of the musician. As Quantz writes (XI, 5) *"The good effect of the music depends almost as much on the performers as on the composers."*

Geminiani, in his *Treatise of Good Taste* (1749) advises the performer who wishes *"to inspire his Audience to be first inspired himself, which he cannot fail to be if he chuses a Work of Genius, if he makes himself thoroughly acquainted with all its Beauties; and if while his Imagination is warm and glowing he pours the same exalted Spirit into his own Performance."*[5]

186

Dr. Charles Burney's celebrated description of C. P. E. Bach's performance at the clavichord is another example of the validity of the performer's input and commitment: he *"grew so animated, that he not only played, but looked like one inspired."*[6] Descriptions of Corelli as an inspired performer were quoted in Lesson 10.

Sound comes in many colors and can express a whole gamut of emotions. Occasionally we may indeed choose a sound that seems to express nothing at all, but that is rare, a special effect. Most sounds need to be alive in some way and I spend much time in lessons urging students to breathe life into their sound, to put themselves into the sound, or to ensure that there is blood flowing through its veins.

To play with a basically 'white' sound, one that lacks evidence of that "exalted Spirit" mentioned by Geminiani suggests, I believe, more of a reaction against the modern sound than an educated guess as to the kind of sound that moved the audiences of our erstwhile colleagues such as Biber, Corelli, or Jean-Marie Leclair. I am not speaking here about vibrato, although that may be one element in the living sound: Lesson 22 will deal in detail with that topic.

I would consider sounds that express nothing at all as lifeless misrepresentations of the written notes. However short or insignificant, a sound must still be alive in some appropriate way; for just as in nature there is a borderline between what is alive and what is inanimate, so there exists in music a borderline between a living sound and that which has no life or quality, a mere auditory occurrence.

❦ ❦ ❦

Although we can quantify certain aspects of a single sound, for example its volume or its duration, we cannot unequivocally communicate in words its exact nature. The obvious way of communicating sound in a lesson is for the teacher to demonstrate and the pupil to imitate. That method, though seemingly effective in the short term, is arguably less beneficial in the long term and may conceivably stunt artistic growth if applied too consistently. In the context of the present book, such imitation is in any case irrelevant.

If music is sound, listening must be the key to the sound world. By 'listening' I do not mean mere 'hearing,' the unavoidable perception of sound. By listening, I mean a mental activity that creates sound, one that imagines it into being, fashioning it as it happens and monitoring it throughout its existence from silence to silence.

> Listening is the act of creating sound,
> not the perception of sound already created.

Playing the violin involves activating a higher percentage of the nervous system than any other activity. This vastly complicated process is controlled by a continuous act of listening that molds the sound every second of the way.

> When we imagine sound, we conjure up what will be.
> When we judge sound, we evaluate what is already past.

When we listen, we focus on what is now.
To illustrate this to students, I put two fingers together, ready to click them.
"Can you hear the click?" I ask.
"No."
I click my fingers.
"Can you hear it now?"
"No."
"Exactly, you can only hear sound when it is now."

Perhaps the principal barrier to active listening is thought. I ask students this question: "What goes on in your mind while you are playing?" The answer is an astounding catalogue of thoughts regarding the dos and don'ts, the dynamics, phrasing, preparation for shifting, and wondering what to do after the lesson is over—some students' heads positively buzz with activity!

The problem is that thinking and listening are mutually exclusive activities. When we listen, there is no room in the mind for thought, for to listen is to be in a state of total awareness. Listening excludes all other forms of concurrent mental activity. It is entirely about the now, about being at one with the living sound.

Thoughts are barriers that drift between the ear and the sound; for the duration of those thoughts, the ear is no longer in total control.

The faster we play, the faster we must listen. Thoughts may come into the mind at precisely those critical moments when the listening needs to be at its most intense, for example, while playing a difficult passage. Yet if we disengage our listening for an instant, the sound will be temporarily out of control.

I encourage my students to learn to meditate, for the art of listening and the art of meditation have much in common. In meditation, one focuses the mind on one's breathing, a repeated word (mantra), or a mental image, thus emptying the mind from thought. Meditation raises awareness of the now, calming the mind and the body. Listening focuses the mind on the sound we make and similarly dispels thought. Meditation helps us to listen and listening helps us to play convincingly.

ક ક ક

We have seen how important a thorough analysis of the text is in the preliminary stages of interpretation. By the performance stage, however, the mind will be focused entirely on listening. It follows, therefore, that listening must gradually replace conscious thinking in the course of our practice until there is nothing left in the mind but a constant awareness of the sound itself. This state of total listening and awareness may be considered the ultimate goal of practicing.

However well thought-out one's objective interpretation may have been, true authenticity is achieved only when the impact one's playing makes on the audience meets the criteria formulated in Geminiani's famous sentence; the audience, after all, is there to be moved, not to be lectured at.

If we are to be convincing, we must first be convinced, not merely of a thought, an idea or a phrasing, but of the sounds our instrument must make in order to convey that thought compellingly to the audience. Here lies the crux of the matter: how are our musical convictions and decisions transformed into sound, and how is that sound conceived? Copying other people can be inspirational and instructive, but ultimately the most important person to copy is oneself: by having the courage to do this we will achieve independence and learn to be ourselves.

> The most important teachers we can ever have are our imagination and our powers of listening.

Drawing up sound from the well of one's inner musicality gives expression to our inherent and individual artistry. The more one draws on the imagination, the richer that imagination becomes. In addition, the ability to identify the sound that we want, rather than copying that prescribed by a teacher or other role model, is an important step on the road to artistic independence.

Each sound is like a tiny stone in a mosaic. To create a mosaic, there must first be a design: that is the artist's job. The craftsman then chooses a stone of the right color, cuts it, shapes it, polishes it, and finally eases it into place. The musician is both artist and craftsman: he draws on his understanding and imagination to decide how a phrase should sound, but before his goal can be achieved he must craft each sound within that phrase until it too fits perfectly and organically into place.

It is best to conceive the long phrase first. Once we have an overview and understand how the details that make up the whole should fit into place, we can begin working on a fragment or on a single sound. Working to make each sound as beautiful as possible without first understanding its context in the whole phrase will prejudice the flow of that phrase, just as a speaker, declaiming each syllable of a poem as lovingly and expressively as possible, will fail to make the meaning of the poem intelligible to his or her audience.

❧ ❧ ❧

Between the sounds we hear in our imagination, our inner singing voice, and those we hear when we play, our 'violin-singing voice,' there is often an accumulation of experience that can act as a barrier. This barrier is compounded of all manner of elements: rules and techniques we have been taught, movements we have been conditioned to make, problems real or imagined, personal convictions, other people's recordings, and so on. Wading through this minefield to reach the desired sound is frustrating and time-consuming. The smart thing to do, therefore, is to sidestep the barriers and go straight to the sound.

Exercise 83 is one I use to put the student in touch with his or her inner voice and imagination. By removing blockages that exist between the conception of a sound and its realization, it helps us to achieve that vital transition from imagined sound to perceptible sound.

Exercise 83: Transforming our inner voice into sound

This exercise is best practiced in a quiet environment. It can be applied to anything from an entire movement to a single note, but I would advise starting with small fragments of one or two bars.

1. Place your violin and bow on a table: in this way you will not be tempted to simulate actual playing while performing stages 2 and 3 of the exercise.
2. Choose a fragment of the piece you are studying. Before proceeding, recall to mind what it is you are trying to achieve with regard to dynamics, articulation, phrasing, etc.
3. In your imagination, listen intently to that fragment, ensuring that all your artistic decisions are incorporated into what you hear. Be sure to hear it with the most perfectly expressive sound you can imagine your violin ever capable of making. It is essential to hear it as the sound of your violin, not with words such as "la-la" or "tumty-tum" or in solfège.
4. When you have achieved this 'visualisation in sound' and are inspired by the violin sound you have heard, take up your violin and play the fragment, imitating as exactly as possible what you heard in your imagination.
5. Compare what you have just played with your conception. On a scale of one to ten, evaluate how close the two were. You can note what the differences were before repeating stages 3 and 4.

The score students award themselves after doing this exercise is very telling and often amusing too: some proudly proclaim a score of nine and a half while others admit to no more than zero point one! Whatever score you have given yourself, closing the gap between the sounds in your imagination and those that your outer ear hears is one of the most important aims of your practicing.

Students usually ask "but *how* do I find the sound?" The simple answer is "look for it," or more accurately "listen it into existence." It is clearly impossible to prescribe an exact technical formula for every nano-second that one plays: x grams of pressure on a stick traveling at y centimeters per second at a distance of z millimeters from the bridge, for example. But if you have a clear sound image in your mind, you will know what you are aiming for and can seek to reproduce it. If you have no clear sound in your mind, you will not know what you are seeking—unless your aim is merely to copy someone else or to produce an acceptably 'beautiful' sound rather than an appropriate or meaningful one.

The physical machine by itself cannot create meaningful sound, for sound is conceived deep within us, in our imaginative, artistic soul. It is for the craftsman in us to labor, to mold that inner voice into a physical reality and to bring it forth into the outer world. Our physical movements are merely the reflection of our musical will, that inner singing voice, that oracle within us that we all possess but do not always have the courage or the patience to consult.

If we are in touch with our inner voice it will teach us much of what we seek to learn from others. Our task is to open the channels and allow our inner voice to flow through our physical body and out into the world of sound. It is our inner voice, not our thinking mind, which fires up and powers our physical machine.

The belief that the perfection of a formalized physical technique covering each of the countless separate aspects of violin playing can somehow create an impeccably functioning machine able to bring to life every conceivable musical nuance is surely misguided. On the contrary, such an eclectic, physical approach—I call it 'instrumentalism,' epitomized by the obsessively comprehensive exercises of Ševčík, however useful they may be if used wisely—fails to take account of the inspirational input of the musician and to give due place to the more elusive inner workings of the musician's mind, the mysteries of his craft.

༜ ༜ ༜

Listening is not, of course, exclusively about expression. The player who hears clearly all the notes of a rapid passage guarantees their existence in sound: it is as if every note in turn is swiftly checked off. The player who hears the same passage indistinctly, as a passing blur or vague impression, is not in a position to guarantee that all the notes are there and sounding the way they should. The difference between the two players may be put down to varying degrees of concentration, but a more accurate term for that concentration is "listening."

> If our audience does not hear a note, it is because *we* have not heard it.

Listening, being at one with the sound, is the art not only of creating a living sound but also of eliminating its flaws. A parallel may be found in the saying of the great Florentine sculptor, Michelangelo, who described sculpture as the art of chiseling away from the marble block all that which is not needed. In a similar way, the violinist 'listens away' that which is not wanted. An example of this is given in Exercise 84.

Exercise 84: 'Listening away' unwanted sounds

1. Play the following two notes slowly, in a single bow and using the upper fingering. Listen carefully to the moment that the second note replaces the first, a flawless transition.

2. Play the same notes using the lower fingering. What do you hear between the sounds now: sliding, whistling, or simply a gap?

> 3. Listen again to No. 1 and then imitate that sound as exactly as possible using the lower fingering.
> 4. There is no need to think *how* to perform this shift. By the active listening of the first sound turning seamlessly into the second you will have found the technique of the shift and will have 'listened away' what is not needed.

Perhaps the most difficult problem the listening violinist faces is achieving objectivity with regard to the actual sound, observing a clear distinction between the imagined sound and the true result. The ideal state is somehow to be dispassionate even while feeling the passion of the moment.

Driving a wedge between intention and reality involves awareness of the extent to which the body itself is feeling and expressing emotion, thus diverting it away from the sound, instead of channeling it directly into it.

Rather than 'acting, the sound in this way (communicating emotion by transforming the body and the face into mediums of expression), students who have this problem should be encouraged to flush away all symptoms of purely physical expression, emptying body and face from the intensity the music suggests.

Having achieved this state of physical neutrality, the challenge then is to produce the desired quality of sound while giving the visual impression of feeling no emotion at all. To sum up, I use this formula:

The Violinist's Trinity
A warm heart to feel
A singing soul to express
A cool head to listen

The great eighteenth-century Scottish poet, Robert Burns, wrote the following lines in his 1785 poem 'To a Louse.' The language is Scots, a mixture of Gaelic and English:

"O wad some power the giftie gie us to see oursels as ithers see us."

Translated into English, this means: "O would some power give us the gift to see ourselves as others see us." I like to transcribe Burns's thought thus:

"O would some power the giftie gie us to *hear* ourselves as others *hear* us."

Notes

1. Mattheson, *DVC*, Part I, Chapter 3, § 1 (p. 94).
2. Descartes, *Compendium of Music*, p. 11.
3. Mattheson, *DVC*, Part I, Chapter 3, § 2 (p. 94).
4. Mersenne, *Harmonie universelle*, II, iii, p. 177, quoted in Donnington, p. 537.
5. Geminiani, *A Treatise on Good Taste in the Art of Musick*, p. 4.
6. Charles Burney, *The Present State of Music in Germany, the Netherlands, and United Provinces*, Vol. 2, pp. 235–79.

Lesson 19

In the Footsteps of Corelli

Antonio Vivaldi: Sonata, op. 2,
no. 1, Preludio

In this lesson, we explore the first movement of a sonata that, at first sight, may appear ▶ simple and straightforward: surely everyone knows how to play Vivaldi? Our investiga- Score 19.1 tion will incorporate discussions on the art of gesture and the use of second position, will reveal what the sources say about using open strings, and explain why it is important to ▶ spot ornamentation within a written text. Score 19.2

> Composed just before his "L'estro armonico" concertos, Vivaldi's op. 2 sonatas were published in Venice in 1709. They contain all the passion and virtuosity, the lyricism and emotion that have made Vivaldi so eternally popular a composer. The influence of Corelli's landmark op. 5 sonatas, published in Rome just nine years before, is very evident and will be frequently referred to.

Observations

The key signature has just one flat. Clearly, we are in G minor, but Vivaldi is looking back over his shoulder to the old modal system, as did many composers of his time. G minor was considered a serious, sad, graceful, and tender key by theorists of the period. This is an important clue, a first step toward understanding the basic emotion, or affect, of the movement, for *"the performer of a piece"* writes Quantz (XI, §15) *"must seek to enter into the principal and related passions that he is to express."*

By *"principal and related passions"* Quantz recognizes that aside from the affect suggested by the basic tonality, the music will be strewn with myriad events that cause or reflect shifting affects. Thus *"since in the majority of pieces, one passion constantly alternates with another,"* he continues, *"the performer must know how to judge the nature of the passion that each idea contains, and constantly make his execution conform to it. Only in this manner will he do justice to the intentions of the composer, and to the ideas that he had in mind when he wrote the piece."*

The following elements may be considered central to a meaningful interpretation:

1. An unceasing observation and scrutiny of detail.
2. An appraisal of the implications of each detail.
3. The identification and internalization of the emotions inherent in the music at any given moment.

This Preludio is marked Andante, so even though the C time signature suggests we feel it in 4, the tempo should not be too slow; in fact, the tactus is fairly similar to that of Corelli's Preludio. Vivaldi's word "Andante" is the only difference between the two composers' markings. The dances in the rest of the sonata are the same as Corelli's, although they are not placed in the same order.

The opening bears a clear thematic resemblance to that of Corelli's eighth sonata (Figure a). Although Corelli's is in triple time, the overall arch of the first phrase and the imitative bass line could well have been in Vivaldi's mind when he wrote his sonata.

Figure a

Opening of Corelli's Sonata 8 from his op. 5 set.

Bar 1: one general guiding principle to consider is that the dynamic scheme often follows the graphic contour of the notes: when the notes rise there is a crescendo, when they fall, a diminuendo. This is by no means an immutable law, but it does serve the music well here. The first bar of our sonata implies a steady intensification, climaxing in the first beat of Bar 2; then it falls, resurging with the leap of a seventh in Bar 3, only to fall again through the bar into the cadence. In addition to the overall dynamics, remember to keep the individual sounds constantly alive.

Bar 2: we will regard the sixteenth notes as passing notes, for they cannot be considered essential to the harmony. Their role is therefore ornamental, and as with all ornaments they should be lighter than the main notes (d″ and a′) with a subtle rhythm, neither metronomic nor wooden in feeling, as if improvised. Try extending the main notes a little, playing the others a little hurriedly, with less pressure on the bow. The f♯ must not sound static, it needs to live: shaping it as a Messa di voce would be effective here.

Bar 3: with the first note, d′, we are back were we started, but the surprising leap of a seventh combined with the syncopation constitutes a dramatic momentary re-energizing of the phrase.

Links between musical ideas and literary ones abound; we could describe this syncopated c'' as a kind of 'exclamation' an important rhetorical interjection. It is not, I believe, a violent or shocking gesture, but an uplifting one, perhaps corresponding to the word "behold!" The speed of the gesture dictates the speed of the bow that is to portray it: here, I would use a slowish bow, allowing the sound to grow and then diminish as if hovering before deciding to continue.

Such interjections mark out specific events that occur in the course of the music, sometimes interrupting its flow by contradicting the established affect, sometimes occurring at a moment of heightened emotion, a decisive sound that serves to establish or reinforce an affect.

Exclamations can express all manner of emotions: they can be joyous or tragic, tender or violent; they can evoke pity, corresponding to words such as 'alas,' or conflict, inherent in words like 'away!' Perhaps in this instance a gentle but firm interruption implying some kind of warning would be more appropriate.

We refer to the expression of such events as 'gestures,' for their execution necessitates specific movements of the bow that correspond to the motion implied within the sound of the event. Such movements of the bow spring from the feeling self, the bow acting as a living extension of the inner workings of the soul. They correspond to the kind of gesture a dancer or an actor might make when expressing just such an emotion.

Gesture

The art of gesture, like that of rhetoric, has its roots in classical culture, being used by public speakers and actors to portray and heighten the expression of their words through the movements of their bodies. It had been revived in the Renaissance and remained an essential aspect of music, art, theater, and dance throughout the Baroque period.

A gesture can be defined as an emotional or spiritual state expressed in movement or in the representation of movement. The gestures and facial expressions of a dancer or an actor are not intended to be merely 'beautiful' and are certainly not random: they are calculated to suggest and symbolize deeper levels of meaning, striking emotional chords that will resonate within the collective psyche of the audience.

This language of gesture can serve to clarify and enhance a text: a singer may direct his gaze and stretch his hand upward when singing the word 'God,' or reach forward for the word 'behold.' The entire body may thus be pressed into the service of the voice, an additional instrument for the communication of meaning and emotion, a powerful weapon in the rhetorical arsenal.

In the art of painting, such gestures are of course both silent and static, but the impression of movement is real and will carry within it the insinuation of noise or even, to the musician, the suggestion of harmony, dynamics, and tempo. Imagining and realizing the implied sound track of visual gestures in a painting or sculpture is an exercise well worth attempting. In the Roman Interlude that follows Lesson 29, we will explore how our identification with a work of sculpture can augment the expressiveness of our playing in specific contexts.

The parallel I wish to draw is clear: viewing a movement such as the one under consideration here as a series of gestures, each representing a more or less specific emotion joined (or separated) by material of lesser impact, is an approach that will provide greater insight into the music than if we merely focus on producing a beautiful, singing, flowing sound.

જ જ જ

Bar 3 (continued): since the beginning of the movement, the bass line has been absolutely equal to the violin part, imitating it exactly: in this, Vivaldi is clearly under the influence of Corelli. Here, however, the bass loses its lyrical equality, ending the phrase with an almost clichéd cadence. This change of role and the resulting diminishing intensity in the bass have the effect of taking the wind out of the violin's sails. The lowering of intensity, thereby providing the opportunity for heightening it again later is a common compositional technique, providing relief and contrast.

The + over the f♯ indicates a trill, which should start on the upper note (g'). Give this upper note an expressive Messa di voce, and start to trill only at the end of it. It is not the trill but the appoggiatura that contains the expression: on the contrary, the trill itself is a kind of emotional release. It can start slowly and accelerate, but in a context such as this one it must never be too fast. We are revealing the depth of our expressive powers, not vaunting the speed of our trills!

Tartini tells us that the *"slow trill is suitable in serious, pathetic and sad pieces; the moderate trill in moderately gay ones; the fast in pieces which are gay, lively and swift. A good player must master trills at all these speeds; it is clear that a trill in a cheeky, swaggering allegro must not be the same as in a grave or an andante malinconico, nor one on the E string the same as one on the G string. . . . On a cadential note, which is not tied to the beat, the best trill is one which begins slowly and gradually speeds up to become very fast."*[1]

Bar 4: the bass takes the lead, and the violin imitates. This sequence lasts two whole bars, the parts gently overlapping. However, as with all sequences, the emotional information or 'message' of each element is actually quite different. Awareness of these subtly transforming emotions will necessitate some variation of tone color. Note also that the bass part in Bars 4 and 5 splits into what is effectively two voices, an upper and a lower one.

Bar 6: the bass leaps up more than an octave before broadening out to glide through the rest of the bar. The violin, moving in contrary motion, soars upward. These are clues: a higher tessitura has emotional implications that impact the quality of the sound. Here it will be sweeter and more cantabile perhaps, or more noble and grand.

Bars 7 and 8: the bass takes on a different role, no longer imitating or being imitated by the violin, while the delicious seventh discords on the half bars provide heightened emotion. Enjoy these discords each in its own way, for they are by no means equal in emotional strength: play them separately, one after the other, investigating their distinct messages. Squeeze the bow into the string as Tartini and Geminiani taught us to do in Lesson 9, so that you can both feel and communicate the ecstatic quality of the first one, the yearning of the second, and the possibly regretful feeling of the third. You can also linger a little on them, savoring them more so as to encourage the listener to wallow momentarily in their emotional potency.

The trills at the start of these bars should begin on the main notes, not the upper ones. In Bar 7 this will emphasize the seventh in the harmony, and in Bar 8 the g″ will clash with both the F and the A of the harmony: were we to stress the upper notes we would lose those dissonances and dilute the flavor.

The trill in Bar 7 will, if we are in the second position, be played with a fourth finger. Although Quantz (XVII, II, § 33) advocates avoiding fourth-finger trills because they are *"generally better made with the third rather than the little finger,"* I personally am reluctant to accept such advice as a principle, especially in a slow tempo.

❧ ❧ ❧

Shifting: How, When, and Whither?

In order to execute the trill in Bar 7, we need to shift. The second position is the best and least disruptive option, and we can shift in one of two ways:

1. By leaving the thumb in the first position, hoisting only the fingers up to the second. This makes it very easy to return, as the thumb acts as an anchor to the rest of the hand. If you feel your hand is too small, check that the space between the thumb and the first finger is open to the fullest possible extent.
2. By shifting the whole hand up: you can then shift the fingers back down, leaving the thumb behind in the second position until it is convenient to normalize the hand by returning the thumb to the first position (Geminiani's method, see Lesson 12, Part One).

There are also a number of possible places to shift:

1. During the rest.
2. On the g″.
3. On the last note of the bar, switching from a fourth to a third finger.

We can return to the first position in Bar 7 by

1. Shifting down during the rest.
2. Shifting down in the middle of the bar (this could be useful in emphasizing the stress on the dissonance).
3. Shifting down on the last note of the bar.

As to where to shift, Tartini gives us this advice: *"If the hand has to be shifted several times during a passage, it should be done between the staccato notes, not the legato, in order that no gaps are heard in the latter case."*[2]

Leopold Mozart (VIII, § 16) advises us to *"await a good and easy opportunity to descend in such a fashion that the listener does not perceive the change."* Although he goes on to say that *"this can be most conveniently achieved if you wait for a note which can be taken on the open string, when the descent can be made quite comfortably,"* it is clear that in the passage under discussion here, the first option (shifting up and down during the rests) is the simplest and most practical.

Bar 8, Beat 4: the e″♮ could be played with an open string, but using a fourth finger could be said to produce a more 'cultivated' sound. Can the sources help us on this issue?

❧ ❧ ❧

Open Strings: Use or Misuse

The ubiquitous use of the open E string by many HIP practitioners today, especially on long notes, is questionable both aesthetically and historically. Justification on the grounds that open gut strings are not as shrill as open metal ones, although undoubtedly true, surely misses the point.

Quantz (XVII, II, § 33) argues that playing in positions is *"particularly useful . . . in avoiding the open strings, which sound differently than when stopped with the fingers."* Leopold Mozart is equally clear: *"he who plays a solo,"* he writes (V, §13) *"does well if he allows the open strings to be heard but rarely or not at all."* He also (VIII § 12) decries the use of open strings in double stops as the tone *"contrasts too sharply with that of the stopped notes, and the inequality arising therefrom offends the ears of the listener."*

A similar view had previously been expressed by Roger North, who talks about the advantage of *"sounding all the notes under the touch, and none with the strings open; for those are an harder sound than when stopt, and not always in tune. . . . And besides all this, the power of the finger in giving temper and commixture to the notes, hath a superlative effect of sweetness."*[3]

Leopold Mozart (VIII, §2) gives three justifications for the use of the positions: *"necessity, convenience and elegance."* The latter is important *"when notes which are Cantabile occur closely together and can be played easily on one string. Not only is equality of tone obtained thereby, but also a more consistent and singing style of delivery."*

❧ ❧ ❧

Bar 9: we are expecting the sequence of dissonances to continue, but instead we are surprised: the first chord of Bar 9 is an open and consonant one of A major. Express the unexpected purity and tenderness of it, no longer squeezing the string on the e″, but instead floating along it.

Observe how the bass sinks chromatically downward, implying an ebbing away of energy. The seventh in the middle of the bar can be felt as a sweeter kind of pain than in the previous two bars, while the "cliché" cadence in Bar 10 again acts as a valve to release the tension.

Preludio: Second Half

Bar 11: the two parts are equal again, the violin initiating a sequence that lasts for two bars before taking an unexpected turn in Bar 13. The phrasing is interesting here: if we take away all the non-essential notes from the violin part, we are left with the bare skeleton of an f″♯ (Beat 1) and a g″ (Beat 3). Now, the D major chord is surely stronger than the G major one, so we shall probably decide that the f″♯ is the stronger note and that we should not accent the g″.

Applying the same logic to the bass part, the G major chord we just decided is weak for the violin is strong for the bass, resolving onto the C major chord at the beginning of Bar 12. Thus the two parts intertwine: what is strong for the top is weak for the bottom, and vice versa.

Bar 12: the same observations apply as in Bar 11, but this bar has a gentler feel than the previous one. We should be even softer as we approach Bar 13 so as to be able to start the new sequence in a *piano*.

Bar 13: the rhythmic motive we heard in the first six notes of the second half is now repeated three times, rising graphically and in an obvious crescendo, goaded on by the bass. The feeling of agitated activity can be helped by a subtle *accelerando*, by elongating the eighth notes and by hurrying through the sixteenths to make them sound almost frantic.

Bar 14: the frenzy started in Bar 13 is calmed by the cantabile quality of six notes floating down under the only slur in the piece. Be sure to play a true *legato*, like a bird sailing effortlessly through the air, for although *legato* is one of the glories of which bowed instruments are capable, yet it is often corrupted by an element of nervous *portato* that produces quite the opposite effect.

The highest note under the slur, b″♭, being the climax of a long crescendo, can be elongated, hovering momentarily before the descent, and there is an inevitable diminuendo leading into Bar 14.

In the bass, the agitated three-note motive we have heard since Bar 13 is extended under the slur, thereby adding to the cathartic feeling.

Bar 15: as the first note of the bar is the end of a phrase, the continuo player(s) will want to take a little time before leaping up an octave and leading us from B♭ major to G major. This delicious transformation of affect can be expressed by the bass easing gently into the unexpected B♮, then sweetening the note with a Messa di voce.

The violin's anacrusis note d″, the start of a tender five-note motive, could be long, growing through to the g″ in a cantabile manner. A more interesting and sensuous option, however, would be to make the d″ breathy and slightly shortened, with a brief silence or articulation before the g″. We could then play an opulent Messa di voce on the g″ itself.

Bar 16: the bass repeats the pattern of the previous bar, taking us from C major to A major. The five-note motive of the violin is not as calm now as it was before and we should adapt the articulation to reflect this shifting of affect.

Bar 17: the chromatically rising bass turns up the heat much as it did in Bar 13. The violin reacts to this intensification, the intervals between the notes becoming ever greater: they climax with a leap of two and a half octaves to the top c‴, the highest note in the entire movement.

Emphasize the drama here by making these leaps sound like hard physical work, as if you really have to struggle to reach that top note: communicate this feeling even throughout the silence of the long journey upward. Reaching the top c‴ may therefore take time: by delaying your arrival slightly, you will better communicate this labor and your sense of achievement in gaining this highest of peaks.

> Sometimes we seek to make difficult passages sound easy; at other times the music demands that we make technically easy passages sound like a struggle.

Consider the rising fourths in Bars 15–17 as individual gestures: what do they express? How would a dancer portray each one through physical movements, and how should we translate them into movements of the bow? Each of the top notes may incorporate a

Messa di voce, but how different are they? Notice that although the first three top notes descend into consonances, the last one (c‴) is longer and ends in a dissonance.

Bar 18: the dissonance at the start of the bar is resolved, and the intense drama of Bar 17 gradually diminishes. Nevertheless, the b″♭, like the c‴ before it, needs to grow into the dissonance that follows, and the trill at the end can have an *affetuoso* quality, despite the obvious diminuendo into Bar 19.

Bar 19: we have returned to the tonic key of G minor, so the rest of the movement is something of a coda, albeit an intense one. Pause after the first note to emphasize this tonal homecoming.

Bars 19 and 20: the bass ebbs away chromatically, implying a gradual diminuendo. However, within that overall scheme there are dissonances: the end of each tied note clashes with the violin part, so both parts need to grow into those dissonances. The bass players should ensure that the sixteenth notes do not sound relentlessly mathematical: instead, they should lighten them, giving them a feeling of gentle swing. Likewise, the sixteenth notes in the violin part can totter toward the dissonances: elongating the preceding eighth notes and speeding up the sixteenth notes will give that impression.

In the violin part, the bottom a in Bar 19 and the bottom g in Bar 20 are effectively the resolutions of the preceding dissonances. They are therefore not to be played as pickups to the notes that follow. However, there is no dissonance in the middle of Bar 20: the bottom d′ can thus be treated as a pickup to the c″, forming a rising seventh reminiscent of Bar 3. This is then echoed by the bass, which leaps down a seventh into Bar 21. The violin needs to grow through to the dissonance at the start of the final bar.

Bar 21: the dissonance at the start is resolved, but another dissonance is indicated by the figure below the trill. As there is a G in the harmony, starting the trill with an upper note appoggiatura would cancel it out. I would therefore savor the dissonance by squeezing the bow into the open string and releasing the pressure just before starting a slow, ebbing trill. I would also stop the trill when the bass descends to the lower octave, which is when the G resolves down to an F♯. I would then enjoy a second dissonance, which occurs when my penultimate note grates against this F♯, holding it as long as I dare before moving on to the G minor chord that closes the movement.

৺ঙ ৺ঙ ৺ঙ

Notes Essential and Notes Ornamental

We have not yet tackled the subject of ornamentation with regard to this movement, although the Messa di voce and vibrato (when applied with discernment and good taste) may indeed be considered as valid ornamental devices. Improvising ornaments is perhaps one of the aspects of Baroque violin playing that takes us farthest away from our training as 'modern' violinists. In Lesson 21 we will begin a structured program of ornamentation, taking us right through the repertoire from the early 1600s to the mid-1750s.

However, before we start adding ornaments of our own, it is important to realize that Vivaldi has already ornamented this movement, for trills, passing notes, repetitions, rhythmic figures, and florid passages—anything, in short, that goes beyond the essential notes of the harmony in order to enhance expression may be considered an embellishment and treated as such. By highlighting essential notes and lightening ornamental ones, we can add perspective, color, and interest to the music. Vivaldi writes trills at the cadences: this is unusual, as the convention of cadential trills was already established by this time.

Figure b shows Bars 4 and 5 stripped of all ornamentation. Vivaldi ornaments these bars with passing notes to add flow and with repeated notes, perhaps to add a sense of urgency to the line. At the ends of both bars, the fourth repeated note is ornamented to relieve the repetitiveness and lead us gently into the following bar.

Figure b
Bars 4 and 5 in a non-ornamented version.

Similarly, Figure c shows Bar 21 reduced to basics. Vivaldi adds decorative notes, a trill and a pickup to the final note.

Figure c
Bar 21 in a non-ornamented version.

Notes

1. Tartini, *Traité des Agrémens*, II. Hermann Moeck Edition p. 76).
2. Tartini, *Regole* (Rules for Bowing). Hermann Moeck Edition p. 58).
3. North, *Roger North on Music*, p. 234.

Lesson 20

In the Footsteps of Corelli
Antonio Vivaldi: Sonata, op. 2, no. 1 (Conclusion)

Giga. Allegro

It is almost inconceivable that this Giga was not modeled to some extent on the one by Corelli that we studied in Lesson 17. At the start of both dances, for example, the violin plays alone, with the same articulation and with the exact same number of notes before the bass enters in imitation, an octave below.

The dialogue between the voices in Vivaldi's Giga is more intense than Corelli's and is sometimes, as in Bars 33–37, almost confrontational in feel. There is a greater variety of rhythmic patterns and of bow strokes, and Vivaldi also specifies the bowings for the bass instrument, which Corelli does not.

The basic bowing pattern at the start of both Gigas is that of two slurred notes and a detached one. You will need to experiment to find the location in your bow where this works best: it will be somewhere in the lower half of the bow, where the hair and the stick are farther apart and the bow is at its nimblest.

Exercises 85 and 86 are designed to help you master this bow stroke both in a basic technical context and in a variety of musical ones.

Exercise 85: Practicing the basic bowing pattern of the Giga

Play the following bars very slowly:

1. Start the first note from just above the string, dropping it onto the string with a soft consonant sound like a 'p,' before allowing the bow to sink into the string.
2. Lean on the first note, then gradually lighten the pressure so that the second note (b') starts softer; use very little bow. In the left hand, take the second finger off in a passive way to avoid an accent on the b'.

3. Do not sustain the second note: instead, cut it slightly short by lifting the bow from the string,

4. During the rest, bring the bow back to where you started.

5. The last note of the bar drops back onto the string with the same soft 'p' consonant sound as in No. 1, but in an up-bow direction.

6. Lift the last note off the string so you can begin the second bar as you did the first.

7. When you have absorbed these movements, speed the bars up very gradually. You will eventually break into triple time, at which point you will be playing the bowing pattern of the Giga. At this faster tempo, there will no longer be time to actively bring the bow back (as described in No. 4, above). Nevertheless, the articulation achieved through practicing this exercise will still be audible.

Having learned the basic technique of this bowing pattern, we now practice varying the dynamics and articulations so we can use it convincingly in different musical contexts.

Exercise 86: Varying the dynamics and articulation of the basic bowing pattern of the Giga

1. Start by playing the bowing pattern learned in Exercise 85.

2. Gradually allow the bow to move down toward the point. Observe the natural qualities of the bow as the sound becomes softer and the articulation smoother.

3. Without stopping, creep slowly back up the bow until you reach the frog; observe how the sound becomes louder and the articulation livelier.

4. Play the following dynamic patterns in rhythm, traveling up and down the bow as in Nos. 2 and 3.

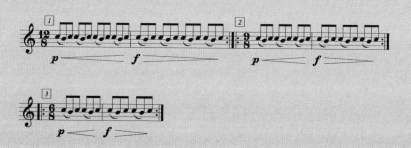

Observations

In contrast with the movements on either side of it, the Giga has a predominantly sprightly and nimble character void of any trace of pomposity, although it does have its more *cantabile* moments.

The thematic material of the opening six bars bears a striking resemblance to that of the first movement and can be seen to be a kind of ornamented version of it. As in the first movement, the bass line switches back and forth between being a direct imitation of the violin part and a harmonic supporting line. Observe that in Bars 37–43 and 56–60 the roles are reversed, the bass being the more active part.

Bars 1–6: the dynamics follow the graphic line charted by the first note of every group of three. Practice this first, before adding Vivaldi's 'ornamentation' (Figure a).

Figure a
Dynamic plan of the opening, following the graphic line of the notes.

Bar 5: the last note (b″♭) can be seen as a pickup to the next bar, thus setting a precedent for the following phrase (Bar 8) and the bass imitation a bar later. Give it a little extra energy, thus interrupting the dynamic scheme outlined above.

Bars 7 and 9: the long notes should not sound lifeless. Give them meaning by shaping them a little; then retake the bow during the rests.

Bars 10–15: the tessitura in both parts sinks throughout this section, indicating a gradual diminuendo.

The long notes in the bass and the bar-long slurs in the violin part are in contrast with the high nervous energy of the previous bowing patterns and require a freer, more floating sound.

The first note of each bar from Bar 11 to Bar 15 forms a dissonance with the bass. Elongate those notes, squeezing the bow into the string a little more to express the dissonances. To make it sound less pedantic, however, do not play each bar in the same way: Bars 11 and 13 can be stronger than the others.

If you are playing with a string bass, ensure that each of the long bass notes crescendos into the dissonance.

Bars 15–16: the violin part changes to three notes in a bow and the bass to a single note, thus leading into the cadence with a more sprightly character.

Bars 17–21: the bass revives the energy of the opening and the violin imitates it. Notice that the original three-note pattern is reversed, the middle note rising rather than falling. The chromatic rising of the bass indicates a crescendo that lasts until Bar 21.

Bars 21–25: with the triumphal high note (b″♭) in the violin (we could linger a little on that note), the bowing changes to groups of three notes under a slur. This gives a more generous feel to the music and should be acknowledged by a more *cantabile* sound.

★Note: the lack of a slur at the start of Bar 23 in the facsimile is surely a mistake, either by Vivaldi or by his copyist.

Bars 23–27: a descending D minor scale begins in the middle of the Bar 23. We should start it *forte,* in preparation for the echo in Bar 25, marked *piano.* Note that the equivalent place in the second half (Bar 60) is indeed marked *forte,* an indication omitted here.

Bars 24 and 26: notice the rapid chord change within the second half of these bars. The $\frac{6}{4}$ indicates a second inversion of a D-major chord which then changes to 5♯, meaning an A major chord.

Notice once again how Vivaldi is following in Corelli's footsteps: both halves close with a *piano* repetition of previous material, exactly as in Corelli's Sonata 7.

Giga: Second Half

Bar 33: the c″♯ is the last note of a diminuendo extending through Bar 32, while the second note (e″) is the start of a new motive. Cut the C♯ short, then retake the bow slightly and make that upward fourth to the top a″ sound energetic and triumphant.

Bars 33–43: make the most of the rhythmic element, especially during the playful tussle with the bass (Bars 33–37.) The notes should sound nimble, not cantabile. You can achieve this by

1. Not using too much bow.
2. Articulating after the long notes (there are no dissonances here).
3. Giving an impish energy to the shorter notes with a hyperactive right hand.

Bar 43: after the gradual winding-down of the previous bars, where the bass was the more active part, we land in B♭ major. The whole bar appears to be under one slur, but the imitative bass in the following bar has just five slurred notes. If we regard our first note (b″♭) as the end of one section and the second note (d″) as the start of a new one, then taking a little time between them (there is no moving bass to take account of) and starting the new section (from the d″) on an up-bow would have a triple advantage: it would make the sections clear, predict the bass in the next bar, and enable us to reach Bar 44 on a down-bow, which is preferable. We have already noted two possible errors in the facsimile in this movement, so taking the considered decision to alter this bar is, I feel, justified.

Bar 49: the strong diminished chord on the first beat requires a matching gesture. It is worth stretching the first note (e″♭) a little in order to savor the full flavor of the harmony (the static bass note will make this easy to carry out.) Afterward, we will need to drop down to a *piano* by the end of the bar, as the start of Bar 50 is a low point.

Bars 49–50: to mark the start of the long crescendo (Bars 50–54) we can make a slight articulation over the bar line, slightly delaying or 'placing' the first note of Bar 50.

Bar 52: the excitement is increased as the bass switches to playing eighth notes.

Bar 54: the violin scale should predictably have ended on a g″ here, as part of a G-minor harmony; instead it leaps up a sixth to a b″♭ over an E♭ chord. Express this surprise modulation with a strong bow gesture on the b″♭ and continue the feeling of crescendo until the harmony finally arrives at G minor in Bar 56.

Bars 54–55: as the bass in Bar 54 still has slurs and is leading through to Bar 56, the single notes spilling out of the long b″♭ should be long. In Bar 55, on the other hand, the notes can be short and forceful, as they are neither slurred nor preceding stepwise.

The trill in Bar 55 should start with the lower note to avoid parallel fifths with the bass.

Bars 56–60: the active, leaping bass line within the *piano* marking suggests a quicksilver energy that needs to be replicated in the violin part, even though it is clearly the less interesting part. The bow should have a nervous energy, producing mini-electric shocks at the start of each note to give 'vitamins' to the sounds; the dotted quarter notes should not be sustained but should decay so as to be more clearly articulated.

Bars 57 and 59 could be considered stronger than Bars 58 and 60: this hierarchy will avoid too many accents and ensure a better flow of the music.

> Note values should be seen as approximate, giving us information about a note in relation to the other notes in the bar, but not necessarily about its actual length; this should be decided on by musical, aesthetic, stylistic, and practical criteria, not purely mathematical ones. Phrases such as "a short quarter note" or "a long eighth note" need to become part of our vocabulary, throwing pedantry to the wind in our mission to bring the music to life!

Bars 60–end: the two G minor descending scales are like the ringing out of bells. As the second one is an echo, one could argue against adding any *ritardando* at all in the last three bars. If the penultimate note were not slurred to the previous one, we could pause a little before it, thus slowing the music down at the last moment without a break in sound over the bar line. The slur, however, makes that solution rather unnatural: instead, we could put a comma over the bar line, thus breaking the sound before 'placing' the final note.

> Playing straight out without slowing down leaves the audience in a state of heightened activity: those few seconds of doubt as to whether the music is to continue or not produces an intense, silent prolongation of the music itself, an effect that cannot be achieved if we herald the end by slowing down.

The final note can be cut short the first time, allowing you and the music to breathe before returning to Bar 28. The second time it can either be discreetly shaped or cut short again, leaving the audience in a state of suspense.

Sarabanda Largo

Vivaldi's beautiful Sarabanda is longer and more complex than Corelli's, although it too is marked "Largo." It features a bass that, instead of elegantly dancing, wends its way lyrically throughout the movement.

The second beats vary in their importance relative to the first:

- In Bars 1 and 3 they rise up the octave in such a gloriously expansive way that they could be said to be stronger in expression than the first beats.
- In Bars 2 and 4, on the other hand, they are clearly weak.
- In Bars 9 and 11, the two beats form a single expressive unit with no obvious hierarchy. However, the bass line could be said to lean on the second beats, so a gentle nudge in the violin part, using a slow bow and shaping the sound, would be justified.
- Bars 19–20 and 21–22 form single melodic units in the violin part, with each first bar leaning toward the second. As neither the harmony nor the violin note changes in these first bars, the second beats cannot be said to be stronger than the first ones; rather, they grow in sound toward the stronger bar. The bass line, on the other hand does leap up to the second beat, an event we cannot entirely ignore. A slight articulation

before the second note will reflect this, clarifying the rhythm and giving the music a pleasing lilt.

৩৯ ৩৯ ৩৯

The first visual impression we have is surely the bass line's ceaselessly undulating flow. This "walking bass" is yet another aspect of Corelli's style that we find in Vivaldi's op. 2. Quite possibly, the model for this Sarabanda was the one from Corelli's Sonata 8 (Figure b). The first two bars are virtually the same in the bass part, and the violin part has striking rhythmic and intervallic similarities.

Figure b

Opening bars of the Sarabanda from Corelli's Sonata 8 from his op. 5.

Our first task is to play the bass part through in the manner of an expressive cellist, keeping the line flowing and the rhythm supple. Think of it as a meandering narrative, a well laid-out path for us to explore, with no feeling of plodding. If there is a special moment, such as the climax of a scale or an unexpected turn, savor that moment by lingering just a little on the important notes; remember that equal in theory does not mean equal in practice.

The bass line will furnish us with clues as to phrasing and dynamics. If we are able to harmonize it on a keyboard, our understanding will be further enhanced, but if that is not feasible, we can attempt a harmonization on the violin, arpeggiating the chords to savor the harmonies.

Reading a figured bass may seem a daunting task for those string players with little or no ability at the keyboard. Nevertheless, it is an absorbing and very rewarding skill to acquire as, even at a very basic level, it deepens our understanding of the music we play. Realizing the harmony on the violin is also a useful basis for acquiring ornamentation skills.

Observations

Remembering that "Largo" means "broad," we will need to arrive at a tempo that allows the bass line to flow coherently but without any feeling of haste. However, we should avoid being fixated on the issue of tempo too early in the interpretative process: a convincing tempo will gradually become apparent as our understanding of the movement deepens.

Bar 1: although this is not a sarabanda to be danced, it does contain an important dance element and even the more melodic parts can be felt more as dance than as song. Here, for example, we need employ no craft to glue the first two notes together: on the contrary, the journey up the octave from g' to g'' is more meaningful when the upward flight is implicit in the brief but active silence that separates the notes.

As a rule, the dynamic scheme of the bass follows the graphic line: thus Bar 1 naturally crescendos into Bar 2. The progression from G minor into D major is also one that creates the feeling of moving forward into Bar 2: we thus crescendo through the g'' and a'' (both notes are on up-bows) into Bar 2.

Bars 2–3: the rising semitone in the bass is emotionally very powerful, enhanced by the clash with the violin's f''♯: your bass player will wish to emphasize it to express its almost menacing quality. The falling semitone that follows suggests relief, so lighten your second note (g'').

We may wish to avoid the same bowing for every bar that has the same rhythm as Bar 1. In Bar 2, therefore, the a'' could arguably be played down-bow, because in Bar 3 the radiant high d''' will sound freer and more glowing on a down-bow. This means starting Bar 3 on an up-bow, sanctioned by Geminiani's celebrated rant (Example VIII, page 4) about *"taking care not to follow that wretched Rule of drawing the bow down at the first note of every bar."*

Tartini would have agreed with Geminiani on this: "As regards bowing," he writes in his *Rules for Bowing*, "there are no definite rules for determining whether one should begin with a down-bow or up-bow." Then, donning his pedagogue's hat, he adds decisively: "All passages should be practised both ways, in order to gain complete mastery of the bow."[1]

Bar 4: the start of the bar is strong, the second beat weak. As the drop from G minor into D minor in the next bar suggests a more subdued character, we can use the eighth-note rest as an opportunity to transform our feelings, swapping one affect for another as an actor swaps his mask, thus enabling us to enter D minor with a more tender sound. We achieve this with a lighter bow, playing a little farther away from the bridge and more toward the upper half: there is no need to retake the bow too much during the rest.

Bar 5: from the last note of Bar 4 we need a lighter sound. However, the e''♭ (on an up-bow) leading to the c''♯ expresses anguish, so we need more texture in the sound here: use more bow pressure, not more speed. This interval will be more poignant if the e''♭ is not too low and the c''♯ not too high.

Bars 6–8 form a hemiola (Figure c). If we follow the graphic line of the bass dynamically, we will discover where the strong and weak beats fall:

- In the first bar, Beat 1 is the strongest.
- In the second bar, Beat 2 is the strongest.

The violin part follows the bass line's phrase. As much rhythmic as melodic, the hemiola should dance graciously. We must be careful to lighten the eighth notes in both bars, using very little bow while skimming featherlike over the string.

Figure c

Bars 6–8: hemiola.

That hemiolas exist is beyond dispute: we even find them written out for purposes of clarity, for example by Corelli in his Sonata, op. 5, no. 3 (see Figure d). We find them discussed in theoretical writings such as Rousseau's *Dictionnaire de musique* (1768) but curiously, no mention of a hemiola is found in any treatise on the violin: the manner of their execution is thus left to us to decide.

Figure d

Written-out hemiola at the end of movement 3 of Corelli's Sonata op. 5, no. 3

Bar 7: the trill will ring better on the open E string, so we should stay in the first position. Harmonically, I would prefer to start the trill on the e″, since that would evoke the maximum of dissonance. Melodically, I would rather start it on the upper note (f″), played as a full and expressive eighth-note appoggiatura. Try it both ways before deciding.

To achieve the plaintive quality of the appoggiatura (literally and musically a 'leaning' note) sink the bow slowly and gently into the string (too much speed will produce a hollow accent) and play a Messa di voce. Start the trill just as you are releasing the pressure, without any hint of a separate impetus from the bow. It should not be fast or virtuosic but slow, like a gentle sobbing, so as to be well integrated into the affect. It may then speed up, but it should not last too long: stop it in time to leave a trail of pure e″ shortly before playing the final eighth note of the bar.

Sarabanda: Second Half

Bar 9: the diminished chord at the start of the bar brings an upsurge of passion that subsides gradually through this bar and into Bar 10.

Bars 11–12: the diminished chord here is stronger than the one in Bar 9. Although it too subsides, it reaches Bar 12 on a D major chord, a more optimistic harmony than the C minor of Bar 10. This change affects the color of our sound: the f‴♯ should not be as weak as the e‴♭ was.

Bar 12: the octave leap in the bass is followed by the same semitone rise and fall that we heard in Bar 2. This time, however, the E♭, coming just after the e‴♮ in the violin part, sounds a note of conflict contradicting the optimism of D major, and we are led back to G minor with a diminuendo into Bar 13.

Bar 13: after four eventful bars, this one has but a single note throughout, the interest lying more in the bass part; nevertheless, the repeated monotone has its own inherent drama that can be enhanced if the rhythmic element is exploited. Articulate between the first two beats, making sure the second is no weaker than the first and that it reaches forward to Bar 14.

Bar 14: the f″♯ grates against the C minor harmony and should therefore not be played too weakly. In this bar, as in Bar 12, Beat 2 in the violin part is weak, but the bass has the Sarabande feel about it.

Bar 15: as we are heading for a hemiola and an augmented fourth, this bar can have more sense of drive than Bar 13.

Bars 16–17: a hemiola, as in Bars 6–7. The trill in Bar 17 should start on the upper note.

Bars 19–24: the bass sinks chromatically at the start of each bar, indicating a gradual diminishing of energy as we pass from E♭ major in Bar 19 to D major in Bar 20, then to D minor (Bar 21), C major (Bar 22), and C minor (Bar 23).

Thus, although Bar 19 leans toward Bar 20 (the augmented fourth (e″♭–a″♮) adding an extra touch of poignancy) we should avoid merely turning up the volume switch. An intensification of feeling can be expressed in many ways, paradoxically even through a diminuendo. Here, the emotion is perhaps one of anguish rather than confidence.

The same is true of Bars 21–22, where the emotion, reflecting the change from D major to D minor, feels more introverted, possibly expressing acceptance. Try playing these two bars with a whispering sound, as if they were within brackets.

> Sound may be manufactured in the laboratory of the physical and the physiological, but it has its origins in our imagination, in the depth of our feelings, in our ability to identify and distinguish emotions and in our will to express.

In Bar 23, the single-note motive of Bars 19 and 21 is laid aside as the violin part rises, then plunges via a dramatic diminished seventh into D major in Bar 24, the start of another hemiola. This D major is once again menaced by an E♭ in the bass.

Bars 23–end: Play the trill as in Bar 7, but on the repeat time leave a small gap (caesura) before the final note.

Corrente

In this Corrente, rhythmic interest is at the forefront of Vivaldi's expressive armory. Syncopations, hemiolas, ambiguous time signatures, and tussles with the bass all combine to give the movement a constantly engaging energy.

Emotional Information in Rhythm

Rhythm contains emotional information just as harmony does. A composer chooses the meter of his composition with the same care as the poet, knowing that different rhythms produce different reactions in the listener. It follows that greater awareness of the emotional power of rhythm will enhance the expressive quality of our performance.

"The power of rhythm in the composition of melody is uncommonly great," writes Mattheson. He attributes specific qualities to the various rhythmic meters: the spondee (---) is *"respectable and serious,"* for instance, while the trochee (-u) *"expresses, melodically, a little of the sarcastic and brittle in tones."*[2]

Let me illustrate this by examining the instrumental introduction to the second movement, *Cujus animam gementem* of the *Stabat Mater* by Giovanni Battista Pergolesi (1736) (Figure e)

Referring to Mary, the mother of Jesus, the text reads *"Through her heart, His sorrow sharing, all His bitter anguish bearing, now at length the sword has passed."*

Figure e
Giovanni Battista Pergolesi, *Stabat Mater*. Opening of "Cujus animam gementem."

Although Pergolesi writes "Andante amoroso" for this movement, the first four bars more than likely have to do with the metaphorical sword passing through Mary's heart. The Iambic meter, an unaccented syllable followed by an accented one, suggests a feeling of alarm or panic, with the climactic fourth bar expressing horror or violence. Had the rhythm been that of a trochee, as in Figure f, the affect would be far less dramatic.

Figure f
The opening four bars in a trochee meter.

In Bars 9 and 10 the rhythm changes to an anapestic meter, producing a gentle rolling feeling. Were we to add dots to these bars, the affect would change to one of dance-like merriment (Figure g).

Figure g
Bars 9–14. The dots transform these bars into a gigue-like dance.

In Bars 15–18, the relentless, rhythmic pounding of this repititio figure, with its dissonant harmony, searing appoggiaturas, and trills, describes outrage, the shrill screams of a mother helplessly watching her son die.

In Bars 19–20, the relatively long legato slows down the tempo of the melody that, with its sinking chromatic line indicates despair or resignation, a wailing rather than a shrieking.

❧ ❧ ❧

To maximize the impact of rhythm in Vivaldi's Corrente, I propose Exercise 87.

Exercise 87: Seeking maximum rhythmic impact in Vivaldi's Corrente

On an open string, play only the rhythm of the movement. Notice which bars are unequivocally in $\frac{3}{8}$ and which combine with the following one to imply a time signature of $\frac{3}{4}$, sometimes forming an unambiguous hemiola.

- Bars 6 and 7 combined, for example, may be said to suggest a $\frac{3}{4}$ time signature, although they do not form a hemiola.
- Bars 8 and 9 are both firmly in $\frac{3}{8}$.
- Bars 10–11 form a clear hemiola in both parts.

When you play you should

1. Vary the dynamics as much as possible, distinguishing between strong and weak notes. It must sound lively, not monotonous.
2. Accent the syncopations: those that lead into a dissonance (Bars 3–4) should be more sustained than those that do not (Bars 12–13).
3. Play adjacent notes smoothly.
4. Play leaping notes with short bow strokes.
5. Breathe quickly during the rests

The bow hand must be constantly vivacious and alert, pulsating with energy! Ensure that it is totally free from interference from other parts of the body: drop your shoulders, free your back, and do not allow your right shoulder or elbow to influence the subtle and intricate movements of the hand that guides the bow.

Remember that for the important notes to sound important, the less important ones must sound less important! Getting that perspective right is vital—without it, all notes will sound the same. For example, in Bars 5 and 6 the first notes are strong and the second ones weak.

To get the full flavor of the rhythm, try tapping it on a drum. As the bass line is equally intricate, get someone to tap that too!

Our Corrente movement is marked "Allegro" and has a time signature of $\frac{3}{8}$, indicating a quicker tempo than if it were in $\frac{3}{4}$. Nevertheless, a glance at the mass of figures in the continuo part (see Bars 13–24, for example) tells us that for the harmony to be at all comprehensible (not to mention playable) the tempo cannot be too rapid. The leaps in both parts also suggest a not too fast tempo: I suggest a metronome marking of somewhere around 70 clicks per minute.

Bow strokes should be swift, crisp, and well defined, executed in the lower half of the bow, where the bow is at its nimblest. To clarify the phrasing and differentiate new motives I would take extra down-bows in the following places:

- Bar 12, on the second note, because a new phrase begins there.
- Bars 14 and 16, on the second note, to clarify the repeat of the motive.
- Bar 18, on the second note, because it is the start of a sequence in which the top note bounces off the bottom one.

Observations

It is not advisable to pause too much between the Sarabanda and the Corrente. Allow the effect of the last note of the Sarabanda to fade and then begin as soon as you feel it is natural to do so. If you wait too long, you risk sending the audience into a neutral emotional state from which it will be hard to resuscitate them.

Think of the first four bars as being a single bar in $\frac{12}{8}$ time, one that you can beat in four. However, many details there may be in the sound, we need to respect this long phrase.

Bar 1: Play the rest at the beginning of the bar, making a discreet gesture for the downbeat as if you were leading a small ensemble. This will help you as well as the audience.

The bow stroke must not be stiff or the sound too controlled. We would do well here to heed Geminiani's advice in p. 5 of *The Art of Playing on the Violin: "Employ the Wrist much, the Arm but little, and the Shoulder not at all."*

Bars 2–3: the first two notes in these bars are played strong/weak. In Bar 3, the tied note (g″) should crescendo over the bar line as it forms a dissonance with the bass in Bar 4.

Bar 4: the first note is a suspension and the rest of the bar is an ornamented resolution of that suspension. Lean on the suspension and lighten the bow for the resolution. Play the sixteenth notes lightly, almost skittishly: they should be rhythmic but not pedantically so!

Bars 7–8: there are dissonances at the start of both these bars; grow into Bar 7 and continue the *crescendo* through to Bar 8.

Bars 10–11: a clear hemiola. The natural way to phrase the violin part would be to stress the first beat (f″#) a little and the second beat (g″) of the hemiola the most. In the bass part, there is a single stress on the first beat, after which there is a *diminuendo* through to the end: the B♭ at the end of Bar 10 can be acknowledged as significant with no more than an implied stress.

Bars 12–18: perhaps Vivaldi is tempting us to hear these bars in $\frac{3}{4}$ time (see Figure h). The question to decide is whether the motive begins on the first or second note of Bars 12, 14, and 16. The bass motive in Bars 13 and 15 clearly starts on the first note, but one could argue that the first note of Bar 12 is weak, being the end of the hemiola, and that starting the motive on the second beat with an extra down-bow gives more rhythmic interest to these bars. If that makes it different from the bass, the passage will be all the more fascinating.

Figure h
Bars 12–18 transcribed into $\frac{3}{4}$ time.

Bars 18–20: more inconsistency between bass and violin accents. The bass's accents are on the first and arguably on the third beats, while the violin's are on the second: use short bow strokes to assure clarity.

Bars 21–22: the first beats are both dissonances, implying longer strokes than in the previous bars. Note the complex rhythms in the bass part from Bar 20 to 22.

Bars 23–25: a hemiola. A string bass should play the first beat of Bar 24 on an up-bow to avoid an accent on the second beat of the hemiola.

213

Bar 23: the e‴♭ should not be too low nor the c‴♯ too high. This will give the interval more character; otherwise, they could sound like a sharp d″ followed by a flat one!

Corrente: Second Half

Bars 32 and 34: Shorten the first notes of these bars by almost taking the bow off the string; then hit the string for the trills, producing a syncopated effect. The trills start from the upper note, with a short, crisp appoggiatura.

Bar 34: play the trill on an open string for greater resonance. Cross nimbly over to the A string for the termination of the trill, using a slight flick of the wrist to get you there. Play the last note of the bar (e″) with a fourth finger.

Bars 36–45: each note tied over to the next bar (in either part) is syncopated and needs its own accent, but the quality of the accents should vary. Bars 37–41 all begin with a dissonance. In Bars 36–41, therefore, we should crescendo through the ties (in both parts) in order to stress those dissonances. In addition, both parts need to grow through the eighth notes that follow the ties, so as to arrive strongly on the next dissonance. These eighth notes can have a *cantabile* quality, in keeping with the emotional heat given off by the ubiquitous dissonances, and the accents on the syncopations can be more pleading than precise.

In addition to this micro-dynamic scheme, these bars have an overall dynamic scheme, a long *decrescendo* ending in Bar 42, where the first consonance occurs.

In Bars 42–46 the ties end in consonances and do not require the same amount of sustaining. Their function is more rhythmic, so the attack can be more impish, like little darts. Shorten the notes before the ties and shorten the ties themselves. The passage starts softly but as it crescendos these articulations can vary, the better to hold the listener's attention: for example, the second note of Bar 45 could be long, as an exception.

Bars 47–49: the rhythm is very complex here and needs to be well communicated. Each slur should have its accent, but the second note in it should be shorter and quieter. The separate leaping notes too will be short.

Bars 48–49: in the bass here is an obvious hemiola, but in the violin part we would have to lighten the g″ on the first beat of Bar 49 to clarify the hemiola, possibly even playing it on an up-bow. In a case like this, I would find it more natural to allow the violin part to remain ambiguous, thus adding to the rhythmic complexity of the passage, rather than 'enforcing' a hemiola.

Bars 51 and 53: the trills add a syncopated quality to these bars, but as the bass is smoother and more lyrical here, especially in comparison with the preceding bars, the violin part too should be more *cantabile*, less agile than in Bars 32 and 34.

Bars 55–62: the danger here is of having too many first-beat accents, especially as the two parts are overlapping. We can avoid this by bowing out the entire passage and by taking a longer view of the phrasing: imagine beating the whole passage from Bar 56 to Bar 64 as if it were two long bars written in $\frac{12}{8}$ time, with stresses only on the first beat of each bar. In the bass the $\frac{12}{8}$ begins a bar earlier, in Bar 55.

Bars 55–56: play stepwise notes smoother than the leaping ones.

Bar 57: staying in first position will add energy and interest to the motive.

Bar 59: the first note is the end of a phrase, the second note the beginning of the next. Clarify the phrasing by articulating between the notes.

Bar 65–end: the *piano* is a coda, not an echo, an exact transposition of the end of the first half (Bars 21–25.)

Concluding Suggestion

Having studied these two sonatas by Corelli and Vivaldi in great detail, I would recommend that you take another sonata by each composer and write your own lessons. In this way you will sharpen your powers of observation, the key to interpretation!

Postscript: Learning to Read Vivaldi's Sonata in the Original Notation

Of the two freely available facsimiles of this sonata, that of the first edition (Venice, 1709) uses printing techniques similar to those used throughout the seventeenth century and even earlier; the second, published in Amsterdam by Estienne Roger in 1711, uses the more modern technique of engraving that was to remain in use throughout the rest of the Baroque period.

Learning how to read sixteenth and seventeenth century facsimiles, an essential skill for the interpreter of Baroque music, is a topic that will be dealt with in Part Three. However, as you are by now more than familiar with this sonata, reading it from the first edition will be a good way of familiarizing yourself with some of the earlier conventions.

Notes

1. Tartini, *Regole* (Rules for Bowing). Hermann Moeck Edition p. 56).
2. Mattheson, *DVC*, Part II, Chapter 6, § 3 (p. 344).

Lesson 21

Nurturing Spontaneity
Ornamentation, Module One

We have thus far avoided the issue of ornamentation—no more! This lesson is the first of five modules designed to guide the reader through the first steps in improvised ornamentation: the other modules are in Lessons 24, 30, 34, and 39.

Roger North's warning that this *"hath bin attempted, and in print, but with Woefull Effect"* is sobering, but although some people are clearly more adept at this ancient art than others, I cannot altogether agree with North that *"the Spirit of that art is Incommunicable by wrighting,"* or with his conclusion that *"therefore it is almost Inexcusable to attempt it."*[1]

Ornamentation: Diversion or Essence?

When we enter a Baroque church and stand gazing up at the altarpiece, we may initially feel overwhelmed by the mass of lavish detail crammed together to form a seemingly chaotic whole (Figure a). Paintings and marble sculptures, representative or decorative, are adorned with gold, silver, and bronze; stucco, alabaster, plaster, wrought iron, and *trompe l'oeil* abound. Not an inch of space, it seems, has been left plain in this multi-dimensional tribute to the power of God, as commissioned by popes or bishops and executed by a host of artists and artisans.

And yet, as we slowly step back to observe the overall design, the essential message that this extravagantly rich statement of faith is intended to convey is gradually revealed. The ornamentation is no longer the main focus of perception and its purpose has become clear: to enhance, beautify, and impress, but not to dominate.

In much of the music of the Baroque period, the composer confines his role to that of architect, writing down the essential outline of a piece but leaving its realization to the imagination of the performer. In such cases the performer's task is to understand the composer's concept and, by enhancing and embellishing it more or less spontaneously, bring it to life. *"The good effect of a piece of music,"* Quantz writes, (XI, § 5) *"depends almost as much on the performer as upon the composer himself."*

Figure a
Baroque altarpiece,
Peterskirche, Vienna.

Few compositions, however, can be said to exist in this entirely skeletal form. Later in this lesson we discuss how notes written by the composer that are not absolutely essential to the harmony may in themselves be considered ornamental.

A composer may equally choose to conceive of a piece in its totality: overriding the freedom of the performer, he composes both the outline and his own elaborate embellishments, leaving the performer with the difficult task of reproducing them in a pseudo–spontaneous manner. The most important examples of this in our repertoire are the opening movements of Bach's G minor and A minor solo sonatas. I shall discuss the illusion of spontaneity in the context of Bach's written-out ornamentation in Lesson 41.

"*It is not likely,*" writes Carl Philipp Emanuel Bach, who worked alongside Quantz in Berlin, "*that anybody could question the necessity of ornaments. They are found everywhere in music, and are not only useful, but indispensable. They connect the notes; they give them life. They emphasize them, and besides giving accent and meaning they render them graceful; they illustrate the sentiments, be they sad or merry, and take an important part in the general effect. They give to the player an opportunity to show off his technical skill and powers of expression. A mediocre composition can be made attractive by their aid, and the best melody without them may seem obscure and meaningless.*"[2]

Our colleagues of the past were indeed the spontaneous creators of their performances. Improvisation was an integral part of their skill, much as it is with jazz artists today. Hearing two identical performances of a movement from a Baroque sonata would thus have been as unlikely as hearing two identical performances of a classic jazz number.

The continuo players improvised one hundred per cent of the time, not merely filling in the chords to complete the harmonies suggested by the bass line, which was written out, but doing so in a way that expressed the mood of the moment most appropriately and complemented whatever the top-part performer or performers were doing. That is why being privileged to play with great continuo players, the true heroes of improvisation, is one of the most inspiring aspects of our Baroque music making even today!

The top-part player or singer would also embellish the written part whenever he or she felt the music required something extra, something personal and spontaneous, something of the moment. It is important that we understand the word 'embellish': it literally means 'to beautify.' The first function of ornamentation, as far as we are concerned, is thus to add to the beauty of a line when it is appropriate and seemly to do so.

Even at this early stage in our investigation, it is important to point out that throughout the Baroque period, voices were raised against those who abused their freedom of embellishment. *"Divisions have been invented, not because they are necessary unto a good fashion of Singing,"* protests Giulio Romolo Caccini in 1602, *"but rather for a certain tickling of the ears of those who do not well understand what it is to sing Passionately."*[3]

At the other end of the period, a century and a half later, C. P. E. Bach echoes Caccini's annoyance, warning us of the danger of indigestion caused by adding too many ornaments, for they can be *"like spices which may ruin the best dish."*[4]

On the other hand, *"a Deficiency of Ornaments,"* Pier Francesco Tosi (1723) warns, *"displeases as much as the too great Abundance of them."*[5]

Quantz, although he also writes disparagingly (XI, § 6) of people who *"believe that they will appear learned if they crowd an Adagio with many graces,"* sums up his views with some sobering wisdom. *"There is more art in saying much with little,"* he writes, *"than little with much"* (XI, § 6).

❧ ❧ ❧

Overcoming Our Fear of Playing the Unwritten

Ornamentation and improvisation are not part of the training that we, as 'modern' violinists and violists, normally receive. Quite the contrary, we have been conditioned to play what is written, nothing more and nothing less. This insistence on the absolute authority of the written text places our Western art music from the late eighteenth century until the jazz and 'aleatoric' music of the twentieth century in a quite unique position among the vast array of global musical cultures. No wonder many classical musicians harbor a fear, almost a phobia, of casting off from the security of the printed page, relying on their ears, imagination, understanding of harmony, and technical skill to guide them through terrifying nothingness back to musical terra firma.

Yet is it not a timeless human instinct for a young child to improvise a song while playing, or for a shepherd to hum while watching over his sheep? Both will alter the details of the song to suit their mood, adding some extra notes or dwelling a little longer on this word or that. How rare is the teacher today who has the patience to listen to his young pupils playing melodies by ear or who encourages them to improvise their own compositions! How swift, on the other hand, is he to pounce when a rhythm is not strictly enough executed or when a written crescendo is begun too early or too late. No wonder, then, that the illiterate musician, one who has learned by ear rather than by years of obeying written texts, can so easily outshine the classically trained one, recreating with ease melodies and harmonies heard but briefly on the radio or in the cinema!

I encourage students to spend time improvising melodies, playing whatever comes into their heads, or to improvise dances: the important thing is not to care about failing, but to keep trying. To some it feels like time wasted, time that could be better spent practicing intonation in a Bach fugue. To others, to play without printed notes in front of them feels like standing on the edge of a terrifying abyss. But with time, most people overcome that feeling and start to be more courageous and to really enjoy it. We will take further steps in that direction in Lesson 24.

Ornamentation and National Styles

Baroque ornamentation, like Baroque music, is a misleading term: in every musical culture the style of ornamentation was different, appropriate to and reflecting the current, local style of composition. The most extreme divide is perhaps to be found between the Italian composers of the early seventeenth century and the French composers of the seventeenth and eighteenth centuries. The latter had set formulae, known as 'agréments' (from the word 'agréable,' meaning 'pleasant') written in by the composer, that had generally to be played exactly as the composer indicated: they were not to be left out, nothing more was to be added and only very limited variation was permitted:

"*I declare, then,*" wrote François Couperin in the introduction to his *Third Book of Harpsichord Pieces* (1722), "*that my pieces must be performed as I have marked them, and that they will make a certain impression on people of good taste only if everything which I have marked is observed to the letter, without addition or subtraction.*"

The Italians, on the other hand were, from the earliest times, both mentally apt and highly trained to add ornamentation spontaneously, regarding the written text merely as a rough guide, a bare platform on which to exercise their skills as improvisers. No wonder, then, that the highly opinionated Abbé François Raguenet, in his famous *Parallèle des italiens et des françois* (1702) expresses his contempt for what he perceives to be the lack of taste of those unruly musicians from south of the Alps. "*The French,*" he writes with an audibly indignant sigh, "*would think themselves undone if they offended in the least against the rules. . . . The more hardy Italian . . . makes double or treble cadences of seven or eight bars together upon tones we should think incapable of the least division. . . . He'll have passages of such an extent as will perfectly confound his auditors at first, and upon such irregular tones as shall instill a terror as well as surprise into the audience, who will immediately conclude that the whole concert is degenerating into a dreadful dissonance.*"[6]

෴ ෴ ෴

219

Composed Ornamentation

Undeterred by the good Abbé's scorn, we begin our study of Italian ornamentation with the Sarabanda from the Corelli sonata that we have recently studied. We shall study French ornamentation in Lesson 34 and ornamentation attributed to Corelli himself in Lesson 30. Before we proceed, however, we need to consider two basic questions:

1. Should notes written by a composer that are not absolutely essential to the harmony be considered ornamental?
2. If yes, how does this affect the way we play these ornamental notes?

Cadences often demand a special measure of ornamentation: is not the word 'cadence' etymologically linked to the word 'cadenza'? In the second cadence (Bars 7–8) of the Sarabanda, Corelli has written his own simple ornamentation: he could have left it plain, as he did in Bar 12 of the Preludio (Figure b) where the harmonic sequence is identical. Instead, he adds three eighth notes, one on either side of the main note (Figure c).

Figure b

Preludio, Bar 12.

Figure c

Sarabanda, Bars 7–8.

I would consider these added notes to be ornamental. Therefore, rather than play them as predetermined melody notes, I would aim to make them sound spontaneously improvised, lightening the bow and giving a certain lilt to the rhythm, shortening the first and third notes to produce a faintly dotted effect. *"Passage-work in music composed of many notes or divisions,"* Jean-Jacques Rousseau writes in his *Dictionnaire de musique* (Paris, 1768) *"are sung and played very lightly."*[7]

Working on embellishments of this kind will help us clarify the distinction between what is 'essential' in a piece of music and what can be considered 'non-essential ornamentation' written in by the composer himself. These two elements should be approached in different ways: the ornamentation element should sound unplanned, rhythmically imaginative, possibly more whimsical, and played with a less assertive bow than the 'essential notes.' To illustrate this distinction, I have chosen two short extracts from Handel's A major violin sonata and one from his E major sonata.

In the third movement of the A major sonata (Figure d) Georg Friedrich Handel writes only a minimum of 'essential' notes, adding his own embellishments as if improvising at the keyboard. He omits trills, mordents, and other ornaments of the kind, presumably taking it for granted that the performer would feel free to add them.

As there is a moving bass, the ornaments must not be allowed to interrupt the flow of the music; nevertheless, they do need to sound as if they are the product of the performer's spontaneous imagination. The rhythm, therefore, needs to be flexible, rather than mathematically "accurate," *"stealing the Time exactly on the True Motion of the Bass"* as Pier Francesco Tosi puts it, the perspective between essential and improvised non-essential notes alluded to by the shifting colors of the sound.[8]

Note that although Handel omits any slurs in the first three bars, it would seem unnatural not to add some: that too may be considered an element of our improvisational freedom.

In the penultimate bar, the single bass note suggests a more cadenza-like freedom, possibly including the filling out with additional notes of what may be seen as a skeletal outline.

Figure d

Handel, Sonata in A Major, third movement.

In the opening bars of the first movement of the same sonata (Figure e) Handel's essential harmony notes and his ornamentation are more integrated: here too, it is our task to discern the distinction between them and to make that distinction clear to our audience, playing the ornaments as if they were the result of our spontaneous creativity. The long notes may be considered the skeleton of the music, the shorter notes an ornamental filling-out by the composer himself. We will return to this movement in Lesson 38.

Figure e

Handel, Sonata in A major, first movement, opening bars.

Handel's E major sonata abounds in written-out ornamentation. Bars 3–5 of the first movement, for example, (Figure f) consist of a rising scale, each essential step decorated with three notes under a slur: the violin part has effectively been divided into two voices in dialogue with each other. Playing each four-note unit as equally important melody notes would be a mistake: the essential notes need to be highlighted, possibly even stretched, while the slurred ones react to them like murmured comments. Of the three slurred notes, the second is dissonant and we can enjoy the momentary pleasure they give, teasing the ear by nudging them just a little with the bow.

Figure f

Handel, Sonata in E Major, first movement 1, Bars 3–5.

Learning to perceive notes as ornamental or decorative is an essential part of the HIP musician's training; stripping a composed line down to its essentials is one way of training the eye for this task. In Exercise 88 we do just that, but we also attempt to substitute Handel's ornamentation for our own.

> ### Exercise 88: Removing and replacing ornamentation
>
> 1. Play the first line of the Handel A major sonata (Figure e) missing out all 'non-essential' notes. The first bar, for example, has just two essential notes, c″ sharp and e″.
> 2. Having reduced the ornamented line to its essential skeleton, play it again, modifying Handel's ornaments or even replacing them with your own.
> 3. Work through the rest of the movement in this way.

First Steps in Ornamenting: Corelli's Sarabanda

The most basic way spontaneously to embellish a line is to fill in the gaps between the notes. Figure g shows the first half of the Corelli Sarabanda: examples of ornamentation for each bar, based on the simple joining up of notes, follow. These examples will necessarily be simple and are not intended to emulate the complex ornamentation Corelli himself might have indulged in: an in-depth examination of ornaments attributed to Corelli will follow in Lesson 30.

Figure g
Sarabanda, Bars 1–8.

Figure h shows Bar 1 ornamented in five different ways: notice how each rhythm conveys a different shade of emotional information. The first is the most basic and possibly the least expressive; the second is wistful, while the throbbing back-dotting of the third is emotionally more powerful. The last two are the most complicated: here, the rhythms are identical, but the bowing in version a) is different from version b), demonstrating how varying the articulation also affects the quality and intensity of the emotional message.

Figure h
Bar 1, with simple ornamentation and examples of rhythmic alteration.

The ornament connecting Bars 1–2 (Figure i) is known in rhetoric as a 'tirata.' The speed of execution impacts its emotional meaning. It can be played in an unhurried manner, giving the ornament a dignified feel; alternatively, the first note can be lengthened and the four last notes bunched together, rushing upward toward the top note in Bar 2.

Figure i
Bars 1–2, with tirata.

Bars 3–4 (Figure j): the slur leads us gently into Bar 4; omitting it could make the ornament disruptively energetic.

Figure j
Bars 3–4.

Bar 4: the dynamic hierarchy of the original notes should not be disturbed by these three ornamented versions (Figure k). Thus the e″ will always be stronger than the d″.

Figure k
Bar 4.

Bar 5: despite having identical notes to those in Bar 1, the context and feeling are different. Your choice of rhythm (see Figure h) should reflect this.

Bar 6 (Figure l): the a″ is harmonically weaker than the e″, so a diminuendo within the ornamented version would be appropriate. The same applies to the more elaborate second version of the ornament.

Figure l
Bars 6–7.

Bars 7–8 (Figure m): to give the illusion of an off-the-cuff moment of inspiration, the rhythm of these ornaments must not sound too calculated. They should have the same subtlety as the words whose rhythm we worked on in the early lessons.

Figure m
Bars 7–8.

Bar 8 (Figure n): the tirata, or bridge passage, leading back to Bar 1 can be slow or fast; it could also start slowly and accelerate. The speed/dynamic formula is crucial to obtaining exactly the affect required. If a more vigorous affect is needed, the tirata could be played without the slur. On the repeat time we could use a similar ornament to lead us into the second half. However, as the structure of this piece is so beautifully symmetrical, you may prefer to rest after the final note and breathe before continuing. Silence is often the most effective transition, so beware of overusing any ornament!

Figure n
Bar 8 leading back
to Bar 1.

Writing out ornaments is legitimate in the early stages but is no substitute for spontaneous invention: that is a skill we will acquire only if we practice it. Written ornaments should be played as if they are being spontaneously improvised, that is with a certain freedom, especially of rhythm, *"that They do not appear studied,"* as Tosi (1723) puts it *"in order to be the more regarded."*[9]

There is substantial evidence that cadential trills were taken for granted in Baroque music and were therefore not even marked. Without a trill, writes Bénigne de Bacilly in 1668, *"the melody is very imperfect."*[10]

Indeed, the word 'cadence' came to be used as the French word for a trill, although 'tremblement' was more common. Cadential trills, writes Tosi, are *"for the most part . . . very essential."*[11]

The speed of the trill should always be appropriate to the emotional context. Too fast a trill in a gentle or melancholic affect such as in our Sarabanda will shock the listener, making it sound *"like a squirrell scratching her ear,"* as Roger North so eloquently puts it.[12]

Trills are appropriate in the following places, starting on the upper note.

- Bar 4, on the e″. After an appoggiatura lasting about one eighth note, the trill should have a moderate tempo and should cease altogether for the last quarter note of the bar.
- Bar 8: because it has a more final feeling, I would play a lingering upper note appoggiatura of about one quarter note's length, followed by a trill that starts slowly and hesitantly before accelerating a little. The trill should cease by the third quarter note, allowing the c″♯ to be heard as it fades out. Ensure that the c″♯ is not too high.

    The following non-cadential trills could add drama to the first half.

- In Bar 2, an upper note appoggiatura of an eighth note will strengthen the emotional impact of the bar to an almost shocking degree, being dissonant with both the third and the fifth of the chord. Be sure to cease trilling one eighth note before the a″ that follows.
- In Bar 3, a trill on the f″ will add a touch of gravitas to the second beat, although it will not have the emotional value of the trills listed above.

Playing all of the trills and ornaments suggested above within a mere eight bars must not be allowed to *"confuse the melody and obscure its beauty,"* to quote Jean Rousseau who, in his *Traité de la viole* (1687) exhorts us to *"avoid a profusion of ornamental figures."*[13]

We conclude Module One of our ornamentation program by attempting to apply to the second part of our Sarabanda (Figure o) what we learned in the first. Keeping your eyes on the score, join up the notes and experiment with the various ornamental fragments we learned in this Lesson. Further suggestions are given below.

Figure o
Sarabanda, Bars 9–16.

Ornamenting the Second Half of the Sarabanda

Bar 9: join the first two notes, aware that the bar is in D major, so your scale will need an f″♯. The rhythm does not need to be accurate: the effect could be one of cascading down.

Bar 10: add a trill. Here, it will have to start on the lower note; otherwise you will have consecutive fifths with the bass.

Bar 11: as Bar 9. The key is C major.

Bar 12: as Bar 10.

Bars 12–13: a scale linking these two bars is possible. In view of the delicate nature of Bar 13, the scale should not be abrupt but should float gently upward in a diminuendo. An e″♮ will make the transition from F major to D minor sweeter and more poignant.

Bar 13: we can join the e″♭ to the g″ and, in one continuous line, tumble over the bar line into Bar 14

Bar 14: if we add a trill to the first c″♯, starting on the upper note, it must not detract from the dramatic interval of the diminished fifth. The appoggiatura should therefore be loud and forceful, the trill itself having a wild quality, starting slowly and accelerating.

Bar 15: add a trill on Beat 2. If we start on the upper note, we will hear a D, an E, and an F all at once. If that is too much of a cluster, a lower note trill will be preferable.

Corelli's Sarabanda Ornamented by Dubourg

Corelli's sonatas were so popular in the eighteenth century that many examples of ornamented versions, especially of slow movements, are to be found: we will explore some of these in Lesson 30. The Sarabanda from our Sonata 7 exists in an ornamented version by Matthew Dubourg (Figure p).

Dubourg (1703–1767), a pupil of Geminiani, was Master and Composer of State Music in Ireland, in which capacity he led the orchestra at the first performance of Handel's *Messiah*. On one famous occasion, he unexpectedly improvised a lengthy cadenza in the middle of an Air. Handel waited impatiently for him to finish and, when the cadenza finally came to an end, was heard to exclaim, "*Welcome home, Mr Dubourg.*"[14]

Figure p
Matthew Dubourg's ornaments to Corelli's Sarabanda. It should be noted that Dubourg wrote ornamented versions of quick movements as well as slow ones.

Notes

1. North, "The Art of Gracing," in *Roger North on Music*, p. 149.
2. C. P. E. Bach, *Essay*, Chapter 2, §9.
3. Caccini, Preface to *Le Nuove Musiche*, quoted in Donnington, p. 154.
4. C. P. E. Bach, *Essay*, Chapter 2, "Embellishments, General," §9, p. 81.
5. Tosi, *Opinioni de' Cantori Antichie Moderni*, Chapter 9, §52.
6. Quoted in Strunk, *Source Readings in Music History*, p. 117.
7. Jean-Jacques Rousseau, *Dictionnaire de musique*, quoted in Donnington, p 159.
8. Tosi, *Opinioni de' Cantori Antichie Moderni*, Chapter 8, §5.
9. Tosi, *Opinioni de' Cantori Antichie Moderni*, Chapter 10, §13.
10. Bacilly, *Remarques curieuses*, p. 164.
11. Tosi, *Opinioni de' Cantori Antichie Moderni*, Chapter 3, §3.
12. North, *Roger North on Music*, p. 166.
13. Jean Rousseau, *Traité de la viole*, p. 73. International Music Score Library Project (IMSLP), quoted in Donnington, p. 192.
14. Charles Burney, *An Account of the Musical Performances in Westminster Abbey . . . in Commemoration of Handel*. "Sketch of the Life of Handel," p. 27.

Lesson 22

Straight from the Heart: The Great Vibrato Debate

In this lesson, we attempt to establish a balanced HIP standpoint on the thorny and controversial question of vibrato. We begin our enquiry with sources not from the Baroque period but, intriguingly, from the twentieth century, working back in time to the start of the nineteenth. The oft-voiced myth that vibrato somehow claimed its 'de rigueur' status the instant the last Baroque composer was lowered into his grave will itself be laid to rest.

Following this, we explore sources from 1529 until 1778, asking such questions as why, why not, by what means, how much, and when vibrato might have been used by our colleagues of that far-off age. If no clear, satisfactory answers are seen to emerge from these sources, we shall be obliged to conclude that, within certain parameters, vibrato was a question of individual taste and must therefore be so today. We will delay discussing so-called bow vibrato until we deal with the repertoire of the early seventeenth century in Part Three.

❧ ❧ ❧

If there is one single component of violin technique liable to ignite the passions both of those who expound HIP and those who denigrate it, it is vibrato (the term 'vibrato,' by the way, is a nineteenth-century one). Its use, misuse, over-use, and under-use seem bizarrely almost to define the aesthetic priorities of the opposing sides, with ardent exponents of HIP claiming that the modern players' vibrato is like a lava flow smothering articulation, sweeping away all hope of rhetorical expression and, happily for them, burying dubious intonation. For their part, the diehard 'modern' players deride the white vibrato-less tone of some HIP violinists as bland, soulless, and in any case unhistorical.

"Vibrato," one of my teachers, the great Sandor Vegh, used to cry, vigorously thrusting his left arm back and forth, "comes straight from the heart!" Although it is clear that a continuous vibrato has become an integral part of contemporary left-hand technique (rarely is a pure vibrato-less note heard in the modern sound world), nevertheless, one cannot argue that today's great violinists use vibrato in an altogether thoughtless way. Violinists there are, it is undeniable, who use such unremitting, wide vibratos that we are hard-pushed to tell which notes they are playing! But the critical ear can observe how the more nuanced players use differing speeds and widths of vibrato and even, occasionally, no vibrato at all.

If we listen to good HIP violinists we will also hear vibrato, but used more sparingly, with the specific purpose of warming up the more expressive notes, rather than as an essential and constant element in sound production.

The issue, as I will shortly demonstrate, is far from being one spawned by the rise of fashionable, historical authenticity in recent times. It is part of an ancient and ongoing argument between great artists and pedagogues, on the one hand, appalled by what they considered to be the excessive and vulgar use of a cherished, expressive device, and musicians judged by them to possess dubious taste, on the other.

The fact that so many great musicians of the past have felt the need to criticize the over-use of vibrato rather suggests that at all times there have been violinists open to the charge of over-indulgence. HIP advocates today are arguably joining forces with those critics of the past who, rather than condemning vibrato, struggled to defend it as an ornament whose ubiquitous overuse devalued it and rendered its true purpose obsolete.

In a detailed discussion on vibrato in his book *Principles of Violin Playing and Teaching* (1962), Ivan Galamian, one of the most influential violin teachers of the twentieth century, stresses the importance of varying the speed, width, and intensity of vibrato *"from the 'white' sound of no vibrato to that of the greatest intensity."*[1]

Although Galamian does not say as much, the white, vibrato-less sound is presumably to be used sparingly, a special effect, an emotional cooling off: how paradoxical that it had once been the very inclusion of vibrato that had been considered a special effect to be used in moderation!

Over the course of the twentieth century, a continuous vibrato came to be accepted as the norm; yet many important teachers of the day were vehemently opposed to it. The great pedagogue Carl Flesch, writing in 1923, insisted that vibrato be used only when the need for heightened expression in the music justified it. He cited three of the greatest virtuosi of the mid-nineteenth century, Joseph Joachim, Ernesto Camillo Sivori, and Pablo de Sarasate, as opposing continuous vibrato. Furthermore, he bemoaned the increased breadth of the vibrato cycle.[2]

Adopting a more philosophical tone, Flesch deplored the superficiality of his era, the hectic quality of modern life, and the profligacy that together were conspiring to drive out spiritual values. For him, vibrato had become nothing less than a metaphor for contemporary decadence, the triumph of hedonism over spirituality, true artistry drowning in waves of sensuous sound.

The teacher's mission was to save art by denouncing this habit. Donning his prophet's cloak, he peered into the future: the day may well come, he pondered, when the tide will turn and sophisticated audiences will reject the continuous, hyper-activity of the left hand.[3]

Others were rather less philosophical: an outraged contributor to the *Strad* in 1908 complained how seldom it had become to hear *"four bars of a violin solo, even by the greatest artists, played without the "vibrato" effect! Every note longer than a quaver is sure to be delivered by a left hand which trembles like jelly on a plate in the hand of a nervous waiter."*[4]

It could be argued that HIP, born partly as a reaction against the relentless intensity of the modern sound ideal, represents the vanguard seeking to fulfill Flesch's prophecy. For there is little doubt that purely aesthetic considerations play an important initial role in directing many musicians of today, young and old, toward the exploration of the

228

Baroque repertoire and away from the more highly charged way of music making prevalent elsewhere.

Although the trend toward elevating the status of vibrato within the total sound ideal was widely noticeable in the first part of the twentieth century, Fritz Kreisler (1875–1962) may be regarded as the first iconic violinist to play with a continuous vibrato. An outstanding artist, he had no lessons after the age of twelve and developed a unique sound and technique which, because he was one of the most recorded violinists of his time, became something of an ideal for the next generation. Interestingly, he failed to gain a position in the orchestra of the Vienna Court Opera because Arnold Rosé, the leader from 1081 until 1938, would not allow vibrato in the orchestra! The thought of every member of his string section varying the pitch of each note in differing degrees by means of a constant vibrato seemed quite absurd to Rosé: how could it possibly lead to a homogenous sound, a sound in which all parts would be clearly audible?

In the same year that Carl Flesch published *The Art of Violin Playing*, Leopold Auer, another highly influential teacher, wrote in his book *Violin Playing as I Teach It*, "*the excessive vibrato is a habit for which I have no tolerance. As a rule, I forbid my students using the vibrato at all on notes which are not sustained.*" Auer, who had studied with Jakob Dont and Joseph Joachim and counted Jascha Heifetz, Nathan Milstein, and Mischa Elman among his eminent pupils in St. Petersburg, considered the vibrato to be "*an effect, an embellishment; it can lend a touch of divine pathos to the climax of a phrase or the course of a passage, but only if the player has cultivated a delicate sense of proportion in the use of it.*"[5]

Furthermore, Auer considered resorting to vibrato as "*an ostrich-like endeavour to conceal bad tone production and intonation from oneself and from others.*" The vibrato should be "*primarily used as a means to heighten effect, to embellish or beautify a singing passage or tone. Unfortunately, both singers and players of string instruments frequently abuse this effect . . . and by doing so they have called into being a plague of the most inartistic nature.*"[6]

A similar criticism of this "plague" comes, perhaps surprisingly, from the composer Arnold Schönberg. Writing in 1940, the man who had revolutionized twentieth-century music castigated contemporary artists for their over-use of vibrato. Where once it had been used sparingly to breathe life into the sound, as he recalled from his youth, vibrato had sunk to the level of a sensationalist mannerism that sounded like the bleating of goats and was every bit as dreadful as the current fashion for audible shifts! Great artists, declares the man whose string sextet *Verklärte Nacht* had provoked a riot at its premiere in 1902, use very little vibrato and only on long notes that need a touch of extra color; they are also careful to vibrate at the appropriate speed and not to allow the vibrato to affect intonation.[7]

The books of Flesch and Auer were not the first in the twentieth century to criticize the use or abuse of vibrato. In his *Violin School*, written with Andreas Moser in 1902–5, the great Joseph Joachim, who had premiered Brahms's Violin Concerto in 1878 and was a close friend of Brahms, Mendelssohn, and Schumann, appeals to his readers to avoid the indiscriminate use of vibrato, or 'tremolo.' *"The pupil cannot be sufficiently warned against the habitual use of the tremolo,"* he writes, *"especially in the wrong place. A violinist whose taste is refined and healthy will always recognise the steady tone as the ruling one and will use the vibrato only where the expression seems to demand it."*[8]

Away from the restrictions of academic respectability, Joachim is more forthright. In a letter to his student Franz von Vescey, dated 1904, he advises thus: *"Break yourself of the habit of an overdone vibrato and the slow wobbling of the fingers in Cantabile passages—it is really the result of weakness in the fingers, and reminds one of the lamentations of old women."* Vibrato should, he insists, only be used *"when you wish to lay a particular stress on a note, which your feeling will suggest."* Elsewhere, he is quoted as saying to another pupil, Jelly d'Aranyi, never to use too much vibrato: *"that was for the circus artists!"*[9]

Joachim himself was revered as a great artist in the service of music. He used vibrato when he felt it would benefit the music, not as a way merely to beautify the sound. One of his pupils, the Scottish violinist Marion Ranken, describes how he played the *"slow themes of Beethoven, allowing himself not one single slide when avoidable or one hint of vibrato."* Having heard him play, she adds, *"the sickly wobble of most modern playing, in such places, becomes very painful."*[10]

Joachim had been a pupil of Joseph Böhm, who had himself studied with Pierre Rode. Rode had studied in Paris with Giovanni Battista Viotti (1755–1824), the founder of the French school of violin playing, renowned for his strong, full tone, his penetrating, singing legato, and his great diversity of bowing.

Viotti advocated vibrato on selected notes only. Figure a shows an extract from his 19th Violin Concerto, in which the wavy lines indicate where vibrato is considered appropriate. The extract appears in Pierre Baillot's *L'art du violon* of 1834. A disciple of Viotti, Baillot warns against endangering expression through the use of too much vibrato:

> *"In order that the ear does not suffer from vibrato ('ondulation' in French) . . . one should start (a note) pure and in tune. Vibrato placed with discretion gives to the sound of the instrument much similarity to the voice when it is strongly moved. This means of expression is very powerful, but if it were often used it would soon have lost the virtue to move and would have only the most dangerous inconvenience of denaturising the melody."*[11]

Figure a

Extract from Giovanni Battista Viotti's 19th Violin Concerto, from Pierre Baillot's *L'art du violon* (1834). The wavy lines indicate the places where an "Ondulation modérée" (moderate vibrato) is recommended. Note that these places always coincide with a dynamic swelling, the old Messa di voce.

Louis Spohr (1832) agrees with Baillot: "[The player] *must beware of introducing it too often or in unsuitable places,"* he writes, demonstrating how the French and German schools saw eye-to-eye on this issue.[12]

ঙ ঙ ঙ

The sometimes virulent criticisms leveled by those quoted above would not have been relevant had not many of their contemporaries been playing with the excessive vibrato of which they complained. Would they have written with such passion if only a small minority of players were transgressing their aesthetic boundaries? Would they have immortalized their views in print had not the offenders been prominent professionals, rather than chamber music aficionados playing string quartets in their drawing rooms at weekends? Could playing with a constant or near-constant vibrato, therefore, be any less 'historical' than playing with little or no vibrato at all?

Here lies our dilemma: do we follow the advice of those who preached moderation, discretion, and artistically motivated usage, or do we turn a blind eye to them and choose to emulate those whom they took such pains to criticize? What must we who aspire to play music in an historically informed manner understand to be the right approach to take vis-à-vis this complicated issue? Let us examine the evidence more thoroughly.

∾ ∾ ∾

If we choose to explore the advice of the overwhelming majority of sources from the Baroque period until recent times, we will be faced with four issues:

1. For what purpose was vibrato used?
2. How much was it used?
3. By what technical means was the vibrato produced?
4. To what extent did vibrato alter the pitch of a note?

We have ample evidence that vibrato was used as an expressive device both vocally and instrumentally throughout the Baroque period and indeed long before, as the following examples will show.

- 1529: the German theorist Martin Agricola writes in his *Musica instrumentalis deudsch* that a finger that trembles will produce a sweeter sound:
  "Auch schafft man mit dem Zittern frey
  Das susser laut die Melodey
  Denn auff den andern geschen mag."
  This delightful verse, translated by Curt Sachs, reads:
  "Who, while their stopping finger teeter
  Produce a melody much sweeter
  Than 'tis on other fiddles done."[13]
- 1542: Sylvestro Ganassi, in his treatise on the Viola da Gamba *Regola rubertina* advocates the use of both a bow and a left hand vibrato. *"With sad music,"* he writes *"the bow should be drawn lightly and at times, one should even make the bowing arm tremble and do the same thing on the fingerboard to achieve the necessary effect."*[14]
- 1619: in his "Syntagma musicum," Michael Praetorius speaks about the shimmering of the voice as being an essential part of the singer's art, possibly implying a varying of intensity rather than an actual changing of the pitch. A good singer, he writes, must *"have a beautiful, lovely, agile [zittern] and vibrating [bebende] voice."*[15]
- 1620: Francesco Rognoni, in Part Two of his *Selva* (see Lesson 26), mentions two types of *tremolo* (vibrato). He criticizes those who vibrate with one finger, varying the pitch both upward and downward and thus playing out of tune. The *tremolo* should, he says, be played with two fingers, as it is by nature a rising [accrescimento] of the note, not a falling. The rather exotic effect of this vibrato/trill hybrid clearly produces pitch fluctuation, but only upward (see Exercise 89).

Exercise 89: A possible reconstruction of Rognoni's tremolo

1. Play a c″♯ with the second finger on the A string,
2. Place your third finger lightly on the nail of the second, the tip very slightly above the string.
3. Using a wrist movement, rock the hand to and fro so that the tip of the third finger lightly touches the string.
4. The third finger does not move independently of the second finger.

- 1636: in his *Harmonie universlle*, Marin Mersenne devotes much space to explain different kinds of vibrato ("tremblemens") on the lute. One of these is the "Battement," described as "*a violent shaking of the hand while not allowing the finger to leave the string,*" an ornament "*more often used on the violin than on the lute.*"[16]

- 1687: in his *Traité de la viole*, Jean Rousseau advocates playing vibrato on all long notes: "*The vibrato imitates a certain gentle agitation of the voice in the sounds. That is why one uses it in all places when the value of the note permits, and it must last as long as the note.*" One kind of vibrato (*le batement*) involves pressing two fingers together, one on the string and the other tapping very lightly on it. Rousseau also advocates a gentler kind of vibrato (*langeuer*) played with one finger.[17]

- 1695 (?): in the Chapter "As to Musick" of Roger North's autobiography *Notes of Me*, North illustrates three kinds of vocal or bowed ornaments:
  1. The "plaine note," basically a Messa di voce, without vibrato.
  2. The "waived note." This begins like a Messa di voce, but as it blooms an audible vibrato is added that lasts throughout the note, diminishing toward the end.
  3. The "trillo note" begins as above, but vibrato is wide enough to distinguish two clear pitches (as in a trill); the vibrato accelerates, becomes thinner and vanishes. North warns that the latter is "*dangerous for a scollar to medle with, till he hath mastery of the sound, els it will make him apt to loos the principall tone; and that spoiles all.*"[18]

A distinction should thus be made between a type of vibrato that does not alter the pitch of a note and one that does, which North describes as "dangerous." Any pitch fluctuation due to vibrato poses a risk to the enharmonic distinctions (between E♭ and D♯, for example) that meantone temperaments demand. Losing the center of the sound, says North, spoils everything.

- 1706: In his *Musicalischer-Trichter*, a treatise on singing, Martin Heinrich Fuhrmann uses the term *tremoletto* to describe a type of vibrato related to the "Ribattuta di Gola" or "re-beating of the throat," the term used by Caccini (see Lesson 25).

Fuhrmann's illustration (Figure b) of the *tremoletto*, like Caccini's, shows just a single note. Sing the word "ha" on each note, quite slowly and clearly articulated, and then quicken the pace until you reach your maximum speed, gradually losing the "h" until you have something more like an "ah." There is now no articulation between sounds, just a wave within a single note. Caccini's bleating has become gentler, "*almost not struck at all,*" as Fuhrmann writes.[19]

Figure b

Martin Heinrich
Fuhrmann's illustration
of the *tremoletto*.

This effect, he says, is best demonstrated on the violin *"when one lets the finger remain on the string and as with the shake, slightly moves and makes the tone shimmer."* Was Fuhrmann merely seeking to illustrate on a violin the effect of a vocal technique, or was he comparing his vocal *tremoletto* to a kind of vibrato being used by violinists at the time, a finger vibrato with no fluctuation in pitch? Exercise 90 is an attempt to reconstruct this technique, reproducing the "shimmer" Fuhrmann describes.

Exercise 90: Producing a vibrato without pitch fluctuation

1. On any open string, play a trill with your third fingor.
2. Repeat, but this time without entirely lifting the finger from the string. The fluctuation in pressure produces a vibrato effect without any fluctuation of pitch. The speed of this type of vibrato will be rather moderate.
3. Practice with each finger above open strings.
4. Practice on a scale, keeping the fingers down normally: the vibrato produced will be subtle but perceptible.

- 1715: the French flute virtuoso Jacques-Martin Hotteterre, describes the "flattement" or vibrato as being done by playing a trill without covering up the entire hole with the finger. *"One will observe,"* he writes in the Preface to his *Premier Livre de Pieces Pour la Flute Traversiere, "that one must do the 'flattements' on almost all long notes . . . slower or faster, according to the character of the Pieces."* This technique has much in common with that of Fuhrmann described above and, as in the quote from Rousseau (above), implies that vibrato on long notes was common on both flute and viol in French music of this time. [20]

- 1739: Johann Mattheson, in *Der Vollkommene Capellmeister,* seems to advocate no fluctuation of pitch when he says that the *"tremolo . . . is the slightest possible oscillation on a single fixed tone . . . on instruments merely bending the fingertips without yielding the positioning accomplishes this very thing to some degree. . . . [N]othing more is required for it than a single pitch."*

  "Whoever is acquainted with the tremolos in organ works," Mattheson continues, *"will know that simply the wavering air itself performs the effect and no higher or lower keys are touched on the keyboard: for such a tremolo is only a valve in the windpipe of the organ which causes an oscillation of the sound as rapid as one wants. On violins the same trembling can also be accomplished on one tone within one bowing without another being necessary for it."* [21]

- 1748: Francesco Geminiani in *A Treatise of Good Taste in the Art of Musick* and reprinted in *The Art of Playing on the Violin* (1751) writes, in the section entitled *"Of the Close Shake,"* (Example XVIII, 8) *"This cannot possibly be described by Notes as in former Examples. To perform it, you must press the Finger strongly upon the String of the Instrument, and move the Wrist in and out slowly and equally, when it is long continued swelling the Sound by Degrees, drawing the Bow nearer to the Bridge, and ending it very strong it may express*

233

Majesty, Dignity &c. But making it shorter, lower and softer, it may denote Affliction, Fear, &c. and when it is made on short Notes, it only contributes to make their Sound more agreable and for this Reason it should be made use of as often as possible."

This last phrase is something of a thorn in the flesh of some in today's HIP community. Geminiani is the single most important role model for many Baroque violinists, his writing a gold mine of information directly informing many aspects of their playing—except for this sentence on vibrato. Geminiani, a pupil of Corelli, does appear here to be advocating a generous, if not a continuous, use of vibrato. As will be seen below, however, he was quickly taken to task by one of his own pupils.

- 1777: Robert Bremner, a Scottish music publisher who *"had the honour to be the pupil of the once eminent Geminiani"* challenged his teacher's view. *"Many gentlemen players on bow instruments are so exceeding fond of the tremolo,"* he writes in *Some Thoughts on the Performance of Concert Music,* *"that they apply it wherever they possibly can. This grace has a resemblance to that wavering sound given by two of the unisons of an organ, a little out of tune; or to the voice of one who is paralytic."* Although a little vibrato was admissible *"for the sake of variety . . . at times on a long note in simple melody,"* Bremner concedes, *"yet, if it be introduced into harmony, where all the parts [should be] exactly in tune with each other, it becomes hurtful. The proper stop is a fixed point, from which the least deviation is erroneous; consequently the tremolo, which is a departure from this point will not only confuse the harmony . . . but also enfeeble it."*[22]

  Bremner was so adamant on this point that when he republished the "once eminent" Geminiani's treatise, he censored it, omitting the passage on vibrato with which he disagreed.

- 1756: Leopold Mozart bemoans the fact that some violinists were playing with a constant vibrato involving pitch fluctuation. *"Now because the tremolo is not purely on one note but sounds undulating,"* he writes (Chapter XI, § 3), *"so would it be an error if every note were played with the tremolo. Performers there are who tremble consistently on each note as if they had the palsy."*

On the other hand, he did consider vibrato to be a natural phenomenon: *"The Tremolo is an ornamentation which arises from Nature herself and which can be used charmingly on a long note, not only by good instrumentalists but by clever singers,"* he says at the start of Chapter XI. *"For if we strike a slack string or a bell sharply, we hear after the stroke a certain wave-like undulation (ondeggiamento) of the struck note. And this trembling after-sound is called tremolo. . . . "Take pains,"* Leopold continues, *"to imitate this natural quivering on the violin."* He then describes how to vibrate: *"The finger is pressed strongly down on the string, and one makes a small movement with the whole hand . . . forwards toward the bridge and backwards toward the scroll."*

Does this mean that the pitch fluctuation resulting from this movement both sharpens and flattens the note? It would appear so: *"For as, when the remaining trembling sound of a struck string or bell is not pure and continues to sound not on one note only but sways first too high, then too low, just so by the movement of the hand forward and backward must you endeavour to imitate exactly the swaying of these intermediate tones."*

Almost everything that Leopold writes about vibrato in his *Versuch* (1756) was shamelessly plagiarized from Tartini's *Regole* (Rules for playing the violin), written around 1753. At the time Leopold was writing, the *Regole* was circulating in handwritten copies only (presumably that is why Leopold felt he could get away with copying so much of it!) The *Regole* was eventually published in France in 1771.

"This kind of ornament," Tartini had written, *"is by its very nature more suitable for instruments than for voices. . . . The sound of harpsichord strings, of bells and of the open strings of any bowed instrument, leaves naturally behind it a wave motion in the air which has been disturbed. This wave motion comes from the quivering of the little parts that make up the metal or from the continuation of the vibrations of the string struck by a bow or a jack."*

"This effect," Tartini continues, *"can be imitated on the violin, the viol and violoncello by a finger pressing on the string and being caused to vibrate by a movement of the wrist; the finger does not leave the string, though it is raised a little. If the finger vibrates slowly, the wave motion in the air, which is the vibrato of the tone, will be slow. If it is quick, the wave motion will be quick. The speed of the wave motion can thus be increased gradually by starting slowly and quickening it by degrees."* [23]

In Figure c, this increase is shown by little semi-circles, whose relative sizes indicate the slowness and quickness and consequently the increase.

Exercise 91 seeks to provide the student with a methodical approach to vibrato when playing chinless, gleaned from the above sources. Naturally, the 'chin on' player will find it easier to control and vary the vibrato, but this may lead him or her into a sound world too close to our modern one. I would therefore recommend 'chin on' players to explore vibrato from a chinless perspective.

"This ornament," adds Tartini *"makes the final note of a phrase sound excellent, when that note is long. It flatters both the tone and the melody. . . . It sounds very well, likewise, in the long notes of any singing passage. . . . "[it] must never be used for semitone intervals where not only must the human voice be imitated but in addition the intonation must be perfect with mathematical precision."*[24]

This last caveat, that vibrato must never be used for semitone intervals, goes some way toward clarifying Tartini's stance on the issue of pitch fluctuation. In the section on trills, on the other hand, he mentions a hybrid vibrato, not unlike the "batement" of Rousseau, halfway between a trill and a vibrato, presumably used for moments of greater passion. This technique clearly involves a sharpening of the main note:

> There is another kind of trill that is best performed on the violin. The two notes that make it up join in such a way that the two fingers never quite leave the string. It is not done, like the others, by raising the finger but by using the wrist to carry the whole hand and thus also the finger, in a rippling motion, so that this kind of trill is "rippled" and not "struck" (Liée et non battue). It sounds well in playing con affetto and when the two notes are only a semitone apart.[25]

235

Exercise 91: Toward a technique of vibrato when playing chinless

1. Hold the violin like a guitar.
2. Place the first finger on any string and roll it back and forth along the trajectory of the string in a slow, measured way. Do not move the arm, or consider the wrist as the primary source of movement: it is the finger that is the primary mover, with the help of the wrist. Begin practicing at a speed of 60 cycles of vibrato per minute, using a metronome.
3. Still in a measured way, increase the speed of the metronome by one notch at a time, staying in each new tempo for one minute.
4. When you have reached the fastest tempo possible without losing control, hold the violin in a chinless way and repeat this exercise from the beginning.
5. Take up the bow and repeat the entire exercise. As vibrato is essentially a disturbance of the string's natural oscillation, the bow will need to be more firmly placed on the string as the vibrato speeds up.

- 1791: Francesco Galeazzi (1758–1819) in his *Elementi teorico-pratici di musica con un saggio sopra l'arte di suonare il violino analizzata, ed a dimostrabili principi ridotta* describes vibrato as a *"discordant tremolo"* produced by a *"paralytic and trembling motion,"* adding that it *"should be banished from music by anyone who has good taste."*[26]

ᵛᵍ ᵛᵍ ᵛᵍ

I leave the last word to Mozart, not the father, for once, but the son. On June 12, 1778, Wolfgang Amadeus wrote to his father from Paris complaining about the Salzburg singer Joseph Dominik Nikolaus Meissner whose vibrato he intensely disliked. *"Meissner, as you know, has the bad habit of making his voice tremble at times, turning a note that should be sustained into distinct crotchets, or even quavers—and this I never could endure in him. And really it is a detestable habit and one which is quite contrary to nature. The human voice trembles naturally—but in its own way—and only to such a degree that the effect is beautiful. Such is the nature of the voice; and people imitate it not only on wind instruments, but on stringed instruments too and even on the clavichord. But the moment the proper limit is overstepped, it is no longer beautiful—because it is contrary to nature. It reminds me of when, on the organ, the bellows are jolted."*[27]

Mozart's reference to vibrato on the clavichord may strike one as strange, but there is evidence of vibrato having being used on keyboard instruments, notably the organ and clavichord, from the sixteenth to the late eighteenth centuries.

- Michael Praetorius (1610) mentions a harpsichord with a mechanism for bowing the strings that can produce vibrato *"by trembling and shaking slowly or rapidly with a free hand."*[28]
- Friedrich Wilhelm Marpurg, in his treatise of 1750, also mentions vibrato, known in old German as "Bebung," being executed by moving the fingers although, he notes, this is not as effective as on a "bowed" harpsichord.[29]

- C. P. E. Bach in his *Versuch* (1753) notes that *"a good* clavichord . . . offers all the beauties of [a fortepiano]. Moreover *"A long, expressive note can well accommodate a Bebung, executed as it were by rocking the key with the finger remaining on it."* [30]
- Daniel Gottlob Türk, in his *Clavierschule* (1789) states that the Bebung enables the player to *"play with much more expression than is possible, for example, on the harpsichord. . . . The Bebung can only be used effectively over long notes, particularly in compositions of melancholy character and the like. . . . The finger is allowed to remain on the key for as long as is required by the duration of the given note and attempts to reinforce the note with a repeated and gentle pressure. I scarcely need mention that after each pressure there is a lessening, but that the finger should not be completely lifted off the key."* But he cautions that *"one ought to be wary of the frequent use of the Bebung and when it is used, one must guard against ugly exaggeration of the tone by too violent a pressure."* [31]

Conclusions

There are three types of vibrato that can be used in Baroque violin playing:

1. Bow vibrato (a fluctuation of pressure on the stick) to be discussed in Part Three.
2. Finger vibrato of intensity, as described in Exercise 90 (the finger rising and falling vertically as if playing a trill but without leaving the string).
3. Hand (wrist) vibrato with pitch fluctuation, (the finger oscillating both forward and backward from the note, thereby sharpening and flattening the pitch).

Without the use of the chin to steady the instrument, the wrist vibrato is more restricted than its modern equivalent and is consequently not as wide. The arm vibrato that is so prevalent today is technically impossible without the use of the chin, and even then very difficult to do without a chinrest: as this device was invented by Spohr around the turn of the nineteenth century, we can disregard this technique in the present discussion.

Sources written over a period of around two centuries agree that the expressive quality of vibrato is not to be devalued by excessive use. Ultimately, I believe that the amount of vibrato a player uses is a question of individual taste. Some will use more than others: I am sure it was ever thus.

237

Notes

1. Ivan Galamian, *Principles of Violin Playing and Teaching*, p. 37.
2. Carl Flesch, *The Art of Violin Playing*, Book One, p. 40.
3. Flesch, *The Art of Violin Playing*, Book One, p. 40.
4. *The Strad*, January 1908. The contributor wrote under the pen name "The Strolling Player."
5. Leopold Auer, *Violin Playing as I Teach It*, p. 23.
6. Leopold Auer, *Violin Playing as I Teach It*, p. 22.
7. *Style and Idea*, selected writings of Arnold Schönberg, pp. 345–47.
8. Joseph Joachim, *Violin School*, p. 94.
9. Joseph MacLeod, *The Sisters d'Aranyi*, p. 48.

10. Marion Bruce Ranken, *Some Points of Violin Playing and Musical Performance as learnt in the Hochschule für Musik (Joachim School) in Berlin during the time I was a Student There,* 1902–1909, p. 16.

11. Baillot, *L'art du violon,* p. 138.

12. Louis Spohr, *Violin School,* Henry Holmes translation, p. 157,

13. Quoted in Boyden, p. 91.

14. Ganassi, *Regola rubertina,* Section 1, Chapter II.

15. *Performers' Guide to the Seventeenth Century,* p. 19.

16. Mersenne, *Harmonie universelle,* Livre Second, Proposition IX, Article VII, p. 81. "Le battement est plus pratiqué sur le Violon que sur le Luth," quoted in Boyden, p. 178.

17. Jean Rousseau, *Traité de la Viole.* Troisiéme Partie, Des Agrémens. Chapitre XI "Du Batement, de la Langueur & de la Plainte," pp. 100–101.

18. Roger North, *Notes of Me,* p. 150.

19. *Performers' Guide to the Seventeenth Century,* p. 19.

20. *Pieces pour la Flute Traversiere et Autres Instruments,* . . . par M. Hotteterre-le-Romain, Flûte de la Chambre du Roy. Preface.

21. Mattheson, DVC, Part II, Chapter 3, § 27, (p 270).

22. Robert Bremner: *Some Thoughts on the Performance of Concert Music.* Introduction to *Six Quarttetos for two Violins, a Tenor and Violincello* (Opus 6) by J. G. C. Schetky.

23. Tartini: *Traité des Agréments* III. Hermann Moeck Edition p. 85).

24. Tartini: *Traité des Agréments* III. (Hermann Moeck Edition p. 84-87).

25. Tartini: *Traité des Agréments* II. (Hermann Moeck Edition pp. 78-79).

26. Galeazzi: *Elementi teorico-pratici di musica con un saggio sopra l'arte di suonare il violino analizzata, ed a dimostrabili principi ridotta,* Vol. 1, p. 171. Quoted in Neal Zaslaw, "Vibrato in Eighteenth Century Orchestras," Performance Practice Review: Vol. 4: No. 1, Article 4, 1991.

27. Letter of 12 June 1778. English translation by Emily Anderson in *The Letters of Mozart and His Family.* vol. 2, pp. 816-17, London, 1938. Quoted in Neal Zaslaw, "Vibrato in Eighteenth Century Orchestras," Performance Practice Review: Vol. 4: No. 1, Article 4, 1991.

28. Praetorius, *Syntagma Musicum,* Vol. II. Quoted in Brauchli, The Clavichord, p 271.

29. Marpurg, *Die Kunst das Klavier zu spielen,* quoted in Brauchli, The Clavichord, p 271.

30. C.P.E Bach, *Essay,* Introduction, 11 and III, 20. Quoted in Brauchli, The Clavichord, p 271.

31. Türk, *Clavierschule,* Section 88, quoted in Donnington, p. 192.

Lesson 23

Rhetoric

The Power to Persuade

In this lesson, after a brief historical introduction to the subject of rhetoric, I give further indications of what playing in a rhetorical style means in practice and how it differs from the 'modern' approach to playing. We will also investigate some key rhetorical figures with the help of Prince Hamlet.

The rhetorical element in both the composition and performance of Baroque music has already been explored in previous lessons:

- In Lesson 4 we learned to play words, investigating their rhythm and other aspects of their enunciation, first individually and then in complete texts.
- In Lesson 5 (on Jan Pieterszoon Sweelinck's *Garrula rondinella*) we worked on that same aspect of rhetoric in more detail, not merely imitating the rhythm of words and enunciating specific vowels and consonants with our bow, but also seeking to communicate in sound the emotions of each phrase.
- In Lesson 8 we discussed how sound affects us and how, by intensifying our awareness of the emotional information contained within different intervals, we are better able to *"express Sentiments, strike the Imagination, affect the Mind, and command the Passions."*
- In Lesson 13 we discussed the importance of flexibility in rhythm, dynamics, and articulation.

The Origins of Rhetoric

The word "rhetoric" comes from the Greek "rhekorike" meaning the art of the public speaker, or "rhetor." From "rhetor," via the Latin, we get our words "oratory" and "orator." We first find the word "rhetor" in Plato's dialogue *Gorgias*, written in the fourth century BC, where it is defined as "a worker of persuasion."

Athenian democracy and the Athenian system of justice depended, like ours, on debate and argument, so it was necessary for Athenian citizens who wished to involve themselves in politics and the legal system to perfect their ability to speak persuasively in public.

This art of persuasion was to become a kind of pseudo-science: many handbooks and manuals were written on the subject, the principal texts in Greek being by Aristotle and Demetrius. These were widely distributed throughout the Hellenic world and many were also translated into Latin. The Roman writers Cicero and Quintilian added their masterpieces to the literature of rhetoric, and from the Middle Ages onward, both Greek and Roman texts were circulating among the intellectual elite of Europe, forming the basis for more textbooks on the subject, written both in Latin and in other languages. Rhetoric was to form one of the cornerstones of European classical education until modern times.

In biblical Hebrew the word "shir" can mean either "song" or "poem," so the "Song of Songs," traditionally written by King Solomon, could equally be known as the "Poem of Poems." Adding a melodic element to the recitation of a poem, as Homer is known to have done, was known as melopoeia by the ancient Greeks but was normal practice throughout the ancient world; indeed, it is hard to imagine poetry spoken without an element of chant.

Rhetoric and Music

Quintilian recognized that a careful study of music was beneficial to the orator's art. *"Music,"* he wrote, *"by means of the tone and modulation of the voice, expresses sublime thoughts with grandeur, pleasant ones with sweetness, and ordinary ones with calmness, and sympathizes in its whole art with the feelings attendant on what is expressed. In oratory, accordingly, the raising, lowering, or other inflection of the voice tends to move the feelings of the hearers. We try to excite the indignation of the judges in one modulation of phrase and voice . . . and their pity in another, for we see that minds are affected in different ways even by musical instruments, though words cannot be uttered by them."*[1]

Nearly 1,600 years later, Marin Mersenne, the French philosopher, theologian, music theorist, and disciple of Descartes, was to concur: *"There is nothing of any importance in elocution,"* he writes, *"that is not subject to the rules and the science of music."* Musicians must therefore study *"the art of the harmonic orator, who must know all the degrees, rhythms, and proper accents to excite everything he wishes in his audiences."*[2]

Quintilian (Marcus Fabius Quintilianus) was born in Spain but was sent to Rome to study rhetoric. His *Institutio Oratoria* (Institutes of Oratory) published in about 95 C.E., gives a detailed account of the theory and practice of rhetoric, but also covers huge areas of interest including the early education of children. The book was widely read in the ancient world and throughout the Middle Ages. In 1416, a complete manuscript was discovered in the monastery of St. Gall, and Quintilian was thereafter seen as an inspiration to the Humanist movement. He was revered by many leading intellectuals, from Francesco Petrarch and Martin Luther to John Stuart Mill.

Conversely, the study of rhetoric was later to be seen as an essential part of the musician's art. Compare Quintilian's words with those of Quantz:

Musical execution may be compared with the delivery of an orator. The orator and the musician have . . . the same aim . . . namely to make themselves masters of the hearts of their listeners. . . . Thus it is advantageous to both, if each has some knowledge of the duties of the other. (XI, § 1)

The declared links between the art of the orator and that of the Baroque musician, both composer and performer, are ubiquitous and numerous: *"As all good Musick should be composed in Imitation of a Discourse,"* writes Geminiani, *"these two Ornaments (piano and forte) are designed to produce the same Effects that an Orator does by raising and falling his Voice."*[3]

That "all good Musick should be composed in Imitation of a Discourse" is one of the pivotal concepts that divide musicians with an interest in historically informed performance from those who have none. The realization that much of the music we play is not in fact melodic in the sense that Classical and Romantic music later came to be, is a crucially important event in our search for an authentic and convincing approach to the interpretation of the Baroque repertoire. To play rhetorically conceived music as if it were melodic, forcing it indeed to *become* melodic through the use of techniques developed for later styles of music, is to choose an approach that is unhistorical, misleading, and fundamentally flawed.

Music composed "in Imitation of a Discourse" demands to be performed "in Imitation of a Discourse."

The Musician as Orator

To produce *"the same Effects that an Orator does"* means learning to play using much the same means as a public speaker attempting to persuade his audience to think and believe as he does. When we listen to a politician angling for our vote, or indeed to one of those charismatic leaders who have no time for democracy at all, he or she will be intent on manipulating us into a state of believing that *his* or *her* political agenda is the one that is best for us and for the nation. Similarly, when we watch courtroom dramas, we see lawyers using their skills of oratory to persuade a jury that Mr. X was, or could not possibly have been, murdered by Mr. Y. Their power of persuasion (not necessarily in harmony with the truth) is what will eventually sway the jury.

As an example, let us take the iconic "I have a dream" speech of Martin Luther King (1963).

"I have a dream that one day this nation will rise up and live out the true meaning of its creed: 'We hold these truths to be self-evident: that all men are created equal.'"

1. Read the lines through silently.
2. Read them again, this time out loud.
3. Declaim them as if you were standing in front of 250,000 people!

These three stages illustrate the progression from mere reading toward true oratory. Now watch Dr. King declaim it himself, on YouTube. It's worth watching the speech right through from the beginning, observing how at first he carefully sets out his case, spoken with the measured voice of the historian. He then gradually turns up the heat to move his public with a more visionary tone of voice as he foresees the future, his "dream," leading us toward the rapturous, triumphant climax.

The term "rhetorical style" can apply to most aspects of our art, anything indeed that we do to affect our audience before, during, and after we play: how we walk out on stage and bow, how we are dressed, how we tune, and how we pause to prepare ourselves for the first sounds, drawing the audience subtly into a state of empathy and expectation of our performance.

Almost every single device the orator can employ to hold the attention of his audience, we too can use to make our performance persuasive and convincing. The pacing of his speech, the fluctuating tempi that he uses, now slow and ponderous, now more rapid; his voice rising and falling, now almost whispering as if imparting a very special truth just for you, now trembling with passion, now fuming with rage, now pausing to share a joke; his use of silences, pausing to allow some more meaningful and significant thought he has just imparted to sink in, or to create a feeling of expectation as to what he is about to disclose next; his accentuated stressing of certain words, allowing others to slip by discreetly; some words are almost sung, others rattled out dryly; some words are spoken in a high voice, others in a medium or low voice, each with a different color. Some words or syllables are lingered upon for special emphasis, others not; some passages are delivered with a smile, for relief, others with a frown or a knowing wink; perhaps he remains stock still or perhaps he moves about on the podium making gestures with his eyes, his hands, and his head: all these devices and more form the arsenal of the orator and his musical equivalent, the rhetorical performer.

"*The accents of the voice,*" writes Jean-Jacques Rousseau in 1775, "*reach into the soul; for they are the natural Expression of the passions, and by painting the passions, these accents arouse them. It is through these accents that music becomes oratorical, eloquent and imitative; they form the language of music. It is through them that music paints objects for the imagination, that it transmits sentiments to the heart.*"[4]

The accents Rousseau writes about may convey myriad different emotions, from a cry of anguish or horror to an intimate sigh of grief, from an exuberant whoop of joy or the expression of astonishment to a lingering and questioning doubt. They can be slow, drawn out and languishing, or as quick as a sudden gasp of breath. They can be spoken or played prematurely or they can be delayed, with an expectant silence before, or a poignant, shocked silence after.

In his *Les Principes du clavecin* (1702), Saint Lambert compares the arts of rhetoric and music. "*A Piece of Music,*" he writes, "*resembles a Piece of Rhetoric, [une pièce d'Eloquence] or rather it is the Piece of Rhetoric that resembles the Piece of Music.*" Saint Lambert's prioritizing of music contains an important idea: that music expresses absolute truths that transcend language. More specific links between the two do exist: "*The notes*" he writes, "*correspond to letters, the bars to words, the cadences to sentences, the sections to parts, and the whole to the whole.*"[5]

Much later, Bernard Germain de Lacépède (1785) was to write that *"instrumental music as such is none other than ordinary speech from which all the consonants have been removed."*[6]

Rhetorical Playing versus Pure Instrumentalism

The modern approach to sound production, with its emphasis on legato bowing, a continuous vibrato, and a constantly singing sound, cannot achieve the variety of articulation and gesture that typifies the orator's art: neither does it seek to do so. The distinction between the two approaches is both aesthetic and ideological. Thus, whereas the 'modern' player is convinced of the expressive validity of a cherished instrumentalism, the rhetorical player is tempted to decry instrumentalism as the sacrifice of meaning on the altar of sensuality.

We may liken the rhetorical instrumentalist to the singer who prioritizes the text and, having explored its meaning, understood its implications, followed the ebb and flow of the poet's thoughts, and observed the subtle ways in which the composer has struggled to strengthen the impact of the poem, will put his or her voice at the service of the text in order to convey these subtleties to the audience.

On the other hand, there are singers who, even if they have explored the text in the same way, nonetheless prioritize the beauty of their voice and the power of their own personality, and by doing so risk obscuring not only the implications of the text but even the text itself.

In rhetorical playing, the elements that went into the conception and composition of a piece of music must first be identified. The "Observations" that form much of the content of the lessons in this book constitute an attempt to do just that. We must then seek to exploit every detail of the written text and to extract from it every possible appropriate ounce of expression, drama, and interest for, as Quantz reminds us (XVII, V, §12) *"the "purpose of music—to constantly arouse and still the passions—must never be forgotten."*

Learning to be a musician has many parallels with learning the art of public speaking. The public speaker cannot make his speech in the voice that he uses when he reads stories to his children or discusses philosophy over a glass of wine. In public he must exude a larger than life persona; he must be eloquent and stylish, and his voice cannot drone but must constantly hold the attention of his audience, both by the content of his speech and by his manner of delivery.

Just as we have learned to play words, we can learn to speak music. Exercise 92 is designed to help you perceive and play in a more rhetorical way.

Exercise 92: Learning to speak music

1. Play the opening of the Preludio from the Corelli sonata we studied in Lesson 16, or the one from the Vivaldi sonata we studied in Lesson 19.
2. Improvise words that fit the rhythm: they need not be coherent.
3. Declaim these words as if giving a speech before a large audience.
4. Play the movement again, imitating the speech you have just made.

When we practice, we should always have in mind that there is an audience out there with whom we have a duty to communicate, asking ourselves in every bar if what we are playing has the quality needed to *"affect the Mind, and command the Passions."* Like the orator, we need to speak the notes clearly, not slurring them together like a drone. We need to determine which notes are to be stressed and which are of lesser importance, ensuring that this distinction is clearly audible.

❧ ❧ ❧

Some Rhetorical Figures

There are literally hundreds of rhetorical figures, or devices, mentioned in the literature, many with Greek names that are complicated to retain: fortunately, it is not necessary for us to do so. Once we are clear about the overall rhetorical nature of Baroque music, however, there is little danger that we might fail to notice such figures when we see them, even if we cannot name them. It will then be left to our imaginations to express these motives clearly, rather than playing the notes with a 'beautiful' but less than meaningful sound.

> "Do not play the violin," I tell my students, "play words, music, gestures! Your sound cannot be merely beautiful: it must be meaningful and convincing!"

Many aspects of rhetorical playing, such as the emotional information contained in intervals and in rhythms, the gestures and exclamations, have already been explored in previous lessons. A few are summarized below, with more examples added. It is to be hoped that these will help train the eye to perceive the black dots on the page as forming rhetorical fragments that together combine to map out a broader truth.

Dynamics

Dynamic markings rarely occur in Baroque music, but varying the dynamics is an essential part of the rhetorical art. Speaking in a monotonous way will result in the loss of attention on the part of one's listeners, possibly even sending them to sleep! So it is with the performer. Dynamics are determined by the ebb and flow of the harmony, or by the simple geography of the line: a crescendo when it rises, a diminuendo when it falls (although the opposite can also be convincing).

If the harmony at the end of a single note is stronger than at its beginning, for example because it is dissonant, a crescendo on that note will give more life to the note as well as ensuring that the full emotional content of that dissonance can be made clear. In order to have sufficient bow left to sing the dissonance, our bow speed must be carefully controlled. A diminuendo on a note can similarly engage the audience's attention, arousing mystery and expectation as to what might follow, especially if it fades away to silence.

> When the orator ceases to declaim and, seeming to adopt a more personal tone aimed at the individual rather than at the crowd, speaks softly to a hushed audience, the effect is the same as the performer who, exploiting the enormous power of the *pianissimo,* draws his audience into sharing his most intimate musical thoughts.

Parentheses

Fluctuations of intensity are central to holding an audience's attention. When you declaim the following sentence, it is probable that the words in parentheses will be intoned at a lower pitch. To make the meaning clear, you will also pause briefly both before and after the brackets:

"I believe wholeheartedly" (he added) "in democracy, justice and equality."

So it is in music: in Bars 10–12 of Schmelzer's third "Sonata unarum fidium" (Figure a) the three descending notes (notes 4–6) in the first and second bars, as well as the entire second half of the third bar could be said to form 'asides' to the main line of the music. We would be justified, therefore, to place them in parentheses, playing them softer than the rest of the musical sentence and pausing briefly both before and after to clarify the rhetorical narrative.

Figure a
Bars 10–12 of Schmelzer's third *Sonata unarum fidium.*

245

Repetition

The orator's insistent repeating of a word is similar to the composer's insistent repetition of a note or group of notes. This can have various effects, depending on the context. In the following sentence, the gradual speeding up of the word "never" within a crescendo will serve to impress on the audience the speaker's determination to be honest and trustworthy.

"I shall never / never/ **never** / break this oath."

In act 2, scene 2, of Hamlet, on the other hand, Hamlet's repetition of "words" could be phrased in any number of intriguing ways.

Polonius: What do you read, my lord?
Hamlet: Words, words, words.

The intonation, both within individual units and in the sentence as a whole, can be varied; tempo, timing, dynamics, accent, and stress likewise have limitless possibilities of inflection. Thus the music of just three words has the power to inform, confuse, alarm, or amuse an audience struggling to comprehend Hamlet's state of mind.

In the opening bars (Figure b) of the first sonata from his 1681 set, Heinrich Ignaz Franz von Biber uses repetition in a similar way, although the affect is very different. As in Hamlet, the number three is prevalent and the potential for rhetorical nuance through the means listed above is vast.

The fanfare-like opening two notes are followed by a rapid A major flourish. There are three statements of this opening, but the third statement is extended, with three flourishes in quick succession. From the end of Bar 4, the A major triad is inverted and is paired with a further triad, spiced with an added g'♯ that alters the affect toward something possibly more sinister. Coiling snake-like, the two triads are heard three times before disappearing.

Figure b

Biber, Sonata 1 from the 1681 set, opening bars.

Direction, Punctuation, and Intonation

In speech, we use punctuation and intonation to help articulate thoughts clearly. In Hamlet's phrase "To die, to sleep—No more" (act 3, scene 1), each two-word thought has a distinct intonation and tempo, additionally clarified through punctuation. The meaning would be corrupted if this were not so: "To die? To sleep no more?" is one example of such corruption. In music, successive two-note fragments can also have meanings that need to be clearly expressed.

Another crucial element in purveying the multifarious nuances possible within these three fragments is intonation. Speaking the words "To die" on a single note, or with a rising or falling voice will alter our audience's perception of Hamlet's mindset at this pivotal moment in the speech.

In the following fragment (Figure c) from Biber's Annunciation Sonata, Bars 45–47, the gestures are so distinct they could be easily choreographed: the rising interval (a″– c‴) leading into the third bar may suggest a yearning, or reaching upward, while the descending second (g″–f″) that follows may symbolize resignation or regret. The rest of the extract is less fragmented and more forward-looking: after the pain of the dissonance at the start of the final bar we move on to a glowingly optimistic D major harmony.

Having identified these four contrasting gestures, we can find our way to a meaningful and nuanced portrayal of each of them in sound before exploring how they relate to each other, just as "to die" and "to sleep" do: we could even declaim the first two gestures with those words, observing the resultant effect.

Naturally, if there is no stated programmatic context, identifying sentiments remains little more than an exercise in subjectivity. Nevertheless, the performer who has a clear personal concept of the emotion inherent in a piece or fragment of a piece is more likely to play it in a convincing way. Failure to make such decisions could result in a papering over of the inherent rhetorical content, thus rendering the fragment inconsequential.

Figure c
Biber, Mystery Sonata 1 (Annunciation), Adagio (Bars 45-48).

Tonality

Ascribing specific characters to individual tonalities (we touched on this in Lesson 11) is as fraught with subjectivity as ascribing specific emotions to rhetorical figures. Nevertheless, both lines of investigation are important and can contribute valuable additional information to the process we call "interpretation."

The connection between tonality and emotion was already established in ancient times. Aristotle, in Book VIII of his *Politics*, describes how specific musical modes affect the soul: the Mixolydian, for example, makes one sad and serious, the Dorian produces a moderate and stable temper, while the Phrygian inspires enthusiasm.[7]

Plato, in *The Republic*, also discusses the individual qualities of the modes: the Mixolydian and Extreme Lydian modes are deemed suitable for dirges, he writes, whereas the Ionian and Lydian modes are good for relaxing and for drinking songs—and therefore of no use in the training of soldiers![8]

Judy Tarling has devised a helpful table comparing the key characteristics as described by Jean Rousseau and Marc-Antoine Charpentier in 1691 and 1693, respectively, and by Johann Mattheson (1713–19) and Jean-Philippe Rameau (1722). You will find Charpentier's complete table "The Energies of the Modes" in Appendix III of this book.

There are inevitably some jarring disagreements: A major is "joyful" according to Charpentier and Rameau but "devotional" for Rousseau and "lamenting, sad, playful and jesting" according to Mattheson, while E major is "quarrelsome" to Charpentier, has a "fatal sadness" for Mattheson, and is "grand and tender" to Rameau. Nevertheless, there is on the whole a striking similarity between their descriptions. Remember that with equal temperament such individual qualities are in any case diluted or lost.[9]

Dissonance

Dissonances are used to express a variety of emotions such as grief, pain, sorrow, regret, protest, horror, and ecstasy in varying dosages according to the context. The sound of a dissonance can thus be anything from gentle, sweet, searing, or ecstatic to raw and even violent; the latter two occur more rarely in Baroque music than in the music of later periods.

Identifying the emotion implicit in each dissonant chord is important, for that emotion will suggest a quality of sound appropriate to its expression and that sound will in turn determine the technique appropriate for its realization. To express tender pain, for example, we may need a slow bow, one that sinks gently into the strings; in three- or four-part chords the bow may roll gently over the strings after lingering on the bass note, the remaining notes following with only a slight degree of actual merging. With more aggressive emotions, the bow will probably need to move faster, with a greater degree of merging (by "merging" I mean two or more notes sounding simultaneously.) In all chord playing, the danger of yielding to pure instrumentalism in the form of a limited number of set technical formulae is to be avoided.

A resolution may be slurred to its dissonance or, in order to obtain a certain effect such as stuttering or staggering, played with a separate bow. In both cases, care must be taken not to accent the resolution by playing it with too fast a bow or with too much pressure: it should usually be weaker than its dissonance, but not so weak as to be inaudible!

Let us examine two contrasting examples of dissonance from Biber's solo *Passagaglia*. In Figure d, the string of repeated thirty-second notes hardly prepares us for the intensity of the strident dissonance at the beginning of the second line. This dissonance, suggesting horror and extreme pain, is sustained for an entire quarter note. Immediately following the resolution, another dissonance replaces it, although this second one is less extreme.

Figure d
Biber, *Passagaglia*,
Bars 69–82.

In the second example, (Figure e) each dissonant harmony may be said to express suffering of a more intimate but quite distinct nature. Here, the pain is not raw, but refined, exquisite, pious, perhaps even ecstatic. From the third to the sixth bar the overall tessitura sinks, and although it rises up again into the last bar, it immediately resumes its downward trend. There is much chromaticism here, adding ambiguity to the overall affect, as emotions dissolve and re-form like shadows.

The technical variables are

- The speed and rhythm of the string crossings.
- The extent to which the parts merge into each other.
- The amount of time spent on the bass note.
- The time spent on the dissonance itself.
- The articulation of the eighth notes.
- The amount of pressure on the stick.

From the breathiness of a chord suggesting hushed awe to the searing lyricism expressing hope or redemption, each chord requires thought as to its meaning, both in itself and in relation to the surrounding harmonies.

Figure e
Biber, *Passagaglia*, Bars 93–101.

Tessitura

Tessitura is a rhetorical device of great significance. In language, we talk about "deep sorrow" or the "heights of happiness" rather than "high sorrow" or the "depths of happiness." In declamation, the same word (for example "yes") spoken in a low, medium, or high voice will have different nuances and connotations.

The tessitura of the orator's voice is a vital aspect of his power of persuasion at any given time. Quintilian tells us of *"Caius Gracchus, the most eminent orator of his time, behind whom, when he spoke in public, a musician used to stand and give, with a pitch-pipe, the tones in which his voice was to be exerted."*[10]

In music, low notes tend to have a greater sense of gravitas than high ones. Compare the first note of Bach's G minor solo sonata, a low g, with the first notes of the D minor Partita a fifth higher or the start of the E major Partita, a high e′′′ (one of the highest notes Bach wrote) that certainly suggests a joyous affect.

On the other hand, high notes can sometimes suggest a floating, celestial sound: take the opening of the Sonata no. 5 in E minor from the 1681 set by Biber, (Figure f). At the start, the violin is three octaves higher than the bass note, by far the highest opening note of the set. In Bar 5, Biber repeats the opening motive down an octave, adding the open E string for extra resonance and drama.

249

Figure f
Biber, Sonata 5 from the 1681 set, opening bars.

The tessitura of the bass also impacts on the sound of the violin, perhaps suggesting a more ethereal sound when it rises high and more gravitas when it is low.

Tempo

The choice of tempo is an important factor. Just as in a Mass, a fast and skittish "Kyrie" or a slow ponderous "Gloria" would send incorrect and confusing messages to the congregation, so the tempo we choose has expressive and rhetorical implications. Too slow a tempo could risk losing the long line of a phrase as well as the listeners' attention, while a too fast tempo runs the risk of sacrificing detail and causing amusement instead of the intended effect.

It is usually best to explore all aspects of a piece before deciding on the final tempo, rather than first deciding on the tempo and then struggling to manage the details within it. In any case, tempo depends to a certain extent on the acoustics of the concert venue. In a resonant church, too fast a tempo may result in notes becoming blurred and the music incomprehensible.

Meter

"The power of rhythm in the composition of melody," Mattheson tells us *"is uncommonly great."* To demonstrate this, he gives entertaining examples of dances with their rhythms removed, transformed thereby into church chorales, and of church chorales with rhythms inserted so as to make them into Minuets and Polonaises *"without at all altering the flow of melody itself, nor the tone or pitch."*[11]

Throughout this book we refer to the emotional information conveyed through rhythm and meter. At a basic level, there is clearly an emotional distinction to be made between long notes and short ones, for example, or between movements in triple time and those in quadruple time. Each rhythmic formula derived from the basic ingredients of 'short' and 'long' (Mattheson lists twenty-six of them used in poetry) can be said to have its own emotional impact; music, by its very nature has an infinite number of variations.

Acoustic

It is our duty to engage the audience with every note that we play. Too often we practice in small studios that encourage us to play in a miniature fashion: we are then overwhelmed when we realize what a vast space we need to fill on the day of the concert! Practicing in a large hall or in a church will help us to develop the art of projection as well as how to cope with resonant acoustics, for our practice studios too often have very dry acoustics.

Short notes are often swallowed up in resonant churches, so divisions and ornaments may need to be played slower, more emphatically, or in some cases cut out altogether. Weak notes, low notes, resolutions of dissonances, etc. will be in danger of getting lost in the wake of the stronger notes that precede them and in the general wash of sound; there may also need for clearer consonants to penetrate that wash.

Imagery

Just as the orator inspires the listener with images, symbols, and metaphors, so it can be useful to have some kind of visual association in our minds when studying a piece of music.

Sometimes the composer provides this imagery for us: Figure g shows the start of the final section from Biber's Crucifixion Sonata. Biber writes no program (see Lesson 33) but we can assume that the rushing thirty-second notes and the pulsating eighth notes represent the earthquake following the death of Jesus: "and the earth did quake, and the rocks rent" (Matthew 27, 51).

Figure g

Text-painting. Biber's Crucifixion Sonata, the earthquake.

When no obvious image is present, it may be left to our own imagination to create one. Metaphors and similes, as well as poetic and visual images and literary references can be immensely powerful means of suggestion, both for teachers to inspire students and for performers to inspire themselves when working on a piece.

Figure h shows another extract from the first of Biber's 1681 sonatas. Visually, there are so many disparate elements and obvious events: how unlike a melody it is! Conjuring up images and 'spotting' some rhetorical figures will build an image of this fragment that can help us to play it more convincingly.

In the first bar, the top line trembles while other notes leap down like sparks. Later, those sparks turn into a raging fire.

The Adagio resembles a chorale, a moment of order and calm. The soprano and bass parts move in contrary motion, evoking a feeling of elation, or perhaps a vision of a glorious sunrise. In rhetoric, this is an *anabasis* or an *ascensio,* defined by Athanasius Kircher as "*a musical passage through which we express exalted, rising, or elevated and eminent thoughts.*"[12]

In the third bar, the high bass line and low violin notes suggest a more hushed communion of sounds, after which the violin parts rise again. In the fourth bar, the upper violin part transforms itself into the lower one as if a new voice, the a″, has suddenly appeared out of the blue. This crossing of parts is known in rhetoric as *metabasis* or *transgresso.*

The descending scale, or *tirata,* swoops swiftly down like one of Homer's goddesses from Mount Olympus, then rises and swoops again, this time disappearing into a silence. The rhetorical term *Abruptio, "used by Virgil to denote a breaking off in the middle of a speech,"* is appropriate here: Biber makes frequent and often startling use of this device.[13]

In order to prolong the effect of the *Abruptio,* the bass should wait before rising up the octave to continue, possibly cutting out the sound altogether. The next two chords (A and B major) have a quality of doubt, a questioning uncertainty after the *Abruptio.* Naturally, the 'question' is a common occurrence in rhetoric: we can call this harmonic progression by the rhetorical name of *interrogatio.* The silence before it could be a sigh of regret, a *suspiratio,* whereas the silence after it is more decisive, its purpose being to energize the eighth note double stops that follow: these eighth notes have an air of purposeful, stately walking.

251

Figure h

Biber, Sonata No. 1
from the 1681 set,
Bars 17–30.

The penultimate bar is visually fragmented and incoherent, the notes limping and strained, without any obvious sense of line; each pair should be practiced as a separate unit to reveal its individual rhetorical expression. The D♯ appoggiaturas have a yearning or pleading quality (try enhancing their impact by flattening those sharps) while the contrasting rising fourth in Beat 3 carries an element of surprise.

Presentation

Elegance on stage, whether of speaker or performer, was considered highly important throughout the Baroque period. In the very first chapter of his *Regola rubertina* (1542), Sylvestro Ganassi stresses the importance of *"beauty and quality in all things." "You must know,"* he writes, *"that in the art of playing, one's limbs are the servants of one's body and that the body is not the servant of one's limbs. It would be ugly to see one make ungainly body movements just to move one's hands just as it would, to see the master wrest a broom from his servant's hand to do the sweeping himself."* He adds that *"there would be no purpose in acting as though you were doing some kind of Moorish dance, for that would not be the most graceful or beautiful way of holding the instrument. . . . I certainly do not want you to hold the viol in such a disturbed foetal position."*[14]

François Couperin, in the Preface to the 1717 edition of his *L'art de toucher le clavecin* remarks, *"It is best, and more becoming, not to mark time with one's head, body or feet. One should have an air of ease at the harpsichord, without fixing one's gaze too much on any object nor looking too vague."*[15] He also advocates placing a mirror in front of students to cure them of facial grimaces! C. P. E. Bach concurs that *"ugly grimaces are . . . inappropriate and harmful,"* adding that *"fitting expressions help the listener to understand our meaning."*[16]

In Lesson 2, we had similar good advice from Leopold Mozart on the subject of appearance and the need to be wary of bad habits on stage. The risk, he warns, is that the audience will be *"moved either to laughter or pity at the sight of so laborious a wood-chopper"* (Chapter II, § 6). Similarly, Mattheson asks whether *"the attentive listener [can] be moved to pleasure if he . . . sees a dozen violinists who contort their bodies as if they are ill?"*[17]

A degree of elegance is also important to modern audiences. Musicians who slouch onto the platform as if apologizing for their very existence do not inspire confidence, while those who move around too much, leaping and bobbing up and down in an ungainly fashion, can cause audiences gathered in expectation of a moving musical experience to titter.

Audiences also set much store by the way the performers communicate with each other on stage. Musicians who stare into their music without any visual contact with their colleagues can be as disturbing to the audience as those who smile during moments of deep sadness or who look glum when the music suggests a light-hearted, amusing atmosphere.

Thus appearances are an important element in the performer's communication system with the audience. C. P. E. Bach writes about manipulating one's feelings in order to be able to communicate the appropriate affect. *"In languishing, sad passages, the performer must languish and grow sad,"* he writes, whereas *"in lively, joyous passages, the executant must again put himself in the appropriate mood."* But he goes further: one should

253

adopt appropriate physical expressions, for *"fitting expressions help the listener to understand our meaning."*[18]

Notes

1. Quintilian, *Institutes of Oratory*, Book 1, Chapter 10, 24.
2. Mersenne, *Harmonie universelle*, 2:365, translation by David Allen Duncan, "Persuading the Affections: Rhetorical Theory and Mersenne's Advice to Harmonic Orators," in *French Musical Thought, 1600–1800*, ed. Georgia Cowart (Ann Arbor; University of Michigan Research Press, 1989), quoted in Mark Evan Bonds, *Absolute Music: The History of an Idea* (New York: Oxford University Press, 2016), p. 62.
3. Geminiani, *A Treatise on Good Taste in the Art of Musick*, p 3: "Of Piano and Forte."
4. Patricia Ranum, *The Harmonic Orator*, p. 8.
5. Saint Lambert, *Les principes du clavecin*, Chapitre VIII, pp. 35–36.
6. Lacépède, *La poétique de la musique* Paris 1785, quoted in Patricia Ranum, *The Harmonic Orator*, p. 2.
7. Aristotle, *Politics*, Book VIII.
8. Plato, *The Republic*, Book 3, 398.
9. Tarling, *BSP*, p. 7.
10. Quintilian, *Institutes of Oratory*, Book 1, Chapter 10, No. 27.
11. Mattheson, *DVC*, Part II, Chapter 6, § 3 (p. 344).
12. Quoted in Bartel, *Musica Poetica: Musical-Rhetorical Figures in German Baroque Music*, p. 180.
13. Bartel, *Musica Poetica*, p. 167.
14. Ganassi, *Regola rubertina*, Section 1, Chapter I.
15. François Couperin, *L'art de toucher le clavecin*, Preface (1717)
16. C.P.E Bach, Essay, Chapter 3, Performance, § 13 (p152).
17. Mattheson, DVC, Part I, Chapter 6, § 16 (p135).
18. C.P.E. Bach, Essay. Chapter 3, Performance, § 13 (p152).

BIBLIOGRAPHY

Notes

The most oft-quoted primary sources, Johann Joachim Quantz's *Versuch einer Anweisung die Flöte Traversière zu spielen* (On Playing the Flute) and Leopold Mozart's *Versuch einer gründlichen Violinschule* (Treatise on the Fundamental Principles of Violin Playing) are referenced within the text. The formula (XVII, VI, § 12) for example, means Chapter XVII, Section VI, paragraph 12.

Abbreviations

Boyden:	Boyden, *The History of Violin Playing from Its Origins to 1761.*
C.P.E. Bach, *Essay*:	C. P. E. Bach, *Essay on the True Art of Playing Keyboard Instruments.*
Donnington:	Donnington, *The Interpretation of Early Music.*
Mattheson *DVC*:	Mattheson, *Der Vollkommene Capellmeister.*
GMPP:	*Georg Muffat on Performance Practice.*
NBR:	*New Bach Reader.*
SRMH:	Strunk, *Source Readings in Music History: The Baroque Era.*
Tarling, *BSP*:	Tarling, *Baroque String Playing for Ingenious Learners.*
Tarling, *WOR*:	Tarling, *Weapons of Rhetoric A Guide for Musicians and Audience.*
Tosi:	*Observations on the Florid Song.*

Primary sources listed by country of publication

Many of these sources are available on IMSLP or are published in facsimile form or in transcription. The most complete collection of instrumental treatises in facsimile is *Méthodes et Traités* by Anne Fuzeau Productions, Paris.

Seventeenth-Century Italian Ornamentation Treatises in Chronological Order

Ganassi dal Fontego, Sylvestrodi. *Opera Intitulata Fontegara*. Venice, 1535; Robert Lienau Musik Verlag, 1997.

Ortiz, Diego. *"Trattado de glosas sobre clausulas y otros generos de puntos en la musica de violones,"* Rome, 1553. Bärenreiter Editions, Kassel, 1936. English Translation by Ian Gammie published as *Treatise on Divisions, Cadences and other kinds of points in the music of viols*. Corda Music Publications, St. Albans, UK, 1978.

Dalla Casa, Girolamo. *Il vero modo di diminuir con tute le sorte le Stromenti*. Venice, 1584. IMSLP.

Bassano, Giovanni. *Ricercate, passaggi et cadentie per potersi essercitar nel diminuir terminatamente con ogni sorte d'Istrumento; & anco diversi passaggi per la semplice voce*. Venice, 1585; published by Musedita, 2009.

Rogniono, Riccardo. *Passaggi per potersi essercitare nel diminuire terminatamente con ogni sorte d'instromenti*. Libro Secondo: *Il Vero Modo di Diminuire*. Venice, 1591. English version, with a preface on this work and Francesco Rognoni's treatise by Bruce Dickey, published by Forni, Bologna, 2002.

Zacconi, Lodovico. *Prattica di musica.* Venice, 1592. IMSLP and Google Books.

Bovicelli, Giovanni Battista. Regole. *Passaggi di musica, madrigali e motetti passaeggiati.* Venice, 1594; transcribed and published by Musedita Edizioni, Albese con Cassano, 2009.

Virgiliano, Aurelio. *Il dolcimelo d'Aurelio Virgiliano, dove si contengono variati passaggi, e diminutioni cosi per voci, come per tutte sorte d'instrumenti musicale; con loro accordi, e modi di sonare.* IMSLP and Anne Fuzeau Productions

Rognoni, Francesco. *Selva de varii passaggi secondo l'uso moderno, per cantare e suonare con ogni sorte de stromenti, divisa in due parti.* Milan, 1620; transcription by Musedita Edizioni, Albese con Cassano, 2014.

Spadi, Giovanni Battista. *Libro de passaggi ascendenti et descendenti . . . Con alter cadenze & madrigali diminuiti per sonare con ogni sorte di stromenti, & anco per cantare con la semplice voce.* Venice, 1624. IMSLP.

Doni, Giovanni Battista. *Annotazioni sopra il compendio de generi e de'modi della musica.* Rome, 1640. IMSLP.

Additional Italian Sources

Caccini, Giulio. Preface to *Le nuove musiche,* Florence, 1602 Complete transcription (without English translation) by Musedita Edizioni, Albese con Cassano, 2009.

Bardi, Pietro de. Letter to G. B. Doni (1634). Reproduced in W. Oliver Strunk, *Source Readings in Music History: The Baroque Era.* New York: W. W. Norton, 1966, p. 3.

Peri, Jacopo. Preface to Euridice. Reproduced in W. Oliver Strunk, *Source Readings in Music History: The Baroque Era.* New York: W. W. Norton, 1966, p.14.

Castiglione, Baldassare. *Il libro del Cortegiano,* Venice, 1528. Translated by George Bull as *The Book of the Courtier.* Baltimore, MD: Penguin Classics, 1967.

Vasari, Giorgio. *Le Vite de' più eccellenti pittori, scultori, ed architettori* (Lives of the Most Excellent Painters, Sculptors and Architects). Florence, 1550 Published as *Lives of the Artists* by George Bull. Baltimore, MD. Penguin Books, 1965.

Italian Violin Treatises in Chronological Order

Zanetti, Gasparo. *Il scolaro per imparar a suonare di violino, et altri stromenti.* Milan, 1645. Firenze: Studio per edizioni scelte, 1984.

Bismantova, Bartolomeo. Chapter about violin in *Compendio musicale.* Ferrara, 1677. IMSLP.

Tessarini, Carlo. *Gramatica di musica: insegna il modo facile e breve per bene imparare di sonare il violino sù la parte.* Rome, 1741. Published in English as *An accurate method to attain the art of playing ye violin. With graces in all the different keys, how to make proper cadences, & ye nature of all ye shifts, with several duets and lessons for that instrument.* London, 1765.

Tartini, Giuseppe. *L'arte dell'arco.* Paris, 1758.

Tartini, Giuseppe. *Lettera del defonto Signor Giuseppe Tartini* alla *Signora Maddalena Lombardini Inserviente ad una importante Lezione per I Suonatori di Violino.* Published with a translation by Dr. Burney: *A letter from the late Signor Tartini to Signora Maddalena Lombardini (now Signora Sirmen) Published as an Important Lesson to Performers on the Violin.* London, 1779. IMSLP.

Tartini, Giuseppe. *Regole per arrivare a saper ben suonar il violino.* First published as *Traité des agréments de la musique.* Paris, 1771. Modern edition: Hermann Moeck Verlag, Celle and Bärenreiter, New York.

Signoretti, Pietro. *Méthode de la musique et du violon.* Den Haag, 1777. Fuzeau.

Galeazzi, Francesco. *Elementi teorico-pratici di musica con un saggio sopra l'arte di suonare il violino analizzata, ed a dimostrabili principi ridotta,* Rome, 1791. Fuzeau.

Campagnoli, Bartolomeo. *Nuovo metodo della mecanica progressiva per suonare il violino* (Original bilingual edition). Milan/Florence, 1797. Fuzeau.

French Violin Treatises in Chronological Order

Jambe de Fer, Philibert. *Epitome musical.* Lyon, 1556. Available on website of Bibliothèque nationale de France (gallica.bnf.fr).

Mersenne, Marin. *Harmonie universelle.* Paris, 1636. Part II, Book II, *Des instruments à chordes.* IMSLP. English translation by Roger Chapman, 1957. Republished by Springer, Dordrecht, Netherlands.

Brossard, Sébastien de. *Méthode de violon.* 1711.

Montéclair, Michel Pignolet de. *Méthode facile pour apprendre à joüer du violon.* 1711.

Dupont, Pierre. *Principes de violon par Demandes et par Réponce.* Paris, 1718. The later (1740) edition is available online at gallica.bnf.fr

Corrette, Michel. *L'Ecole d'Orphée, méthode pour apprendre facilement à jouer du violon.* Paris, 1738.

Mondonville, Jean-Joseph de. Introduction to *Les sons harmoniques,* op. 4. Paris and Lille, 1738.

Geminiani, Francesco. *L'art de jouer du violon.* 1752.

Herrando, José. *Arte y puntual explicación del modo de tocar el violin.* Paris, 1756.

L'Abbé le fils (Joseph-Barnabé de Saint-Sevin). *Principes du violon.* Paris, 1761.

Mozart, Leopold. *Méthode raisonnée pour apprendre à jouer du violon.* 1770.

Tarade, Théodore-Jean. *Traité du violon.* Paris, 1774.

Corrette, Michel. *L'Art de se perfectionner dans le Violon.* Paris, 1782.

Bornet l'ainé. *Nouvelle méthode de violon.* 1786.

Woldemar, Michel. *Méthode pour le violon.* Paris, 1795–98.

Bailleux, Antoine. *Méthode raisonée pour apprendre à joüer du violon.* Paris 1798–99.

Cartier, Jean Baptiste. *L'art du violon* [including *L'arte dell'arco* by G. Tartini]. Paris, 1798. Reprinted New York: Performers Editions, 1989.

German Violin Treatises in Chronological Order

Agricola, Martin. *Musica instrumentalis deudsch,* Wittenberg, 1529. English translation by William E. Hettrick. New York: Cambridge University Press, 1994.

Prinner, Johann Jacob. Chapter 13 from *Musicalischer Schlissl,* 1677.

Falck, Georg. *Anleitung zum Violin-Streichen für die Incipienten,* from *Idea bonis cantoris.* Nürnberg, 1688.

Merck, Daniel. *Compendium musicae instrumentalis Chelicae.* Augsburg, 1695.

Muffat, Georg. Prefaces to *Florilegium primum* (1695), *Florilegium secundum* (1698), and *Auserlesene Instrumentalmusik* (1701). See *Georg Muffat on Performance Practice.* Edited and translated by David K Wilson. Bloomington: Indiana University Press, 2001.

Mozart, Leopold. *Versuch einer gründlichen Violinschule,* Augsburg 1756. English translation by Editha Knocker. *A Treatise on the Fundamental Principles of Violin Playing,* 2nd ed. Oxford: Oxford University Press, 1951.

Reichardt, Johann Friedrich. *Über die Pflichten des Ripien-Violinisten.* Berlin and Leipzig 1776.

Lolli, Antonio. *L'école du violon en quatuor.* Berlin and Amsterdam, 1784.

English Violin Treatises in Chronological Order

Playford, John. *A Brief Introduction to the Playing on the Treble-Violin.* Extract from *An Introduction to the skill of Musick.* London, 1674. Facsimile published London: Travis and Emery.

Lenton, John. *The Gentleman's Diversion, or the Violin Explained.* London, 1693.

Anon. *Nolens volens, or You Shall Learn to Play on the Violin Whether You Will or No.* London, 1695.

Anon. *The Self-Instructor on the Violin.* London, 1695.

Prelleur, Peter. *The Art of Playing on the Violin.* Part V of *The Modern Musick-Master, or the Universal Musician.* London, 1730. IMSLP.

Crome, Robert. *The Fiddle New Model'd or a Useful Introduction to the Violin.* London, 1735(?).

Geminiani, Francesco. *The Art of Playing on the Violin.* London, 1751. London: Oxford University Press, 1952.

Zuccari, Carlo. *The true Method of Playing an Adagio . . . Adapted for those who study the Violin.* London, 1762.

Nineteenth and Twentieth Century Violin Methods in Chronological Order

Spohr, Louis. *Violinschule.* Vienna, 1832 (?). English translation by Henry Holmes. Published London: Boosey and Co., 1878.

Baillot, Pierre Marie Francois de Sales. *L'art du violon,* 1834. English translation by Louise Goldberg. Evanston, IL: Northwestern University Press, 1991.

Joseph Joachim and Andreas Moser. *Violinschule,* 3 vols. Berlin, 1902–5. Translated by A. Moffat. Berlin, 1905.

Flesch Carl. *The Art of Violin Playing:* Book One, *Technique in General. Applied Technique.* English edition, 1924.

Flesch Carl. *The Art of Violin Playing:* Book Two, *Artistic Realization and Instruction.* English edition, 1930.

Auer, Leopold. *Violin Playing as I Teach It.* New York: Dover, 1921.

Galamian, Ivan. *Principles of Violin Playing and Teaching.* 1962. Republished by Dover, New York, , 2013.

Other Instrumental and Voice Treatises in Chronological Order

Ganassi dal Fontego, Sylvestro di. *Regola rubertina and Lettione Seconda.* Venice, 1542–53. Translated by Richard Bodig. Stony Creek, Queensland, Australia: Saraband Music, 2002.

Burwell, Mary. *The Mary Burwell Lute Tutor,* c 1670. Facsimile available online or in an edition with an introductory study by Robert Spencer. Leeds: Boethius Press, 1974

Bacilly, Bénigne de. *Remarques curieuses sur l'art de bien chanter et particulierement pour ce qui regarde le chant François.* 1668. IMSLP.

Rousseau, Jean *Traité de la viole.* Paris, 1687. IMSLP.

Freillon Poncein, Jean-Pierre. *La véritable maniere d'apprendre à jouer en perfection du haut-bois de la flute et du flageolet.* Paris, 1700.

Saint Lambert, Monsieur de. *Les principes du clavecin avec de remarques nécessaires pour l'intelligence de plusieurs difficultés de la musique.* Paris, 1702. IMSLP.

Fuhrmann, Martin Heinrich. *Musicalischer-Trichter,* Franckfurt an der Spree, 1706. IMSLP.

Hotteterre, Jacques, dit le Romain: *Principes de la Flute Traversière, de la Flute à Bec, et du Hautbois.* Paris, 1707.

Couperin, François. *L'art de toucher le clavecin.* Paris, 1716. Edited and translated by Margery Halford. Van Nuys, CA: Alfred Publishing, 1974.

Tosi, Pier Francesco. *Opinioni de'cantori antichie moderni* (1723). Translated as *Observations on the Florid Song* by Johann Ernst Galliard (1742). London: Dodo Press and London: Travis and Emery.

Montéclair, Michel Pignolet de. *Principes de musique.* Paris, 1736.

Geminiani, Francesco. *A Treatise on Good Taste in the Art of Musick.* London 1749 Facsimile edition by King's Music.

Tonelli, Antonio. Harmonic realization of the complete op. 5 of Corelli. Undated MS in Biblioteca Estense Universitaria, Modena. IMSLP.

Quantz, Johann Joachim. *Versuch einer Anweisung die Flöte Traversière zu spielen,* Berlin, 1752. English edition, *On Playing the Flute.* Translated by Edward R. Reilly. Faber and Faber.

Anonymous. *Easy and Fundamental Instructions whereby either vocal or instrumental performers unacquainted with composition, may from the mere knowledge of the most common intervals in music, learn how to introduce extempore embellishments or variations; as also ornamental cadences with propriety, taste and regularity, translated from a famous treatise on music, written by Johann Joachim Quantz, composer to his Majesty the King of Prussia.* London, 1780 (?) IMSLP.

Bach, Carl Philipp Emanuel., *Versuch über die wahre Art das Clavier zu spielen.* Berlin, 1753. Translated as *Essay on the True Art of Playing Keyboard Instruments* and edited by William J. Mitchell. New York: W.W. Norton, 1949; London: Eulenburg Books.

Engramelle, Marie Dominique Joseph. *La tonotechnie ou l'art de noter les cylindres et tout ce qui est susceptible de notage dans les instrumentsde concerts mécaniques,* 1775. IMSLP.

Hiller, Johann Adam. *Anweisung zum musikalisch-zierlichen Gesange* (1780). Translated as *Treatise on Vocal Performance and Ornamentation* and edited by Suzanne J Beicken, University of Maryland. New York: Cambridge University Press, 2004.

Books on or Relevant to Performance Practice in Chronological Order

Morley, Thomas. *A Plaine and Easie Introduction to Practicall Musicke.* London, 1597.

Praetorius, Michael. *Syntagma musicum.* published in Wittenberg and Wolfenbüttel, 1614–20. Volume III edited by Jeffery T. Kite-Powell. Oxford: Oxford University Press, 2004.

Descartes, René. *Compendium musicae,* 1618. Translated by Walter Robert. Stuttgart: American Institute of Musicology, 1961.

North, Roger. *Notes of Me: The Autobiography of Roger North by Roger North.* Edited by Peter Millard. Toronto: University of Toronto Press, 2000.

Kircher, Athanasius. *Musurgia universalis*, 1650. IMSLP.

Mace, Thomas. *Musick's Monument*. London, 1676. IMSLP.

Charpentier, Marc–Antoine. *Règles de composition*, 1690. Available online (in French) at musebaroque.fr

North, Roger. *Roger North on Music, Being a Selection from his Essays written during the years c. 1695–1728*. Transcribed from the Manuscripts and Edited by John Wilson. London: Novello, 1959.

L'Affilard, Michel. *Principes très-faciles pour bien apprendre la musique*. Paris, 1694. Reprinted many times up to 1747.

Loulié, Étienne. *Eléments*. Published by Christophe Ballard. Paris, 1696. IMSLP.

Masson, Charles. *Nouveau traité des regles pour la composition de la musique*. Paris, 1697. IMSLP

Georg Muffat. Prefaces, collected in *Georg Muffat on Performance Practice*, edited and translated by David K Wilson. Bloomington: Indiana University Press, 2001.

Raguenet, François. *Parallèle des italiens et des françois en ce qui regarde la musique et les opéras*, Paris, Barbin, 1702. English version in **Strunk, W. Oliver.** *Source Readings in Music History: The Baroque Era*. New York: W. W. Norton, 1966.

Brossard, Sébastien de. *Dictionaire de Musique*, 1703. IMSLP.

Masson, Charles. *Nouveau traité des regles pour la composition de la musique*, 3rd ed. Paris, 1705. Available to read online at gallica.bnf.fr

Walther, Johann Gottfried. *Musicalisches Lexicon, oder Musicalische Bibliothec*. Leipzig, 1732. IMSLP.

David, François. *Méthode nouvelle ou principes généraux pour apprendre facilement la musique ou l'art de chanter*, 1737. Published 1760 by Mr de la Chevardière Paris. Available to read online at gallica.bnf.fr Digitalized by University of North Carolina at Chapel Hill 2013.

Mattheson, Johann. *Der Vollkommene Capellmeister*. Hamburg, 1739. Revised translation with critical commentary by Ernest C Harriss. Ann Arbor, MI: UMI Research Press, 1981.

Trévoux. *Dictionnaire universel françois et latin, vulgairement appellé Dictionnaire de Trévoux*. 1740.

Grassineau, James. *Musical Dictionary*. London, 1740. IMSLP.

Marpurg, Friedrich Wilhelm. *Die Kunst das Clavier zu spielen, durch den Verfasser des critischen Musicus an der Spree*. Berlin, 1750.

Marpurg, Friedrich Wilhelm. *Anleitung zum Clavierspielen*. Berlin 1755; and *Principes du Clavecin*. Berlin, 1756. Translated by E. L. Hays, PhD diss., Stanford University, 1977.

Rousseau, Jean-Jacques. *Dictionnaire de musique*. Paris, 1768. IMSLP.

Burney, Charles. *The Present State of Music in France and Italy: Or, The Journal Of A Tour Through Those Countries, Undertaken To Collect Materials For A General History Of Music*. 1771. Republished Cambridge: Cambridge University Press, 2014.

Burney Charles. *The Present State of Music in Germany, the Netherlands, and United Provinces*. London, 1773. Republished as *An Eighteenth Century Musical Tour in Central Europe and the Netherlands*. Edited by Percy Scholes. Oxford: Oxford University Press, 1959.

Kirnberger, Johann Philipp. *Die Kunst des reinen Satzes in der Musik*, Berlin and Köningsberg, 1774. IMSLP. Translated by David Beach and Jurgen Thym as *The Art of Strict Musical Composition*. New Haven, CT: Yale University Press, 1982.

Hawkins, Sir John. *A General History of the Science and Practice of Music*. London, 1776. IMSLP.

Bremner, Robert. *Some Thoughts on the Performance of Concert-Music*. Preface to *Six Quarttetos for two Violins, a Tenor and Violincello*, op. 6 by J. G. C. Schetky. London, 1777. British Library.

Türk, Daniel Gottlob. *Clavierschule, oder Anweisung zum Clavierspielen für Lehrer und Lernende . . . nebst 12 Handstücken*. Leipzig and Halle, 1789.

Books on Louis XIV and Versailles

François-Athénaïs de Rochechouart de Mortemart Montespan (1640-1707) *Memoirs of Madame de Montespan.* Public Domain Books, available on Kindle.

Saint-Simon, Duc de. *Memoirs of Louis XIV and His Court and of the Regency (1691–1709).* Public Domain Books, available on Kindle.

Durant, Will and Ariel. *The Age of Louis XIV.* New York: Simon and Schuster, 1963.

Books on the Baroque Violin in Alphabetical Order

Boyden, David. *The History of Violin Playing from Its Origins to 1761, and Its Relationship to the Violin and Violin Music.* Oxford: Oxford University Press, 1965. Reprint, Oxford: Clarendon Press, 1990.

Ritchie, Stanley. *Before the Chinrest. A Violinist's Guide to the Mysteries of Pre-Chinrest Technique and Style.* Publications of the Early Music Institute, Indiana University, 2012.

Stowell, Robin, Editor. *The Cambridge Companion to the Violin.* New York: Cambridge University Press, 1992.

Tarling, Judy. *Baroque String Playing for Ingenious Learners.* St. Albans, UK: Corda Music Publications, 2001.

Modern Books on Performance Practice in Alphabetical Order

Allsop, Peter. *Arcangelo Corelli: 'New Orpheus of Our Times'* (Oxford Monographs on Music). New York: Oxford University Press, 1999.

Anthony, James. *French Baroque Music from Beaujoyeulx to Rameau.* Milwaukee, WI: Hal Leonard, 2003.

Brauchli, Bernard. *The Clavichord.* Cambridge Musical Texts and Monographs. New York: Cambridge University Press, 2008.

Brewer, Charles E. *The Instrumental Music of Schmeltzer, Biber, Muffat and Their Contemporaries.* London: Taylor and Francis Books, 2016.

Brown, Howard Mayer. *Embellishing 16th-Century Music.* Oxford: Oxford University Press, 1976.

Bukofzer, Manfred F. *Music in the Baroque Era.* New York: W.W. Norton, 1947.

Carter, Stewart, Editor. A Performer's Guide to Seventeenth-Century Music Revised by **Kite-Powell, Jeffery.** Bloomington: Indiana University Press, 2012.

Carter, **Tim** and **John Butt**, Editors. *The Cambridge History of Seventeenth-Century Music.* New York: Cambridge University Press, 2014.

Cyr, Mary. *Style and Performance for Bowed String Instruments in French Baroque Music.* London: Routledge, 2016.

Donnington, Robert. *The Interpretation of Early Music.* London: Faber and Faber, 1989.

Donnington, Robert. *Performer's Guide to Baroque Music.* London: Faber and Faber, 1973.

Duffin, Ross W. *How Equal Temperament Ruined Harmony (and Why You Should Care).* New York: W.W. Norton, 2008.

Harnoncourt, Nikolaus. *Baroque Music Today: Music as Speech, Ways to a New Understanding of Music.* Translated by Mary O'Neil. Portland, OR: Amadeus Press, 1995.

Hauck, Werner. *Vibrato on the Violin.* Translated by Dr. Kitty Rokos. London: Bosworth, 1975.

261

Haynes, Bruce. *A History of Performing Pitch: the Story of "A."* Lanham, MD: Scarecrow Press, 2002.

Haynes, Bruce. *The End of Early Music: A Period Performer's History of Music for the Twenty-First Century.* New York: Oxford University Press, 2007.

Hefling, Stephen E. *Rhythmic Alteration in Seventeenth and Eighteenth Century Music. Notes Inégales and Overdotting.* New York: Schirmer Books, 1993.

Houle, George. *Meter in Music, 1600–1800: Performance, Perception, and Notation.* Bloomington: Indiana University Press, 2000.

Kolneder, Walter. *Das Buch der Violine.* Zurich: Atlantis, 1972. Kindle Edition.

MacLeod, Joseph. *The Sisters d'Aranyi.* London: Allen and Unwin, 1969.

Martens, Frederick H. *Violin Mastery, Talks with Master Violinists and Teachers.* New York: Frederick A. Stokes, 1919. Reprinted by London: Forgotten Books, 2017. Also available on Kindle.

Mellers, Wilfred. *François Couperin and the French Classical Tradition.* London: Faber and Faber, 1987. Also published London: Travis and Emery.

Neumann, Frederick. *Ornamentation in Baroque and Post-Baroque Music, with Special Emphasis on J. S. Bach.* Princeton, NJ: Princeton University Press, 1983.

Neumann, Frederick. *The Vibrato Controversy, New Essays on Performance Practice.* Rochester: University of Rochester Press, 1991.

Parsons, John Lewis. *Stylistic Change in Violin Performance 1900–1960 with Special Reference to Recordings of the Hungarian Violin School.* Chapter 3: "Vibrato." PhD diss., Cardiff University, 2005.

Ranken, Marion Bruce. *Some Points of Violin Playing and Musical Performance as learnt in the Hochschule für Musik (Joachim School) in Berlin during the time I was a Student there, 1902–1909.* Edinburgh, privately printed, 1939.

Strunk, W. Oliver. *Source Readings in Music History: The Baroque Era.* New York: W. W. Norton, 1966.

Veilhan, Jean-Claude. *Les Règles de l'Interprétation Musicale à l'Époque Baroque.* Paris: Alphonse Leduc, 1977.

Webber, Oliver. *Rethinking Gut Strings: A Guide for Players of Baroque Instruments.* King's Music, London, 2006.

Books on Vocal Technique in Alphabetical Order

Moriarty, John. *Diction.* New York: Schirmer, 1975.

Trusler, Ivan and **Walter Ehret.** *Functional Lessons in Singing.* Englewood Cliffs, NJ: Prentice-Hall, 1960.

Vaccai, Nicola. *Practical Method of Italian Singing.* New York: G. Schirmer, 1832.

Books on Bach in Alphabetical Order

Butt, John, Editor. *The Cambridge Companion to Bach.* Cambridge: Cambridge University Press, 1997.

David, Hans T., and **Arthur Mendel,** Editors. *The New Bach Reader, A Life of Johann Sebastian Bach in Letters and Documents.* Revised and expanded by Christoph Wolff. New York: W. W. Norton, 1998.

Forkel, Johann Nikolaus. *Über Johann Sebastian Bachs Leben, Kunst und Kunstwerke: Für patriotische Verehrer echter musikalischer Kunst, 1802.* Translated by (?) A. F. C Kollman as On Johann Sebastian Bach's Life, Genius and Works, included in *The New Bach Reader.*

Gaines, James. *Evening in the Palace of Reason: Bach Meets Frederick the Great in the Age of Enlightenment.* New York: Harper Perennial, 2005.

Ledbetter, David. *Unaccompanied Bach, Performing the Solo Works.* New Haven, CT: Yale University Press, 2009.

Lester, Joel. *Bach's Works for Solo Violin. Style, Structure, Performance.* New York: Oxford University Press, 1999.

Little, Meredith and Natalie Jenne. *Dance and the Music of J. S. Bach.* Bloomington: Indiana University Press, 2009.

Schröder, Jaap. *Bach's Solo Violin Works, A Performer's Guide.* New Haven, CT: Yale University Press, 2007.

Shute, Benjamin. *Sei Solo: Symbolum? The Theology of J. S. Bach's Solo Violin Works.* Eugene, OR: Pickwick Publications, 2016.

Thoene, Helga. *Johann Sebastian Bach. Ciaccona—Tanz oder Tombeau?* (Dance or Tombeau?) Eine analytische Studie. Oschersleben, Germany: Ziethen Verlag, 2009.

Wolff, Christoph. *Johann Sebastian Bach: The Learned Musician.* New York: Oxford University Press, 2005.

Books on Rhetoric in Alphabetical Order

Aristotle. *The Art of Rhetoric.* 4th century BCE. Translated by Hugh Lawson-Tancred. New York: Penguin Classics, 1991.

Bartel, Dietrich. *Musica Poetica: Musical-Rhetorical Figures in German Baroque Music.* Lincoln: University of Nebraska Press, 1997.

Quintilian, Marcus Fabius. *Institutes of Oratory.* 81–96 CE. Edited by Lee Honeycutt. Translated by John Selby Watson (1873). Kindle edition, 2010.

Ranum, Patricia M. *The Harmonic Orator. The phrasing and Rhetoric of the Melody in French Baroque Airs.* Boydell & Brewer, 2001.

Tarling, Judy. *Weapons of Rhetoric A Guide for Musicians and Audience.* Corda Music Publications, 2004.

Miscellaneous Books in Alphabetical Order

Flesch, Carl. *Urstudien,* Basic Studies for Violin. Carl Fischer Music.

Helmholtz, Hermann. *On the Sensations of Tone as a Physiological Basis for the Theory of Music* (1863.) English translation by Alexander J. Ellis. Cambridge University Press, 2009.

Jesús, Santa Teresa de (Santa Teresa de Avila). Libro de la vida. Ivory Falls Books, Kindle Edition, 2017.

Schoenberg, Arnold. *Style and Idea,* selected writings of Arnold Schoenberg, Edited by Leonard Stein, Faber and Faber, 1975

Schubart, Christian Friedrich Daniel. *Ideen zu einer Ästhetik der Tonkunst.* Vienna, 1806. Available in IMSLP (in German)

INDEX

Bold numbers denote reference to the specially devised exercises

Aaron, Pietro, *Thoscanello de la musica*, 100

Abbé le fils, L' (Joseph-Barnabé de Saint-Sévin),
 Principes du violon:
 use of bow, 23
 violin hold, 18

abruptio, 251

acoustics, 250

affetti
 subjectivity in, 247
 tables of, 100–1, 166–7, 247
 theory of, 71
 tonality and, 100–1, 107, 166–7, 175, 193, 247

Affektenlehre see affects, tables of; affects, theory of

agogic accent, 129, 172

agréments, 219; *see also* ornamentation

Agricola, Martin, 231

Albinoni, Tomaso Giovanni, *Trattenimenti Armonici*, 127
 Sonata op. 6, no. 2, Allegro, **132–8**, **150–1**

Amati, Andrea, 4

Amsterdam:
 Oude Kerk, 36
 Rijksmuseum, 13

anabasis, 251

anacrusis, 160, 170, 178–9, 199

anapestic meter, 211

appoggiaturas, 209

Arányi, Jelly d', 230

Aristotle, *Politics*:
 modes, 247
 rhetoric, 239–40

articulation, 28, **30**, **131**
 importance of varying, **61–2**, **132**, **203**

artistic independence, 189

ascensio, 251

Athens, 239

Auer, Leopold, *Violin Playing as I Teach It*, 229

Babitz, Sol, 113

Bach, Carl Philipp Emanuel:
 Bebung, 237
 emotions, manipulation of, 70
 fifths, narrow, 102
 human voice, imitation of, 30
 ornamentation, 217, 218
 as performer, 187
 presentation, 253

Bach, Johann Sebastian:
 Brandenburg Concerto no. 3, 28

 Cello Suites, 157–8
 Inventions and Sinfonias, 148
 Sei Solo, Partita no. 2 in D minor, Sarabanda, 177
 Sei Solo, Partita no. 3 in E major, 159
 singing style of playing, 148

Bacilly, Bénigne de, 224

back:
 ideal position, **45–6**, 47
 letting go of, **48**

Baillot, Pierre, *L'Art du violon*:
 left hand, expressive possibilities of, 148
 vibrato, excessive, 230

ballet du cour, 177

bariolage, 47

Baroque churches, ornamentation in, 216–17

Bartók, Béla, 31

bass instrument, bowings for, 202

bass line:
 importance of, 52–3, 207
 playing on the violin, 207
 see also ground bass; walking bass

Bebung, 236–7

Biber, Heinrich Ignatz Franz von:
 Mystery sonata no. 1, The Annunciation, 246–7
 Mystery sonata no. 10, The Crucifixion, 251
 Passagaglia, 248–9
 Sonata no. 1 (1681), 246, 251–3
 Sonata no. 5 (1681), 249

Bismantova, Bartolomeo, 23

body scan, 140

Bononcini, Giovanni Maria, *Arie. . . .a violono e
 violone o spinetta*, 157

Bornet *l'aîné*, 14

bow:
 active and passive impulses, 54–5
 breathing, 91
 contact with string, **139–45**
 control, 176
 dynamics, inherent, **26**, 63
 expressive power of, 75
 as extension of soul, 195
 fourth finger on, **143**
 mastery of, 74–5, 208
 point of contact, 139
 pressure, **83**, 139
 speaking and singing, **30**, 31–4, 62, 63, **243–4**
 speed, **83**, 139, 195
 strokes, categorization of, 133, 160

bow (*cont.*)
  use of, 23
  see also bow hold; bow vibrato; bowings; bows;
    elbow (right)
bow hold, 23–5, 140
  in England, 24
  French grip, 23–4
  thumb under stick, 13, 23–4
bow vibrato, 231
bowings:
  for bass instruments, specified by Vivaldi, 202
  choice of, 208
  dotted rhythms, **58–60**
  down bow, rule of, 208
  down bows, double, 54–5, 177
  indicated by composer, 134, 202
  giga, **202–3**
  marked, 42–4
  ricochet, imitation of, 64, **182**
  slurs, 64, 133–4, 137
  see also slurs; bow vibrato
bows:
  Baroque, 5, 6, 26, 139
  choosing, 5–6
  classical, 5
  detachable frogs, 6
  screw mechanism, 6
  transitional, 5
  'twig', 5
breathing, importance of, 50, **87–8**, 162
Bremner, Robert, 'Some Thoughts on the
    Performance of Concert Music':
  Corelli and powerful sound, 96
  swell (Messa di voce), 86
  vibrato, excessive, 234
Brossard, Sébastien de, 7
Burney, Charles:
  Bach, C. P. E., as performer, 187
  Farinelli's Messa di voce, 75
  shifting, expressive, 119
Burns, Robert, 192
Burwell, Mary, 6–7

Caccini, Giulio, *Le nuove musiche*:
  Messa di voce, 75
  ornamentation, 218
  ribattuta di gola, 232
cadences, ornamentation of, 201, 220, 224
caesura, 55–6
Cammerton see pitch
Campagnoli, Bartolomeo, 18
chacony, second beat of, 53–4
character of a piece, 53; *see also* affects
Charpentier, Marc-Antoine, 'The Energies of the
    Modes', 101, 107, 166–7, 247
chinless *see* chin-off playing; holding the instrument,
    chin-off

chin-off (chinless) playing:
  advantages, 20, 86, 179
  exercises in, **45–50**
  shifts and shifting, **108-19**, **124–5**
  vibrato, **235–6**
  see also holding the instrument
Cicero, 240
clichés, importance of avoiding, 160
'close shake', 233–4; *see also* vibrato
consonance, relation to dissonance, 43, 86, **87**
consonants, single and double, **41–2**
copying other people, pros and cons, 189
Corelli, Arcangelo:
  allegros, how to practise, 132
  bow, speaking, 30
  description of, 96
  exercise for powerful sound, **97**
  influence of, 96–7
  see also Corelli, Sonatas. op. 5
Corelli, Sonatas, op. 5, 155
  dynamic markings, 159
  influence of, 193, 194, 196, 202, 204, 207
  instrumentation, 157–8
  ornamented versions by Dubourg, 225
  tactus, 158–9
  tempo, 158–9
  walking bass, 207
  works:
    Sonata no. 1, Allegro, 47
    Sonata no. 3, Adagio, **85–95**
    Sonata no. 7, Preludio, **69–70**, **159–67**, **243**
    Sonata no. 7, Corrente, 169–76
    Sonata no. 7, Sarabanda, 177–81, 220, 222–5
    Sonata no. 7, Giga, **181–4**
'correct' way of playing, danger of, 186
corrente, 169–70
  Corelli op. 5, no. 7, 169–76
  Vivaldi op. 2, no. 1, **210–15**
Corrette, Michel, *L'École d'Orphée*, xv
  bow hold, 24
  violin hold, chin-on, **15–16**
Couperin, François:
  art de toucher le clavecin, L', 253
  ornamentation, forbidden, 219
  presentation, 253
courante (corrente, corant, coranto), 169–70; *see also*
    corrente
Cowper, William, 67
crescendo, silent, 179
Crome, Robert, *The Fiddle new Model'd*, 14, 15
custos (guida, guidon, Wächter), 162

dance:
  element, importance of recognising, 207–8
  rhythm of, 53, 55
Dante Alighieri, *Paradiso*, 181
Descartes, René:

Compendium musicae, 185
Passions de l'âme, Les, 66
sound, raw material of music, 185
diphthongs, 40–1
direction, 246–7
dissonance:
    relation to consonance, 43, 86, **87**
    rhetorical device, 248–9
    variety of expression in, 90
dotted notes, **58–60**
down bows *see* bowings
Dubourg, Matthew, ornamented versions of
    Corelli, 225
Dupont, Pierre, *Principes de violon*, 108–9
dynamics, 185, **201**
    of bow, inherent, **26**, 63
    crescendo, silent, 179
    flexibility of, 130
    markings, absence of markings, 52–3, 81, 136, 159,
        174, 194
    pianissimo, power of, 245
    relation to graphic contour of notes, 194, 204
    rhetorical device, 244–5
    terraced, 136

editions, modern, 52, 157
elbow (right), 25–6
emotional information:
    exploring, **67–73**
    in intervals, **68–70**
    in ornamentation, 222
    in rhythm, 210–**12**, 250
emotional keypad, **72–3**, 167
emotions:
    awareness of, 66–7
    identification of, 72, **166–7**, 193–4, 248–9
    manipulation of, **70–3**, **166–7**, 193–4
Engramelle, Marie Dominique Joseph, *La
    tonotechnie*, 57–8
equal notes, flexibility in, **127–32**, 207
    articulation, 131
    dynamics, **130**
    rhythm, **128–9**
equal temperament, 100–1, 104, 105
equal tension strings, 7; *see also* gut strings
exclamations, 195
expression, 95–7
    exaggeration in, 132
    more important than velocity, 128, 132

facsimiles, 52, 157, 162
    learning to read, 215
Farinel (Faronell), Michel, 'A Division on a
    Ground', 51–65
Farinelli (Carlo Broschi), 75
fifths, narrow, 10, 100, 101–2
figured bass, learning to read, 207

fingerings:
    chart, by Prelleur, 105–6
    chromatic, 93–4
fingers, left hand, 146–51; *see also* fingering; fourth
        finger trills
first position, the 'natural place', 169
flattement, 233; *see also* vibrato
Flesch, Carl:
    shifting, 113
    vibrato, 228
fourth finger, on bow, **143**
fourth finger trills, 92, 197
Fuhrmann, Martin Heinrich,
        Musicalischer-Trichter, 232–3

Galamian, Ivan, 228
Galeazzi, Francesco, *Elementi teorico-pratici di musica*, 236
Ganassi dal Fontego, Sylvestro di:
    bow, speaking with, 33
    bow vibrato, 231
    Fontegara, 29
    human voice, imitation of, 29
    Regola rubertina, 231, 253
    rhetorical device of presentation, 253
Gasparini, Francesco, *L'armonico pratico al cimbalo*, 171
gauge *see* gut strings, gauge of
Geige, 181
Geminiani, Francesco, *A Treatise of Good Taste in the
        Art of Musick*:
    'close shake', 233–4
    performer, emotional input of, 186
    see also Geminiani, Francesco, *The Art of Playing on
        the Violin*
Geminiani, Francesco, *The Art of Playing on the Violin*, xv
    bow hold, 24
    bow, use of, 23
    'close shake', 233–4
    down bow, rule of, 208
    fingerings, 94
    French edition (*L'art de jouer du violon*), 16
    German edition (*Gründliche Anleitung oder
        Violinschule*), 17
    good taste, 86
    left hand finger pressure, 146, 147
    Messa di voce, 75–6, **78–9**, **80**
    music, emotional power of, 66
    music, purpose of, 66
    musician as orator, 241
    scale studies, **120–6**
    semitones, major and minor, 93–4
    shifting, 108, 113, 118, **124–5**
    slurs, 133
    vibrato, continuous (?), 234
    violin hold, 14, 16–17, 19
    wrist, use of, 213
    see also Geminiani, Francesco, *A Treatise of Good
        Taste in the Art of Musick*

Geminiani grip, 21
gesture, 69–70
  in art, 195
  definition of, 195
  importance in music, 195–6
  relation to bow speed, 195
  roots of, 195
  translated into movements of bow, 199
  used to enhance a text, 195
giga:
  bowings, **202–3**
  Corelli op. 5, **181–4**
  Vivaldi op. 2, **202–6**
  see also gigue
gigue (jig, jigg, *giga*), 181
giguer, meaning of, 181
ground bass, 52, 53
gut strings:
  characteristics of, 147
  covered, 9
  equal tension, 7
  false, 8–9
  from sheep gut, 6
  G strings, 6, 7
  gauge of, 6–7
  putting them on, 7–9
  tuning, 8
  under the bow, **139–45**
  under the fingers, **146–51**

half position *see* second position
Handel, George Frideric:
  Lascia ch'io pianga from *Rinaldo*, 178
  ornamentation, written, 220–2
  Violin Sonata in A major, op. 1, no. 3, 220–2
  Violin Sonata in F major, op. 1, no. 12, **73**
  Violin Sonata in E major, op. 1, no. 15, 220, 221
hands, independent, **46–7**
harmony:
  expression in, 53
  realisation of, 207
Haynes, Bruce, *A History of Performing Pitch: The Story of "A"*, 10
Hebrew, biblical, 240
Helmholtz, Hermann von, 107
Helmholtz system, 2
hemiolas, 93, 208–9
  marked or ambiguous?, 172
  not mentioned in treatises, 209
  written out in Corelli, 95, 209
Herrando, José de, 16
Hiller, Johann Adam, 75
holding the instrument, 11–21
  chin-off (chinless), 14, 18, 19, 20
  chin-on, 15–17, 18, 19
  iconographic evidence, 12–13, 15–16, 17–18

textual evidence, 14–15, 16–18
  see also chin-off (chinless) playing
Homer, 240
Honthorst, Gerard van, *The Violin Player*, 13
Hotteterre, Jacques-Martin 'le Romain', 233
human voice, imitation of, 27, **29–34**, 36–8
  consonants, single and double, **41–2**
  diphthongs, 40–1
  rhythm, 30–4, **38–9**
  vowels, **39–40**

iambic meter, 211
imagery, 251–3
imagination, learning to use, 189
improvisation:
  by continuo players, 217
  fear of, 218–19
  in jazz, 217
  of ornaments, 200, 217, 218, 222–5
  timeless human instinct, 218–19
independence, artistic, 189
inégales see *notes inégales*
inner voice, xii, 70, 87, 115, 146
  connecting with, **147–51**, 167
  copying, 190–1, 210
  importance of listening to, 189–90
Institutio Oratoria, see Quintillian
instrumentalism, 35, 69, 191, 243
instrumentation in Corelli Sonatas, op. 5, 157–8
instruments, choice of, 4–5
interpretation, 155–8
interrogatio, 251
intervals, 102–4
  emotional information in, **68–70**
  fifths, narrow, 10, 100, 101–2
  octaves, 101
  semitones, major and minor, 93, 101
intonation:
  historical, 99–101
  pure, 101–56, **120–6**
  pure, comparison with equal
    temperament, **104–5**
  in relation to bass line, **124–5**
  rhetorical device, 246–7
  when strings are out of tune, **125–6**
  see also temperaments; tuning
Italian musicians, Raguenet on, 96, 219

Jambe de Fer, Philibert, *Epitome musical*, 14
jig *see* gigue
Joachim, Joseph:
  letter to Franz von Vescey, 230
  vibrato, excessive, 228, 229, 230

King, Martin Luther, 241–2
Kircher, Athanasius, 251

Kirnberger, Johann Philipp, 71
Kreisler, Fritz, 229
Kreutzer, Rodolphe:
   Étude for shifting, **118**
   Étude for sound fluctuation, **83**

Lacépède, Bernard Germain de, *La poétique de la*
      musique, 243
Leclair, Jean-Marie, xvi
left hand:
   expressive possibilities of, 148
   finger action, active and passive, **148–51**
   finger pressure, **146–7**
   fourth finger trills, 92, 197
   singing through the fingers, **147–51**
   see also fingering
Lenton, John, *The Gentleman's Diversion*, xv, 14
listening:
   importance of, 111, 120, 139, 187–8, 189, 191
   objective, difficulties of, 192
   in rapid passages, 191
   thought a barrier to, 188
Lolli, Antonio, 14
Lombardini, Maddalena, 74–5, 91, 132
Louis XIV, king of France, 55
Lully, Jean-Baptiste, 23
   rules of bowing, 54–5

Mace, Thomas, *Musick's Monument*, 53
Mannes, David, 11
Marpurg, Friedrich Wilhelm, *The Art of Harpsichord*
      Playing, xxi
   Bebung, 236
   musical expression, 71
   studying, xxi
Matham, Adriaen, *Oude Vioolspeler*, 13
Matteis, Nicola, 14
Mattheson, Johann, *Der Volkommene Capellmeister*:
   Affektenlehre, 71, 166–7
   Descartes, *Les Passions de l'âme*, 66
   presentation, 253
   rhythm, emotional information in, 211, 250
   soul, expansion and contraction of, 71
   sound, raw material of music, 185, 186
   temperaments, 126
   vibrato, without pitch fluctuation, 233
Mazas, Jacques-Féréol, 83
meantone temperaments, 100, 105–6
meditation, comparable to listening, 188
melody, moving by leap or by step, 132
melopoeia, 240
mensural system, 55
Merck, Daniel, 14
Mersenne, Marin, *Harmonie universelle*:
   rhetoric, 240
   sound, emotional effect of, 186

vibrato, 232
Messa di voce, 32, 33
   application of, **85–91**, 92–5
   avoiding the 'Baroque bulge', 86
   as breath, **87–8**
   execution of, **74–8**
   finger pressure, **77–8**
   left hand technique, 77
   multiple, **81–2**
   nineteenth-century examples, 83
   point of contact, **77–8**
   qualities of, 87
   rolling the bow, **77–8**
   in short notes, **78–80**
   vibrato, **78**
metabasis, 251
meter:
   anapestic, 211
   choice of, by composers and poets, 210–11
   iambic, 211
   rhetorical device, 250
metronome, learning to cheat, **176–7**
Michelangelo, 191
minutiae, importance of, 37, 194
modes, ancient Greek, 100
Molière, *Le Bourgeois gentilhomme*, 66
Montéclair, Michel Pignolet de:
   son glissé, 119
   violin hold, 14, 19
Mozart, Leopold, *Versuch einer gründlichen*
      Violinschule, xv, 20
   bow, contact with string, 140
   bow hold, 25
   bow, use of, 23
   elbow (right), 25
   fingerings, 94
   fourth finger, on bow, 143
   French edition (*Méthode raisonnée pour apprendre à*
      jouer du violon), 18
   gut strings, gauge of, 6, 7
   intonation, 105
   left hand finger pressure, 146
   Messa di voce, 76, 77, 81–2
   open strings, use and misuse of, 198
   overtones, 102–5
   presentation, 179
   second position, 91
   shifting, 118, 119, 197
   slurs, 133, 137
   sound quality, 130, 141
   sustained sound, 97
   trills, 89
   triplets, 122
   vibrato, 77, 234–5
   violin holds, 14, 17, 18, 19, 20, 21
Mozart, Wolfgang Amadeus, 236

Muffat, Georg:
  bow hold, 23–4
  double down bows, 54–5
  Florilegium secundum, 54–5, 146
  left hand finger pressure, 146
  syncopations, 160–1
music:
  emotional power of, 66–73
  purpose of, 66, 243

Nolens volens, or You Shall Learn to Play on the Violin Whether You Will or No, xv
North, Roger:
  Corelli, influence of, 96
  Messa di voce, 78
  open strings, use and misuse of, 198
  ornamentation, 216
  trills, speed of, 224
  vibrato, pitch fluctuation in, 232
  violin hold, 14
note values, written and sounded, 57–8, 206
notes inégales, 58
notes, principal and passing, 128, 129
notes, strong and weak, 53, 54, 60–1, 128, 159, 161, 201

observation and analysis, **156–67**
octaves, 101
open strings, use and misuse of, 198
orator, the musician as, 240–4
oratory, 239–44; *see also* rhetoric; rhetorical devices; rhetorical style
ornamentation:
  appoggiaturas, 209
  in Baroque churches, 216–17
  of cadences, 220
  deficiency of, 218
  emotional information in, 222
  excessive, 218, 224
  first steps in, **222**
  forbidden by François Couperin, 219
  function of, 89, 218
  impossibility of teaching, 216
  improvised, 200
  national styles of, 219
  necessity of, 217
  passing notes, 194
  perceiving, **222**
  performance of, 220–2, 224
  ribattuta di gola, 232
  writing out one's own, 224
  written, 200–1, 220–2, 224
  see also Messa di voce; trills
overtones, harmonic series of, **102–5**

parentheses, 245
passing notes, 129, 194

performance, preaching and avoiding preaching in, 93, 164, 189
performer:
  emotional input of, 96, 186–7
  role of, 185, 216–18
Pergolesi, Giovanni Battista, *Stabat Mater*, 211
phrasing, importance of clarity in, 56
Piani, Giovanni Antonio:
  dynamics, 81
  second position, 92
  Sonata no. 8, Preludio, 81
pianissimo, power of, 245
Pietà, La, Venice, xv
pitch, 9–10
Plato, 239, 247
Playford, John:
  bow hold, 24
  Division Violin, The, 51
  gut strings, covered, 9
  violin hold, 14
polyphony, within a single line, **170–1**
positions:
  choice of, 169, 198
  first, 169
  second, 91–2, 165
  see also shifts and shifting
Praetorius, Michael:
  strings, 9
  vibrato, 231
  vibrato in keyboard instruments, 236
Prelleur, Peter, fingering chart, 105–6
presentation, 179, 253–4
principal and passing notes, 129
Prinner, Johann Jacob, *Musicalischer Schlissl*, 15
printing techniques, 215
punctuation, 55–6, 245, 246–7
pure intonation, 101–6, **120–6**
Pythagoras, 100

Quantz, Johann Joachim, *Versuch*:
  Adagio, playing the, 74
  affects, tonality and, 100–1, 193
  dissonance, its relation to consonance, 86, **87**
  emotions, awareness and manipulation of, 70, 193–4
  expression, 128, 132
  good teaching, xiv
  gut G strings, wound, 7
  human voice, imitation of, 29
  intonation, 124
  listening, 120
  Messa di voce, 79
  minutiae, importance of, 37
  music, purpose of, 243
  musician as orator, 241
  notes, strong and weak, 60, 128
  open strings, use and misuse of, 198

ornamentation, 218
performer, role of, 186, 216
pitches, diversity of, 9–10
principal and passing notes, 129
second position, 92
trills, 92, 197
tuning, 102
as violinist, 21
Quintilian (Marcus Fabius Quintilianus), *Institutio Oratoria* (*Institutes of Oratory*):
emotions, manipulation of, 71
influence of, 240
music and oratory, 240
rhetoric, 240
tessitura, 249

Raguenet, François, *Parallèle des italiens et des François*:
gauge of gut strings, 6
Italian musicians, 96, 219
ornamentation, 219
Rameau, Jean-Philippe, 167
Ranken, Marion, 230
repititio, 211; *see also* rhetorical devices
resonance, natural, of violin, **12**
rhetoric, 38, 195, 239–44
rhetorical devices, 242–3, 244–54
abruptio, 251
acoustic, 250
anabasis and *ascensio*, 251
direction, punctuation and intonation, 246–7
dissonance, 248–9
dynamics, 244–5
imagery, 251–3
interrogatio, 251
metabasis and *transgresso*, 251
meter, 250
parentheses, 245
presentation, 179, 252–4
repetition (*repititio*), 211, 245–6
suspiratio, 251
tempo, 250
tessitura, 249–50
tirata, 222–3, 251
tonality, 247
see also exclamations; gesture; intervals, emotional
information in; rhythm, emotional
information in
rhetorical style, 241, 242, **243**
versus instrumentalism, 243
versus melody, 241
rhythm:
dance, 53, 55
dotted, 58–60
emotional information in, 210–12, 250
flexibility of, 128–9, 176–7
metronome, learning to cheat, 176–7
rubato, 129, 220

syncopations, 160–1
triplets, 122
of words, 30–4, 38–9, 42
see also hemiolas
ribattuta di gola, 232
ricochet, 64, 182
ritardando, lack of, effect on audience, 206
Roger, Estienne, 215
Rognoni, Francesco, 231–32
Romantic tradition, 28
Rosé, Arnold, 229
Rousseau, Jean, *Traité de la viole*:
affects, tonality and, 166–7
ornamentation, excessive, 224
vibrato with two fingers, 232
Rousseau, Jean-Jacques, *Dictionnaire de musique*:
hemiolas, 209
ornamentation, 220
rhetorical style, 242
rubato, 129, 220

Saint Lambert, Monsieur de, *Les principes du clavecin*, 242
Saint-Sévin, Joseph-Barnabé *see* Abbé le fils, L'
saraband (sarabanda, sarabande, zarabanda):
Corelli op. 5, no. 7, 177–81, 220, 222–5
history of, 177
second beat of, 53–4, 177–8, 206–7
Vivaldi op. 2, no. 1, 206–10
Sarasate, Pablo de, 228
scale studies, Geminiani, 120–6
scales:
chromatic fingering, 93-4
as exercises for chin-off (chinless) shifting, **112**, **113**
monitoring bow pressure, **144–5**
monitoring left hand finger pressure, **147**
on one string, **117**
see also Geminiani, scale studies
Schmelzer, Johann Heinrich, *Sonatae unarum fidium*, 245
Schönberg, Arnold, 229
'Scuola delle Nazioni' *see* Tartini
second beat of chacony, 53–4
second beat of saraband, 53–4, 177–8, 206–7
second position:
importance of, 91–2, 165
shifting into, 197
semitones, major and minor, 93–4
sequences:
definition, 134
shifting emotions in, **134–8**
Ševčík, Otakar, exercises, 49, 83, **115–16**, 191
Shakespeare, William:
Hamlet, 20, 34, 72, 156, 239, 245–6
Julius Caesar, 34
Much Ado about Nothing, 6, 181
Romeo and Juliet, 34

shifts and shifting, 63–4
    audible and inaudible, 91, 118–19
    chin-off (chinless), **108–19**, **124–6**
    consecutive positions, **115–16**
    creeping, **110–11**, **112**
    deciding where to shift, 197
    displacement scales, **112**
    down, **112–15**
    exercises, **110–18**
    expressive, 119
    four springs (wrist, forearm, elbow, thumb),
        109–10, **111**
    over two positions, **116–17**
    over two strings, **116**
    practice of, **124–5**
    role of listening, **111**
    into second position, 197
    security in, 12, 19
    son glissé, 119
    techniques of, **108–19**, **124–5**, 197
Signoretti, Pietro, 14
silence:
    effect of, 223
    expressive power of, 91
silk strings, 9
slurs:
    adding, 133–4
    first note accented, 137
    as ornaments, 134
    written, 64
son glissé, 119; *see also* shifts and shifting
sound, 95–7
    eliminating flaws in by listening, **191–2**
    emotional effect of, **67–73**, 186
    living, 187
    musical decisions transformed into, 189
    powerful, **96–7**
    raw material of music, 185–6
    searching for, 190
    sustained, 97
    'white', 187
sound production, 139
sound quality, 130, 141
sound world, Baroque, 186
Spohr, Louis, 230, 237
Stainer, Jacob, 4, 25
Strad, The, 1908 article on vibrato, 228
Stradivarius, Antonio, 4
Strauss, Johann, 13
string-crossing patterns, exploiting, 169, 170
strings, 6–9
    names of, 169
    open, use and misuse of, 198
        see also equal tension, advantages of; gut strings; silk
        strings; wire strings

Suppig, Friedrich, *Labyrinthus musicus*, 100
suspiratio, 251
Sweelinck, Jan Pieterszoon, 36
    'Garrula rondinella' from *Rimes françoises et
        italiennes*, 37–44
syncopations, varieties of, 160–1

tactus, 158–9, 194
Tarling, Judy, 247
Tartini, Giuseppe:
    arte dell'arco, L', xv
    articulation, 132
    bow, expressive power of, 75
    bow hold, 25
    bow, mastery of, 208
    bow technique, 74–5
    bowings, choice of, 208
    Corelli Allegros, how to practise, 132
    letter to Maddalena Lombardini, 74–5, 91, 132
    melody, 132
    Messa di voce, 75
    Regole, 75
    Regole, plagiarised by Leopold Mozart, 235
    'Scuola delle Nazioni', 74
    second position, 91
    shifting, 108, 118, 197
    slurs, 133
    'terzo suono', 102–5
    trills, speed of, 196
    vibrato, 235
    vibrato/trill hybrid, 235
technical problems, overcoming, 167
Telemann, Georg Philipp, *Methodical Sonatas*, xv–xvi
temperaments:
    comma, the, 99
    equal, 100–1, 104, 105
    explanation of, 99–101
    initial choice of, 120
    meantone, 100, 105–6
    personal taste in, 126
    quarter-comma meantone, 100
    syntonic comma, 100
    Vallotti, 120
tempo, 53, 158–9, 194, 207, 212
    rhetorical device, 250
tension:
    emotional factors, 49–50
    nervous, 50
    releasing, 140
    technical factors, 49
'terzo suono', 102–5
    learning to hear, **103–4**
tessitura, 63, 64–5, 249–50
The Hague, Mauritshuis, 13
tirata (tirade), 222–3, 251

tonality, 100–1, 107, 166–7, 175, 193, 247

Tonelli, Antonio, harmonic realizations of Corelli, 89, 90, 93, 171, 174

Tosi, Pier Francesco:
  Messa di voce, 33
  ornamentation, 218, 224
  rubato, 129, 220
  semitones, major and minor, 101
  trills, cadential, 224

transgresso, 251

tremoletto, 232–3; *see also* vibrato

tremolo, **231–2**; *see also* vibrato

trills:
  with appoggiatura, expressive, 209
  cadential, 201, 224
  expressive purpose of, 89
  fourth finger, 92, 197
  importance of, 224
  speed of, 89, 196, 224
  starting on the note, 172–4, 209
  upper note, 173–4
  see also ornamentation, vibrato/trill hybrid

triplets, 122

tuning, 7, 8, 9, 10, 101–2
  see also intonation; pitch; temperaments

Türk, Daniel Gottlob, *Clavierschule*, 237

Vallotti temperament, 120

Venice, La Pietà, xv

Veracini, Francesco Maria:
  bowings, 134
  dynamics, 81
  Sonate accademiche, 81
  violin hold, 18

Vescey, Franz von, Joachim's letter to, 230

vibrato:
  arm, 237
  chin-off players, **235–6**
  'close shake', 233–4
  continuous, 37, 78, 105, 227, 228, 229, 231, 232, 234
  as embellishment, 229, 230, 234
  excessive, 228–30, 234, 236
  flattement, 233

hiding bad intonation, 229
  Joachim's minimum use of, 230
  in keyboard instruments, 236–7
  nineteenth-century term, 227
  pitch fluctuation in, 231, **232**, 234
  speed, 77
  Strad, The, 1908 article on, 228
  tremoletto, **232–3**
  tremolo, **231–2**
  with two fingers, 232
  without pitch fluctuation, **233**
  see also bow vibrato; vibrato/trill hybrid

vibrato/trill hybrid, **231–2**, 235

Vienna, statue of Johann Strauss, 13

Vincentino, Nicola, *archicembalo*, 100

viola repertoire, xiii

violinist's trinity, 192

Viotti, Giovanni Battista, 230

Vivaldi, Antonio, xv
  bowings specified for bass instruments, 202
  Corelli's influence on, 193, 194, 196, 202, 204, 207
  Sonata op. 2, no. 1, Preludio, 193–201, **243**
  Sonata op. 2, no. 1, Giga, **202–6**
  Sonata op. 2, no. 1, Sarabanda, 206–10
  Sonata op. 2, no. 1, Corrente, **210–15**
  walking bass, 207

vowels, **39–40**

walking bass, in Corelli and Vivaldi, 207

Watkin, David, instrumentation in Corelli op. 5, 157–8

Wilde, Oscar, *The Picture of Dorian Grey*, 156

wire strings, 9

words:
  consonants, single and double, **41–2**
  diphthongs, 40–1
  imitation of, 27, 29–34, 36–8, 42–4
  rhythm of, **30–4**, **38–9**, 42
  vowels, **39–40**

wrist, use of, 213

zarabanda *see* saraband

Printed in the USA/Agawam, MA
July 28, 2021

778134.030